APPRAISING RESIDENCES
&
INCOME PROPERTIES

HENRY S. HARRISON, MAI, SRPA, ASA, CSA

PUBLISHED BY THE H2 COMPANY.
315 WHITNEY AVENUE • NEW HAVEN, CONNECTICUT 06511

The H2 Company, New Haven, Connecticut 06511

©1989 by The H2 Company
All rights reserved. Published 1989
Printed in the United States of America

First Printing

Library of Congress Catalog Card Number
89-83459

Harrison, Henry.
Appraising Residences & Income Properties

ISBN 0-927054-01-9
ISBN 0-927054-00-0 pbk.

FORWARD

Real estate appraisers enjoy a unique position of trust in the real estate profession and in the whole community. They help people buy homes, investment properties and many other kinds of real estate. They help lenders determine the suitability of property being offered as loan security, estimate value for insurance purposes, help the courts set condemnation awards, settle estates, and establish property tax rates just to mention a few of the hundreds of reasons why their estimates of the value of real estate are required.

My goal in writing this book is to help students learn about real estate appraising by presenting the materials in a straight-forward easy-to-understand manner.

It would have been impossible to write this book without a lot of help and encouragement. My wife and partner (marital and business) Ruth Lambert acted as editor, proofreader and major supporter of this project. She and my children H Alex (age 6), Kate (age 10), Eve (soon to be married) and Julie (newlywed and Yale Law School Graduate) always give up time that would have been theirs each time I write a book.

Most of the type was set by Naomi Corso on our MacIntosh Desktop Publishing System - even pregnancy never slowed her down. Nita Romer, Editor of Residential Valuation Magazine, assisted with editing and proofreading. Maura Gianakos (my long-time secretary) typed the model appraisal and helped keep me organized.

Frank Tassche from Freddie Mac and Mark Simpson from Fannie Mae always answered my questions and kept me posted about their latest guidelines and forms as they were being developed. Frank Mongillo, MAI researched Truth-In-Lending for me.

The model appraisal was developed by Barbara Kaye, my former appraisal associate, who is now a bank Vice President, with additional photographs taken by Richard Chamberlin, Sr. Even my father, Dr. J.M. Harrison (age 87) sent material for the model appraisal from Florida. This is the third book in which my father-in-law, Dr. Joseph M. Lambert's "bell curve" drawing has appeared.

Several hundred Residential Valuation readers responded to my request for help to write a definition for the word "Appraisal".

The beautiful cover was designed by graphic artist Lauri Wirta using the house drawings of Joseph Jaqua.

A special thanks to my partners at our appraisal firm (ABC America's Home Buying Consultants, Inc.) Leonard D'Agostino RM and Arthur Greenlaw, and our 15 staff appraisers who keep me grounded in reality.

I am often asked, "How long does it take you to write a book?" My wife usually replies, "About twice as long as he thought it would." This is quite true, even if it isn't a direct answer to the question. The real answer is thousands of hours. I spend a portion of almost every day writing. When deadlines are closing in, I often write 12 hours a day, taking only brief breaks for food and family.

Since I usually listen to classical music on Public Radio as I write, my musical literacy has improved immensely. I just recently started taking Susuki piano lessons, so I'll be able to make music as well as listen to it.

Finally, I am looking forward to meeting many of you at my seminars sometime in the future. I hope this book is just the first step in your appraisal education.

H² April, 1989

In memory of my mother

HELEN S. HARRISON

She never doubted I could do anything
I wanted to, even write books.

and

Dr. George F. Bloom, MAI, SRPA
Professor of Real Estate, Indiana University

His words from our book *Appraising The Single Family Residence*

"The close relationship that this project necessitated between the authors has produced an even closer friendship. Many hours spent together have produced not only a tangible product but a distinct camaraderie, compassion and total respect for each other. May it last forever."

If a man does not keep pace with his companions,
perhaps it is because he hears a different drummer.
Let him step to the music which he hears,
however measured or far away.

Thoreau: Walden XVIII

CONTENTS

All of the house style pictures used to illustrate this book were taken from my first book, <u>Houses The Illustrated Guide to Construction Design and Systems,</u> published by the Realtors National Marketing Institute of the National Association of Realtors. In this book a full page is devoted to each of the 58 house styles. Below is a typical page illustrating the "Octagon House". It is my favorite style because it is 100% American. Its inventor, Orsen Squire Fowler was the Dr. Rubens of the 1800's. His popular books expounded his theory that living in an octagon house improved the occupants health and sex life (similar to the recent pyramid house theory). As a result of his books and lectures, over 10,000 octagon houses were built around 1850, in all 50 states.

Nineteenth Century American

OCTAGON HOUSE (Octagon - 704)

Key Distinguishing Characteristics

The most distinguishing characteristic of this style is the octagonal shape.

Other Distinguishing Characteristics

    Stone, wood or concrete walls
    Flat roofs
    Chimney or beleveder in the center
    Variety of window and door types used

History

Most of these houses were built around 1850. They were a result of an idea put forth by Orson Squire Fowler, a popular author of the time who wrote about love, marital happiness, sex and phrenology. In several of his popular books he expounded the theory of a happy life in an octagon-shaped house. He thought that this design made for good interior circulation, heating and lighting. Octagon houses were built throughout the U.S. and several hundred are still lived in today. The house was explained in detail in his book, *A Home for All, or the Gravel Wall and Octagon Mode of Building, New, Cheap, Convenient, Superior and Adapted to Rich and Poor.*

1 The Appraisal Profession

Millions of real estate appraisals are made every year, ranging from those of a simple house lot, to those of multi-million dollar mansions and large residential complexes. Although the purpose of this text is to concentrate on the appraisal of residences, a brief overview of the various needs for residential appraisals serves as an introduction.

KINDS OF RESIDENTIAL APPRAISAL ASSIGNMENTS

Residential real estate appraisals are generally made by staff appraisers of organizations requiring such appraisals or by fee appraisers, who are independent contractors. Almost anyone the appraiser meets can be a potential source of business. The list of those seeking the services of a real estate appraiser includes:

--**Buyers and sellers of homes.** Appraisers assist them in setting listing and offering prices and in making final decisions to complete a sale or purchase.

--**Lending institutions** such as savings and loan associations, savings banks, commercial banks, credit unions, insurance companies, pension funds and investment trusts. Appraisers estimate the market value of residences being accepted as loan security. The trust departments of these organizations use appraisers for estate planning and estate disposal. Real estate departments use appraisers to help manage and plan their own activities.

--**Investors.** Appraisers help them acquire and dispose of real estate investments.

--**Architects.** Appraisers help judge the economic feasibility of proposed projects as well as site selection and acquisitions.

--**Builders and developers.** Appraisers help them to make site acquisitions, develop sites to highest and best use, test the feasibility of projects, obtain mortgages and equity financing, attract investors, and assist in the sale of projects.

--**Lawyers**. Appraisers are often hired on behalf of clients. Lawyers also recommend appraisers to help divide property between disputing heirs, partners or clients. They use appraisers for condemnation, tax appeals, estate planning and disposal of estates and a variety of other uses.

--**Tenants.** Appraisers help them estimate fair rental. In condemnation proceedings, tenants need appraisers to estimate their leasehold value (leasehold interests are those of the lessee, tenant or renter).

--**Insurers** and the insured. Appraisers estimate the insurable value of property to aid in determining the proper amount of insurance. Appraisers also play an important role in claims adjustments.

--**Accountants**. Appraisers are hired for clients to help estimate the value of assets and to establish rates of depreciation.

--**Business corporations.** Appraisers help acquire and dispose of residential property, assist in the transfer of employees, evaluate real estate assets, develop real estate programs and plan real estate activities.

--**Non-profit organizations.** Appraisers help buy and sell real estate and value holdings.

--**Government agencies at federal, state and local levels.** These are all large users of appraisals. Some federal agencies that use appraisals are the Veterans Administration, Federal Housing Administration, Federal Home Loan Mortgage Corporation, General Services Administration, Internal Revenue Service, Post Office Department, and Farm Home Administration. States condemn and purchase residential land for schools and other government buildings, parks, open space programs and wetlands. Local governments depend on appraisers in the process of acquiring property for schools and other government buildings. Redevelopment programs require appraisers for both acquisition and reuse programs. Ad valorem (property) taxes are based on real estate assessments (appraisals).

--**Public Utility companies.** Appraisers are needed for the acquisition of rights-of-way for their wires, pipelines and other real estate acquisitions.

The list of users of residential appraisals is almost endless. It is an expanding function and the need for appraisers appears to be constantly increasing. The field presents good opportunities for those who are willing to acquire the necessary skills to serve the public as professionals.

THE DEFINITION OF AN APPRAISAL

In the November/December 1988 issue of *Residential Valuation Magazine* I wrote an article in which offered a possible definition on "What is an Appraisal". I requested suggestions from appraisers on what they believed was an appropriate definition and received several hundred replies. As a result of those suggestions I have compiled a definition which encompasses the following seven concepts:

1. An appraisal is an opinion of value.
2. The opinion must be appropriately supported with general and specific data.
3. It must be as of a specific date.
4. The value estimated must be defined.
5. The property being appraised must be adequately and accurately described.
6. The person making the appraisal must be qualified by reason of adequate education and experience.
7. The person making the appraisal is unbiased and has no undisclosed interest in the property.

An appraisal is an appropriately supported objective and unbiased opinion of the value as of a specific date of an adequately and accurately described property made by a qualified person who has no undisclosed interest in the property.

It may include such complicated considerations as various interests, equities, historic and future values and other conditions which are present.

It may be based on assumed conditions, provided they are clearly stated and there is a reasonable probability that the assumptions will take place some time in the near future.

PURPOSE AND USE OF A RESIDENTIAL APPRAISAL

The fundamental purpose of an appraisal is to estimate some kind of value. The need for an appraisal of market value may arise from many situations, including:

1) Transfer of ownership.
2) Financing and credit.
3) Just compensation in condemnation (eminent domain) proceedings.
4) As a basis for taxation.
5) To establish rental schedules and lease provisions.
6) Feasibility analysis.

In addition to the need for estimating market value, appraisals are also made to estimate:

1) Insurable value.
2) Going-concern value.
3) Liquidation value.
4) Assessed value (May be a percentage of market value).

Although the list does not include all the needs for appraisals, it does indicate the broad scope of the professional appraiser's typical activities.

THE IMPORTANCE OF THE RESIDENTIAL APPRAISER

The appraiser is frequently regarded by lenders and the public as the expert in evaluating a neighborhood's strengths and weaknesses. Accordingly, the appraiser must exercise this responsibility with care and be certain that a considered judgment about a community's trend is supportable by objective facts. Emotional arguments or advocacy must never affect the professional appraiser's presentation of demonstrable facts.

GROWTH OF PROFESSIONALISM IN REAL ESTATE APPRAISING

A profession is, by definition, a vocation that involves primarily intellectual activities and requires high levels of technical competence, individual responsibility and personal integrity. Historically, the first professionals were physicians and surgeons, professors, lawyers, accountants, engineers and the clergy. Today a professional is a member of an organized vital vocation or activity in which the membership is highly competent, thoroughly honest and devoted to the ideal of performing a service to the maximum of their capacity, regardless of compensation. A professional has a responsibility to help make the world a better place in which to live.

Appraisers have aspired to professional status in the eyes of the public and the rest of the real estate field for many years. Today appraisals written by appraisers who have achieved some level of professionally recognized expertise usually receive greater acceptance than those prepared by the non-professional.

The need for professional real estate appraisers came into focus with the collapse of real estate values during the depression of the 1930's. Prior to that time, real estate appraising as a vocation had been unstructured and little educational material was available, although as early as 1929, the National Association of Real Estate Boards had a publication called Standards of Appraisal Practice. To the early appraiser, "market price" meant "market value".

PROFESSIONAL ORGANIZATIONS AND DESIGNATIONS

Some lenders will only use appraisers who have designations from certain appraisal organizations. They believe that a designated appraiser will be qualified.

Unfortunately, not all designations are the same. There are at least 30 national appraisal organizations which award designations to their members. Requirements vary widely (see Addenda C).

Two of these organizations have existed since before World War II. They both have a long history of rigid standards for awarding their designations. They are the American Institute of Real Estate Appraisers (which awards the RM and MAI designations) and the Society of Real Estate Appraisers (which awards the SRA, SRPA and the SREA designations). To earn any of these designations, an appraiser must have taken several courses, have years of proven experience, produced demonstration appraisals and passed several examinations.

The designation requirements of the other national appraisal organizations range from those similar to the AIREA and SREA, to none other than making an application and sending in the required fee. To complicate matters further, some of the organizations which have strict designation requirements now, have a past history of lax requirements.

There are also some good appraisers who, for various reasons, have decided not to apply for any designation. Lenders who refuse to consider appraisers who do not have designations may be eliminating some well-qualified appraisers who are capable of doing their work.

WHAT APPRAISERS HAVE TO SELL

An appraiser basically has five things to sell a client:

      A. Adequate Knowledge
      E. Experience
      I. Integrity

O. **Objectivity**
U. **Uncompromised willingness to do the work on a timely basis for a mutually agreed upon fee.**

ADEQUATE KNOWLEDGE

A qualified appraiser should have had a good general education, taken a variety of appraisal courses and seminars, and be keeping current with continuing education in the field.

In a profession as complex as real estate appraising, most lenders feel that a minimum of a high school education is required. The AIREA and SREA now require a college degree for their designations. However, this is a recent requirement and many of their older members are not college graduates.

Unfortunately, there are appraisers in the field who have never even taken a basic appraisal course. Others have only been to a few one-day seminars. Why lenders accept work from these appraisers is hard to understand. At a bare minimum, every appraiser should have taken a basic appraisal course given by an accredited educational institution or national appraisal organization.

Since the appraisal profession and appraisal requirements are changing all the time, it is necessary that the appraiser keep up with current appraisal practice. Many feel the best way to insure this is to require appraisers to attend continuing educa-tion courses and/or seminars on a regular basis. However, it should be kept in mind that it is possible for an appraiser to keep current by reading the available appraisal journals and other appraisal publications.

EXPERIENCE

There is an old saying that nothing is a substitute for experience. This is not what a new appraiser wants to hear. The reality is that appraising is still not a science but rather an art. Often when is comes to making adjustments, rating the neighborhood and/or the improvements and reconciling differences throughout the appraisal, the appraiser must rely primarily upon judgment.

Since no one is born with experience, a substitute has to be found for the new appraiser. Appraisal experience can be obtained by working as an appraiser, lender, contractor or Realtor. At least some of the required experience should be obtained by actually making residential appraisals.

It is appropriate for an inexperienced appraiser to work with a seasoned appraiser who reviews their work and jointly assumes responsibility for it by signing the appraisal report as the review appraiser. It is a good policy to require that the review appraiser, who jointly signs the appraisal, also inspect the interior of the subject property when the primary appraiser is very inexperienced, when the value of the house is high, when the house is old, or when the property has some significant atypical characteristics. Many people feel that at least two years experience is a minimum requirement for an appraiser to be able to sign an appraisal without supervisory review.

INTEGRITY

There are a variety of ways a client can check on the integrity of an appraiser. The most common is by checking personal, general business and professional references. Others include talking with other appraisers. The participation of the appraiser in community activities and their professional association are other indicators of reputation in the community and among peers.

OBJECTIVITY

The appraiser signs a certificate with each appraisal saying that he or she has no present or future contemplated interest in the property being appraised. This includes making appraisals for friends and relatives.

Unfortunately clients are sometimes their own worst enemy when it comes to appraiser objectivity. It does not take long for an appraiser to figure out whether a client is primarily interested in making loans regardless of the value of the loan security or whether they are primarily interested in obtaining the true value of the property in order to protect their loan portfolio.

The amount of pressure that some clients put on appraisers is well documented. Many people (including the author) feel it is the primary cause of poor appraisals. It is up to the client to communicate to the appraiser how they really feel. If they want true value estimates, they must make it clear to the appraiser that the assignments and payments they receive in the future will not be in jeopardy if they produce appraisals where the appraised value is less than the contract pirice of the pending loan application.

UNCOMPROMISED WILLINGNESS TO DO WORK ON A TIMELY BASIS FOR A MUTUALLY AGREED UPON FEE

The final step in selecting appraisers is finding those who are willing (and able) to do the client's work on a timely basis for a mutually agreed upon fee. The client should investigate the appraiser's capacity to produce work. If the appraiser is a one, two or three person operation, the amount of work they can turn out is limited. Usually the appraiser has other clients who also want their work done on a timely basis. The best arrangement is when the client and appraiser agree upon the approximate number of appraisals that will be ordered in any given period of time When the appraiser receives a smooth flow of work, they are better able to produce it without undue delay. Unfortunately, the clients cannot always control the number of appraisals they need and when they get busy, often give appraisers more work than they can handle. The appraisers, in turn, try to expand their capacity by hiring additional support help and additional appraisers. They also work longer hours. However, in spite of this, it seems to be a pattern that in the Spring when business traditionally picks up, appraisers become swamped and get behind in their work.

Clients have different policies on how they pay appraisers. Some large lenders have a published fee schedule. Appraisers must decide whether they are willing to accept the offered fee in order to get assignments from the lender. Other lenders negotiate fee schedules with each appraiser, taking into consideration the appraiser's knowledge, experience and the length of time they have been working together. Clients should recognize that some appraisal assignments require substantially more work than others. Often the fee will be adjusted to reflect the extra work required to make an appraisal of a high value home, waterfront property, historic property, contemporary house and other houses with significant atypical characteristics.

PROFESSIONAL CONDUCT

The essence of our civilization is that people acknowledge the limited right of society to control the activities of individuals for the benefit of the public. In addition, many people conduct their own activities at a higher level than is required by the law or by their fellow humans.

There are several levels of conduct. The first deals with the laws the apply to all the people. In the United States, there are federal, state and local laws. Everyone is required to obey these laws. It makes little difference if one agrees or disagrees with them. If someone does not obey a law, society has the right to punish the lawbreaker. (Of course, not all laws are enforced uniformly, and many people break laws and are not caught or punished.)

The second level of conduct consists of the laws that apply to certain groups of people. These are laws and rules that regulate special activities such as those of lawyers and doctors. Often one has to obtain a license or permit to participate in such activities. For example, in the real estate field, one must have a license to sell or rent real estate for compensation. Real estate brokers are subject to special laws that control their activities. Other common examples at this level are the laws pertaining to driving automobiles, building houses, practicing medicine, or running a store. Such regulatory laws apply only when one voluntarily engages in a special activity controlled by the legislation or regulation which applies. In some states, real estate appraising falls into this category of control.

The third level consists of The Uniform Standards of Professional Practice and the various codes of ethics that have been developed by the professional organizations to control the activities of their members. The members of the organization agree to be governed by its code of ethics as one of the conditions of membership. The organization itself develops and enforces the code of ethics. Violators may be disciplined in a variety of ways. The maximum penalty usually is expulsion from the group. The American Medical Association, the American Bar Association, the National Association of Realtors as well as many other organizations have these codes governing the conduct of their members with the public, their clients and among their own members.

The fourth level encompasses the personal rules people set for themselves to control their own lives according to their personal (and religious) beliefs. Many everyday decisions people make about their professional activities and conduct fall outside the scope of the three preceding levels of conduct. The decision regarding how to act must be made by the individual based on personal standards of conduct. The rewards for functioning at this higher level are personal satisfaction and approval by one's family and peers. The punishment is from one's own conscience and disapproval by others.

SUMMARY

The needs and reasons for real estate appraisals are as varied as the clients who request them. Broadly, a real estate appraisal is "a supported estimate of a defined value." The clients' specific needs will give further refinement and shape to the objective of the appraisal report. The validity of the report is strongly based on the knowledge and experience, integrity and objectivity of the person performing the appraisal. Over the last 50-plus years, real estate appraising has grown as a profession, based on the development of standards of professional practice.

2 The Nature of Real Property and Value

Real property has economic value and significance only as it satisfies the needs and desires of human beings. The utilization of and the collective desire for real property gives it value. Although land acquires value when it is desired and has a feasible use, the value assigned to a parcel of real estate is not limited to the individual whose desires create it. Reflections of that value have significance for everyone whose welfare might be affected by its utilization. Before value can be discussed, however, the nature of real property must be understood.

"Under all is the land"[1] . Land is the major source of all mineral, vegetable and animal substance. It is the foundation for the social and economic activities of people; it is a commodity and the wellspring of wealth.

Land has been the subject of human study throughout recorded history because it is essential to human existence. This study is divided into various disciplines including geography, law, sociology and economics. Each discipline studies land in a different way and has developed different concepts of land.

The appraiser's concept of land includes the concepts of all the other disciplines. By understanding these concepts a foundation is laid to form the background against which appraisal activities are conducted.

Value is the principal subject of inquiry in a residential appraisal. In order to estimate the value of any property it is first necessary to understand value theory. This theory includes anticipation, change, supply and demand, substitution, balance and externalities. Other theories the appraiser needs to understand are highest and best use, the forces that influence real property values (social, economic, government and environmental), and the factors of value (utility, scarcity, desire and effective purchase power). Such comprehension provides the foundation necessary for a competent appraisal and an objective, systematic analysis of events and motivations that effect residential property value (market value, use value, investment value, insurable value and assessed value).

---

[1]These famous words begin *The Appraisal of Real Estate*, 9th Edition, American Institute of Real Estate Appraisers, Chicago, Ill 1988.

CONCEPTS OF LAND AND REAL ESTATE

GEOGRAPHIC CONCEPT OF REAL ESTATE

Geography focuses on describing the physical elements of land and the distribution and activities of people who use it. It recognizes the diverse physical characteristics and the significance of the combination of these characteristics in a particular area.

Land is affected by a number of processes. Ongoing physical and chemical processes modify the land's surface; biological processes affect the distribution of all life forms; and socioeconomic processes direct human habitation and activity on the land. Together, these processes influence land capability and, therefore, land use.

Land may be used for many purposes, including agriculture, commerce, industry, residence, and recreation. Land-use decisions are influenced by climate, topography, and the distribution of natural resources, population centers, and conditions, population pressures, technological practices, and cultural influences. The degree of influence of each of these varies, depending on the geographic area.

These subjects of geographic study are particularly significant for appraisers. The importance of the land's physical characteristics - climate, geology, soils, water, and vegetation - is obvious. Just as important are the distribution of people and their facilities, as are services and the movement of goods and people. With its emphasis on such matters as resources and resource bases, industrial location, and actual and potential markets, the geographic concept of land forms much of the background knowledge about land that is required in any real estate appraisal.

LEGAL CONCEPT OF REAL ESTATE

The original legal concept of real estate is more comprehensive than is generally realized. By definition it

> ...includes not only the ground, or soil, but everything that is attached to the earth, whether by course of nature, as trees and herbage, or by...(society), as houses and other buildings. It includes not only the surface of the earth, but everything under it and over it. Thus, in legal theory, a tract of land consists not only of the portion on the surface of the earth, but is an inverted pyramid having its tip or apex at the center of the earth, extending outward through the surface of the earth at the boundary lines of the tract, and continuing on upward to the heavens.[2]

This, theoretically, is full and complete ownership. However, acts passed by Congress in 1926 and 1938 give the United States complete sovereignty over the air space above the nation. In general, the courts have held that an owner can control only as much air space above the land as can be reasonably utilized, depending upon its location, zoning and other factors governing the use of the property.

A variety of terms describe land and the structures thereon, either natural or synthetic.

---

[2]Robert Kratovil, *Real Estate Law*, 6th Ed., (Englewood Cliffs, NJ: Prentice-Hall, Inc., 1974), p. 5.

Definition of Terms

-- Real Estate. The physical land and appurtenances, including structures affixed thereon. In some states, by statute, this term is synonymous with real property.

-- Property. Synonymous with rights as used in the "bundle of rights". It includes the rights to future benefits by ownership or possession of economic goods.
   a. Real property. The interests, benefits and rights inherent in the ownership of the physical real estate. It is the bundle of rights with which such ownership is endowed. This term does not include personal property.
   b. Personal property. Movable items, those not permanently fixed to and part of real estate. In deciding whether an item is personal property or real estate, four factors must be considered: (1) the manner in which it is annexed, (2) the intention of the party responsible for the annexation (i.e., to leave it permanently or to remove it at some time), (3) the purpose for which the premises are used, and (4) the cost of the item. With some exceptions, items remain personal property if they can be removed easily and without damage to the real estate or the item itself.

-- Chattel. A legal term referring to any property other than a freehold or fee estate in land. Chattels are treated as personal property but are divided into two subcategories:

   a. Chattels real. All interest in real estate that does not constitute a freehold or fee estate in land, including leasehold estates and other interests issuing out of or annexed to real estate.
   b. Chattels personal. All movable things.

-- Fixtures. Tangible items that previously were personal property and have been attached to or installed on land or in a structure in such a way as to become a part of the real estate.

Thus, real estate, real property, personal property, chattels and fixtures are different and precise concepts. The distinctions between them are significant and the appraiser must have a thorough understanding of them.

The chief characteristics of real estate are its immobility and tangibility. Real estate is land and all things of a permanent and substantial nature affixed thereto, whether by nature or people. Real property, however, embraces in its broadest sense the tangible elements of real estate plus the intangible attributes that are the rights of ownership. The appraiser is concerned with real property, since the estimate of value made in an appraisal is of the rights and benefits to be derived from the ownership and/or use of real estate.

The major characteristic of personal property is its mobility. Furniture and furnishings, machinery, mortgages and securities of every type comprise personal property.

Chattel is a legal concept referring to non-ownership interests in real estate or personal property.

Because the distinction between real estate and personal property is not always evident and because it is important in the evaluation of real estate, appraisers should be familiar with the law of fixtures as it applies in their area. In the case of controversial items, the appraiser may abide by local custom; however, the appraisal report should clearly state the distinction.

SOCIAL CONCEPT OF REAL ESTATE

As physical characteristics and legal limitations increasingly affect land use, many different groups in society become concerned with how land is used and how rights are distributed. Because the supply of land is fixed, the demand for land in modern American society causes pressure for its more intensive use. Conflicts often arise between groups whose views on proper use of the land differ. Certain people believe that land is a resource to be shared by all. They want to preserve the land's scenic beauty and important ecological functions. Other persons view land primarily as a marketable commodity and believe that society is best served by private, unrestricted ownership. The fact that land is both a resource and a commodity prevents clear-cut solutions to these group conflicts.[3]

Both groups have won support for their beliefs. As a resource, land is protected for the good of society. Because land is also a marketable commodity, its ownership, use, and disposal are regulated so that unjust infringement on individual rights is precluded.

The government's right to regulate "the manner in which (a citizen) shall own his own property when such regulation becomes necessary for the public good" was established in 1876 by the U.S. Supreme Court, which repeated the words of England's Lord Chief Justice Hale: "When private property is 'affected with a public interest,' it ceases to be juris privati only."[4]

Even earlier, land ownership had been recognized as fundamental to America's institutions. John Adams wrote, "If the multitude is possessed of real estate, the multitude will take care of the liberty, virtue, and interest of the multitude in all acts of government."[5]

The restrictions that society may fix in the public interest include building restrictions, zoning and building ordinances, development and subdivision regulations, and environmental controls. The latter include provisions to prohibit the pollution of air and water through dumping wastes, emitting dirt and chemicals, and causing excessive noise. Concern for preserving the natural state has made possible certain regulations that protect wetlands, beaches, and navigable waters.

ECONOMIC CONCEPT OF REAL ESTATE

Land is a physical substance imbued with ownership rights that can be legally limited for the good of society. Further, land is a major source of wealth. In economic terms, wealth is measured in relation to money value or exchange value. Land and its products are of economic value only as they are converted into goods or services that are useful to, and desired and paid for by, consumers. The economic concept of land as a source of wealth and object of value is central to appraisal knowledge and inquiry.

---

[3]Richard N.L. Andrews, *Land in America* (Lexington, Mass: D.C. Heath and Company, 1979), p. ix.

[4]Andrews, op cit., p. 31

[5]Andrews, op cit., p. 31

APPRAISER'S CONCEPT OF REAL ESTATE

The geographic, legal, social, and economic concepts of land all are germane to the real estate appraiser's concept of land. Land, as defined legally to include everything attached to it, constitutes real estate. The appraiser studies the value of physical real estate and its accompanying ownership rights. The potential uses of land are influenced by geographic, legal, social, and economic considerations. These considerations form the background against which appraisal activities are conducted.

RIGHTS AND INTERESTS

The rights and interests in real estate can be divided into public rights and private rights. Public rights are included in the bundle of rights. Private rights may be classified further as (1) undivided fractional interests or (2) divisions based on physical separation.

PUBLIC RIGHTS

Bundle of Rights Theory

The bundle of rights theory holds that the ownership of real property may be compared to a bundle of sticks wherein each stick represents a distinct and separate right or privilege of ownership. These rights, inherent in ownership of real property and guaranteed by law (but subject to certain limitations and restrictions), include the right to occupy and to use real property, to sell it in whole or in part, to bequeath it, and to transfer by contract for specified periods of time the benefits to be derived by occupancy and use of the real estate ("beneficial interests").

Absolute fee simple title to real property is the most complete degree of ownership but some restrictions and reservations are included. It does not guarantee the unrestricted exercise of the entire bundle of rights. These rights and privileges are limited by four powers of government:

FIG. 2-1 BUNDLE OF RIGHTS

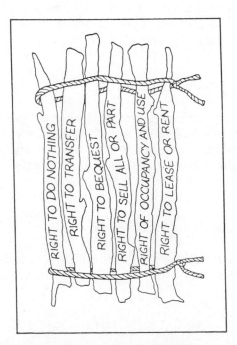

BUNDLE OF RIGHTS THEORY

--Ad valorem taxation. The right of the state to levy and collect a tax varying with the assessed value of the property. It is a compulsory contribution exacted from all owners of real estate for the general support of the state and for the maintenance of public services. Also included are special assessments that may be levied against certain real estate benefitting from public improvements, usually to offset directly the cost of such improvements.

--Eminent domain. The right reserved by government to take private property by condemnation for public benefit, provided just compensation is paid. As the concept of what constitutes public benefit broadens, there is an apparent trend toward broader interpretation of this right, which has been extended to quasi-government or public bodies such as housing authorities and public utilities.

--Police power. The right to regulate property to promote the safety, health, morals and general welfare of the community via zoning ordinances, building codes, traffic regulations and other restrictions such as fair housing laws.

--Escheat. The reversion to the state of property ownership if the owner dies without a will and with no known legal heirs.

PRIVATE RIGHTS

In addition to the controls and restrictions resulting from the four powers of government, appropriate provisions may be inserted into deeds, by which properties are transferred, that will further restrict property uses. Through private deed restrictions owners can limit property uses, establish building restrictions, regulate land coverage, and control property in other ways. Such restrictions may apply to one property or to an entire area. Deed restrictions should be enforced by the original owners, subsequent owners or other affected individuals or organizations. Where restrictions are conditions upon which the deed is given, a reversionary clause may provide that the property will revert to the seller if violations are claimed and can be proven.

Federal, state and local fair housing laws guarantee persons the right to buy, sell, lease, hold and convey property without being subjected to discrimination on the basis of race, color, religion, sex or national origin. These laws have nullified private deed restrictions which limit occupancy on racial, ethnical or religious grounds. They also prohibit all types of discrimination in housing and rental transactions, so that equal housing opportunity is now often regarded as one of the basic property rights.

Undivided Fractional Interest

Division of earnings or productivity occurs when ownership is in undivided fractional interests such as either tenancy-in-common or joint tenancy. The value of such fractional interests is usually less than the fraction the ownership bears to the value of the entire property, particularly where the ownership is less than a 50 percent interest in the property. Some examples of fractional ownership are:

--Land Trusts. Title is held by a trustee (usually a bank or trust company) for the benefit of the fractional owners.

--General and Limited Partnerships. Limited partners share proportionately in the net earnings and other benefits and depreciation but have no voice in the management decisions or responsibility. General partners are usually the persons who develop the partnership, retain special benefits, including the right of management decisions, and are solely liable for all obligations.

--Cooperative Ownership. Usually ownership of stock in a corporation owning the entire property. Each stockholder is given a proprietary lease on a unit, subject to certain conditions and obligations as to its use, sub-leasing and sale. Usually the lease or sale is subject to the approval of a board of directors of the cooperative.

--Corporate Ownership. Stock ownership in a property that has been incorporated. One of the disadvantages of corporate ownership is that depreciation for income tax purposes cannot be passed through directly to the owner of the fractional interest.

FIG. 2-2 TYPES OF OWNERSHIP

COOPERATIVE   CONDOMINIUM

Physical Division

The second category of fractional ownership or interest is a division of the physical use of the property.

--Horizontal and Vertical Subdivision. Horizontal subdivision is the definition of the boundaries of surface areas of a property. Vertical subdivision refers to the division of air rights and subsurface rights. Subsurface rights in the form of oil or mineral rights are commonly leased or sold. Their exclusion may have little effect on surface land values if the terms of conveyance protect the surface from interference. Subsurface rights may also involve underground pipes and cable lines.

--**Air Rights.** Within the distances normally encompassed above or below the land surface, real estate ownership may be considered to be between vertical boundaries above and below the site. Practically, this means that a 100-by-100 foot parcel of land is not a square surface but a cube. Accordingly, this cube may be divided not only vertically, similar to a slice of a layer of cake, but also horizontally, as in the individual layers of the cake. The useful height or depth of this cube (number of stories) is limited only by the practicalities of engineering, economics (highest and best use) and zoning.

--**Mineral Rights.** Like air and other rights, mineral rights may be owned, sold, bought and transferred. The estimation of value of each right is becoming a more common appraisal assignment.

--**Easement.** A non-possessing interest held by one person in land of another person whereby the first person is accorded partial use of such land for a specific purpose. Easements are created to allow access to property whether it be from public or private land. An easement may be vertical and/or horizontal, such as underground utility lines. Where an easement is granted to allow specific access to or through a property, it may be called a right-of-way.

--**Condominiums.** Ownership of a condominium unit is basically ownership of the cubical area within the confines of its outer walls, floor and ceiling plus common ownership rights in all public space which, together with all the units, comprise the entire property. The condominium unit is a separate ownership, the title to which is in the name of the owner(s). It may be leased, sold, mortgaged or refinanced separately.

Lease Interests

Lease interests are another type of partial interest in real estate, which can be divided into two types.

--**Leased Fees.** An owner may lease real estate, relinquishing the right of occupancy but retaining the title to the fee, subject to the lease, including the recovery of use at the expiration of the lease, known as the reversionary rights. The value of a leased fee interest is profoundly affected by its length and terms, which may cover a wide range of provisions agreed upon between the parties.

--**Leasehold or Possessory Interest.** That portion of the rights including occupancy that is transferred from the owner of the fee to a tenant. This is usually done by a lease, permit, license, concession or other type of contract. It is the opposite of the leased fee. The value of possessory interests usually refers to the value of the interest leased (i.e., the value of the use and occupancy of the property for the lease term, known as a leasehold interest).

Knowing exactly which rights are under consideration is fundamental in appraising. Precise definition is customarily a matter of documentation. In the absence of such definition, it may be necessary to obtain a legal opinion. The appraiser, however, should be generally familiar with the broad range of property rights, their more common characteristics, and the usual manner in which they are utilized and transferred.

APPRAISAL PRINCIPLES

The basic principles defined, explained, and illustrated in this section are concerned with their impact upon real property value. This section begins with the traditional agents of production and surplus productivity. Next the broad principle of supply and demand is discussed, followed by more specific real estate principles: anticipation, balance, change, competition and excess profit, conformity, contribution, externalities and substitution.

The last to be discussed, highest and best use, is the most fundamental principle in understanding real property value. Estimating highest and best use has been described by many appraisers as the most critical step in the total appraisal process. Some steps of the process may be more technical, others may lead more directly to the value conclusion, but none is more basic or fundamental than the concept of highest and best use.

FOUR AGENTS OF PRODUCTION

Economic theory holds that for any good or service to be produced, expenditures must be made for the agents of production: land, labor, capital, and coordination.

Definitions

--**Land** refers to the earth and all its resources, which include water, fish, game, woods, and minerals in their natural state. Land provides the basic space and the raw materials needed for all production.

--**Labor** is the work required to obtain and process natural resources, to shape them into salable products, and to transport these products to a location where buyers will purchase them. Management and highly skilled labor such as that provided by an engineer or architect are not included in this category.

--**Capital** refers to the money committed to the creation and operation of an enterprise apart from the money needed for the other three agents of production. Materials, tools, machinery, warehouses, and buildings, which are the physical parts of the enterprise and not part of the natural land, represent forms of invested capital.

--**Coordination** refers to the knowledge, skill, business acumen, managerial talent, and entrepreneurial ability that are typically required to provide beneficial items efficiently. Successful production of some items requires more or less coordination, but all items require this agent of production in some degree.

Because a limited amount of each of these agents is available in any one area at any one time, production costs are largely shaped by competition in the local market. There is competition for land in real estate markets; for labor in employment markets; for capital in financial markets; and for coordination in markets for trained professionals, skilled entrepreneurs, and effective business managers. Naturally, local markets are often influenced by the broader markets for these agents and by external economic conditions. Therefore, for example, residential appraisers must follow trends that affect local construction costs to analyze supply and understand the data used in the cost approach. These supply-side costs will be discussed further in Chapters 6 and 13.

SURPLUS PRODUCTIVITY

Surplus productivity is defined as the net income remaining after the four agents of production have been paid. It may be attributed to the land in its present use. Surplus productivity is dependent upon the principles of balance and increasing and decreasing returns and the proper apportionment of the four agents of production.

SUPPLY AND DEMAND

The principle of supply and demand involves the interrelationship of the desire for a commodity and its scarcity. Demand for a commodity is created by its utility (ability to satisfy a need) and its scarcity and is limited by the financial ability of people to purchase it. The greater the supply of a commodity, the lower its price will tend to be. There is a point, at least theoretically, at which supply and demand are in balance. At this point, market value tends to reflect the cost of production or replacement. As the supply increases or demand decreases, the price in the market decreases. Recently this market phenomenon has been called a soft market.

Abstract demand is unlimited--that is, people continually desire more goods. But effective demand is limited in the economic sense by the purchasing power of the participants in the market. Because demand is closely related to desire, both advertising and education can greatly influence demand.

Among the factors affecting supply and demand for housing are population changes, purchasing power, and price levels. The supply of housing, for example, is controlled in part by rentals and sales prices and the relationship these bear to the temper of the market. A certain combination of factors must be present in the housing market to stimulate additions to the housing supply. There must be a shortage in the supply of units, a strong demand for housing, and effective purchasing power to satisfy the demand at the rentals and prices offered, which in turn must be high enough to encourage builders to construct new units. If demand is very strong and purchasing power is increasing faster than the ability of the supply to satisfy the increased need, rentals and sale prices for available units rise (inflation results when demand exceeds supply). When increased rentals or sales prices continue to find a ready market, more builders enter the scene, accelerating the pace of additions to the supply. Should this result in an excess of units, prices fall (deflation results when supply exceeds demand).

Other factors influencing the real estate market are the cost of labor, taxation of property, the money supply and the cost of financing, rent controls, zoning and other government regulations.

The following principles operate within the structure of the market. Market activity is composed of supply and demand; the interaction of the two is expressed as a price. To understand the influence of the market on prices (as well as on values and costs), the appraiser must understand and apply the concept of micro- and macro-economics. Micro-economics is the study of the individual property in the market. Macro-economics is the study of the industry; in real estate appraising it applies to all the properties of a certain type and their activity in the market.

Obviously a substantial difference exists between the study of an individual residence in its market and the analysis of all such residences as a segment of the market. The basic principles that follow are applicable to both micro and macro situations although the application and interpretation may vary.

Although all of these relationships and reactions are stated definitely, there may be exceptions (called "phenomena"); furthermore, these are indicated as "tendencies," that is, "the price tends to increase," etc.

ANTICIPATION

Value is created by the expectation of benefits to be derived in the future. The future, not the past, is important in deriving estimates of value. The primary use of past experience is in its significance in forecasting possible future trends and conditions.

Value may be defined as the present worth of the rights to all prospective future benefits, tangible and intangible, accruing to the ownership of real estate. In most cases the quantity, quality and duration of future benefits may be estimated in the light of past experience as disclosed by analysis of the property being appraised and comparable properties.

An illustration of changing attitudes and wants on the part of a segment of the residential market is found in the reactions during the energy crunch in 1974 and 1975. Some consumers in the market altered their desires for housing, from larger to smaller units within closer proximity to employment and schools, with more attention to the costs to heat and cool the structure. Such a significant change in a major part of the market must be considered by the professional appraiser in his or her analysis.

Recent sales prices of comparable houses indicate the attitudes of informed buyers and investors in the market concerning the present value of the anticipated benefits of ownership of a particular property. However, the market value of an individual property is not necessarily established by past selling price or by the cost to create it.

BALANCE

Maximum value is achieved when the agents of production are in economic balance. The value of a property depends on the balance of these four:

1. Land (rents).
2. Labor (wages).
3. Capital (the investment in buildings and equipment).
4. Coordination (management or entrepreneurial contribution).

The classical economists, especially David Ricardo, recognized the importance of the agents of production. They are used today to help explain the principle of balance and the residual nature of the value of the land.

There is a theoretical point of equilibrium in each property that will produce the greatest net return. An imbalance exists when a building represents an under-improvement or overimprovement in relation to its site; one also is present when the cost and amount of special services to the occupants are inadequate or excessive when related to the character of the building or neighborhood. These conditions illustrate the principle of balance, affirming that a disadvantage or loss in value attends any excess or deficiency in the contribution of the four agents of production.

The use of goods and services resulting from these agents produces gross income. Gross income is first applied to labor, capital, coordination and finally to land.

The principle of balance is applied in the process of estimating highest and best use in appraisal practice. Thus the proper apportionment of the agents of production is essential if maximum net return is to be produced and maximum land value developed. Because land has last claim on the gross income produced by the proper apportionment of the four agents, the land value is residual.

The natural operation of the market is towards balance. This concept applies to individual productive units as well as to all units in a market. It is difficult to alter the relationship the units of production in an existing building, although it might be accomplished by a renovation program, refinancing or new ownership. New units added to the market use the experience of existing units to maximize their chances of reaching balance.

Three sub-elements of the principle of balance are contribution, increasing and decreasing returns and surplus productivity, each involving the agents of production.

CHANGE

Change is constantly occurring; in real estate it affects individual properties, neighborhoods and cities. Change can evolve so slowly that it is almost indiscernible. The appraiser must be sensitive to subtle as well as obvious indications of change. The future, not the past, is of primary importance in the valuation of real estate.

The appraiser's concern is with the market's view of transition. Recognition must be made of the social, economic, governmental and environmental forces at work and their present and future effect on the market value of single family residences.

Individual properties, districts, neighborhoods and entire communities often follow a four-phase life span:

--**Growth.** A period during which there are gains in public favor and acceptance.

--**Stability.** A period of equilibrium without marked gains or losses.

--**Decline.** A period of diminishing demand and acceptance.

--**Renewal.** A period of rejuvenation and rebirth of market demand.

In the market the basis of the value of a property is neither the price paid for it in the past nor the cost of its creation, but rather the prospective amenities and uses that buyers and sellers believe it will provide for them in the future. The actions of the market (sales) reflect informed buyers' opinions of the probable future benefits of ownership. The attitude of the market towards property in a specific neighborhood reflects the probable future trend of that neighborhood. For example, following World War II, more ranch-style houses were built than two-story houses. Buyers in the market developed a preference for one-story houses, reducing the demand for two-story houses.

COMPETITION AND EXCESS PROFIT

Profit tends to breed competition and excess profit tends to encourage ruinous competition. Profit is defined as that portion of the net income produced by real property over and above the costs of labor, capital, coordination and land (the agents of production).

Profit as applied to real property is not the same as profit obtained from the operation of a business. Normal business profit is the monetary incentive and reward for capital investment. The yield on real property investments also is the monetary incentive for investment in land and buildings. But profit, as it is considered by the appraiser, is the prospective net income remaining after operating costs and adequate returns on land and building(s) have been satisfied. In other words, it is what remains after providing for the agents of production.

Competition is one of the most familiar and easily recognized forces present at all levels of economic activity. Reasonable competition stimulates further creative contribution, but in excess it can destroy profits. A lack of competition, such as created by a monopolistic situation, must be recognized by the appraiser as being outside the realm of market value definition and consider it accordingly in his or her analysis. The appraiser not only recognizes competition in normal situations but also perceives those situations in which it is excessive and, if unchecked, may undermine value. Competition is a product of supply and demand; a proper study of the highest and best use of a property includes current supply and demand factors.

CONFORMITY

Maximum value is realized when a reasonable degree of architectural homogeneity exists and land uses are compatible. Conformity in use is usually a highly desirable feature of real property since it tends to create and maintain value; and maximum value affords the owner maximum return. Reasonable homogeneity implies reasonable similarity; it does not mean monotonous uniformity. Generally, the most satisfactory use of land is realized when it conforms to the standards governing the area in which it is located.

The standards of conformity are subject to the principle of change. For example, racial homogeneity was once considered a sign of social conformity and neighborhood stability. Conversely, racial integration was once considered a sign of social non-conformity and neighborhood decline. Social perceptions and attitudes have changed. The notion that racial or ethnic homogeneity is a requirement for maximum value is without empirical support. Many strong and stable neighborhoods are composed of residents of varied and diverse racial, religious and cultural backgrounds.

Other signs of change may be observed in architectural design and urban planning. The trend toward multipurpose urban structures and a deliberate mixing of land uses reflects an increasing awareness of the interdependence of land uses to maximize utility and value.

The elements of conformity are not preconceived standards of development but have evolved as cities have grown and land uses have multiplied. Homeowners have recognized the advantages of living in neighborhoods designed and developed to provide facilities or amenities which add to the benefits of ownership, and they have protected those assets by maintaining conformity through zoning.

CONTRIBUTION

The principle of contribution (also known as the principle of marginal productivity) is the principle of increasing and decreasing returns applied to a portion or portions of real property. It affirms that the value of any individual agent in production depends on how much it contributes to value by its presence or detracts by its absence. An example of this principle in the appraisal of residential properties is the valuation of lots of varying depths. The appraiser must estimate the value, if any, that additional depth contributes to a parcel over and above the value of lots of standard depth in the area. If the lot is of less than standard depth, its value would reflect a loss of contribution attributable to the missing piece.

This principle has practical application in estimating the degree of overimprovement, underimprovement, or misplaced improvement in highest and best use analysis.

--Increasing and Decreasing Returns. Larger amounts of the agents of production produce a greater net income up to a point, at which the maximum value has been developed; any additional expenditures will not produce a return commensurate with such investment. The fertilization of farmland affords a simple example of this principle. Up to a certain point, increasing use of fertilizer results in a greater crop yield; beyond that point, it will not produce an additional return sufficient to warrant th additional cost.

It is frequently necessary to determine the character and size of the structural improvements that will enable the land to produce the greatest net yield. To ascertain this point, hypothetical combinations of probable income and expenses and capital requirements for improvements of various types and sizes should be analyzed. Different combinations may represent higher or lower probable yields.

The process of developing hypothetical improvements to determine that combination of the agents of production providing the greatest yield illustrates the principle of increasing and decreasing returns.

EXTERNALITIES

The principle of externalities is that external economics result from goods, products, or conditions that have a positive or negative effect on people other than those who produce or own the goods or products, or who create the conditions. For example, an external economy occurs when one group of ticket purchasers for a concert pays a price higher than the cost of its seats so that others may attend at a lower, subsidized price. When external economics affect great numbers of people, the product or service will probably be provided by government. Bridges, highways, police and fire protection, and other commonly needed services are provided more cheaply per user through common purchase by the government than through separate purchase by each individual.

External economics occur when costs or inconveniences are imposed on other people by an individual or a firm. For example, a person who litters imposes the cleanup costs on other people. A business firm that erects an unattractive sign imposes the cost of offensive visual sensations on people who see the sign.

Real estate is affected by externalities more than any other type of economic good, service, or commodity. Its physical immobility subjects it to many types of external influences. Such influences emanate from all levels - international, national, regional, community, and neighborhood. The influences may be as broad as international currency and gold prices or as narrow as a neighbor's standard of maintenance. An appraiser should be knowledgeable about, and analyze the impact of, all such influences on a parcel of real estate.

At the international and national levels, such influences as international trade policy, manufacturing efficiency, interest rates, and socioeconomic priorities affect real estate values greatly. For example, the combination of these influences caused many U.S. real estate values in the early 1980's to fall or to increase less rapidly than in previous years. Foreign imports tended to make U.S. manufacturing operations and equipment less efficient than certain foreign counterparts. High interest rates tended to depress home buying and industrial expansion.

Moreover, a lesser emphasis on homeownership as a national priority resulted in competition for credit. Borrowers who wanted to buy a home had to compete with government and industry.

At the regional level, real estate values during these years prospered better in some areas than in others. Generally, the population migration to the Sunbelt tended to enhance values there at the expense of older, northern regions, where values tended to stabilize or decline. Industrial areas with manufacturing operations most susceptible to foreign competition suffered more than areas less reliant on such

At the community and neighborhood levels, property values are affected by local laws, local government policies and administration, property taxes, economic growth, and social attitudes. Different trends in property values often are noted among communities in the same state or region and among neighborhoods in the same community. An appraiser should be familiar with such externalities and be able to assess their impact on individual property values.

SUBSTITUTION

When several commodities or services with substantially the same utility or benefit are available, the one with the lowest price attracts the greatest demand and widest distribution. The importance and application of this principle can be found in many segments of the economy. In real estate, for example, if two homes offer approximately the same advantages, the prospective buyer will select the one with the lower price.

The principle of substitution is found in each of the three approaches to value:

--Sales Comparison Approach. When there are alternate choices of like or similar residences, market value tends to be set at the price of acquiring an equally desirable substitute property, assuming that no costly delay is encountered in making the substitution.

--Cost Approach. No rational person will pay more for a property than that amount for which one can obtain, by purchase of a site and construction of a building without undue delay, a property of equal desirability and utility.

--Income Approach. Value tends to be set by the effective investment necessary to acquire, without undue delay, a comparable substitute income property offering an equally desirable net income return.

The principle of substitution is the basis for these premises:

1. The market value of property tends to match the value indicated by the actions of informed buyers in the market for comparable real estate having similar physical and locational characteristics.

2. The cost of producing, through new construction, an equally desirable substitute property may set the upper limit of value, if new construction can be completed in a reasonable period of time.

3. The value of a property tends to be related to its competitive position among alternative investment choices producing the same net income.

HIGHEST AND BEST USE

Fundamental to the concept of value is the theory of highest, best and most profitable use. Highest and best use is defined as: "The reasonable and probable use that will support the highest present value, as defined, as of the effective date of the appraisal". It is also defined as: "The use, from among reasonably probable and legal alternative uses, found to be physically possible, appropriately supported and financially feasible and which results in highest land value".

This definition applies specifically to the highest and best use of land. Where a site has existing improvements, the highest and best use of the site as if vacant may be different from the existing use. The existing use will continue, however, unless and until land value in its highest and best use exceeds the total value of the property in its current use.

Implied in the definition of highest and best use is the concept that, in addition to the maximazation of profit for the property owner, consideration must also be given to the effect on the community environment and to the overall community development goals. Also implied is that the determination of highest and best use results from the appraiser's judgment and analytical skill--that is, that the use determined from analysis represents opinion, not a fact. In appraisal practice, the concept of highest and best use represents the premise on which value is based. In the context for most probable selling price (market value), another appropriate term to reflect highest and best use would be most probable use.

The most profitable likely use cannot always be interpreted in terms of money. Net return sometimes takes the form of amenities, usually more applicable to houses than other kinds of properties.

Deed restriction, zoning and government regulations may not conform to current market requirements, and thus the site may remain undeveloped to its highest and best use. If the site has more valuable use potential then allowed by law, and if there is a reasonable probability that a change in use will be permitted, its value will be affected to the extent that a buyer or seller might recognize this potential, after giving due consideration to the expense involved in the change.

FORCES THAT INFLUENCE REAL PROPERTY VALUE

The value of all real property--including residential property--is created, maintained, modified or destroyed by the interplay of four great forces that affect human behavior.

1. Social ideals and standards.
2. Economic activities and trends.
3. Government regulations and actions.

4. Physical or environmental forces.

These dynamic forces set the pattern for the variables affecting real estate market values. Combined, they are the essence of cause and effect that influences every parcel of real estate on earth and directly affects both the demand and the supply side of the market.

SOCIAL IDEALS AND STANDARDS

When these forces are closely examined, it becomes apparent that they are composed of many complex factors that are constantly changing. A partial list of social forces includes:

1. Population growth, decline or stability.
2. Shifts in population density.
3. Changes in family size.
4. Geographical distribution of social groups.
5. Attitudes toward education and social activities.
6. Attitudes toward architectural design and utility.
7. Factors emerging from human social instincts, ideals, moral codes, likes and dislikes.

ECONOMIC ACTIVITIES AND TRENDS

Economic forces, including the resources and efforts of society to achieve its social goals, are made up of factors such as:

1. Gross national product.
2. Economic trends and activity.
3. Employment trends and wage levels.
4. Availability of money and credit.
5. Price levels. Interest rates and tax burdens.
6. All other factors having an effect upon purchasing power.

GOVERNMENT REGULATIONS AND ACTIONS

Forces created by government regulations and activities include:

1. Zoning laws.
2. Building codes.
3. Environmental regulations.
4. Police and fire regulations.
5. Rent controls, national defense measures, special-use permits, and credit controls.
6. Government-sponsored housing and guaranteed mortgage loans.
7. Monetary policies, including all forms of taxation, that affect the free use of real estate.

PHYSICAL OR ENVIRONMENTAL FORCES

Physical or environmental forces created by either nature or society encompass:

1. Natural resources.
2. Climate and topography

3. Characteristics of soil and subsoil to support improvements.
4. Soil fertility.
5. Mineral resources.
6. Flood control and soil conservation.
7. Technological advances affecting land use.

Because all these factors affect cost, price and value, their impact--whether direct or indirect---must be considered in estimating the cost, the probable price or the value of real property. These four forces and the factors comprising them constitute the basic raw material for making an appraisal of value. Any decision on or action about the market value of real estate is based upon an appraisal, whether it is a formal narrative written report or a verbal estimate of value.

Students of real property valuation are prone to attempt to categorize a factor specifically and concisely under one of the four forces. Often, however, a factor may appear in two or more of the classifications. The reason for itemizing the four major forces is to assist both beginning and experienced appraisers in making a comprehensive analysis of all possible factors and conditions that may affect a real estate decision. To assist in classifying activities and trends in the most appropriate categories, greatest emphasis is given to the force from which the factor tends to stem. For example, the impact of population statistics is typically classified under social forces but the appraiser recognizes that it may be expressed in terms of economic impact as well.

The conclusions drawn from all the forces must be expressed in terms of dollars, but this does not justify the inclusion of all activities under the economic force. Another example of potential conflict in classifying has to do with natural resources. As illustrated so dramatically in the energy crisis, a shortage of fuel is typically expressed economically although the matter is originally and primarily classified as a physical and environmental force.

FACTORS OF VALUE

Because the term value has many possible interpretations, its meaning for the appraisal of real property must be precise. Value has been defined as the quantity of one thing that can be obtained in exchange for another or the ratio of exchange of one commodity for another. Money is the common denominator by which real property value is usually measured.

An appraisal of value is based on an interpretation by the appraiser of facts and value indications processed and reconciled to produce an estimate as of a specific date. Because the term appraised value is too general, the type of value must be precisely defined in the appraisal report. The value most commonly sought in an appraisal is market value, although there are other types of value that may be considered depending on the use for which the client requires the appraisal and the nature of the valuation problem being solved. Obviously, the reliability of an appraised value depends on the basic competence and integrity of the appraiser and on the skill with which pertinent data is processed.

The emphasis in appraising is on the relationship between a thing desired and the potential purchaser or consumer. The idea that need alone is responsible for the creation of value would imply that value is a characteristic inherent in the object itself. If this concept were true, bread would be intrinsically valuable because it is needed to satisfy hunger. But hunger is limited; therefore, if bread were produced in excess of the need to satisfy all normal hunger, its value would decrease. The value of any object is not intrinsic but depends upon the relationship between supply and demand.

An object also cannot have value unless it has utility--that is, unless it is able to satisfy the desire for possession; but utility is relative to the satisfaction gained from the object. For example, bread has great utility to a hungry person but much less to one who is not hungry.

Although utility is basic to value, utility alone does not establish value. Scarcity also must be present before significant value exists. For example, air is highly useful but because it is usually so plentiful it has little value. No object, including a parcel of real estate, can have value unless it possesses in some degree the two factors of utility and scarcity.

Utility and scarcity do not alone create value. The other element necessary if an object is to have value (as defined by the appraiser) is purchasing power--the ability of the individual to participate in the market in order to satisfy the desire to possess. For example, if no one has the purchasing power (money) to buy bread, bread becomes valueless.

The appraiser's interpretation of value can be summarized as follows:

1. Value is not a characteristic inherent in real property itself but depends on the desires of people. It varies from person to person and from time to time, as individual wants vary.

2. An object (real property) cannot have value unless it has utility. Usefulness arouses desire for possession and has the power to give satisfaction.

3. An object (real property) must also be relatively scarce to have value.

4. The desire of a purchaser who has the purchasing power to buy must be aroused for the object to have value.

Unlike rapidly consumed goods, the benefits of real property are realized over a much longer period. Land and its improvements have a useful life usually extending over decades. The value of real property, consequently, is equal to the present value of the future benefits forthcoming from the property. Estimating the market value of the highest and best use is the paramount problem in the valuation of real estate. Any such estimate must take into consideration the social, economic, government and environmental forces that may influence the property's highest and best use. A clear understanding of current and future conditions and the perception to recognize the forces that modify and affect these conditions are essential.

In considering these factors, the professional appraiser should never lose sight of the fact that what must really be interpreted are the reactions of typical users and investors. Appraisers do not make value; they interpret it, chiefly from market evidence. The appraiser must sift through large quantities of data to select those that have the greatest significance relative to market value.

DISTINCTIONS AMONG VALUE, PRICE, AND COST

Appraisers make important distinctions among the terms value, price and cost. By traditional definition, value and price are equal only under conditions of a perfect market. Value, as applied to real estate, represents an expected price that should result under specific conditions. Price, commonly referred to as a sale or transaction price, is an accomplished fact. A price represents what a particular purchaser agreed to pay and a particular seller agreed to accept under the particular circumstances surrounding their transaction.

Presumptions requisite for market value - rational behavior by buyer and seller and no undue duress or pressure - are not implicit in any actual sales price. Neither is there a presumption that the transaction was typical in the market. Without making an appraisal, an appraiser does not know whether a price actually paid or received represented the property's value. Although actual prices can provide strong evidence of market value, the appraiser must analyze specific transaction prices carefully before reaching a market value conclusion.

Cost, as used in appraisal procedures, applies to production, not exchange, and is not synonymous with either value or price. Cost is the total dollar expenditure for labor, materials, legal services, architectural design, financing, taxes during construction, interest, contractor's overhead and profit, and entrepreneurial overhead and profit. Cost is either a retrospective fact or a current estimate. It may or may not have a direct relationship to the utility (present or future) of the property created. Consider, for instance, the classic example of the luxury hotel built in an unpopular location. The hotel might cost much to build but have little value because of the lack of business.

Appraisal procedures provide the means to refine conclusions about whether the cost to construct a property equals the property's market value. Such market conditions as oversupply, undersupply, or poor design cause market values to fall below the current cost of duplicate development. Cost will equal market value if the new building represents the highest and best use of the land as though vacant; that is, if there is no accrued depreciation. Value can exceed cost only to the extent that buyers are willing to avoid the delay of constructing a duplicate, or it is not possible to construct or duplicate in a suitable location.

VALUE DEFINITIONS FOR REAL PROPERTY APPRAISAL

By far the majority of residential appraisal assignments are to estimate the market value of the residence. However, appraisers receive a wide variety of other assignments for many different purposes. It is therefore necessary that many types of value be understood.

MARKET VALUE

Market value, or value-in-exchange, is relative. It implies a comparison of available alternative economic goods from which the potential purchaser may make a choice; it also reflects the interaction of buyers, sellers and investors.

Most real estate appraisal assignments involve estimates of market value. Numerous definitions of market value have been devised over the years by professional organizations, government bodies and the courts. These definitions are subject to frequent change, and appraisers performing services that may be subject to litigation are cautioned to seek the exact definition of market value which is accepted in the jurisdiction in which the services are performed. A widely accepted definition of market value accepted by the Federal National Mortgage Corporation and the Federal National Mortgage Association is:

"The highest price in terms of money which a property should bring in a competitive and open market under all conditions requisite to a fair sale, the buyer and seller each acting prudently, knowledgeably and assuming the price is not affected by undue stimulus. Implicit in this definition is the consummation of a sale as of a specified date and the passing of title from seller to buyer under conditions whereby: (1) buyer and seller are typically motivated; (2) both parties are well informed or well advised, and each is acting in what he considers his own best interest; (3) a reasonable time is allowed for exposure in the open market; (4) Payment is made in terms of cash in U.S. Dollars or in terms of financial arrangements comparable thereto; (5) the price represents the normal consideration for the property sold unaffected by special or creative financing or sales concessions* granted by anyone associated with the sale."

*Adjustments to the comparables must be made for special or creative financing or sales concessions. No adjustments are necessary for those costs which are normally paid by sellers as a result of tradition or law in a market area; these costs are readily identifiable since the seller pays these costs in virtually all sales transactions. Special or creative financing adjustments can be made to the comparable property by comparison of financing terms offered by a third party institutional lender not already involved in the property or transaction. Any adjustment should not be calculated on a mechanical dollar-for-dollar cost of the financing or concession but rather, the dollar amount of any adjustment should approximate the market's reaction to the financing or concessions based on the appraiser's judgment.

Because of varied decisions in different legal jurisdictions, there is no "universal" definition of market value. Each definition carries its own parameters and presumptions.

Obviously, different definitions of market value can result in different value estimates, and appraisers should be careful to state the definition they use in an appraisal.[6]

Market value, or value in exchange, is the purpose of most valuations. A market value estimate reflects the appraiser's interpretation of the actions of buyers and sellers in the marketplace.

OTHER VALUES IN RESIDENTIAL APPRAISAL

In the process of solving an appraisal problem, one of the earliest decisions that must be made is the kind of value applicable to the situation i.e., value-in-use or value-in-exchange. The decision is based on the problem to be solved. If it is a question of the most probable selling price, then the appraiser is committed to value-in-exchange. If the problem is related to a proposed renovation program, then the most likely kind of value may be value-in-use to the owner. A financial institution considering a mortgage wants to know the likely selling price of the property; therefore, the market value (value-in-exchange) is the appropriate kind of value. Assessed value historically has been based on costs rather than market prices, which tends to relate such values to "use" rather than "market" values. In recent years, however, there has been a trend to relate assessed values to the market rather than solely to costs to reproduce or replace.

VALUE-IN-USE

Use value is the value or importance of an object to a particular owner who may have no intention of exposing it on the open market. Value-in-use has been defined as the value of an economic good to its owner-user based on its productivity (in the form of income, utility or amenity).

Value-in-use does not necessarily represent market value, unless there are a significant number of buyer-users active in the market place who are willing and able to pursue the commodity or service.

INVESTMENT VALUE

Closely related to use value is investment value. As employed in appraisal assignments, investment value is the value of an investment to a particular investor based on his or her investment requirements. In contrast to market value, investment value is value to an individual, rather than value in the marketplace.

Investment value is the subjective relationship between a particular investor and a given investment. When measured in dollars, it is the highest price an investor would pay for an investment in view of its perceived capacity to satisfy a desire, need, or investment goal. In colloquial use, investment value may refer to the "reasoned value" of a given investment from the viewpoint of a typical, rather than actual, investor. In all appraisals that estimate investment value, specific investment criteria must be known.

Investment value appraisals are fairly common when the appraiser is employed by a potential purchaser of an existing investment or income-producing property, or by a developer of a new property.

INSURABLE VALUE

Insurable value is based on the concept of replacement and/or reproduction cost of physical items subject to lose from hazards. Insurable value designates the amount of insurance that may or should be carried on destructible portions of a property to indemnify the owner in the event of loss.

LIQUIDATION VALUE

Liquidation value is a price that an owner is compelled to accept when the property must be sold with less-than-reasonable market exposure.

ASSESSED VALUE

Assessed value is a value based on a uniform schedule for tax rolls in ad valorem taxation. The schedule may not conform to market value, but usually has some relation to a market value base.

SUMMARY

Real estate has economic value and significance only as it satisfies the needs and desires of human beings. Land has been studied throughout history and these studies have included geography, law, sociology and economics. An appraiser must understand all of these concepts as a required background for their appraisal activities.

Interests in real estate are shared between the government and the property owner. The rights of the property owner may be further limited by restrictions inserted into deeds by prior owners. The rights of the property owner are often described as a "bundle of rights".

Division of earnings or productivity occurs when ownership is an undivided fractional interest such as tenancy-in-common or joint tenancy. Another category of fractional ownership or interest is a division of the physical use of the property. When the property is leased, the interest is divided between the owner and the tenant. The appraiser must be familiar with how these rights are divided.

The value of land depends on its usefulness, including all of its improvements and appurtenant rights. Real property is distinct from personal property and chattels. Title is limited by the four great powers of government and frequently by private restrictions and agreements as well. There are many facets to the term value, but the real estate appraiser is customarily interested in estimating market value (value-in-exchange). The legal definition of market value becomes most significant when an assignment will involve litigation where precise, legally accepted definitions are required.

Several fundamental economic principles provide the basis for analyzing the action of the real estate market, which are of particular interest to the real estate appraiser.

FOUR AGENTS OF PRODUCTION

Economic theory holds that for any good or service to be produced, expenditures must be made for the agents of production: land, labor, capital, and coordination.

SURPLUS PRODUCTIVITY

After the four agents of production are paid for, what ever value is left is attributable to the land.

SUPPLY AND DEMAND

1. Utility and scarcity combined create demand, which is the desire for possession.
2. Demand is effective only when supported by purchasing power.
3. Value is increased if supply is reduced or demand increased.

ANTICIPATION

1. Value is the present worth of the rights to all prospective future benefits accruing to ownership and use of real property.

2. Recent sales prices of comparable properties indicate the market value of such rights and benefits.

BALANCE

1. The value of a property depends on the balance of the four agents of production: labor, capital, coordination, and land.

CHANGE

1. Change is constantly occurring.

2. Cities, neighborhoods and individual properties undergo the process of change.

3. The effect of prospective changes is reflected in the market.

4. Change is fundamentally the law of cause and effect.

CONFORMITY

1. Conformity is the result of a reasonable degree of architectural homo-geneity and compatible land uses.

2. The standards of conformity have changed over the years reflecting changes in market attitudes, social trends, economic conditions and public policy.

3. The highest and best land use is generally realized under circumstances of harmony or conformity.

4. The principal purpose of zoning regulation and private restriction is to maintain conformity.

CONTRIBUTION

1. The principle of contribution deals with increasing and decreasing return applied to a portion or portions of an improvement.

2. The value of an item in production is measured by its contribution to the net return of the enterprise.

3. Application of this principle is basic to any feasibility study or remodeling or modernization program and in the valuation of lots of varying depths.

EXTERNALITIES

The principle externalities says that goods, products or conditions produced by one group of people can have an effect on many other people besides the ones who produce them.

SUBSTITUTION

1. The value of a property tends to be indicated by the value of an equally desirable substitute property.

2. The value of a property tends to coincide with the value indicated by the actions of informed buyers in the market for comparable properties.

3. Disadvantage attends any excess or deficiency in the supply of the agents of production.

4. Equilibrium (balance) in character, amount and location of essential uses of real estate creates and maintains value.

5. The principle of contribution is related to surplus productivity in that the value of an individual agent of production depends upon how much it adds to or detracts from the income because of its presence.

HIGHEST AND BEST USE

1. Highest and best use is that which, at the time of appraisal, is the most profitable, likely use of a property. It may also be defined as the available use and program of future utilization that produces the highest present land value.

2. Existing use may not conform to highest and best use.

3. Highest and best use may comprise a combination of profitable interim (transition) uses and a deferred, more profitable potential use.

4. Highest and best use may be limited by zoning or deed restrictions

5. Improvements must add to the value of the land in order to have value attributed to them.

6. The principle of increasing and decreasing returns affirms the proper apportionment of land and improvement to achieve maximum land value.

7. Balance and consistent use are important collateral considerations in the selection of highest and best use.

FORCES THAT INFLUENCE REAL PROPERTY VALUES

A value is created, maintained, modified or destroyed by the interplay of four great forces that affect human behavior (social, economic, government and physical or environmental). The appraiser expresses conclusions based on these forces in dollars of property value.

THE FACTORS OF VALUE

The meaning of value must be precise in the valuation process. Money is the common denominator by which real property value is measured. Real estate does not have value unless it has utility and scarcity.

DISTINCTIONS AMONG MARKET VALUE, PRICE AND COST

1. Price is the historic amount paid for something.

2. Cost is the total dollar expenditure for labor, materials, legal services, architectural design, etc.

3. Value is the expected price a property should bring under a specific set of assumptions.

VALUE DEFINITIONS FOR REAL PROPERTY VALUATION

Most residential appraisals are to estimate market value which must be defined as part of the report.

Market Value

'It is the highest price in terms of money which a property should bring in a competitive and open market under all conditions requisite to a fair sale. All full definitions expand and clarify this concept.

Other Values In Residential Appraisal

Besides market value the residential appraiser is called upon to estimate value-in-use, investment value, insurable value, assessed value and other special values.

2½ STORIES   PROTRUDING FRONT WING   COLUMNS ON CORNERS OF WING   GABLE ROOF

STONE

Colonial American

FRONT GABLE NEW ENGLAND COLONIAL OR CHARLESTON COLONIAL OR ENGLISH COLONIAL (F Gab NE or Charles or Eng Col - 114)

MANSARD ROOF

MASSIVE CORNICE AND
SUPPORTING BRACKETS

DECORATIVE
IRON WORK

MANY DORMERS

COLORED
GLASS
WINDOWS

FRENCH
DOORS

Nineteenth Century American

AMERICAN MANSARD OR SECOND EMPIRE STYLE
(Mansard or 2nd Emp - 707)

3 Valuation Process

For over 50 years, the appraisal profession has been working to perfect a process for estimating the value of real estate. The process is not stagnant--it improves as time goes on. Appraisers who feel they have an improvement to the process are invited to write an article for one of the appraisal journals published by the professional organizations. If the improvement gains acceptance, the next edition of the APPRAISAL OF REAL ESTATE[1] incorporates the change. (Most appraisers consider this to be the definitive work on real estate appraising.) However, there are many other texts covering different real estate appraising specialties.

The purpose of a professional appraisal is to help the client make a decision. For example, an appraisal helps a Lender decide if a property is adequate security for a proposed loan. Other purposes are to help a buyer or seller decide how much to buy or sell a house for, how much to insure a house for, its value for estate or tax purposes, etc.

The appraisal process, as it is described in this textbook, has been simplified. The author has kept in mind that the reader will be a new appraiser possibly with limited formal appraisal training.

THE VALUATION PROCESS

DEFINITION OF THE PROBLEM
    Identification of the Real Estate
    Identification of the Property Rights to be Valued
    Date of Value Estimate
    Use of the Appraisal
    Definition of Value
    Other Limiting Conditions

PRELIMINARY SURVEY AND APPRAISAL PLAN
    Data Needed
    Data Sources
    Personnel Needed
    Time Schedule
    Flow Chart
    Fee Contract

---

[1]*Appraisal of Real Estate*, 9th Edition, American Institute of Real Estate Appraisers, Chicago, IL 1988.

DATA COLLECTION AND ANALYSIS - GENERAL DATA
Economic
Market Analysis
Financial
Economic Base
Trends
Locational
Region
Community
Neighborhood

DATA COLLECTION AND ANALYSIS - SPECIFIC DATA
Appraised Property
Title & Record Data
Relationship of Site to Land Pattern
Physical Characteristics of the Site and Improvements
Description of the Improvements
Analysis of Highest and Best Use
Comparative Properties
Sales
Listings
Costs
Rentals
Site Value Estimate
Purpose of Separate Site Valuation
Procedures for Estimating Value
Sales Comparison Approach
Financing Terms
Conditions of Sale
Elements of Comparison
Market Conditions
Location
Physical Characteristics
Income Characteristics
Techniques for Making Adjustments
Reconciliation of Adjusted Site Sales Prices
Other Methods of Making Adjustments
The Allocation Method
Extraction Method
Capitalization of Ground Rental
Land Residual Technique

APPLICATION OF THE THREE APPROACHES
Cost Approach
Sales Comparison
Income

RECONCILIATION OF VALUE INDICATIONS INTO A FINAL ESTIMATE OF DEFINED VALUE

APPRAISAL REPORT

It is helpful for many appraisers and students to see the Valuation Process in the form of a flow chart:

FIG. 3-1 THE VALUATION PROCESS

THE VALUATION PROCESS

DEFINITION OF THE PROBLEM

The first step in an appraisal is to define the problem to be solved. There are six major steps in the definition of the problem.

      1. Identification of the Real Estate
         a) Site
         b) Improvements
         c) Personal Property
      2. Identification of the Property Rights to be Valued
      3. Date of Value Estimate
      4. Use of the Appraisal
      5. Definition of Value
      6. Other Limiting Conditions

IDENTIFICATION OF THE REAL ESTATE

It must be crystal clear to the reader of an Appraisal exactly what is being appraised. The appraisal must contain an accurate description of the real estate (Site and Improvements) and also any personal property included in the appraised value.

Identification of the Site

A property is first identified by means of a mailing address or other short description such as a lot number. This is shown in the "Subject" section of the Uniform Residential Appraisal Report (URAR). A more precise identification, such as that provided by a legal description which can be copied from the deed or mortgage, is also required. When available, a survey helps to precisely identify a property. Whether or not a complete legal description is needed in the appraisal is a matter of judgment. When a more complete description is included, it is attached as part of the addenda. More details about the site follow in the "Specific Data" section.

Identification of the Improvements

A required and important part of every appraisal is a complete, accurate description of all of the improvements included in the appraised value. More details about improvement identification follow in the "Specific Data" section.

Identification of the Personal Property

The statutes vary from state to state as to what is personal property and what is real estate. Appraisers should be familiar with the applicable statutes in the areas where they make appraisals. One cannot always tell just by physical inspection what is real estate and what is personal property.

In residential appraising, some typical items that fall into the gray area between real estate and personal property are carpeting, drapes, T.V. antennas, appliances and lighting fixtures.

IDENTIFICATION OF THE PROPERTY RIGHTS TO BE VALUED

An appraisal of real property is not directly a valuation of the physical land and improvements; it is a valuation of the rights of ownership. A specific appraisal may require a value estimate of all property rights, while another will analyze only limited rights in property. Ownership of property may be held by an individual, a partnership, a corporation or a group of heirs. When ownership is vested in more than one interest, each may hold an equal or unequal share.

The property rights or interests to be appraised may be fractional interests such as air rights over a specified property, subsurface rights, an easement, a right-of-way or fee simple subject to an easement. Because the value of real property is not limited to its physical components, the appraiser cannot define the problem precisely until fully aware of which property rights are involved. Without this knowledge, the appraiser may produce an estimate of value that is irrelevant to the problem. A clear conception of the rights being appraised will also help the appraiser evaluate the complexity of the problem and the amount of work it will require.

DATE OF VALUE ESTIMATE

An appraisal must be a value estimate as of a specific date. The value of a property may change from day to day. For example, the sudden announcement of some event that affects of the market will have a significant effect on the value of property. Typical announcements which affect the value of property are the expansion or contraction of business activities in the area which are major sources of employment. Other announcements that suddenly affect value are the additions or relocation of roads and highways or anything else in the close vicinity of the property.

Sudden changes in the physical condition of the property by fire, the environment or man-made additions, demolitions or alterations all affect the property value.

When the date of the appraisal is the same date as the date of last inspection, no assumptions about the future or past are needed. On the other hand, when the date of the appraisal is either before or after the date of last inspection, the appraisal must contain statements that express the assumptions the appraiser made about the property on the date of the appraisal.

It is very customary for an appraisal to be as of some date in the past. The appraiser then makes assumptions about the condition of the property and the site as of that date and uses data that reflect values as of the date of the appraisal.

Appraisals that attempt to estimate the value of the property in the future tend to be speculative. Special care must be take by the appraiser to fully report all of the assumptions that were made (or not made) about the property, the neighborhood, the community and region, the economy (both locally and nationally), and other unknown information about the future. Most appraisals of future value tend to be highly speculative in nature, in spite of the care appraisers use to tell what assumptions were made.

USE OF THE APPRAISAL

The objective of most appraisals is to estimate the value of a property as of a specific date. Market value is by far the most common value that is estimated by appraisers, but there are other kinds of value estimates such as insurable value, investment value, partial interest value, etc. that are becoming a more significant proportion of the assignments available to appraisers.

It is helpful for the appraiser to know the purpose of the appraisal so that the report will provide the reader with all of the information required to make a decision. When the appraisal is made for mortgage lending purposes, the appraiser must know if it should comply with Freddie Mac, Fannie Mae, HUD/FHA, VA, or FmHA requirements. Each of these organizations have their own special appraisal requirements.

DEFINITION OF VALUE

In all cases, it is necessary that the appraisal include a clear statement as to what value is being estimated. Appraisals that are made for loan purposes base their Value Estimate on "Market Value". The current accepted definition of "Market Value" is either attached to each appraisal or a copy is filed by the appraiser with the client and is referred to in the appraisal. Below is that portion of form FHLMC #439-FNMA #1004B which has the Freddie Mac - Fannie Mae accepted "Market Value" definition.

"DEFINITION OF MARKET VALUE: The most probable price which a property should bring in a competitive and open market under all conditions requisite to a fair sale, the buyer and seller, each acting prudently, knowledgeably and assuming the price is not affected by undue stimulus. Implicit in this definition is the consummation of a sale as of specified date and the passing of title from seller to buyer under conditions whereby: (1) buyer and seller are typically motivated; (2) both parties are well informed or well advised, and each acting in what he considers his own best interest; (3) a reasonable time is allowed for exposure in the open market; (4) payment is made in terms of cash in U.S. dollars or in terms of financial arrangements comparable thereto; and (5) the price represents the normal consideration for the property sold unaffected by special or creative financing or sales concessions* granted by anyone associated with the sale.

*Adjustments to the comparables must be made for special or creative financing or sales concessions. No adjustments are necessary for those costs which are normally paid by sellers as a result of tradition or law in a market area; these costs are readily identifiable since the seller pays these costs in virtually all sales transactions. Special or creative financing adjustments can be made to the comparable property by comparisons to financing terms offered by a third party institutional lender that is not already involved in the property or transaction. Any adjustment should not be calculated on a mechanical dollar for dollar cost of the financing or concession but the dollar amount of any adjustment should approximate the market's reaction to the financing or concessions based on the appraiser's judgment."

OTHER LIMITING CONDITIONS

For the appraiser's and client's protection, it is often important to add additional limiting conditions. The following are eight which might be appropriate.[1]

1. Any value estimates provided in the report apply to the entire property, and any portion or division of the total into fractional interests will invalidate the value estimate, unless such portion or division of interests has been set forth in the report.

2. Only preliminary plans and specifications were available in the preparation of this appraisal; the analysis, therefore, is subject to a review of the final plans and specifications when available.

---

[1]*Appraisal of Real Estate*, 9th Edition, American Institute of Real Estate Appraisers, Chicago, IL 1988.

3. Any proposed improvements are assumed to have been completed unless otherwise stipulated; any construction is assumed to conform with the building plans referenced in the report.

4. The appraiser assumes that the reader or user of this report has been provided with copies of available building plans and all leases and amendments, if any, encumbering the property.

5. No legal description or survey was furnished so the appraiser utilized the county tax plat to ascertain the physical dimensions and acreage of the property. Should a survey prove these characteristics inaccurate, it may be necessary for this appraisal to be adjusted.

6. The forecasts, projections, or operating estimates contained herein are based upon current market conditions, anticipated short-term supply and demand factors, and a continued stable economy. These forecasts are, therefore, subject to changes in future conditions.

7. This report should be considered a limited analysis in that the appraiser did not perform all of the requirements for an appraisal as set forth by the American Institute of Real Estate Appraisers (for members and candidates).

8. This limited assignment is not an appraisal, in that a value estimate of the subject property has not been provided.

PRELIMINARY SURVEY AND APPRAISAL PLAN

The second step of the Valuation Process is the Preliminary Survey and Appraisal Plan. There are six steps:

1. Decide which data is needed.

2. Identify the sources of the needed data.

3. Determine what personnel are needed.

4. Make a time schedule.

5. Make a flow chart.

6. Present a fee proposal, agree upon a fee and sign a contract.

DATA NEEDED

The type of data required for an appraisal consists of General Data about the market and location and Specific Data about the property being appraised and the comparative properties.

General data is divided into the broad categories of social, economic, governmental and environmental factors that affect the value of the property. There are a variety of ways to organize the General Data. The most common way is to break the data down into Regional, State, Community, and Neighborhood sections.

An advantage of this system is that once the data is assembled and organized it can be used for other appraisals in the same region, state, community or neighborhood. In some areas, two of the classifications may be combined. For example, the state and regional data are often the same. When the community is small, it may contain only one neighborhood.

The collection of Specific Data is probably the most difficult part of making appraisals. This is especially true when the property is located in a territory that is unfamiliar to the appraiser. Specific data collection about the site and the improvements is described in more detail elsewhere in this textbook.

DATA SOURCES

An appraiser should maintain a reliable data collection and storage system. A large bank of market data should be accumulated in the appraiser's own files and should be organized to serve the appraiser's needs most effectively. Only some of the data will be immediately pertinent; the remainder is collected, filed, and cross-indexed for future use. Sales information usually is collected and recorded on standardized sheets. Many appraisers are using computers for data storage, retrieval and analysis.

PERSONNEL NEEDED

A simple appraisal made in a one-person shop requires only one individual.

The most common configuration of an appraisal company consists of the designated appraiser, who is usually the owner or manager, and an assistant who helps gather data and completes on their own, with supervision, the less complex assignments. A clerical support person is available to staff the office, answer the phone, and do most of the typing, computer entry, filing and billing.

Whether an office is like this typical small office or a large facility, a decision should be made for each assignment about how the work will be divided among the available personnel.

TIME SCHEDULE

The timely production of appraisals is essential to the successful management of an appraisal practice. In many areas, the competition for single family appraisal business requires delivery of the finished work within a few days of receiving the assignment.

A planned schedule of how the work will be performed is a good management tool. This helps the staff begin with a clear understanding of the exact nature of the work to be done by each person, which will go a great way to expedite the efficient completion of an assignment.

FLOW CHART

A commonly used device to keep track of the work in an appraisal office is a flow chart. This can be as simple as a calendar on which are marked the dates when portions of the appraisal are due. Another common type of flow chart is a metal board on which magnetic holders are displayed indicating the steps of the appraisal and when they are due. Larger offices often have computerized flow charts that help them keep track of the status of each job in progress.

FEE PROPOSAL AND CONTRACT

Some large lenders determine how much they will pay for an appraisal and the appraisers only decide if they can afford to do the work for the fee being offered.

Many other clients require the appraiser to quote a fee or a fee range in advance of a commitment to proceed with an appraisal assignment.

The relationship some appraisers have with select regular clients is so well established that these clients permit the appraiser to proceed with an assignment without having previously agreed upon a fee.

The fee an appraiser may charge for the services performed depends on the reputation of the appraiser. Appraisers who, in the view of their clients, have an established reputation for experience and sound judgment command higher fees than those appraisers who do not have the same well-established reputations.

Finally, since appraisers are professionals, competent work is required regardless of the fee. An inadequate fee is not considered a valid excuse for inadequate work, since a professional is obliged to perform competent work regardless of the fee charged. Therefore, the appraiser should be careful to correctly estimate the scope of work an assignment will require, so that a reasonable fee can be charged.

When an assignment is done for a regular client such as a lending institution, mortgage broker, mortgage banker or relocation company, the appraiser often elects to work without a contract. However, even in these situations, a contract or letter of authorization is desirable if it can be obtained. Personnel in large institutions often change jobs; what is authorized and understood by one employee may be objectionable to their replacement.

When making appraisals for the public or their representative, it is very desirable for the appraiser to have a contract that reflects what work will be done, when it will be completed and how and when the appraiser will be paid. It is also customary in many areas for the appraiser to receive a retainer.

DATA COLLECTION AND ANALYSIS - GENERAL DATA

ECONOMIC

Appraisers should consider all the significant social, economic, governmental, and environmental influences that affect property values in their region.

This information is gathered from general and specialized publications including national and local newspapers, financial magazines and real estate appraisal publications. Analysis of current economic conditions such as interest rates, effective purchasing power, construction costs, and availability of financing is included here.

LOCATIONAL

Background data deals with the locational and economic forces outside the appraised property that influence its value. This includes information about the region, community and neighborhood such a population characteristics, price levels, employment opportunities, economic base analysis, etc.

DATA COLLECTION AND ANALYSIS - SPECIFIC DATA - APPRAISED PROPERTY

Specific data pertaining to the appraised property includes title and record data, the relationship of the site to general land patterns, a description and analysis of the physical characteristics of the property, and highest and best use analysis.

TITLE AND RECORD DATA

Pertinent title data may include the identity of the owners, type of ownership, existing easements and encroachments, zoning regulations affecting the property, assessed value and taxation, and deed or other restriction.

RELATIONSHIP OF SITE TO LAND PATTERN

Descriptive data includes a complete evaluation of the site. Site features such as size, shape, topography, lot and building orientation, utilities and relationship to the existing land-use pattern are also analyzed here.

CHARACTERISTICS OF THE SITE AND IMPROVEMENTS

Legal Description

A parcel of land consists of any piece of land that can be identified by a common description in one ownership. A special characteristic of real estate is that every parcel is unique. The best identification of a parcel is a legal description and a survey, which eliminates all confusion because it specifically identifies and locates a parcel of real estate.

The three methods used in the United States to legally describe land are the Metes and Bounds System, the Rectangular Survey System, and the Lot and Block System.

--Metes and Bounds. This is a system that measures and identifies the property by describing the property boundaries. It began in the 1600's in the original 13 colonies where it is still used today. It describes the property's boundaries in terms of reference points.

A metes and bounds description starts at an identified point of beginning (POB). This POB is often described in relationship to some other established point on an adjoining survey. The description then moves clockwise through several other intermediate reference points until finally returning to the POB.

Metes are descriptions of the direction of movement from the POB to each reference point. The direction is the "Course" and is described in degrees, minutes and seconds of angle from north or south.

Bounds are the lines between the points. To describe a bound, it is necessary to know its length in terms of feet and inches and the angle from the point at which it starts to the point at which it ends. Courses are described in degrees, minutes and seconds of angle from north or south.

In addition to being the primary method of describing real property in 21 states, the metes and bounds system is often used as a corollary system in other states.

--Rectangular Survey. The U.S. Rectangular Survey System was established in 1785. It is also known as the Government Survey System. It is the principal survey system used west of the Mississippi River.

The system is based on reference points established by the U.S. government, form which true east-west and north-south lines run; these are called base lines and principal meridians. Each meridian has a unique name and is crossed by its own base line.

The land is then divided by north-south range lines, six miles apart and east-west township lines, also six miles apart. Each square thus created is called a township and contains 36 square miles.

Townships are further divided into 36 sections. Each standard section is one square mile and contains 640 acres. Sections are further divided into quarter sections and fractions of quarter sections.

--Lot and Block System. This is a system used by developers who sub-divide parcels of land into small lots. It is based on a map or survey which is filed in the land records showing the location of the lots, together with identifying numbers.

Other Descriptive Information

The description of the site should also include information about the type of ownership. The property may be in fee simple ownership, Planned Unit Development (PUD), De Minimis PUD, condominium, cooperative or some unique form of fractional ownership. (FNMA & FHLMC permit use of the URAR for single family residences in fee simple ownership, on leased land or when there is a De Minimis PUD. It is not permitted for multi-family residences or ones that are Planned Unit Developments, or cooperative or condominium ownership.)

The appraiser should check for any outstanding apparent rights that may affect the value such as surface or subsurface rights, easements, restrictions, air rights, water rights, mineral rights, obligations for unique lateral support, easements for common walls, etc. The appraiser is not responsible for reporting rights that are not apparent.

The description also includes information about the applicable zoning regulations and other environmental regulations that affect the use of the property. It is the responsibility of the appraiser to determine and report whether the improvements are a non-conforming (legal or illegal) use.

Assessment and Taxes

How a property is taxed affects its value. Real estate taxes are based on ad valorem assessments. At a minimum, the appraisal should report the current taxes. If they are not typical, the appraisal should compare them with typical taxes and estimate the effect of atypical taxes on the value.

Physical Characteristics of the Site

The important physical characteristics to be described consist of the size and shape, corner influence, plottage, excess land, topography, utilities, site improvements, location and environment.

--Size and Shape. The description of the site includes a description of its size and shape. Included in this description are the site dimensions, street frontage, width, depth and any advantages or disadvantages caused by the physical characteristics. Special attention is given to any characteristics that are atypical. Deviations in size and shape may have a substantial effect on the values of some sites. In other instances, these deviations have little effect.

The size of the site should be described in the unit customary for such land use in the area of the appraised property. Acreage is often the unit used for large tracts of land. Smaller parcels are often described in square footage, although acreage is sometimes used even for small residential parcels.

Frontage is usually described separately. It usually is the frontage that abuts the street. Sometimes the frontage is that portion of the site that abuts a stream, lake or a body of water.

The effect on a property of being bordered by two or more streets varies with different types of properties and locations. The appraiser must determine whether the local market considers a corner location favorable or unfavorable.

The advantage of a corner site is that it may have utility not possessed by inside properties. Often, a more flexible building layout is possible. Houses on corner sites often can have their garages more conveniently located. Corner sites also have their disadvantages. The cost of off-site improvements is higher. For residential properties, the assessment is often higher, too. There is a lack of privacy and the requirement for additional sidewalks and other site improvements increases the overall cost of the site.

--Plottage. In a given market there usually is an optimum site size for each of the various permitted uses. When two or more parcels are combined together under a single ownership in such a way that their result is a plot closer to the optimum size, there is a value increment obtained from the combining of two smaller parcels. If the combined parcels have a greater unit value than they did separately, plottage value results.

--Excess Land. It is not uncommon to find that the amount of land involved in the parcel being appraised is greater than that necessary to serve the existing improvements. If it is located in such a way that it is impossible to sever or use it in the future, it probably adds little or no value to the overall property. On the other hand, if the excess land can be used for other purposes, either now or in the future, or it permits expansion of the existing facility, it may add significant value to the property being appraised.

--Topography. The topography of the land should be part of the site description. The topographical description should include information about the contour, grades, drainage, soil conditions, view and general physical usability of the land.

Utilities

This description should include mention of all the utilities and services that are available to the site. Typical facilities are storm and sanitary sewers, water, gas, electricity and telephone service.

The neighborhood description should include all of those utilities available to the neighborhood. Special mention should be made of any utilities available in the neighborhood which are not utilized by the site being appraised. If there is a potential of connecting these unused utilities to the site, an estimate of this cost should be part of the appraisal.

When the cost of utilities is either more advantageous or more burdensome than the typical cost of utilities in the market, it will affect the value of the property.

Site Improvements

The first part of this description is that of off-site improvements and an analysis of their effect on the value of the property. This description includes the quality, condition and adequacy of sewers, curbs, access to utility hook-ups and the potential of these items being available in the future. On-site improvements include landscaping, fences and walls, curbs, gutters, walks, on-site roads and a wide variety of other man-made site improvements.

The location of any existing buildings on the site should also be described. It is very helpful to the reader when the appraiser makes a plot plan which shows all the buildings in relationship to the lot lines.

Location

The location of the site within the neighborhood is an appropriate part of the site description. This description includes information about the access to and from the property, parking, and the size and condition of the streets and highways that bring vehicular traffic to the site.

Residential sites are influenced by the ease with which residents can go to and from work, school, shopping, recreation, places of worship, etc. Public transportation for residents and workers also affects the value of the site.

Environment and Pollution

When there are unique environmental influences or evidence of pollution that affect a particular site, they should be included in the site description. Such influences include unusual wind exposure, exposure to the sun, and inland and tidal wetland use restrictions. Sometimes the development of adjoining properties has an advantageous effect on the value of the site being improved. Examples are adjoining attractive buildings, compatible commercial buildings and a favorable industrial park environment.

PHYSICAL CHARACTERISTICS OF THE IMPROVEMENTS

General Description

All appraisal forms provide room for a general description of the improvements. A mandatory important part is an accurate and adequate description of the property including the improvements.

For appraisal purposes the appraiser estimates both the actual age of the house and its effective age. The actual age is the chronological age. The effective age is how old a house appears to be, based on its design and condition. A property of typical design and average condition will have an effective age approximately the same as its actual age. When a house is modernized or renovated and well-cared-for, its effective age will be less that its actual age. A house in poor condition will have an effective age greater than its actual age.

The description of the improvements can be organized as follows for many improvements. (Unique improvements require special descriptions).

1. Site improvements.
2. Relationship of the improvements to the site.
3. General description and classification of improvements.
4. Exterior.
5. Interior.
6. Mechanical systems and equipment.
7. Items requiring immediate repair.
8. Deferred maintenance items.
9. Overall condition of improvements.
10. Design and layout (functional utility).
11. Renovation: rehabilitation, modernization, and remodeling.

DATA COLLECTION AND ANALYSIS - SPECIFIC DATA - COMPARATIVE PROPERTIES

SALES AND LISTINGS

Sufficient specific data is collected about the sales and listings in the market to apply the Sales Comparison Approach. The Sales Comparison Approach chapter provides details about how to collect and analyze sales and listing data.

COSTS

To process the Cost Approach the appraiser collects information on what it would cost to reproduce the subject property on the date of the appraisal. Information on how this data is collected and analyzed is presented in the Cost Approach chapter of this text.

RENTALS

To process both the Income Capitalization Approach and the Income GMRM Approach it is necessary to obtain information about rentals in the subject's market. This data is used to estimate the market rent of the subject property and also to develop a Gross Monthly Rent Multiplier (GMRM).

ANALYSIS OF HIGHEST AND BEST USE

Two separate highest and best use analyses are made. Some appraisers think this is the most important part of the appraisal process.

HIGHEST AND BEST USE AS THOUGH VACANT

Analyzing the highest and best use of the site as though vacant serves two functions. First, it helps the appraiser identify comparable properties. The comparable properties' highest and best use of the site as though vacant should be similar to that of the subject property.

The second reason to analyze the property's highest and best use as though vacant is to identify the use that would produce maximum income to the site after proper income is allocated to the improvements. In the cost approach and some income capitalization techniques, a separate value estimate of the site is required. Estimating the site's highest and best use as though vacant is a necessary part of deriving a site value estimate.

HIGHEST AND BEST USE AS IMPROVED

There are also two reasons to analyze the highest and best use of the property as improved. The first is to help identify comparable properties. Comparable improved properties should have the same or similar highest and best uses as the improved subject property.

The second reason to analyze the highest and best use of the property as improved is to decide whether the improvements should be demolished, renovated, or retained in their present condition. They should be retained as long as they have some value and the return from the property exceeds the return that would be realized by a new use, after deducting the costs of demolishing the old building and constructing a new one. Identification of the existing property's most profitable use is crucial to this determination.

SITE VALUE ESTIMATE

PURPOSE OF SEPARATE SITE VALUATION

It has been argued that once the site is improved with a house, a separate site valuation is difficult, if not impossible and unnecessary. The claim is that only a total property valuation is possible in such cases and that the two units are inseparable. In spite of the theoretical merits of this argument, however, many practical reasons exist for making separate site valuations even when the property is already improved.

Separate site valuations are required by statute in most states for ad valorem (real estate) tax purposes. The assessed value is almost universally split between the land (or site) and the improvements. Special assessments for public improvements, such as streets, water lines, sewers, etc., are often based on their estimated effect on land or site values. Income tax preparation also requires that the cost of a property be split between the improvements and the site. The first step of the Cost Approach is to estimate a separate market value for the site. Separate site value estimates are also commonly used for establishing condemnation awards, adjusting casualty losses, deciding whether to raze existing improvements to use the site for new structures and establishing site rentals. FNMA, FHLMC, VA and HUD/FHA all require separate site valuations.

PROCEDURES FOR ESTIMATING VALUE

Five basic procedures for estimating the market value of individual residential sites are:

1. Sales Comparison Approach
2. Allocation Procedure
3. Extraction Method
4. Capitalization of Ground Rental
5. Land Residual Technique

Sales Comparison Approach

The Sales Comparison Approach is based on comparing and contrasting pertinent data on comparable sites that have actually sold, with data about the site being appraised. It is the most popular and practical site valuation procedure. The appraiser may also consider offering and listing prices and other market information, but primary attention is given to actual sales of like sites, consummated under typical market conditions, as close to the date of the appraisal as possible. Sellers may offer a property at any price they choose, and potential purchasers may bid any price they like, but the actual selling price of a site (a figure acceptable to both buyer and seller) best reflects market conditions.

Market value is intended to describe the result of the interaction of buyers and sellers operating in an open market, all parties being knowledgeable, willing and able. Thus, having exposed the real estate in the open market for a reasonable period of time, the result is an agreed upon price that is recognized as market value. The Sales Comparison Approach results in the development of market values of sites by converting sales prices (and sometimes other evidence) into market value for the site being appraised.

The process of comparing the property being appraised with others in the market always involves two components - elements of comparison and units of comparison. To better organize the comparison process, a standard format is recommended.

--Elements of Comparison

Appraisers use six elements of comparison when considering the comparability of like sites. They are:

1. Financing Terms
2. Conditions of Sale

3. Market Conditions (Time)
4. Location
5. Physical Characteristics
6. Income Characteristics

Professional appraisers generally accept that these six elements encompass every possible consideration necessary to extract market value from market prices.

--Techniques for Making Adjustments

There are a variety of techniques for making adjustments. For example, a site being appraised is considered to be $500 better than Comparable Site A because of physical terrain. If Comparable Site A sold for $6,000 the adjustments would be made as follows: The comparable is poorer than the site being appraised, therefore a plus $500 adjustment is required, giving an indicated value of the subject site of $6,500 ($6,000 + $500).

Now consider the situation in which the property being appraised is poorer than the comparable. The comparable lot sold for $7,500 and is served by a sanitary sewer; the lot being appraised is not served by a sanitary sewer. The market indicates a preference in the amount of $750 for sanitary sewer. Therefore, the comparable site is superior and a minus $750 adjustment is made. The indicated market value of the site being appraised is $6,750 ($7,500 - $750).

The Allocation Procedure

A relationship exists between the application of the agents of production and the market value of a site. This is confirmed by the application of the principles of balance, contribution, surplus productivity and increasing and decreasing returns. Therefore, site value can be estimated by allocating the total sales price of a comparable between its two utilitarian and productive parts--the lot and the improvements. The appraiser determines what portion of a property's sales price typically may be allocated between the lot and the improvements, estimating the market value of the house and other improvements first. The balance (residual) is then allocated to the site. The National Association of Home Builders reports that land which was about 11% of the cost of a new home after World War II represents nearly 30% of the cost today.

Statistics from the U.S. Census Bureau demonstrate the relationship between the sales price and site value of residential properties. The statistics are presented as a national and regional average. The older the improvements, the higher the ratio of land value to total value. The typical ratio can be affected by a site of unusual size or characteristics and by building costs.

To estimate the value of unimproved property in an area where vacant land sales are lacking, the appraiser can allocate from the total sales price of a comparative property that part which could reasonably be assigned a building value. The remainder, except for intangibles, is the site value.

For example, assume that a property with a 1,500 square foot house sold for $190,000. the appraiser estimates the value of the house at $100 per square foot, or $150,000. The remainder of $40,000 is the residual value of the site, assuming that the house represents typical or highest and best land use and that no extraneous considerations were involved in the transaction.

The advantage of this procedure is that a sense of proportion is retained. If a neighborhood is typically improved with certain types of properties that can justify only a certain land value, the typical vacant lot probably will not be improved to a higher and better use. Where no vacant site sales are available, this method does afford an indication of site value. However, the results may sometimes be inconclusive and need collateral confirmation.

Extraction Method

The extraction method also involves an analysis of improved properties. The contribution of the improvements is estimated and deducted from the total sales price to arrive at a sales price for the land. This technique works best when the contribution of the improvements to the total sales price is small.

Capitalization of Ground Rental

The ground rental attributable to a property can be capitalized into an indication of the value of a site. This procedure is useful when comparable rents, rates, and factors can be developed from an analysis of sales of leased land.

Land Residual Technique

In the land residual technique, the site is assumed to be improved to its highest and best use, and the net operating income attributable to the site is capitalized by the land capitalization rate into an indication of land value. This technique works best on commercial and industrial sites.

RECONCILIATION OF ADJUSTED SITE SALES PRICES

The next step is to reconcile all the adjusted comparable sales prices into an indicated value of the site being appraised. Use of a simple arithmetic average of value indications is not acceptable appraisal practice. Averaging small groups of numbers produces a meaningless measure of central tendency, which may or may not reflect actual market value. The accepted procedure is to review each sale and judge its comparability to the property being appraised. The final value is based on all the information available to the appraiser, with greater weight given to particular comparables for well-explained reasons.

APPLICATION OF THE THREE APPROACHES

The fifth step of the Valuation Process is the Application of the Three Approaches traditionally used by appraisers to estimate the value of a property.

The Uniform Standards of Appraisal Practice require that the appraiser attempt to use all three approaches to estimate the value of each property appraised. However, it is recognized that this is not always possible simply because there may by insufficient data available. When an appraiser elects not to use one or two of the three approaches to value, the reasons for their elimination should be part of the appraisal report.

The three traditional approaches to value are:

1. Cost Approach
2. Sales Comparison Approach
3. Income (Gross Monthly Rent Multiplier, Income Capitalization) Approaches

COST APPROACH

The Cost Approach provides the appraiser with the opportunity to make an additional estimate of the value of the property. This value estimate is arrived at by using different data than that used for the Sales Comparison Approach and the Income Approaches.

The Cost Approach starts with an estimate of the value of the site and site improvements. (This first step is required by FNMA and FHLMC even when the Cost Approach is not used to estimate the value of the improvements. Site Valuation is covered separately in this textbook).

Historically, the Cost Approach was often the only approach used by appraisers for many appraisals. After World War II, it fell out of favor and some states prohibit it for condemnation cases. Many relocation companies also discourage appraisers from using it for relocation appraisals.

Experienced appraisers know that, when correctly used, the Cost Approach is a valuable technique. They feel more confident when they are able to make two or three independent estimates that tend to confirm each other than when their value estimate is based solely on the Sales Comparison Approach.

Unfortunately, some appraisers misuse this approach by backing into the numbers to make them agree with the Sales Comparison Approach.

 The Cost Approach is most appropriate when the site value is well substantiated, when the improvements are new or nearly new and when they are the highest and best use and do not suffer from substantial amounts of depreciation.

To estimate the value of a property using the Cost Approach, the appraiser selects the information that will be required from data gathered when the property was inspected.

STEPS OF THE COST APPROACH

The data is processed following the 5 steps described below:

1. Estimate the value of the site and site improvements (this technique is described elsewhere in this text).

2. Estimate the Reproduction Cost of the improvements (some appraisers use Replacement Cost; when Replacement Cost is used it should be noted in the comments section).

3. Estimate the amount of depreciation from all causes and categorize it into the three major types of depreciation: Physical Deterioration, Functional Obsolescence and External Obsolescence.

4. Deduct the total estimated depreciation from the reproduction or replacement cost of the improvements to derive the amount of value the improvements contribute to the property.

5. Add together the value of the site, the value contributed by the site improvements and landscaping, and the cost of all the improvements less the applicable depreciation.

ESTIMATING THE REPRODUCTION COST OF THE IMPROVEMENTS

 The reproduction cost of the improvements is estimated as of the date of the appraisal (not when they were constructed).

Reproduction cost is an appraisal term for the cost to reproduce an exact replica of the improvements at current costs using the same materials and the same design as the original structure.

Replacement cost is the cost of creating a residence having the same or equivalent utility, using currently available material and current design. When replacement cost is used some of the depreciation that exists is automatically accounted for.

Methods of Cost Estimating

There are a variety of ways for appraisers to estimate the cost of the property being appraised.

Square Foot Method

The comparative method is widely used by residential appraisers. It is a simple, practical approach to cost estimating, based on unit figures applicable to the gross living area of the house. It involves a comparison of the known costs of similar houses which have been reduced to units per square foot of gross living area. In applying this method, the number of square feet of gross living area in the house being appraised is first computed.

The cost of known similar houses is obtained from local builders, lenders or from a cost service.

Building Cost Estimates

A building cost estimate is a detailed breakdown of all the costs that make up a house item by item. This is similar to what a builder prepares when estimating what it will cost to build a house.

These cost estimates are usually prepared by professional cost estimators, builders or cost services.

DEPRECIATION

A simple definition of depreciation is "the difference between the cost of an improvement on the date of the appraisal and the value of the improvement."

Depreciation begins upon construction of the improvements; they immediately begin to age physically and to suffer from functional obsolescence in their design. Negative environmental forces cause immediate external obsolescence.

When the improvements are constructed, their economic life begins. During this period, they should contribute value to the property. If they are the "perfect improvement", the amount of value they contribute would be their total cost. Since few, if any, perfect improvements are constructed, a difference exists between their total cost and their value, which represents some form of depreciation. At the point when an improvement cannot be profitably utilized, or when it no longer contributes to the value of the property, it is at the end of its economic life and depreciation has reached 100%.

Generally, if the house is of average condition and design and conforms to the other houses in a neighborhood that is not subject to unusual economic influences, its effective age and chronological age will be about the same. If the house has had better than average maintenance, rehabilitation or modernization, its effective age probably will be less than its chronological age. If it is in poorer condition than typical houses of the same age or has not been modernized or rehabilitated as other similar houses in the neighborhood, or if some off-site economic or environmental factor is negatively affecting the value, the effective age will be greater than the chronological age.

Techniques for Estimating Accrued Depreciation

Accrued depreciation may be estimated directly through observation and analysis of the components of depreciation affecting the property or through use of a formula based on physical or economic age-life factors. It may also be estimated indirectly by use of the income or market data approaches.

Three techniques are used by appraisers to measure depreciation:

1. The abstraction or market method extracts depreciation directly from the market.

2. The age-life method is accomplished by estimating the typical economic life of the improvements and their effective age.

3. The breakdown method separates charges on the basis of origin of cause of loss (physical deterioration, curable and incurable; functional obsolescence,curable and incurable; and external obsolescence). Each component is estimated separately, using the engineering method or observation techniques.

TYPES OF DEPRECIATION

Depreciation is traditionally divided into three separate components:

1. Physical Deterioration
2. Functional Obsolescence
3. External Obsolescence (economic)

Physical deterioration and functional obsolescence may be further broken down into curable and incurable types. External obsolescence is rarely curable.

ORNAMENTATION

BOX-LIKE SHAPE

FLAT ROOF

BELVEDERE

CHIMNEYS PROTRUDE THROUGH ROOF

BALUSTRADE

Colonial American

FEDERAL (Federal - 101)

4 Financing

Interest rates and the availability of mortgage money have a direct effect on the value of residential real estate.

The complex relationship between financing and the valuation of residences is difficult to recognize, explain and understand. Experts agree that there is a relationship between financing and the price, cost or value of residences. They agree that the market reflects this relationship, but acknowledge it is difficult to "tie down". In spite of this difficulty, the influence of financing must be considered in the appraisal process.

Buyers and Sellers are affected by changes in interest rates and the availability of mortgage money. They play a major role in buying decisions. The appraiser must consider how much of an impact special or unusual conditions of finance have on price, cost and value.

Because a residence is fixed in location and has a relatively long life, it makes excellent security for a loan. Because it is high in cost compared to the assets of a typical buyer, the cost of housing ranges from 25% to 50% of a typical family income after taxes.[1] Residences are almost always financed with a long-term loan secured by a mortgage on the property.

THE MORTGAGE INSTRUMENT

Because long-term financing arrangements are necessary in most cases when a residence is purchased, the mortgage instrument has been developed to fit these needs. It is a legal document comprised of two parts--the mortgage and the note. The use of the mortgage instrument has been commonplace in this country for many decades.

The traditional first mortgage is categorized as a conventional mortgage. Non-conventional mortgages are those which are insured or guaranteed by an agency of the Federal government (Federal Housing Administration or Veterans Administration) or a private insurance company. Since the 1930's the FHA has been insuring loans to persons who require assistance because of their lack of financial capacity. The VA provides a similar service to veterans. Both FHA and VA interest rates tend to be lower than rates for conventional loans. They usually have longer terms and a higher loan-to-value ratio.

---

[1]Cost of housing includes mortgage interest and amortization, property taxes and utilities.

Other types of financing include deeds of trust, privately insured and guaranteed loans, cash, second mortgages and contract purchases.

Legal restrictions and requirements applying to a mortgage vary from state to state. Such legal considerations impact on the mortgage instrument and are two-sided: On one side the homeowner is given as much protection and encouragement as possible, and on the other side risk to the lender must be considered. The best examples of this are the foreclosure laws of the various states. A state having foreclosure legislation excessively favorable to the borrower may attract few funds from outside the state. Those states that give the greatest protection to the mortgagee, with short time periods for foreclosure, tend to attract more funds from around the country.

MORTGAGE MONEY SOURCES

The two primary sources of money for purchase of single family homes are the savings deposits of customers in the nation's thrift institutions and the secondary mortgage market [which is dominated by Freddie Mac (Federal Home Loan Mortgage Company) and Fannie Mae (Federal National Mortgage Association)]. The thrift organizations obtain some of their funds from people who save with them. However, a substantial portion of their mortgage money comes from the secondary mortgage market. Lenders package a portfolio of mortgages and sell them to Freddie Mac, Fannie Mae and other organizations in the secondary mortgage market.

Savings and loan associations and mortgage brokerage companies are the leading sources of funds to the residential buyer. Life insurance companies provide some funds, but they tend to look more towards multi-family and other types of income property. Commercial banks provide a limited supply of funds, usually on much shorter terms. Mutual Savings banks (which are similar to S & L's) also are a large source of mortgage money in their limited geographic areas.

FINANCING AND RISK

Lending institutions and mortgage brokers who are the prime originators of mortgage loans, analyze the risk in making residential loans very much like any other investment. The security of the real estate in the mortgage loan gives added incentive to many institutions and individuals to make mortgage loans. However, certain risks are involved, such as delinquencies which result in the need to foreclose. Another risk is that at some point in the future, the loan will be greater than the value of the real estate (the amount for which the real estate can be sold under pressure), thereby resulting in a loss to the financial institution. The high risk of mortgage loans is now receiving a substantial amount of publicity. It is one of the major causes of the failure of many thrift institutions.

In analyzing the relationship of financing to real estate values, it is necessary to consider the mortgage lending system and the risks involved. The quoted interest rate for a mortgage loan is the cost of the money. The annual rates of interest tend to be commensurate with the risk involved in a specific investment.

Interest rates may be different from the actual yield on an investment. The mortgage market has become active on a much broader basis and so the impact of the secondary market (and the national market in some respects) affects the yield which a mortgage may produce. A 10% interest rate on a $50,000 loan pays, on an annual basis, $5,000. If an individual or institution acquires the loan at a discounted price of $45,000, the yield per year would be $5,000 on a $45,000 investment - a rate of 11.11% ($5,000 divided by $45,000), rather than the contract rate of 10%. Conversely if the investor paid $55,000, the yield is reduced to 9.09%.

To compete in the market, it is necessary at times to charge "points" or to use a discount rate. For example, if a loan were to be made in the amount of $100,000 at the going rate of 9%, the lender may feel that rate is inadequate under the circumstances and make one of the following adjustments: The borrower may be asked to pay points--say, four points--which on a $100,000 loan would be $4,000. Another technique is applying a discount rate. By discounting the loan 3%, the amount of money actually advanced at the time of closing is 3% less than the original $100,000; however, the borrower still pays 9% interest on $100,000. In other words, a 9% return would be earned on $100,000 even though only $97,000 was loaned. This increases the yield to the lender, providing compensation for what the lender perceives to be a higher risk or to match yields in other types of investment opportunities.

COMPETITION FOR FUNDS

When there is a shortage of mortgage money or when interest rates are high, the number of potential home buyers decreases. This has an effect on the value of houses. The appraiser therefore is concerned with the amount of money available, and with the interest rate at which loans are being made, the length of the term and the ratio of loan to value. Each of these variables or combinations thereof are critical to the buyer making a decision in the market. The appraiser's first concern, however, is the total amount of investment funds flowing to the single family housing market. As this book goes to press in early 1989, interest rates are going up. It is too early to determine what effect this will have on the availability of mortgages.

THE MONEY MARKET

Money is defined as all currency plus all deposits in private checking accounts and "near monies", which include time and savings deposits, savings and loan shares, mutual savings bank deposits and short-term U.S. government securities. All are cash or the equivalent to cash; that is, they are available for expenditure without delay. To understand the competition for investment funds, it is necessary to comprehend to a certain extent the nature of the whole money market.

The amount of money available for borrowing is regulated by the U.S. Treasury Department and the Federal Reserve System. It is their obligation to assist the economy by having adequate money available. Originally the "Fed" was charged with the primary responsibility for the money market. The function of the Federal Reserve System is to foster a flow of credit and money that will facilitate orderly economic growth, a stable dollar, and long-run balance in our international payments. Its original purpose, as expressed by the founders, was to give the country a lasting currency, to provide facilities for discounting commercial paper, and to improve the supervision of banking. As the economy changed, broader objectives were outlined, namely to help counteract inflationary and deflationary movements, and to share in creating conditions favorable to a high level of employment, a stable dollar, growth of the country, and a rising level of consumption.

The mortgage market, which provides the basic supply of funds for residential property, is in direct competition for these funds. At times the mortgage market is not competitive with other users. Then the supply of funds goes down, the cost of money goes up, or both occur. At other times, slow decline in the cost of money takes place without a corresponding reduction in the supply of money. It is hard to accurately predict what effect interest rate changes and mortgage money availability will have on the value of houses in a specific market.

THE SECONDARY MORTGAGE MARKET

The financing of real estate has been facilitated greatly by the development of the secondary mortgage market. Many lending institutions formerly made home loans and held them; now they are able to sell loans in the secondary market and thus secure additional funds for home financing. A number of private investors and institutions purchase home mortgages.

A major influence on the secondary mortgage market is the activitiy of the Federal National Mortgage Association (FNMA). "Fannie Mae" purchases mortgages from primary mortgage markets, thus increasing liquidity among primary mortgage lenders. It issues long-term debentures and short-term discount notes to raise most of its funds. FNMA programs emphasize insured and guaranteed mortgages.

The Federal Home Loan Mortgage Corporation (FHLMC) known as The Mortgage Corporation or "Freddie Mac" conducts both mortgage purchase and sales programs. Its main emphasis is on conventional mortgages.

The Government National Mortgage Association (GNMA or "Ginnie Mae") is a government organization that gets its funds from the U.S. Treasury. It is specializing in the purchase of mortgages which require extraordinary support.

ADJUSTABLE RATE MORTGAGES (ARMs)

In the past 20 years, interest rates have changed much more rapidly than in the past. Lending institutions with large portfolios of low interest mortgages found themselves in serious financial trouble when the rates of interest they were forced to pay to keep and attract depositors exceeded the yield on their mortgage portfolios.

To prevent a re-occurrence of the problem, an Adjustable Rate Mortgage (ARM) was developed as an alternative mortgage instrument carrying an interest rate that varies with changes in market rates.

Since 1985, the majority of home buyers have financed the purchase of their homes with an ARM. ARMs now account for about 60% of home mortgages being written.

The interest rate on an ARM is indexed to some other interest rate. This means that when the interest rate changes on the indexing instrument the interest rate also changes on the mortgage.

There is an endless variety of ARMs being offered. They have a few common characteristics:

1. The interest rate on the mortgage changes only once or twice a year (or less often), not every time the interest rate on the index instrument changes.

2. There is a maximum amount the interest may be increased in any one year (often 2%).

3. There is a total maximum amount the interest may be increased (often 6%) over the life of the mortgages.

The following are some of the ARM plans that have been approved by Fannie Mae:

1. One Year Treasury Bills.
2. One year 11th District Federal Reserve Funds.
3. Six month 11th District Federal Reserve Funds.
4. Three Year Treasury Bills.

Other indices which are used are:

5. National Mortgage Contract Rate.
6. National Median Cost of Funds to FSLIC - Insured Savings Institutions.
7. Prime Rate.
8. London Interbank Offering Rate (LIBOR).
9. Certificates of Deposit.

OTHER TYPES OF FINANCING

Second Mortgages

In addition to the first mortgage, a second or "junior" mortgage may be used to facilitate the purchase of a residential property. As its name implies, a second mortgage is secondary to the rights of the first mortgagee. It is used in circumstances in which the buyer is unable to arrange for adequate financing based on one mortgage and so requires a second mortgage. This technique provides additional funds and facilitates the purchase of the property when the buyer may not be able to do so otherwise.

Deed of Trust

While the mortgage is a traditional means of financing the purchase of a property, some states provide vehicles to accomplish the same end but with different kinds of legal arrangements. In some western states, a deed of trust, which is similar to a mortgage, is used. It involves a third party who serves as a trustee. Money is borrowed in the same manner as with a mortgage but the trustee holds the title to the property until the borrower meets all obligations at which time the title is conveyed.

Conditional Sales Contract

A relatively common means of financing property is with a conditional sales contract (buying on contract). This device requires the seller to finance the sale of the property to the new buyer. Title does not pass from the seller to the buyer until the buyer has satisfied the contract--that is, paid it off. Quite often terms are different from those available with first mortgages; a conditional sales contract may have a shorter term or provide for a higher ratio of loan-to-value, traditionally at a higher interest rate than a conventional mortgage.

All Cash Purchases

A few buyers provide all cash for the entire purchase of a property. Through the sale of other property or the accumulation of funds in some manner, they are able to purchase property with a lump-sum cash payment. Such financial arrangements quite often expedite the purchase and affect the negotiating ability of the buyer.

Private Mortgage Insurance

A variation of FHA insured loans has been developed by private mortgage insurance companies for conventional mortgages. Such companies typically insure the risk to the lender on the top 10% above the amount traditionally loaned as a conventional mortgage. If an 80% loan-to-value ratio were available, the next 10% (increasing the loan to 90% of value) is insured by the private mortgage company.

Favorable Purchase Money Mortgages

The most common financing market is the conventional first mortgage loan. In the conventional market, if the going loan for a particular community is 13 1/2%, 20 year term with 80% loan-to-value ratio, sales used as comparables should have a similar type of financing. If financing varies by a quarter percent of interest, a few years differences in length or a few percentage points variation in loan-to-value ratio, these would not be considered adequate differences in conditions of sale to require adjustments. In the above example, however, if a comparable were financed (because of special arrangements) at a 10 1/2% rate for 30 years with a 95% loan-to-value ratio, adjustments must be made before it could be used, on the assumption that such special and favorable conditions of financing affected the sales price. Similarly, a buyer required to pay 16 1/2% interest with a maximum term of only 15 years and a 70% loan-to-value ratio would probably have paid less for the property, and an adjustment would have to be made.

FHA and VA Insured Mortgages

FHA-insured and VA-guaranteed loans tend to be in a market by themselves and when such properties are being appraised, comparables should be those with FHA or VA loans. It is quite common today for investors to seek out subdivisions that have been predominantly FHA- or VA-financed. By doing so, financing terms are typically very favorable--sometimes interest rates are one-half or two-thirds of the going conventional rate. The length of the term may be greater and the original loan-to-value ratio may be very competitive with conventional mortgages as of the date of the purchase. These unique financing arrangements have a marked effect on sale prices. To compare the sale of a house having favorable financing arrangements with the sale of a house subject to conventional financing arrangements cannot be justified unless an appropriate adjustment is made. Rather than attempt to make an adjustment for such differences most appraisers feel that it is better appraisal practice to restrict themselves to using comparable sales from a similar market.

TRUTH IN LENDING

The Board of Governors of the Federal Reserve System has been charged by Public Law 90-321 (as amended) Title I to administer the "Truth-In-Lending Act" which applies to almost everyone who loans money to the public for real estate transactions.

The purpose of this law is to educate the borrower about the true cost of the money they borrow.

To implement this act of Congress the Board of Governors of the FHLBB issued Regulation Z which provides rules and tables with which it is possible to calculate the "Annual Percentage Rate (APR)" for any loan.

The APR is made up of all of the following charges paid by the borrower in addition to the interest:

1. Fees or premiums for title examination, title insurance, or similar purposes.

2. Fees for preparation of a deed, settlement statement, or other documents.

3. Escrows for future payments of taxes and insurance.

4. Fees for notarizing deeds and other documents.

5. Appraisal fees.

6. Credit reports.

Lenders are required to advertise the APR of all loans they advertise and advise all borrowers of the APR of each real estate loan they make.

NEW TYPES OF MORTGAGES (GIMMICKS?)

Recently two types of mortgages have been advertised by lenders as being superior to more traditional types of mortgages.

BI-WEEKLY MORTGAGE

A mortgage in which payments are made every two weeks as opposed to the more typical payment once a month. Payments are calculated initially according to the terms of the contract on a monthly basis and then halved. Payments made on a bi-weekly basis in this manner result in the equivalent of thirteen monthly payments per year.

In order to be sure that the payments are made on a timely basis many lenders require that the payment be transferred directly from the borrower's bank account which must be opened in the lender's institution.

There is no doubt that the total dollars of interest paid over the course of a loan is substantially less than on a similar monthly payment loan, as shown in Fig. 4-1.

FIG. 4-1 BI-WEEKLY MORTGAGE SAVINGS

Conventional Monthly Mortgage Payment

Principal Amount	$100,000
Annual Interest Rate	11.5%

Monthly Payment $1066.43

Term of Mortgage   20 Years

Total Payments over 20 years

	Principal	$100,000
	Interest	$155,943
	Total Payments	$255,943

Mortgage with Bi-weekly payment (1/2 conventional monthly payment)

Principal Amount $100,000

Annual Interest Rate   11.5%

Bi-weekly Payment $533.22

Term of Mortgage   15 years 3 months

Total Payments over 15 years 3 months

	Principal	$100,000
	Interest	$111,155
	Total Payments	$211,155

Total Dollar Savings $ 44,787.88 ($255,943 - $211,155)

By paying 1/2 the conventional mortgage payment bi-weekly the term of the mortgage is reduced from 20 years to 15 years and 3 months. This results in total dollars of interest saved of $44,787.88.

The reason this happens is that the bank gets the mortgage principal paid back faster and therefore less interest is paid on the remaining balance.

"TEASER" RATE MORTGAGES

This is the nick name given to mortgages where the first 6 month's interest or first year's interest is substantially below market rate. "Teaser Loans" are offered by lenders as an enticement to potential borrowers to apply for their ARM mortgage versus that of the competition.

It is poor underwriting practice to qualify the borrower based on the reduced first year payments.

Michael Smilow, Executive Vice President of Fannie Mae is quoted in the 2/27/89 issue of National Thrift News: "As rates rise, the crazies come out of the woodwork". He went on to add: "Fannie Mae will buy only those loans that are properly underwritten."

REVERSE AMORTIZATION MORTGAGES

These are mortgages with low monthly payments. They started as a convenience for elderly borrowers who had large equity in their homes but didn't want to sell to realize their equity. Each month, the base amount of the mortgage is increased by difference between what payment is needed for the mortgage interest and the amount the borrower pays.

CASH EQUIVALENCY

The accepted definitions of Market Value all presume that the value of the subject property will be based on the assumption that it will be purchased by a typical buyer who will finance it with a typical conventional mortgage that is available in the market.

Therefore, whenever a property is sold and financed with some special financing it is assumed that the special financing had an effect (usually upward) on the sales price. When a property was sold with special financing, it usually requires a minus adjustment to reflect the higher price that was received for it as compared to what the sales price would have been if the property had been purchased by a buyer who could not take advantage of the special financing.

There is far from universal agreement between appraisers, underwriters and the secondary mortgage market about how to make so called "cash equivalency" adjustments. All agree that any mathematical formula or method by itself is not sufficient. The appraiser must always try to determine how the market reacts to the special financing which may be different than the raw dollar adjustment indicted by whatever formula is used.

SELLER PAID POINTS

The easiest and least controversial cash equivalency adjustment to make is for seller paid points. Simply put, what points the seller pays are deducted from the sales price to give the cash equivalency price. Even in this situation the appraiser may modify the figure to reflect his or her judgment about how seller paid points actually affected the market value of properties in a specific market at the time of the appraisal.

FIG 4-2 CASH EQUIVALENCY ADJUSTMENT FOR SELLER PAID POINTS

Reported sales price of house	$160,000
(conventional first mortgage $120,000)	
2 points paid by seller	$ -2400
($120,000 x .02)	
Adjusted sales price of house	$157,600
(may be modified by appraiser	
to reflect market)	

Even the simplest adjustment is not universally accepted. The VA and FHA handle points differently. Appraisers who do work for these and other agencies should seek specific instructions about how they want special financing adjustments for seller paid points handled.

LOWER THAN MARKET INTEREST RATES

There are a variety of methods used to estimate the effect below market interest rates on purchase money mortgages has on the value of the property sold subject to the advantageous mortgage.

One method that is used by myself and many other appraisers is to calculate the monthly savings that is enjoyed by the buyer because of the special financing, estimate how long the savings will last assuming that the buyer was a typical buyer and then discount this monthly savings to present value using the current market interest rate. (See Fig. 4-3).

FIG 4-3 ADJUSTMENT FOR DIFFERENCE IN FINANCING

Typical Financing in this market:

$90,000 conventional first mortgage:

11% fixed interest rate
20 year term (monthly payments)
Monthly payment $ 928.80

Special owner provided financing:

$50,000 conventional first mortgage
11% fixed interest rate
20 year term (monthly payments)
Monthly payment $ 516

$40,000 purchase money second mortgage:
9% fixed interest rate
20 year term (monthly payments)
Monthly payment $ 360

Total monthly mortgage payments $ 876

Monthly Savings: $ 52.80

Present value of monthly savings
discounted at market interest rate of 11%
over typical holding period of 10 years $3,774

SUMMARY

There is a strong connection between the availability of mortgage money, interest rates and the value of residential real estate.

Residences have been traditionally financed with long-term mortgages categorized as conventional mortgages and non-conventional mortgages which are insured or guaranteed.

The government, through the Federal Reserve Banking System, attempts to control the economy by changing the interest rate and the reserve requirements of Federal banks.

Risk is an important factor in setting mortgage interest rates. Lenders can make small adjustments to interest rates by also charging a borrower points at the inception of the loan.

Adjustable rate mortgages (ARMs) are now more popular than fixed rate mortgages. Their interest rate is tied to some other financial instrument. Usually, the amount they can change in a year is limited as is their total potential interest change.

Other types of residential purchase financing includes second mortgages, deeds of trust, conditional sales contracts, private mortgages, purchase money mortgages and FHA/VA insured mortgages.

Truth-In-Lending laws require that all lenders who make consumer loans on real estate make known to the borrower the annual percentage rate (APR) of every loan they offer, in person and in their advertising and promotional material.

Several new types of mortgages have recently been introduced by lenders in an attempt to increase their share of the mortgage market. Bi-weekly mortgages, mortgages with low "teaser" rates and mortgages with reverse amortization are being criticized as not being in the public's best interest.

Whenever a property is sold with favorable special financing, the sales price must be split by the appraiser into what was paid for the real estate and what was paid for the special financing. When the property is used as a comparable sale, an adjustment is required to reflect the value of the special financing.

When percentage adjustments are used, special financing and special conditions of sale adjustments are made first.

ASYMMETRICAL;
LOOKS LIKE A CHURCH

HIGH, MASSIVE CHIMNEYS

ONE WALL
MATERIAL

ONE COLOR

TRACERY

GOTHIC
ARCH WINDOWS

WINDOW
TRACERY

Nineteenth Century American

EARLY GOTHIC REVIVAL (E Goth - 701)

5 Collection and Analysis of General Data

TYPES OF GENERAL DATA

General data useful to appraisers can be divided into items of information that help them understand the influence of the four forces originating outside a property and their effect on the value of the property. These forces are social, economic, government and environmental. It is different from Specific Data which includes details about the property being appraised, comparable sales and rental properties, and relevant local market characteristics.

General data is classified as primary or secondary. Primary data includes original elements of information generated by an appraiser or some other group or agency. An example of primary data an appraiser can gather is the number of vacant houses and apartments in the neighborhood of the property being appraised.

Primary data becomes secondary data when it is published and available to the public for general use.

Macrodata comprises information on aggregate phenomena, such as total employment at the national, regional and local levels; national and regional income or product growth or decline; interest rates; or the balance of trade. Macrodata is typically general data obtained from secondary sources.

Microdata is more specific data. The supply of new apartment units in the community, the vacancy rates in a housing submarket, the number of local households in the $25,000 to $49,999 income bracket, and the comparable sale properties used in the sales comparison approach are all examples of microdata. Microdata may be obtained from a primary source, such as a sample of vacant units taken from the local apartment market, or from a secondary source, such as the number of persons employed locally in manufacturing, as reported in the United States Census of Population.

USES OF GENERAL DATA

General data is essential in valuation because it (1) provides a background against which to place specific properties being appraised; (2) supplies information from which possible trends affecting land values can be inferred and figures for appraisal calculations within the three approaches can be derived; and (3) forms a basis for judgments about highest and best use, reconciliation of value indications within the three approaches, and the final estimate of defined value.

An appraiser should have an understanding of all elements that contribute to the market price and market value of all types of real estate. An awareness of social, economic, government, and environmental trends allows an appraiser to interpret specific market phenomena.

In estimating value using sales or cost data, an appraiser uses prices and costs that have been determined in the market, which are the products of the interaction of all value determinants. Similarly, the income capitalization approach to value requires estimation of market-determined rents, interest rates, capitalization rates, and financing terms. When the methodology of the income capitalization approach requires an appraiser to make explicit forecasts of future income or reversion value at the end of an assumed investment holding period, these forecasts are conditioned by judgments concerning the effects of the basic determinants of value embodied in general data.

An appraiser also may do a quantitative analysis in which he or she reports the level, changes, and trends in general data; then applies the quantitative data to the problem under consideration; and finally shows the relative importance of the data trends. For example, the comparison of two local economies among markets for various types of real estate, or the analysis of comparable sales data from a given market, requires consideration of relative trends and cross-sectional differences in the variables appropriate to the problem.

The significance of a 2% population increase in one city depends on the population increases in other cities. The demand for apartments must be considered relative to the demand for detached single family houses. The selection of comparable properties depends on their competitiveness and substitutability relative to the subject property.

SOURCES OF SECONDARY DATA

Today there is an almost unlimited supply of data covering the items outlined in this chapter and the following chapter. Although good unbiased data pertaining to local communities can be difficult to find, it usually is available. Government agencies at all levels and the Federal Reserve System and its district banks around the country are excellent sources of economic data. The Federal Home Loan Bank System, which is closely related to the real estate industry, is also widely known for its economic research with application to local and state areas. Some states have computerized retrieval systems that provide printouts listing historical and current economic, social and governmental data.

Many private organizations also serve as clearing houses for such statistics. Some real estate appraisers and consultants make a practice of collecting pertinent statistical data; such a procedure is costly and justifiable only if kept current. A thorough analysis cannot depend on technique alone; it depends heavily upon sound information.

METROPOLITAN AREA ECONOMIC ANALYSIS

The economic environment of a residential property and the market of which it is a part are of vital concern to the appraiser. A close relationship exists between the economic analysis of a metropolitan area and the analysis of its residential market.

The principal characteristic of real estate is its fixity of location. Although an oversimplification, it is true that real property is either the benefactor or the victim of its surroundings. Most real estate can be no better than that of which it is a part.

One major limiting factor affecting the market value of real estate is the economic potential of the community in which it is located. Any reasonably qualified analyst recognizes that the marketability of real estate depends heavily upon the economic potential of its community. Just as a close relationship exists between economic development and income producing properties, such as office buildings or retail stores, there is also a high correlation between the economic potential of the community and the marketability of residential property. This chapter deals with the steps in analyzing the economic base and its impact on the market value of residential property.

DEFINITION OF METROPOLITAN AREA ECONOMIC ANALYSIS

Metropolitan area economic analysis has many other names. It frequently is referred to as economic base analysis, regional and local economic analysis, and input-output analysis; the term little economies[1] is a more descriptive name because it refers to the economic health of an area and its ability to bring in income from outside the area. It can be compared to international trade situations where countries seek to establish favorable balances of trade. For example, if the United States sells more to Canada than Canada sells to the United States, the balance of trade will be in favor of the United States - that is, gold or the equivalent will flow into the United States, thereby enhancing its economic growth.

It is simple to apply this same concept to the economic area of a local community or metropolitan area. Compare and contrast the growth potential of a particular metropolitan area with other metropolitan areas of similar characteristics, size and physical location. In which community is it most desirable to live? Which community has the greatest growth potential? Which has the greatest protection against unfavorable economic developments? Obviously, the one that rates highest on each of these three questions, is the one that has the most favorable future.

IDENTIFICATION OF A METROPOLITAN AREA

The boundaries of a metropolitan area must be identified before one can analyze such an area. Most simply, it is a geographic area that is contiguous and operates as one unit. It may cross state boundaries, such as the greater Louisville area or the greater St. Louis area. Quite often it encompasses several counties. It may be the Standard Metropolitan Statistical Area (SMSA) as defined by Bureau of the Census. Recent directives from agencies of the federal government delineate certain economic communities; thus, statistical data is most readily available for these standardized areas. Because substantial data is necessary to analyze the potential of a specific area, it is good practice to follow defined areas and regions.

---

[1]Committee for Economic Development, 1958.

GROWTH OF CITIES

To understand the importance of metropolitan area economic analyses, one must understand why cities exist at all and why they grow in a particular location.

Humans are social beings. Historically, they came together for defense and self-protection or to facilitate trade among themselves and outsiders or for religious motives. Usually a combination of reasons brought people together into communities. Problems have developed where many people are clustered together, but these have been offset by the advantages of such groupings.

Why did people gather at a particular geographic point to develop a community? One obvious reason was location on established trade routes or other points of transportation access such as rivers. The specific points along such routes may have been established for convenience -- for example, a day's travel distance from an established point -- or related to access to raw materials and natural resources, such as a waterfall or other source of energy, and to those who were going to be served by the products being developed. Added to these reasons is a catalytic force that has played a greater part in recent community growth -- a favorable climate. The greatest growth in the United States in the latter half of this century has been in warmer, more moderate climates.

ECONOMIC BASE ANALYSIS

Appraisers are concerned primarily with the economic potential of a community as it affects the market value of the property they are appraising. They must look at the economic potential of a community compared to competitive communities.

Real estate markets depend on growth or the expectation of growth. Although there may be short-run market conditions that are favorable without growth, such circumstances are rare. The market for residential properties depends heavily on families and their economic capacity to purchase homes, which depends on their jobs and the competitive position of such jobs. If the average family income within a specific community is higher than the national or state average, the potential for purchase or construction of homes in that community is greater than in other communities.

It may be helpful to understand the relationship between residential values and the community's economic future by pointing out that certain areas in the United States are recognized for their special economic conditions, both good and bad. Much publicity has been given to Appalachia and its economic problems. The federal government has conducted special programs for this geographic area.

Certain sections of the northeast United States are experiencing marginal economic growth because their major industries have moved to other sections of the country or have become obsolete.

In contrast, some geographic areas are undergoing great physical and economic growth. The "sun belt" has had spectacular growth in the last two decades. Parts of Florida and California, as well as sections in other southwest states, have had spectacular population growth. Along with such growth, however, there must be sound economic development. Population increase alone does not imply substantially sound economic growth; there must be a correspondingly strong economic base to ensure that the community can support itself and be competitive with others. Overdependence on one industry, such as oil in the Southwest, can bring about rapid destabilization of the real estate market in such areas when the economics of that industry change.

BASIC AND NON-BASIC EMPLOYMENT

Because the economic potential of a community is dependent on its ability to produce income, metropolitan area economic analysis deals to a great extent with gathering and analyzing employment data. It involves the collection of statistics regarding the total basic employment within the community plus similar statistics for non-basic employment.

Basic employment is the type of employment that attracts dollars from consumers and others outside the metropolitan area being analyzed. This kind of employment is, by definition, the basis for the level of the economy in the area. Non-basic employment generates its income from within the community. Lawyers, doctors and service employees, such as the supermarket clerk or city sanitation worker are included in this category. A community cannot thrive without these people and if they are insufficient in number to satisfy the needs of those in basic employment, the latter will become dissatisfied and less productive. Ideally, there must be both basic and non-basic employment in proper proportion to maximize the prosperity of the whole community.

There is no consistent standard ratio of basic to non-basic employment within an economic community. Such relationships are derived locally and vary in accordance with the income level and nature of the basic employment. If the basic employees are primarily white-collar research and scientific personnel with extremely high levels of income, they will probably require more services; a ratio of two basic to one service employee might be appropriate. In other communities, where basic employees have lower income levels, a ratio of three basic to one service employee might be entirely satisfactory. Certain special kinds of communities occasionally have a ratio of one to one. The ratio itself is not important in the analysis of the level and potential of economic activity; however, it does affect the general social and economic climate in terms of the subjective analysis of the community as a good or less satisfactory place to live.

Data on basic employment is collected on an historical as well as a current basis and divided into three major categories; industry; specialty, such as government and recreation; and trade, including retail, wholesale, finance and transportation. These categories are intended to include all types of basic employment and are considered to be the most critical in the estimation of the economic growth of the community being analyzed. They are rated according to predicted employment trends, diversification, and cyclical fluctuation. The importance of diversification in basic employment and the need for types of basic employment that are not subject to cyclical fluctuation have long been recognized.

--**Industry.** This basic employment category, also called manufacturing, includes all components of fabrication, assembly, manufacturing and extractive activities. Industry is the truly essential, critical and fundamental area of employment for most communities, although there are some communities, such as Washington D.C., that have virtually no industry. Most communities, however, rely on industrial employment to carry the future of their economy. Accordingly, this analysis is made first and typically is given the greatest weight in the conclusion.

--Specialty. This category includes non-industrial types of employment, such as government service, education and recreation. For purposes of this analysis, local government employees are not included. Only those whose salaries are paid by outside sources, such as a federal court in the community which attracts its income from outside that community, are considered. The fire department is paid from local tax revenue and therefore is not considered base employment. Likewise, education is limited to those institutions that attract most of their operating revenue from outside the economic area, such as a state university or a private college. Local elementary, junior and senior high schools are excluded as basic employment.

Recreation communities, such as Miami Beach, Florida or Scottsdale, Arizona, base their employment on providing tourist and retirement services and facilities. In such communities, the waiter employed in a hotel catering to out-of-town people is a basic employee, but the busboy in a restaurant catering primarily to local citizens is a non-basic employee.

--Trade. This category includes positions in retailing, wholesaling, finance and transportation that exist to serve users outside the economic community. A regional shopping center that attracts those outside the community as well as consumers inside the community, is partially a basic employer. Major banks serving the entire state or region obviously attract some of their revenue from outside the local economic community. The headquarters of a national bus service or moving company would be primarily a basic employer.

QUALITY RATING

The procedure for rating the three categories of employment is to look at them individually in light of three quality rating requirements: predicted employment trends, diversification and cyclical fluctuation.

Briefly, the predictable trend for employment opportunities requires the analyst to project the relative position of the types of industry in the local community in competition with other communities and the nation. If the results of the comparison show that the community is in the middle range of all other communities and with national figures, a different kind of future will be forecast than if it is in the top 10% of all communities. In one respect, this technique is similar to the use of GNP for the national compared to a specific community's gross product.

Estimating the predicted employment trend requires the analyst to project soundly and objectively the growth patterns (decline or increased stability of employment) in each of the factories and other types of industry supporting the local economic base. Such an analysis is not to be a Chamber of Commerce projection which, by its nature, tends to be optimistic. To be useful for the appraiser, it must be done thoroughly, carefully and with insight.

The second area of quality rating is diversification. Obviously, if one industrial firm hires 50% of all those employed in industry, the risk to the community is greater if a negative trend develops in this organization (or the industry it represents) than if a major employer hires only 15% of all industrial employees. If the latter plant should be moved, shut down or cut employment by half, the community would not suffer so severely.

The third quality rating deals with cyclical fluctuation. Evaluation of this factor is based on how business in the community will fare in the event of recession or depression. Few types of business are recession or depression proof. The staple food industry tends to be least affected by recession or depression but high-priced luxury goods tend to drop off in sales the minute the consumer has less money.

This step requires a judgment as to how businesses will rate in the event of adverse conditions. If there is a tendency for overall stability and resistance to such cyclical phenomena, the quality rating would be high. If the majority of the firms can be subject to rapid cutbacks in production or services in the event of unfavorable economic changes, the quality rating would be low.

Industrial, specialty and trade categories of employment are evaluated on the three quality ratings in comparison with the nation and other communities. There may be a tendency for much wider variation in the specialty category, which should be recognized and adjusted for.

The final ratings in each of the three categories of employment are totaled to reach a figure applicable to all categories of employment. Such a figure is of value only when it is compared to a rating of competitive communities.

LOCAL RESOURCES

In analyzing the economic potential of a community, consideration is given to its primary physical and human resources. Obviously, a complete and thorough supply of data regarding the people who make up an economic area is essential. Also, information is required regarding its energy sources and physical resources such as mineral and other types of natural resources. Favorable weather and climate conditions may be considered a resource especially in dealing with the recreational potential of a community. Unfavorable factors such as smog, odors, polluted waters or unusual weather conditions obviously are considered a disadvantage. Capital resources or access to capital is affected by the attitudes of bankers, investors, and other financial sources.

FUTURE ECONOMIC ACTIVITY

Economic base analysis is not merely a collection of data; it is developed so that the analyst can project the economic potential of a defined area. It is useless to collect a mass of data and perform a thorough statistical analysis and then fail to draw clear, concise conclusions regarding the future of the economic entity. This latter step is vital in the analysis of the economic potential of a metropolitan area. Concise and definitive projections regarding the competitive position of the community, compared to other communities and the nation as a whole, are essential. If such projections are not made, there is no validity or justification for the economic base analysis.

Economic base analysis is not the only technique used in predicting the economic future of an area. An input/output analysis has been developed by urban economists to rate the economics of a community on an income and expense basis. It may be further analyzed in terms similar to a profit and loss statement. Urban economists have also developed a regional accounting system that compares one part of a region or area with other parts to see which has competitive advantages. A third type of analysis is referred to as a balance of payments, which is basically a study to reveal historical, current, and future projected capacity for the favorable balance of trade in one economic community compared to the world, the nation, and other economic areas. All economic analysis techniques, however, are projections or estimates of the future. The appraiser must recognize that all prognostications about the future must be used wisely and cautiously.

SUMMARY

The whole process of rating the economic base of a community and its future is an attempt to produce an honest and critical analysis. In no way can all subjectivity be removed, of course, but the analyst would be subject to criticism if too many personal likes, dislikes or prejudices are used in developing the ratings.

The process is also a way to measure more scientifically the degree of competitiveness among the "little economies" (economic communities). It adds a degree of reliability to the appraiser's conclusions regarding the community in which the residential property being appraised is located. Communities do vary widely. There are great ones, good ones and some marginal ones. The appraisal process must recognize the impact of the community. The marketability of residential property will be affected accordingly.

General data consists of data about the four forces originating outside a property and what effect they have on the value of the property being appraised. They are known as the social, economic, governmental and environmental forces.

General data is divided into primary data which is original data collected by the appraiser or other groups and agencies. When it becomes published and available to the public it becomes secondary data.

Another way to classify data is Macrodata comprised of information on aggregate phenomena and Microdata which are more specific observations.

General data is essential to the valuation estimate. It provides needed background information about trends that affect property value and form a basis for judgments about highest and best use, reconciliation and final value estimates.

A parcel of real estate reflects what surrounds it: the community of which it is a part; the state, district or region; and, of course, its general location within the nation. The economic potential of the community can be analyzed in a logical and orderly manner. This type of rating emphasizes the future economic potential of the community, not its past or present status. The future is paramount in such analyses.

To analyze a metropolitan area, it must be properly identified and its boundaries located. Typically, it is wise to choose an established type of community for which statistics are readily available, such as an SMSA.

Metropolitan area economic analysis requires identification of local resources, establishment of data sources and development of clear and careful estimates regarding the future economic potential of the area.

SYMMETRICAL

2 OR 3 STORIES

COLUMN-SUPPORTED
COLONNADE ACROSS
FRONT

Colonial American

SOUTHERN COLONIAL (South Co - 113)

LARGE
BAY
WINDOWS

ELABORATE
WINDOWS

LIGHT
IRON
WORK

Colonial American

ADAMS COLONIAL (Adams Co - 103)

6 Residential Real Estate Markets

The market value of a parcel of real estate cannot be estimated without first understanding its relationship to the real estate market. The appraiser must be familiar with the structure of the market and how it functions, its peculiarities and idiosyncrasies, and its degree of effectiveness. In estimating the market value of a single family residence or a small residential income property, the appraiser must have full knowledge of the market in which it is being offered; without this knowledge the estimate may be inaccurate and unreliable.

To obtain this background, the appraiser may use detailed market analyses prepared by experts in that field. The purpose of this chapter is to provide the appraiser with a broad background to facilitate an understanding of market analysis. It is not intended to provide complete instructions on the techniques of making such an analysis. This chapter examines the real estate market, discusses its special economic characteristics and analyzes the relationship of the market and market value estimates.

THE MARKETPLACE

All transactions, purchases, sales, leases, exchanges and like activities occur in a market. The marketplace may be a specific location where business is transacted (e.g., the New York Stock Exchange) or it may refer to the activity of negotiating toward agreement between parties. The real estate market has no central exchange to facilitate its activities of buying and selling; therefore, when reference is made to the real estate market, it refers to the activities of the market.

The major factors in the activity of all markets are demand, supply and price. Demand and supply are causal factors; price is the result or effect of the interaction of the other two, the pressures or lack of activity.

From a brief and general description of the forces operating in the real estate market and the functions they perform, the competitive process may seem to bring about smooth adjustments among supply, demand and prices. This is not necessarily the case. Competition is the main regulative force but the actual operation of the real estate market is far from perfect.

The real estate market is subject to many outside influences such as seasonal activity peaks, general and local economic activity, the availability of financing and government regulations. At any given time these factors can combine to create a buyers' or a sellers' market. When supply is greater than demand, prices tend to fall, making it a buyers' market. When demand exceeds supply, prices tend to rise, creating a sellers' market.

CRITERIA OF AN EFFECTIVE MARKET

Any open and free market has a tendency to move toward a point of equilibrium--that is, a point at which supply equals demand. This basic economic principle is clearly understandable because when prices fall, activity on the demand side of the market tends to increase, which results in increased purchases and lowered supply. As demand increases beyond existing supply, prices tend to rise, thereby automatically encouraging suppliers to produce more goods or services for the market. Because of the inefficiencies of most markets, an oversupply can develop, in which case prices drop again and the cycle starts over again.

These statements about the market are generalized and oversimplified. Most markets are more formal and efficient than real estate markets, so special effort must be made to understand the real estate market. The reason the real estate market does not match other product markets in efficiency is that the real estate market does not possess features essential for maximum efficiency, including:

1. Central marketplace.
2. Standardized product, movable and requiring little care or protection.
3. Non-seasonal and non-cyclical activity.
4. Simplicity of financing.
5. Minimal legal requirements and restrictions.
6. Free, open market not supervised or regulated by governments.

The real estate market has improved in efficiency over the last two decades because of the contribution of brokers, appraisers, lawyers, title companies, financial institutions, and government agencies; however, it still has not reached the efficiency of most other markets.

Certain restrictions are placed on the real estate market that impair its open and effective functioning. To understand these restrictions, one needs to know the criteria of an effective market. Competition can operate more easily if the goods involved are durable and can bear long carriage and if they can be standardized, graded, and bought and sold from samples. Furthermore, a market requires good organization, preferably with a central exchange that is easily accessible to all and where offers to buy and sell can be cleared with a minimum of difficulty. The more buyers and sellers know about the forces bearing on the market, the more effective market competition becomes. Buyers and sellers must be free from compulsion (for example, where some single group dominates the market) if competition is to be effective. Financing must not be difficult or time consuming; and a minimum of legal requirements and few, if any government regulations or restrictions can exist.

In a model competitive market, both buyers and sellers are numerous and they are seen as bidding against each other until a price is reached that is agreeable to both parties. The action of any single buyer or seller in this model has only an infinitesimal effect on the market as a whole; but the interactions of all operators taken together create changes in supply, demand, and price. All that any individual buyer can do is buy or not buy, or buy greater or smaller quantities, as prices change. Likewise, an individual seller can choose to sell, not sell, sell more or sell less. A producer can produce, not produce, or produce different amounts. The quantities supplied will thus be changed and this will affect price.

The real estate market ranks comparatively low in effectiveness among various types of markets, and it differs in several ways from the model of a competitive market outlined above. In general, real estate cannot be standardized, graded, or bought and sold from samples. Also, real estate transactions involve a variety of legal rights that may differ from property to property, and every transfer of real property involves many legal formalities and much documentation. Financing may be a severe restriction on the free action of the market.

In some real estate markets a single buyer may have a significant effect due to the relative "thinness" of the market, such as that for unimproved land. This is similar to the over-the-counter securities market where stocks are traded in limited volume.

ECONOMIC CHARACTERISTICS OF THE SINGLE FAMILY RESIDENCE

To understand the operation of the single family residential market, the appraiser must first appreciate the special economic characteristics of the single family residence. Real estate is different from most economic goods, in terms of its size, the manner in which it is used and the way in which it is marketed. Four special economic characteristics of single family residences make them distinct and separate from most other economic goods: fixity of location, long life, large economic units, and the interdependence of public and private property. These four characteristics affect the reaction of buyers and sellers in the marketplace.

FIXITY OF LOCATION

Land stays where it is; it is location in itself. Added to this is the lack of mobility of the dwellings that are built upon the sites. (Even today's "mobile home" is not truly mobile). Because of fixity of location, each residential property is unique; no two properties can possibly be identical because the site for each is different. Two models of a manufactured home may be built by the same builder with exactly the same interiors and exteriors, but both houses cannot sit on the same lot. The total package may differ in that one may be located on an inside lot and the other on a corner lot. The market will recognize this difference.

The second aspect of fixity of location is that the surroundings of each residence have a direct impact on the marketability and livability of such a residence. This is referred to as "neighborhood impact." A single family residence located in a neighborhood in which all the other houses are much older and in poorer condition will be looked upon by buyers in a different light from the same residence in a neighborhood of its approximate age and in good condition. Other factors on neighborhood are discussed in the next chapter.

The third feature of fixity of location is that by its very nature the markets are more limited. Buyers or users must come to the product; the product cannot be moved to the buyers. Therefore, existing inventories of houses must depend on the market that is active in the community or can be attracted to it. To fully appreciate the operation of the residential market, this pertinent point must be remembered.

The fourth special feature of fixity of location deals with the legal distinctions applicable to real property. Real property has more special legal complications, limitations and provisions than virtually all other types of economic goods. An automobile, for instance, is conveyed from one owner to another by the simple registration certificate. A real estate transaction may involve many title complications and resultant recording requirements. While these may be looked upon as a handicap, the intention is protection for the owners rather than a limitation. The additional complications of legal arrangements obviously affect the marketability or the operation of exchanges in the market.

LONG LIFE

Although land itself, the surface of the earth, is enduring, the buildings built upon it will not last forever. However, in terms of other economic goods, a house has a long life. Most houses are useful for 30 to 50 years; some are still being lived in after 200 years. Most types of houses have an economic life of many decades and even the most poorly built building can probably be used for at least 10 to 20 years.

Long duration and physical existence mean that once constructed, the product will remain in inventory (on the market) for a long time. It is not quickly consumed like other products. Once the product is added to inventory, it will be a factor in a specific locational market for a long time. Further more, it takes a reasonably long period to add new units to a specific market. Six months is probably a minimum period for the most efficient homebuilder; two years or longer may be required under certain circumstances.

LARGE ECONOMIC UNITS

The median sale price of a residential unit in the United States now has exceeded the $100,000 range. Not many people make such a purchase frequently; rather, it may be once in a lifetime. In most cases special financing arrangements are necessary so that the buyer can afford the purchase. This requirement complicates the marketing of the product. While much progress has been made in streamlining the financing process it still is a time-consuming factor and, in some cases, prevents a buyer in the market from becoming an effective bargainer. Obviously, such a matter must be weighed in analyzing the demand aspects of the residential market.

INTERDEPENDENCE OF PRIVATE AND PUBLIC PROPERTY

The fourth economic characteristic of single family residences is the interdependence of private and public property. No matter how well built or architecturally attractive it may be, a house's usability depends upon its accessibility. Because of fixity of location, the residence must be reached by public access It must have street and/or sidewalk access. Many other types of dependence on the public sector are needed to make a house livable. Most houses depend heavily on public utilities--sanitary sewer, water, gas, electricity, and telephone. Public transportation is an important factor in many kinds of living units. The close relationship of schools, public recreation areas and other public activities either enhances or detracts from the marketability of a home.

The four special characteristics outlined above must be related to the economic characteristics of the real estate market. The housing unit is a product in the market; the market is made up of buyers interested in such a product and sellers desirous of selling their commodities. The interaction of the market is directly affected by the special characteristics of the product. The following section analyzes the special economic characteristics of the residential real estate market for small income properties.

ECONOMIC CHARACTERISTICS OF THE SMALL RESIDENTIAL INCOME PROPERTY

The market for small residential income properties operates differently than the market for single family residences. The typical buyer of a single family residence is primarily looking for a place to live with their family. Studies show that the buyers tend to be divided into two broad groups, those who move from one community to another usually because of the requirements of their employment or retirement and those who move within the same region because they wish to upgrade their standard of living by moving into a more desirable neighborhood and/or a better home.

Buyers of small residential income properties do so primarily for investment and potential tax savings purposes. Some also elect to live in their investment properties but they tend to place more emphasis on the quality of the property as an investment than as a residence.

FIXITY OF LOCATION

A distinguishing characteristic of all real estate is its fixity and its permanent location. Small income property investors are usually concerned more with the impact of location on the quality of the investment than on the direct quality of life offered by living in the property. Many owner-occupants of multiple family dwellings will live in neighborhoods they perceive to be less desirable than what they would choose if they were to purchase a single family residence.

The second factor of fixity of location is that the surrounding of each residence is very important. Many buyers of single family residences prefer to select homes that conform with the rest of the neighborhood (the principle of conformity appears to be less important in urban settings than it was in the past in suburban neighborhoods). By contrast, often the best small income investment properties are located in single family neighborhoods where they do not conform to the surrounding homes.

The third feature of fixity of location is that by its very nature the markets are more limited. Buyers of investment properties tend to consider properties over a larger geographic area than the typical single family home buyer would consider.

The fourth feature of fixity of location deals with the legal distinctions applicable to real property. Small income properties have all the special legal complications, limitations and provisions of single family homes plus the additional ones caused by the landlord/tenant relationship such as leases, rental commissions, management contracts, evictions, etc. Many people choose not to buy real estate as an investment because they do not wish to become involved in the many complications of real estate ownership.

LARGE ECONOMIC UNITS

Few small income producing properties are purchased for all cash. In most cases, special financing arrangements are necessary. More favorable financing has a significant impact on the investment. Buyers often seek lower down payments, lower interest rates, longer mortgage terms, etc. While there are many sources of financing for residential income properties, they usually are more limited than the sources of single family mortgages in the same market.

INTERDEPENDENCE OF PRIVATE AND PUBLIC PROPERTY

Small residential income properties are also dependent upon accessibility. A much smaller segment of rental tenants are willing to live in isolated areas than are single family home owners. Therefore, multiple family dwellings tend to be located in areas where there is good access to transportation leading to shopping areas and work places. Because the density of multiple family housing tends to be higher than single family housing in the same community, they are more dependent on public utilities, especially public water and sewers.

ECONOMIC CHARACTERISTICS OF THE MARKET

The following is a partial list of factors that influence the operation of the residential real estate market:

1. The uniqueness of each parcel of real estate.

2. Local restrictive factors, such as taxes, zoning regulations, rent controls, availability of services, environmental controls.

3. The general economic climate and outlook.

4. The lack of mechanisms for selling short.

5. The variability of improvements. Lack of standardization may create desirable features or hidden defects.

6. Long lease periods, causing some properties to be removed from the market for a length of time.

7. Un-informed buyers and sellers.

8. Buyers limited to those who are able to take advantage of bargains or the necessities of the seller.

9. Financing terms, which influence prices.

10. Possibility of legal complications in the exchange. Agreements must be in writing to be legally enforceable.

11. Title, which must be clear and transferable.

12. Sentimental attachment on the part of the seller, creating an unwillingness to sell for the market value.

MARKET VARIATIONS

Real estate markets can be classified according to types of properties, scope, and whether transfers are permanent (sales) or temporary (rentals, leases). The rental and sales markets are not mutually exclusive because they form parts of a larger whole, but the rental market is not characterized by the wide variations that occur in the permanent transfer of properties. The rental market is similar in nature to a consumer goods market and the sale market to a producer goods market. Usually variations in market activity in consumer goods are not so marked as those in producer goods.

The rental market does, however, influence selling prices and the rate of construction. In a sellers' market, prices may move high enough to stimulate new construction. If more new buildings are constructed than can be absorbed at prices characteristic of a sellers' market, a long period of time may be required for absorption to take place, creating a buyers' market as oversupply lowers prices.

DEMAND PRESSURES

An increase in rents and selling prices is normally the result of an increase in the demand for space, although an inflationary trend may result in across-the-board higher prices. In the short-run, demand conditions are of greater importance than those of supply. The basic element in demand is purchasing power, which includes income and the terms and availability of financing. When an increase in demand occurs, an expansion of activity usually follows. Expansion of economic opportunities usually is necessary to attract people or to increase their incomes. Similarly, a loss of such opportunities tends to depress the real estate market.

An increase in population growth does not cause real estate activity to increase substantially unless there is a simultaneous increase in purchasing power on the part of the newcomers. Likewise, the lack of population growth does not necessarily prevent an expansion from occurring if incomes advance and financing terms are liberal.

INFLEXIBLE SUPPLY

Wide variations in real estate activity can be explained largely in terms of the relative inflexibility of the supply of space. People may be willing or need to live in more crowded conditions for a variety of reasons, although they are usually unwilling to live under these conditions when incomes increase. Under depressed economic conditions, new construction tends to decrease because it will not pay to build at the existing low sales prices. But as the population expands in number and in purchasing power, the large supply of vacant units typical of depressed periods tends to be rapidly absorbed. When the percentage of vacant units reaches a low figure, prices begin to rise. Hence, the rate of profit is increased, and it becomes profitable for builders to construct new units again.

MARKET EXPANSION

In the early stages of economic expansion, construction of single family houses tends to dominate because many are constructed for consumers with incomes sufficient to make down payments, even if the houses would not command rents sufficient to yield a normal monetary return on their costs. Similarly, business firms may expand plants or stores. As expansion progresses, however, it becomes profitable to construct apartment buildings, business blocks, industrial structures, shopping centers and office buildings that are financed primarily for return on investment.

A period of construction usually begins with a period of easy credit. During such a period it may be quite easy to finance projects of various types. As new buildings absorb vacant land and subdivision activity gathers momentum, a land boom may result if the pressure to build continues to increase. Large areas may be added to the supply of land available to a community. As outward movement from the city center occurs, the available area increases in a manner comparable to the square of the radius of a circle.

Expenditures for public improvements tend to increase at the same time that the volume of building and subdividing gains momentum. The nature of this type of expansion does not allow it to be done piece by piece or in small quantities. A sewer trunkline, for example, may open many thousands of acres to development.

MARKET CONTRACTION

Inasmuch as the market does not operate "in balance", there tends to be a "teeter-totter" effect. Eventually, supply will begin to exceed demand. It becomes difficult to transfer properties and the sources of credit begin to tighten up, which results in delinquencies. This decline in demand and increase in foreclosures signals a period of economic decline. Many sectors of the real estate market may still maintain a peak level of activity because a marked decline in rents has not yet been experienced. Operating expenses may increase, however, and further foreclosures are likely to take place. The fact that real estate is financed more on a debt than an equity basis probably helps to intensify the variations that occur. Thus those who finance real estate may unsuspectingly make or break the market.

If foreclosures continue to increase as credit tightens, the entire market is affected. Prices fall and land values decline. Just as net rentals rise more rapidly than gross rentals in the early period of expansion, they fall more rapidly because of the fixed charges involved. Hence profits are wiped out and market activity falls to low levels.

A recession in the real estate market is intensified during a simultaneous general recession. As incomes drop, vacancies increase and rents decline. Foreclosures increase rapidly, first in leased properties (apartment and office buildings), as rents decline faster than operating expenses. If a long recession ensues, foreclosures extend to single family residences and owner-occupied business properties. As a result, real estate prices are forced down.

A large volume of foreclosures is characteristic of a depressed real estate market. Following the foreclosure process, properties are refinanced. The financial wreckage is cleared away to make way for a new period of expansion, which usually results from some special impetus to increase demand for real estate.

ANALYSIS OF THE REAL ESTATE MARKET

PURPOSE OF MARKET ANALYSIS

The objective of the analysis governs the pattern it takes, the information employed and the degree of detail used. Because each market analysis is individual and unique, the priority and emphasis assigned to the topics of consideration may vary.

The first step is to state the objective: what is the purpose of the analysis? An analysis may be used for many reasons, such as to learn what has happened in a specific market in the past, to conclude what market conditions prevail currently or to project market activity in the future. It may seek to answer whether a builder should start a new project or a lender should risk financing single family residences.

The problems involved in making market analyses generally fall into two major categories: (1) those pertaining to short-run objectives and (2) those pertaining to long-run objectives. For example, a builder may be concerned with the immediate marketability of his houses; a lender may be concerned with property stability over the next 30 years.

Defining the purpose of the analysis helps to determine which of these two considerations should be given the most weight, the sector of the market that should be emphasized, and the appropriate intensity with which the market should be studied.   In defining the purpose of the market analysis, the particular market segment under discussion must be isolated and identified. The whole market, or general climate, affects the segmented markets within it. These segments may be defined by geographical location, type, age, or value range of the properties.

MAJOR TOPICS OF ANALYSIS

The main topics in the analysis of residential markets are supply factors, demand factors or a combination of both.

--Supply Factors. The first item under this heading is an inventory of the existing stock of all housing units in the defined market area. The Census Bureau's statistics on housing is the primary source of this data, which is updated at regular intervals.

Next under supply factors are new construction volume and costs, including:

1. Recent building rate--new housing starts.

2. Conditions in the building industry as they relate to construction costs-- availability and price of the agents of production.

3. Actual and potential changes in building technology and how they might affect construction costs.

4. Relationship of construction costs to sales prices.

5. Cost of improving raw land and supply available.

Among sources of information will be the Bureau of the Census, Bureau of Labor Statistics, city and county building departments and planning commissions, real estate boards and builders' groups.

The third supply factor is the vacancy rate, one of the important indicators of real estate market conditions and trends. A high vacancy rate results in lowered prices and rents, even when demand is high. Normal vacancy for single family homes is usually less than 5% and for apartments, slightly over 5%. Business units may run somewhat higher. These are general guidelines that may vary from place to place.   If the supply of vacant units exceeds a normal percentage, the market is oversupplied and/or short in demand. Competition may force prices and rents downward, followed by a decrease in new construction. When the vacancy rate declines, rents and prices increase, and optimistic entrepreneurs begin the process of adding more units to the market.

Vacancy information may be obtained from local real estate boards, the post office, local public utility companies and property managers. Vacancy rates for different market segments should be computed separately because one part of the market may have a shortage of space while another has a surplus.

--Demand Factors. First under this heading is general population change (past, present and predictable future trends), including:

1. Changes in population numbers--current population.

2. Changes in population distribution.

3. Ratios of different population segments--for example, ratio between elementary school enrollment and population, net migration figures, marriage and divorce rates.

Again, sources of information include the Census Bureau, utility companies (the current population can be estimated by multiplying the present number of electric or water meters by the ratio of population to number of meters at the time of the last census), local chamber of commerce, county offices, school districts and visitors' bureau.

Changes in preferences and taste are an important demand factor. Within any real estate market, the shifts that occur in the preference and tastes of the consumer may be difficult to identify or evaluate. Many real estate professionals rely on their own experience and observation to guide them, almost intuitively, with respect to such changes. Surveys may not reveal basic shifts in preference, especially for goods that are unfamiliar to consumers, even though once available consumers may flock to buy. Preference and taste are highly subjective and therefore very difficult to quantify and predict.

Any change in market prices or rents that persists for a year or more is a strong market trend indicator. Of special importance is the range between the listing and actual sales price, compared property by property. Similarly, the difference between the rental rate asked and finally paid is a reflection of the strength of the market. The length of time to dispose of properties on the market also indicates its strength. When long periods are required to dispose of property, the market is weakening, assuming, of course, that prices have been set at a reasonably competitive level.

Variations in market activity are reflected in the number of real estate transfers. The county record office can supply figures on the number of deeds, mortgages and foreclosures recorded. Studies of this data covering fairly long periods of time are desirable. This data may be related to population trends, vacancy ratios, prices, rents, cost indices and the volume of construction. Such relationships provide a good indication of the present position of the market with regard to past periods. This overall perspective should allow an accurate prediction for future market activity.

--Combined Supply and Demand Factors. Business conditions, employment and income and financing conditions all fall within this category.

Estimates of general business trends usually precede the analysis of a specific real estate market. Local markets follow national economic trends to the degree that they represent a typical cross-section of the economy. The appraiser must note whether local conditions follow closely or deviate significantly from general trends.

The most important factors to consider when studying local business conditions are employment and income data. Sources for this type of information include local Chambers of Commerce, state employment services, local employers and monthly business reviews published by certain universities and financial institutions. These reports give information on local business activities, including retail sales activity, real estate transfers, new housing starts, and electricity production.

Recent changes in employment or income have a vital influence on all phases of local real estate market activity. Of special significance are potential developments likely to strengthen or diminish the demand for specific types of properties. Such developments must be related directly to the specific market problem under discussion. If local incomes are good and income prospects favorable, the real estate market is likely to be active (unless there has already been a great surge of building and a large unused inventory). Even though no new residents are attracted to the area, higher incomes mean an increase in the demand for housing. Heavier spending leads to greater demand for commercial property. Thus, demand for real estate can rise in a locality even though there has been no major increase in population. Similarly, demand falls with a decline in incomes, even if there has been no loss of population.

It is important in analyzing real estate markets to know what sections of the city are occupied by high, middle or low income families. For cities of 50,000 population or more, data is available on a census tract basis, including the average monthly rent and average value of owner-occupied houses, which gives indications of income ranges in the area. The terms and availability of financing are also primary factors in determining the strength or weakness of demand for real estate. When financing is readily available at attractive interest rates, the demand for property is strengthened. A tight interest market tends to limit demand for real estate. Financing conditions vary not only from region to region but also from one real estate market to another. The availability of funds for the real estate market is dependent on the yield an investor can anticipate from his investment. For instance, if the bond market is offering a higher return on invested funds than the mortgage market, funds are diverted away from the real estate market. Information regarding the real estate finance market can be obtained from many different sources including publications of the Federal Reserve System, Federal Home Loan Bank Board, or from financial newspapers, lending institutions, magazines and journals.

RELATIVE PRICES AND RELATIONSHIPS

Of major importance in market analysis are relative prices. For example, construction costs may be rising but if rents, selling prices and incomes are rising proportionately, further construction is likely to continue. An upward or downward trend in prices and rents may cause buyers, investors and property users to expect still further changes in the same direction and accentuate the trend that has been developing.

An increase in funds available for real estate investment, resulting in more favorable financing terms, may stimulate market activity even though no other basic changes have occurred. The effect of rising incomes may be limited if the price of all goods and services, including real estate, is also increasing. In other words, real income, rather than monetary income, is the primary consideration.

Real estate resources are in competition with other goods and services for a portion of the consumer's income. The real estate market is not isolated from other markets; it is an integral part of the entire economic system. Real estate market changes must always be considered in relation to other developments in the local or national economy.

HOUSING MARKET ANALYSIS

The factors discussed above refer to all types of real estate markets. In making an analysis of the single family residential market, the following factors are considered in detail.

HOUSING DEMAND

Expanding economic opportunities will encourage growth and stimulate the demand for housing. Rising incomes, even without expansion of employment, may also lead to heavier housing demand. Thus economic base and similar types of analyses are often helpful in housing market studies.

In analysis of housing demand, income must be related to house prices. As a rule, families cannot afford to pay more than two to three times their annual income for housing. Consequently, a good housing market analysis requires information on the income distribution of the families in the area. Data of this type is available by census tract in metropolitan regions and for cities, towns and counties. Census reports also indicate the number of owner-occupied and rental units by price in rent brackets.

Closely related to income, cost and price factors, are financing considerations. If financing is available on easy terms, demand may be maintained even though incomes are not advancing. Conversely, if financing terms are not favorable, housing demand may reduce rapidly even though incomes are steady or advancing. Changes in the terms of financing may have an even greater impact on the market than changes in incomes because of the large proportion of borrowed funds that go into most purchases of single family residences.

HOUSING SUPPLY

The supply of new dwelling units can be estimated on the basis of new building permits and the number of water or electric meters added. Data of this type can be broken down by districts and related to base periods such as those for which census information is available.

A long period of strong building activity may point towards a weakening market, especially if vacancies are increasing and new houses are selling slowly. Also, construction costs must be studied in relationship to current prices to determine whether it is profitable to continue high volumes of construction activity.

Efficiency of building and low sale prices stimulate demand. Larger builders, both those with large-scale, on-site operations and prefabricators, have been able to stimulate demand in this way. However, whenever market prices fall below the cost of construction, regardless of scale or methods used, few new housing starts are initiated.

Fashion in design or style may reflect changing tastes and preferences of consumers, thus affecting demand.

SUMMARY

All real estate transactions take place in the real estate market, a term that refers to the activity of the transactions, not to a specific marketplace. An appraiser must gain a thorough understanding of the real estate market before being able to accurately estimate the market value of any parcel of real estate.

Competition from both supply and demand must exist to create an effective market. Demand in excess of supply creates a sellers' market; supply in excess of demand creates a buyers' market.

The restrictions on the open and effective functioning of the real estate market are caused by the uniqueness of each different parcel of real estate and the involvement of legal rights in each transaction. The economic characteristics particularly applicable to the single family residence are: (1) fixity of location; (2) long life; (3) large economic units, and (4) interdependence of private and public property.

Factors that influence market operation are generally dependent upon supply, demand, price, legal procedures and complications, subjective values of both buyers and sellers and the overall economic climate.

The objective of any market analysis influences how it is conducted and what information or data is used in the analysis. Major topics for analysis can be divided into supply factors, demand factors or a combination of both. The analysis of a housing market involves applying factors that are pertinent to the residential sector of the real estate market.

SHINGLES

GABLE ROOF

1½ STORIES

CENTRAL
ENTRANCE

Colonial American

CAPE COD COLONIAL (Cape Cod - 104)

7 Neighborhood Analysis

A house is an integral part of its neighborhood and its community; its market value is affected substantially by the neighborhood in which it is located. Therefore, the primary purpose of neighborhood analysis is to identify the geographic area which is subject to the same influences as the property being appraised. Prices paid for comparable properties in the defined area theoretically reflect the positive and negative influences of that particular neighborhood. Two houses with similar physical characteristics may have significantly different market values, due to location in different neighborhoods.

In the appraisal process, neighborhood analysis provides background for valuation. Information that has no bearing on value is irrelevant and may mislead the reader who can rightfully assume everything in the appraisal report is related to the appraisal process and the final estimate of value. Mis-use of neighborhood analysis can lead to double counting and false conclusions.

Assume, for example, that after complete neighborhood analysis, the appraiser delineates the neighborhood and obtains an indication of value based on recent prices received for similar properties in the same neighborhood. In such a case, it would be incorrect to adjust value for neighborhood influences, because these influences must be assumed to be reflected in the observed market prices.

The depth of analysis varies according to the need, but a neighborhood must be defined in terms of some common characteristics and trends in order to interpret market evidence fairly. The appraiser should avoid reliance on the racial, religious or ethnic characteristics of the residents. Racial and other ethnic factors are not reliable predictors of value trends and use of such factors by the appraiser in neighborhood analysis can be misleading. People's reactions and preferences are so diverse and variable that they are not readily quantifiable in the course of the appraisal process.

OBJECTIVITY IN NEIGHBORHOOD ANALYSIS

Consideration of observable neighborhood conditions and trends is an important aspect of neighborhood analysis and typically includes observation of factors that enhance or detract from property values. Objectivity is essential in identifying and discussing these conditions, trends or factors. For instance, general reference to a presumed "pride of ownership" (or lack thereof) may be too vague and too subjective to be indicative of an actual contribution to or detraction from property values. The presence of special amenities or detrimental conditions should be noted and described clearly and carefully.

The appraiser's findings with respect to neighborhood conditions and the effects of these conditions on property values are considered by buyers, sellers, brokers, lenders, courts, arbiters, public officials and other decision-makers or advisors. Because of this broad influence, the appraiser is often called upon to provide specific evidence of neighborhood conditions and trends and to elaborate the findings in a written appraisal report. The use of photographs and detailed field notes enables the appraiser to recall important evidence and verify the facts considered in the analysis.

The appraiser should avoid generalization with respect to the desirability of particular types of neighborhoods. Older urban neighborhoods, as well as newer suburban subdivisions, can attract a wide range of residents. Neighborhood trends do not necessarily depend upon the age of the neighborhood or the income of neighborhood residents.

NEIGHBORHOODS

What constitutes neighborhood is difficult to describe precisely.[1] In fact its meaning has been changing. Neighborhoods previously were defined as a segment of a community that gave a noticeable impression of unity. This unity might have been based on similar uses of the properties within the neighborhood such as mostly industrial plants, retail stores or multiple or single family housing. It also might have been a unity of structural appearance such as mostly colonial or contemporary style buildings. It sometimes was a unity based on the economic, religious, racial or ethnic status of most of the residents of the neighborhood. For example, some neighborhoods would be occupied predominantly by workers from a local industry or by persons of a particular national origin, race or religion.

Neighborhoods that can be described on these bases are becoming less common. Often industrial, commercial and residential uses all exist in the same neighborhood. Likewise, people with a variety of economic, ethnic, racial and religious backgrounds now often live compatibly together in the same neighborhood.

The criteria for neighborhood analysis are clearly changing, reflecting changes on our social structures and attitudes. Obsolete standards of conformity have no place in modern neighborhood analysis. Broad federal and state Fair Housing laws have made discrimination on the basis of racial, religious or ethnic factors unlawful in the sale, rental and financing of housing. These laws, and changing social norms, have contributed to the establishment and maintenance of many stable, integrated residential areas.

Today a neighborhood tends to be any separately identifiable cohesive area within a community with some commonality of interest shared by its occupants. Some neighborhoods may have recognizable natural or man-made boundaries. Neighborhoods sometimes have their own names, such as Old Town or Pigeon Hills, but frequently neighborhoods of this size actually consist of many sub-neighborhoods with different characteristics. A neighborhood may be as large as an entire community, or as small as a one-or two-block area.

---

[1]An intriguing description. Dr. Robert O. Harvey is "a neighborhood is the area around a lot to a point where changes in land use have no direct effect on the value of the lot." AREA Course Instructors' Manual, Real Estate Certification Program, Indiana University, Revised Edition, August 1977.

BOUNDARIES

The first step in the study of a neighborhood is to identify its boundaries. Sometimes these are natural physical barriers such as lakes, rivers, streams, cliffs, swamps and valleys. They also can be highways, main traffic arteries, railroad tracks, canals and other man-made boundaries. The boundary of a residential neighborhood may also be a change of land use to commercial, industrial, institutional or public park. Some boundaries are clearly defined, while others are more difficult to identify precisely.

1. Inspection of the area's physical characteristics. An appraiser should drive around to develop a sense of the area, particularly the degree of similarity in land uses, types of structures, architectural styles, maintenance and upkeep. On a map of the area, an appraiser should note points where these characteristics show perceptible changes and should note any physical barriers, such as major streets, hills, rivers, and railroads, that coincide with such changes.

2. Drawing preliminary boundaries on a map. An appraiser should draw lines that connect the points where physical characteristics change. The appraiser should identify the streets, hills, rivers, railroads, and so forth, that coincide with or that are near the shifts in physical characteristics.

3. Testing preliminary boundaries against socioeconomic characteristics of the area's population. If possible, an appraiser should obtain accurate data concerning the ages, occupations, incomes and educational levels of the neighborhood occupants. Such data is collected every 10 years by the Bureau of the Census, U.S. Department of Commerce. U.S. Census of Population data that pertain to population and housing characteristics, employment, and earnings are also available.

Reliable data may also be available from local chambers of commerce, universities, and research organizations. In unusual cases, the appraiser may also consider sampling the population of the area to obtain an indication of the relevant characteristics.

The appraiser may informally interview neighborhood occupants, business persons, brokers, and community representatives to determine their perceptions about how far the neighborhood extends.

CHANGE

The analysis of the neighborhood continues with a description of the properties within the neighborhood. In addition to single family housing, a typical residential neighborhood may contain multi-family dwellings, retail stores, service establishments, schools, churches, theaters, municipal buildings, health institutions and sometimes industrial and commercial buildings.

Part of this analysis is the consideration of discernible patterns of urban growth that will influence the neighborhood. Careful analysis can reveal the general trends in the surrounding community area and the patterns of growth, decay and renewal that will affect the neighborhood.

Few neighborhoods are fixed in character. Most are dynamic in nature and are changing at various rates of speed. What is happening in one neighborhood in a community often affects other neighborhoods in the same and nearby communities. As new neighborhoods in a community are developed, they compete with existing neighborhoods. An added supply of new homes also tends to induce shifts from old to new. New neighborhoods may have the advantage of new housing stock. Older neighborhoods may have the advantage of closer location to places of work. Community historic significance, and access to parks, recreational facilities and shopping also affect the competitive position of a neighborhood. All these things being equal, a new house usually has an advantage over an older one.

STAGES OF A NEIGHBORHOOD

Neighborhoods are established when new buildings are constructed together with streets, utilities and other services. Sometimes a new neighborhood is established where an old neighborhood existed. This transition is most common where a residential neighborhood changes into a commercial or industrial neighborhood. With the help of urban renewal, an industrial or commercial neighborhood can be changed into a residential neighborhood.

The first stage of a new residential neighborhood is the growth period. This growth period may last for a year or so, or it may spread over many years. It may continue until all the available land is used or it may stop when the demand for new houses diminishes or when acceptable financing is not available. If the neighborhood is successfully developed, there will be active building. New construction will attract new inhabitants and usually the neighborhood gains public recognition and favor.

When the growth period ends, the neighborhood enters a period of relative equilibrium. Changes rarely stop completely but in this stabilizing period they may slow down considerably. New construction may continue on a limited basis as demand increases or financing terms improve and make building profitable. The period of stability is characterized by the lack of marked gains or losses. Many neighborhoods are stable for long periods of time. There is no preset life expectancy for a neighborhood and decline is not imminent in all older neighborhoods. The period of decline starts when the neighborhood is less able to compete with other neighborhoods. During this period, prices may have to be lowered to attract buyers to the neighborhood. Among the characteristics of a declining neighborhood are properties in a poor state of maintenance, conversions to more intensive uses and a lack of enforcement of building codes and zoning regulations.

The period of decline may end when the neighborhood changes to another land use and a new neighborhood is developed or when it moves into a renewal period. This may be caused by a change in one or more of the economic, social, physical or governmental forces. For example, expansion of commercial activities in the community may increase the demand for housing in the neighborhood.

Neighborhood rejuvenation can also be the result of organized community activities such as redevelopment programs, organized rebuilding and historical renovation. The rebirth of an older neighborhood is often caused by a combination of these factors, some of which are a result of planning and outside aid and some simply because of changing preferences and lifestyles.

After the rebirth of an older neighborhood the life cycle may be repeated in which a period of stability and eventually a period of decline may occur unless, again, a change in the forces that affect desirability and marketability takes place.[2]

EVIDENCE OF CHANGE

An appraiser often detects neighborhood change, or transition, by variations within the neighborhood. For example, a neighborhood in which some homes are well maintained and others are not, may indicate that the neighborhood is in the process of decline or of revitalization. The introduction of different uses, such as rooming houses or offices, into a single family residential neighborhood indicates a possible change. These new uses may indicate potential increases or decreases in neighborhood property values.

The changes in one neighborhood are usually influenced by changes occurring in others and in the larger area of influence. In any relatively stable city, for example, the rapid growth of one neighborhood or district may adversely affect a competitive neighborhood or district. A city's growth may reach the point where accessibility to the center from the more remote districts is difficult. In such instances, the establishment of new, competing business centers may better serve the needs of the outlying neighborhoods. Thus, commercial sub-centers come into being; the city's pattern becomes complex.

Gentrification and Displacement

A relatively recent neighborhood phenomenon is called gentrification, whereby middle and upper-income families and single persons purchase properties and renovate or rehabilitate them and existing residents become displaced. The existing residents are often lower-income families, who moved into certain older neighborhoods in various cities when middle and upper-income residents either left or did not move in because they found the neighborhoods unappealing and unattractive. Often two or more households would occupy what was formerly a single family residence. Some neighborhoods became blighted.

Gentrification appears to be the result of an increase of smaller families and single persons in metropolitan areas who enjoy living in proximity to urban activities.

ANALYSIS OF VALUE-INFLUENCE FORCES

To understand these life cycles and how neighborhoods change involves understanding the relevant physical, social, economic and governmental factors that affect value. The following is an outline of these factors, together with their various considerations. After the outline, each of the considerations is developed in more detail.

---

[2]There are many interpretations regarding the cycles in residential neighborhoods. An interesting concept is presented in a report entitled, "The Dynamics of Neighborhood Change," prepared by Public Affairs Counseling, a division of Real Estate Research Corporation, San Francisco, for HUD, under Contract #H-2151R, dated December, 1975.

PHYSICAL OR ENVIRONMENTAL

1. Location within the Community.
2. Barriers and Boundaries.
3. Topography.
4. Soil, Drainage and Climate.
5. Services and Utilities.
6. Proximity to Supporting Facilities.
7. Street Patterns.
8. Pattern of Land Use.
9. Conformity of Structure.
10. Appearance.
11. Special Amenities.
12. Nuisances and Hazards.
13. Age and Condition of Residences and Other Improvements.

SOCIAL

1. Population Characteristics.
2. Community and Neighborhood Associations.
3. Crime Level.

ECONOMIC

1. Relation to Community Growth.
2. Economic Profile of Residents.
3. New Construction and Vacant Land.
4. Turnover and Vacancy.

GOVERNMENTAL

1. Taxation and Special Assessments.
2. Public and Private Restrictions.
3. Schools.
4. Planning and Subdivision Regulations.

PHYSICAL OR ENVIRONMENTAL FACTORS

These factors cover conditions of the natural and man-made environment that physically define and limit the neighborhood.

--Location within the Community. The location of a neighborhood in relation to the larger community is important. A neighborhood adjacent to the central business district, for example, may benefit from the convenience of local shopping and municipal services, or it may suffer from exposure to a high crime rate and heavy traffic. Locations in the direction of growth may benefit, but those away from growth may suffer.

--Barriers and Boundaries. Both natural and man-made boundaries can effectively protect and define a neighborhood. These boundaries frequently help to reinforce the neighborhood identity, particularly when they are prominent landmarks such as a large park, super highway or river. Explicit boundaries are usually a favorable characteristic.

--Topography. Like barriers and boundaries, topography may be natural or man-made conditions of terrain. Typically, the desirability of various topography depends upon the nature of the residential development. For large-lot, high-value properties, hillside or wooded sites are often at a premium; tract developers, however, usually seek a level area or plateau which is more conducive to subdivision construction. Proximity to a lake, river, swamp or salt marsh may constitute a topographical advantage or disadvantage. Good topography can contribute protection from wind, fog or flood as well as provide an attractive view. The preferred topography is a rolling terrain at a slightly higher elevation than surrounding neighborhoods. Values tend to rise with the elevation of the land in many areas. Values are penalized where the land is very flat or excessively rugged without reasonable access.

--Soil, Drainage and Climate. The natural quality of the soil directly affects the cost to build and the value of residences in the neighborhood. Its bearing quality, ability to support landscaping and lawns, and the absorption rate for water disposal must be considered.

Drainage of surface water and neighborhood susceptibility to flooding also affect values. Flood maps are now available for many communities and the appraisal report should indicate if the neighborhood and residence being appraised are subject to flooding. Even in neighborhoods not subject to flooding, the disposal of storm water is an important consideration. Sometimes because of proximity to water, mountains or other natural conditions, a neighborhood has a different climate than nearby neighborhoods which affects its competitive position, either positively or negatively.

--Services and Utilities. The availability of services and utilities such as electricity, city water, sanitary sewers and natural gas affect the relative desirability of a neighborhood. Large price differentials for obtaining these services would also be detrimental to values.

--Proximity to Support Facilities. In analyzing a neighborhood, an appraiser must consider the proximity of and accessibility to major support facilities, such as public transportation, places of worship, schools, shopping areas, recreational facilities and centers of employment. Some people prefer to live within reasonable walking distance of convenience stores and service establishments, yet such support facilities should not inflict a commercial atmosphere on a residential neighborhood. Convenient access to these facilities often adds to the desirability of a neighborhood and to the values of homes in the area.

--Street Patterns. Streets are an important man-made physical element which can affect value. They are the entrances and exits of a neighborhood. The physical plan of a neighborhood is strongly influenced by its street pattern. The attractiveness of individual settings depends on the effective use of natural contours, wooded areas, ponds and other features. Contemporary planned neighborhoods make use of curving streets, cul-de-sacs with generous turn-around space and circular drives. These act as deterrents to through traffic, which can be a hazard in older neighborhoods. Where well-planned streets reduce such traffic hazards, they make a neighborhood more aesthetically attractive, and help to preserve the communication and unity of the area.

Ideally, expressways and boulevards should be outside the immediate residential neighborhood but should offer easy access from local streets. Traffic within the neighborhood should move easily and slowly.

--Patterns of Land Use. The pattern of land use within a neighborhood often helps an appraiser estimate the stage in the life cycle of that neighborhood. A stable neighborhood has clearly defined areas for various uses, well-buffered areas between uses, and respect for zoning and deed restrictions which helps maintain neighborhood integrity.

--Conformity of Structure. The character of a neighborhood is partially set by its "average" house. The class of ownership, structural nature of the house and its architectural style, combined with its age and condition are physical considerations that have an important impact on the desirability of the neighborhood. Widely diverse styles and levels of care often indicate a transitional period within a neighborhood.

--Appearance. Maintenance of individual homes and their architectural compatibility influence the general appearance of a neighborhood. Landscaping, plantings and open space preservation also directly affect the appearance of a neighborhood. Neatly kept yards and houses as well as community areas reflect on-going care by owners and residents.

--Special Amenities. In neighborhood analysis, the consideration of amenities is of major importance. People tend to live in the best housing they can afford, and a major factor in higher priced housing is amenity value. The homebuyer in the lowest income group purchases "shelter level" housing--that is, the bare necessities exclusive of most amenities. The more prosperous can afford to pay for the availability of external amenities such as parks, beaches, pools, tennis courts, country clubs and libraries. Amenities strongly improve a neighborhood's competitive position in attracting new residents.

--Nuisances and Hazards. Noise, traffic congestion, smoke and other nuisances directly affect the desirability of a neighborhood. Tolerance of nuisances and hazards tends to be inversely related to the income level of the residents. Values of properties tend to be higher in neighborhoods that have higher standards of public health, comfort and safety. A nearby factory complex or the flight path of an adjacent airport usually have a marked negative affect on the property values in a residential neighborhood. Effective barriers against such disturbances tend to create a premium.

--Age and Condition of Improvements. The age and condition of all residences in a neighborhood can affect the marketability of a house located in that neighborhood. Age alone may not be an indication; however, buildings do wear out even with good maintenance or become obsolete and therefore less marketable, or their location in relation to community growth may cause economic obsolescence. Regardless of age, delayed building maintenance may cause rapid loss of marketability in a residence. Several neglected houses in a neighborhood may not cause the entire neighborhood to decline in attractiveness, but as the percentage of neglected houses increases, there is a tendency for the entire neighborhood to follow the same pattern. The presence of community and neighborhood associations (which will be discussed further in the following section) often spurs maintenance and repair programs, thereby preserving market value and preventing decline among residences in the neighborhood.

SOCIAL FACTORS

Social factors include population characteristics, community and neighborhood organizations and crime level.

--Population Characteristics. Population trends and characteristics indicated by U.S. Census figures or statistics compiled by local agencies are important tools in estimating the trend of a neighborhood.

It was once common practice by some appraisers to examine the racial composition of a neighborhood in an effort to detect signs of change which were assumed to be indications of a trend toward lower values. Such an approach is now regarded as misdirected. This evolution in appraisal practice reflects a corresponding evolution in social attitudes and public policy. The old applications of the principle of racial or ethnic conformity have no place in current neighborhood analysis techniques. Changing social standards supported by broad federal and state Fair Housing laws have made it possible for the racial or ethnic composition of a neighborhood to change without values decreasing. They have also encouraged the establishment and maintenance of many stable, integrated residential areas. There is no factual support for the outdated assumption that racial or ethnic homogeneity is a requirement for maximum value.

Changing social standards and lifestyles now support a growing preference on the part of many people for social heterogeneity in their neighborhoods. In these areas, traditional social groupings are changing to reflect these social preferences. Analysis based on traditional, outdated social groupings has no relevance in current appraisal process. Some of the most desirable and dynamic urban neighborhoods reflect extremely wide diversity in all parameters, from income level to racial or ethic make-up.

--Community and Neighborhood Associations. A wide variety of community and neighborhood associations exist. Some are legal entities formed by the original developers of an area, with membership including all the owners within defined boundaries. Many of these organizations were started before World War II, often in coastal communities, around lakes or in other recreational areas. The developer would deed the beach, lakefront or other desirable natural area to the association, which in turn would maintain and control it for the benefit of its members.

Associations were also formed to maintain and guard exclusive subdivisions having common grounds, parks, courts and limited access. In addition to maintenance of common facilities, a major function of the association was to hire guards to keep uninvited guests off the association property. Some of the typical functions of this type of homeowners' association were:

1. Maintaining commonly owned land, beaches, courts, pools, club house and golf course.

2. Collecting rubbish and garbage, removing snow, and sweeping streets.

3. Providing and maintaining sewer disposal systems and water supply systems.

4. Providing police and fire protection.

5. Providing lifeguards on beaches, waterfronts and pools.

These groups often tried to exercise considerable control by enforcing private convenants and restrictions that gave them the right to approve the transfer of title or rental of property and to approve the style and size of any new buildings. They were also empowered to (1) establish an annual charge to be paid by the association members; (2) put a lien on the property of owners who did not pay their charges; (3) borrow money on behalf of the members; and (4) buy and sell property.

After World War II, the planned unit development became popular. Common land was deeded by the developer of a PUD to the local community. When the community accepted the common land, it incurred a financial obligation to maintain it and also lost tax revenue on it. Because of these reasons and also because the land became usable by the whole community, many communities refused to accept such common land. Developers then formed private homeowners' associations to accept the land and maintain it. They found this was a good way to provide recreational facilities and often constructed swimming pools, tennis courts and golf courses on the common land as an added inducement to potential purchasers.

Other types of neighborhood organizations have been formed on a voluntary basis by the residents in a neighborhood or segment of a neighborhood (for example, a block association). The purposes of these organizations are usually neighborhood preservation and enhancement, social interaction among the residents, and political lobbying efforts to prevent zoning changes the community believes to be detrimental to the neighborhood. Such groups also maintain contact with community officials to obtain services, facilities and improvements within the neighborhood. They may also become involved in political activities, supporting local candidates and parties. Neighborhood improvement projects with the members doing all or some of the work themselves, social gatherings, block parties, fairs, parades, etc., are sponsored by such community groups. Membership is voluntary and usually open to everyone within the neighborhood.

Some associations have little or no effect on the value of property; they have limited functions, few activities and low dues or assessments. Other associations have a substantial impact on the value of property in their areas. Often they define a whole neighborhood. Houses that are in the association may have higher values than nearby houses that are not in the association. These associations usually control important recreational facilities and/or provide substantial needed services, security and other amenities.

The appraiser must investigate such associations to determine the facilities or services provided and the additional costs to individual property owners. When these services appear to be substantial or their cost is high, it is usually best to select comparables from within the association. It is often difficult to make a location adjustment to reflect the difference in value between houses in the association and those outside. (The subject of adjustments is covered in detail in later chapters.)

--Crime Level. Unfortunately, the crime level in many communities and neighborhoods continues to increase and so the appraiser must consider the impact of crime level as part of the neighborhood analysis. When a neighborhood obtains the reputation of having an excessively high crime rate, some residents may leave and potential new residents are discouraged from buying homes there. Increased street lighting and police protection as well as vigilance on the part of residents in reporting suspicious activities to the police may help reduce the crime rate.

ECONOMIC CONSIDERATIONS

These are factors that are the result of economic forces affecting a neighborhood.

--Relation to Community Growth. Property values in a neighborhood are directly affected by the growth pattern of the surrounding community. Houses in the path of an expanding community are usually marketable and tend to increase in value. Other neighborhoods less accessible to newly developing community centers or places of employment may be less desirable.

--Economic Profile of Residents. The income and employment profile of the residents of a neighborhood, and the corresponding price levels and rents these support are important economic parameters in the analysis of a neighborhood. The type, stability and location of employment have a strong impact on the value of residential property, since employment determines to a large degree the ability of individuals to purchase or rent in a particular area. Income levels tend to set a value range for a neighborhood. The influence of neighborhood is often obvious; a superior house will be penalized for its location in a neighborhood that does not support its value.

Changes in purchasing power result in changes in property values. Therefore, substantial change affecting the available income of people living in the area as well as of those who constitute the market for property in the neighborhood must be considered. A downward trend in available income for shelter usually previews a dip in property values.

--New Construction and Vacant Land. Vacant land suitable for the construction of additional houses within a neighborhood may exist simply because the owners, for personal reasons, do not wish to develop or sell the land. It may forecast additional future construction activity or indicate a lack of effective demand.

If only a few vacant lots remain in a neighborhood, residential construction on them usually will not substantially affect values in the neighborhood. However, if they are zoned non-residential, or if variances are granted permitting non-residential construction, the non-conforming uses may have an adverse effect on the surrounding properties.

Proposed construction for the larger parcels of vacant land may substantially affect values in the neighborhood. Available information about proposed future development of these parcels is an integral part of the neighborhood analysis.

--Turnover and Vacancy. The rate and duration of vacancies is another statistical indicator of the economic health of a neighborhood. Some turnover of properties within a neighborhood is usually a sign of a healthy market. At the same time, a neighborhood that is stable and attractive continues to hold a majority of its residents. High rates on long-term vacancy may signal decline or the necessity of changes in use. A large number of "For Sale" signs may be a warning that the neighborhood is experiencing a downturn in stability. Reviewing newspaper ads offering available rentals and sale units helps the appraiser estimate the strength of housing demand and the extent of the supply.

GOVERNMENTAL FACTORS

These are based on the activities of government, including taxation, restrictions, schools, planning and building regulations.

--Taxation and Special Assessments. Neighborhoods are competitive with one another and the level of taxation can be an important deciding factor for potential residents. Taxation is often a significant variable in making comparisons from one neighborhood to another. Special assessments should be directly related to the extra services or advantages they provide, such as a private beach association or extra fire protection. When special assessments become high compared to other houses in the market, they may seriously reduce the value of the highly taxed house. An unpaid special assessment lien will often reduce the value of the house by approximately the amount of the lien. This value reduction may be offset by the enhancement that results from the special improvement or service that is the basis of the special assessment.

--Public and Private Restrictions. Zoning regulations and building codes are important guardians of stability for a neighborhood. They provide legal protection against adverse influences, nuisances and hazards. When special exceptions or variances are easily obtained without consideration for their effect on surrounding properties, the value of all houses in the neighborhood may be decreased. A breakdown in the enforcement of existing zoning and building regulations may also cause a decrease in value. Such violations often start with illegal signs, uses for businesses and conversion to higher density use than permitted by zoning.

Deed restrictions can protect properties from the negative impact of incompatible uses; breakdown of their enforcement may lead to lower values. Some deed restrictions written years ago, however, may be obsolete or unenforceable. For example, deed restrictions setting the minimum cost of construction may be meaningless based on today's costs. The courts have ruled that deed restrictions based on race, religion, or national origin are not enforceable. Generally, any deed restriction that is against the public interest is not enforceable.

--Schools. Educational facilities may be a strong attraction for prospective homebuyers. Families may be attracted to a neighborhood, at least in part, by its schools. Schools are of immediate interest to all families with children. Even homeowners with no children may consider the availability of educational facilities when purchasing a house, because future buyers of their home may have children. Neighborhood schools may be of less importance where children are bussed to schools outside the area.

--Planning and Subdivision Regulations. Planning for the future development of a community is an important task of government. Such planning should include protection of the integrity and character of existing neighborhoods, while providing for anticipated future uses of undeveloped areas. Poor planning for recreational facilities, schools, service areas, and other needs of residents may lead to neighborhood disintegration.

Requirements imposed on developers and subdividers influence the types and quality of basic services available to homeowners in the neighborhood and have a strong affect on the value of existing structures. The protection of open space areas such as wetlands will act as a deterrent to developers who may attempt to sacrifice the character of a neighborhood in order to build the maximum number of units.

SOURCES OF NEIGHBORHOOD DATA

Much neighborhood data must be gathered in the field through close observation and analysis of existing conditions, but other sources of information are needed for population statistics, income and employment profiles and vacancy information. In addition to census data, local utility companies and community-level government organizations frequently have pertinent data available. Other sources of information include real estate brokers, local lending institutions, other appraisers and the residents of a neighborhood.

NEIGHBORHOOD ANALYSIS IN FORM REPORTS

Certain organizations and business firms have developed their own appraisal forms. The forms often contain sections in which the appraiser rates and summarizes various elements believed to enhance or detract from value. Probably the most widely used are the FHLMC and FNMA forms for appraisals of properties for which these agencies may later purchase the mortgage.

Note that the neighborhood section of the FNMA-FHLMC form contains a number of items with boxes at their left. By checking the appropriate boxes, an appraiser describes and rates a neighborhood. Although the form includes a number of considerations, it does not afford as complete or thorough an analysis as a narrative report. It is usually fully adequate, and the FNMA-FHLMC form provides space for additional comments. It does not contain any specific provision for an analysis other than that applicable for the subject neighborhood, but appraisers are obligated to extend the neighborhood analysis beyond the guidelines of the form whenever appropriate.

APARTMENT DISTRICTS

In large cities, an apartment district usually covers an extensive area; in smaller cities, the district may be dispersed or limited in size. Apartment design may be multi-story, garden, row, or townhouse. Units may be privately owned as cooperatives or condominiums.

Although apartment districts differ somewhat from single family residential areas, they are subject to many similar influences. Thus, an appraiser can outline the characteristics and amenities that affect an apartment district in a manner similar to that applied to a single family residential neighborhood, but with a change of emphasis. In an apartment district, desirability and value may be influenced by:

1. Access to work places.
2. Transportation service.
3. Access to shopping centers and cultural facilities.
4. School facilities.
5. Neighborhood reputation.
6. Residential atmosphere, neighborhood appearance, and protection against unwanted commercial and industrial intrusion.
7. Proximity to parks, lakes, rivers, or other natural features.

8. Supply of vacant apartment sites that are likely to be built up, with the potential effect of making present accommodations either more or less desirable.
9. Parking for tenants and guests.
10. Economic status of tenants.
11. Vacancy and tenant turnover rate.

Such characteristics and other pertinent data form the background for an appraiser's study of rental housing property. In certain cities, statistics are available concerning the supply of apartments, vacancy, and rent levels. When statistics are not available, an appraiser gathers data from primary research.

SUMMARY

A neighborhood today tends to be any separately identifiable area of a community, usually having recognizable natural or man-made boundaries. Sometimes they are clearly defined and other times they are difficult to identify precisely. The old concepts of unity and conformity no longer apply.

An appraiser's description and opinion of a neighborhood are an important part of an appraisal report. This places a special responsibility upon the appraiser to be objective.

Most neighborhoods are changing at various rates; what happens in one neighborhood affects surrounding neighborhoods. An added supply of new houses tends to induce a shift from older houses to the new ones. However, other factors such as location, community facilities, educational facilities and parks also influence the rate of shift.

The analysis of a neighborhood starts with a description of the area and the properties it contains. It also describes the growth pattern around it.

Neighborhoods go through life cycles that start when the neighborhood is developed. This is called the growth period. When construction slows down or stops, a period of stability follows. This period ends either because the housing stock deteriorates or changes occur in the economic, social, physical and governmental forces that affect the neighborhood. Decline may cease when these forces change again or when there is an organized effort to rejuvenate the neighborhood. This renewal period is comparable to the original growth period. The life cycle is then repeated with another period of stability and a delayed period of decline. If the period of decline is not reversed, the neighborhood will come to the end of its economic life and usually will change to another use.

To understand neighborhood cycles, one must understand the relevant physical, social, governmental, and economic forces that affect value.

Information about the neighborhood and the factors that make up the four great forces must be gathered in the field by close observation and interviewing of information sources and local residents. This information is reconciled to determine what effect the neighborhood has on the value of the house being appraised. The form and depth of this analysis depends on the particular appraisal problem. It must always be objective, supported by facts and based on current social standards.

Most data about a neighborhood is gathered by the appraiser based on observations and interviews. Published data is useful but must be carefully used as it often pertains to areas larger than the neighborhood in which the property being appraised lies.

Many residential appraisal reports are now being made on forms which limit the appraiser's ability to report completely on a neighborhood. Additional space in the form of addenda should be used by the appraiser to provide for complete reporting.

2 OR 3 STORIES

PITCHED ROOF

COMMON SIDE WALLS

BAY
WINDOWS

HEAVILY DECORATED,
PAINTED

Nineteenth Century American

WESTERN ROW HOUSE OR WESTERN TOWNHOUSE
(West Row - 714)

SMALL CHIMNEY
PROTRUDING THROUGH ROOF

LARGE WINDOWS
WITH FIXED GLASS

MULTI-STORY

LARGE,
RECTANGULAR
SHAPE

EXPOSED STRUCTURAL
FRAMING

ROOF
OVERHANGS

SHINGLE ROOF

SHINGLE
WALLS

SLIDING
GLASS
DOORS

Nineteenth Century American

WESTERN STICK (W Stick - 716)

8 Residential Site Description and Analysis

According to tradition, when an appraiser is asked to name the three most important factors affecting value, the answer is: "Location, location, location." More specifically, the answer might be stated: "Community location, neighborhood location and site location."

Because of the fixed nature of real estate, location contributes more than any other single factor to wide variations in value among similar improvements. Therefore, good appraisal practice requires that the exact location of the subject property be clearly and definitively established. An accurate description of the legal boundaries and a detailed review of the physical features are combined with thorough analysis of the site's location in the neighborhood and community.

LAND AND SITE DESCRIPTION

In the specialized vocabulary of the real estate professional, land and site are not synonymous. "Land" means the surface of the earth, which is unimproved by man, plus a wedge-shaped subsurface piece that theoretically extends to the center of the globe and air rights extending upward to the sky. In practice, the use of air rights is limited in the United States by an act of Congress, which holds that navigable air space is public domain. In some areas of the country, subsurface mineral rights are owned by the government or someone other than the owner of the rest of the fee. All natural resources in their original state are also considered to be part of the land, including mineral deposits, fossil fuels, wildlife and timber. In the appraiser's definition, everything that is natural and within the property boundaries is part of the land.

"Site" is the land plus improvements that make it ready for use, including streets, sewer systems and utility connections.

Many appraisers include such items as the cost of clearing the site, grading and landscaping, drainage, water and sewer connections (or septic systems), electric and gas service, private access streets, alleys, drives and sidewalks as part of the site analysis. Occasionally, local custom dictates that some of these items be treated as building improvements rather than site improvements. It is important in making an appraisal to indicate this distinction clearly and treat the comparable market data in a consistent manner. Proper appraisal terminology states that "improvements to the site" are those described above and that "improvements on the site" are house, garage and other out buildings.

LEGAL DESCRIPTIONS

Every appraisal must describe the property so that it is easily and accurately identified and cannot be confused with any other. The best way to establish the exact location of a property is to incorporate a deed description and survey into the appraisal. In addition, a location map showing the site in relation to the surrounding neighborhood should be provided. A reliable way to identify the property is by street name and number if the parcel is within the limits of a defined community. Rural areas also have improved identification systems.

Often the appraiser decides that the use of street address numbers does not provide the required positive identification of the property. In such cases, an accurate legal description of the property must be obtained from the deed, mortgage or other land record sources in the community. Legal descriptions found in these documents are prepared in one or a combination of four ways: (1) lot and block; (2) metes and bounds; (3) geodetic survey; and (4) government survey system.

--Lot and Block System. This system, derived from the rectangular survey system, applies in most urban communities. It originated in the manner in which these communities grew. The early developers had their tracts surveyed and platted in rectangular blocks and lots. Each was numbered and the numbers were entered on a plat map. Copies of the plat were filed in the local government record office for permanent reference. Identification by use of lot and block numbers is usually sufficient in subdivisions where each lot is clearly distinguished from its neighbors. An example of this system is shown in Figure 8-1.

FIG. 8-1 LOT AND BLOCK SYSTEM

SEC. 18, T. 38, R. 14.

--Metes and Bound System. Originally used in colonial America, this system identified property by delineating its boundaries in terms of a series of directions and distances, starting at a fixed point. (Typical points referred to in old deeds are large trees, rocks, streams, etc., which, in some cases, have become difficult, if not impossible, to locate positively). Each boundary line is described in succession, using a compass bearing and distance, until the entire parcel has been enclosed; for example, "Starting at the old oak tree known as Grand Dad's Oak, South 63 degrees 35 minutes for a distance of 185 feet..."(see figure 8-2).

FIG. 8-2 METES AND BOUNDS SYSTEM

--Geodetic Survey. A land survey that was initiated to identify tracts of land owned by the Federal government gradually has been extended throughout the nation. These survey maps are prepared by the United States Geological Survey Division, Department of the Interior. They show, among other things, height contours, latitude and longitude, existing rivers and streams, buildings and railroads. They are available on various scales by named quadrangles. The skeleton of this survey is a network of "benchmarks," which cover the entire country, each of which is located by its latitude and longitude.

--Government Survey System. This system was also developed during colonial times; it provides for a unit of land approximately 24 miles square, bounded by base lines running east and west and meridians extending north and south. Because of the curvature of the earth, the north boundary of the square is slightly shorter than the south. The 24-mile square unit is divided into areas six miles square, called townships. A "tier" is an east/west row of townships between two parallels of latitude six miles apart. Ranges and tiers are assigned numbers from principal meridians and base lines. A township is divided into 36 sections, each one mile square. The sections are numbered consecutively, beginning with the northeast corner and continuing, east to west and west to east, down to Section 36 in the southeast corner. Discrepancies pertaining to the north boundary, and others due to errors in measurement or alignment, are allowed for in the most westerly half mile of the township (see Fig. 8-3).

FIG. 8-3 GOVERNMENT SURVEY SYSTEM

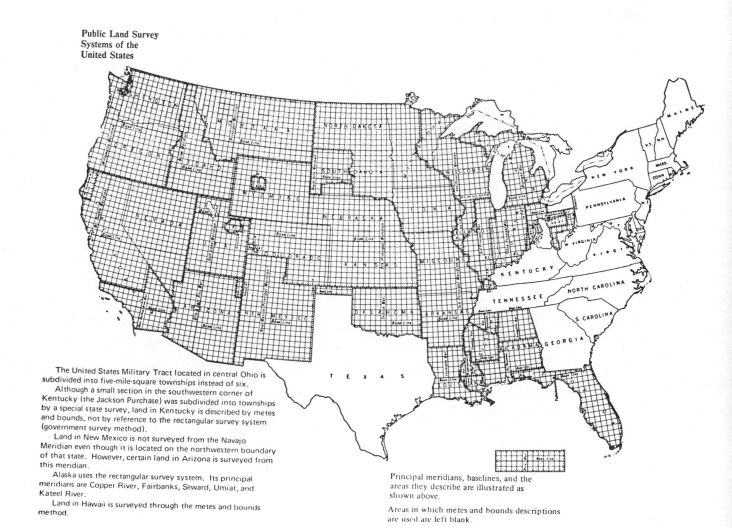

Public Land Survey
Systems of the
United States

The United States Military Tract located in central Ohio is subdivided into five-mile-square townships instead of six.

Although a small section in the southwestern corner of Kentucky (the Jackson Purchase) was subdivided into townships by a special state survey, land in Kentucky is described by metes and bounds, not by reference to the rectangular survey system (government survey method).

Land in New Mexico is not surveyed from the Navajo Meridian even though it is located on the northwestern boundary of that state. However, certain land in Arizona is surveyed from this meridian.

Alaska uses the rectangular survey system. Its principal meridians are Copper River, Fairbanks, Seward, Umiat, and Kateel River.

Land in Hawaii is surveyed through the metes and bounds method.

Principal meridians, baselines, and the areas they describe are illustrated as shown above.

Areas in which metes and bounds descriptions are used are left blank.

8-3   GOVERNMENT SURVEY SYSTEM

FIG. 7-4: Government Survey System

SOURCE: John S. Hoag, *Fundamentals of Land Measurement* (Chicago: Chicago Title Insurance Company).

OTHER TITLE AND RECORD DATA

Ownership information plus data relating to taxes, special assessments, zoning, easements and other restrictions are covered in this section.

OWNERSHIP INFORMATION

A property's legal owner and type of ownership can be ascertained from public records, which are maintained by a county clerk and recorder. Local title or abstract companies may also provide the information.

The most common form of property ownership is ownership in "fee simple". If a property is not appraised in fee simple, the elements of title that are to be excluded must be indicated and carefully analyzed. When an appraiser is asked to estimate the value of a fractional ownership interest, he or she must understand the exact type of legal ownership so that the property rights to be appraised will be accurately defined.

--Building Codes. These are specific restrictions that, like zoning regulations, are based on the police power. They provide design control of permitted buildings and delineate the types of materials that may be used. In addition to a general building code, many communities have separate electric and plumbing codes.

--Deed Restrictions. These limitations may be placed on the use of land by a property owner and will run with the title to the land as it passes on to future owners. Deed restrictions are contractual and are usually imposed by the deeds used to convey title. Sometimes deed restrictions are imposed on an entire tract by the developer of the land. Usually, the goal of such restrictions is to protect the value of all properties in the development.

At one time, racial and religious restrictive convenants were not unusual in single family subdivisions. In the 1930's and 1940's, the Federal Housing Administration sometimes required such restrictions as condition of granting mortgage insurance. Restrictions of this kind have been unlawful for many years, following a 1948 decision of the Supreme Court, and now violate many federal, state and local Fair Housing laws. Occasionally, deeds containing such restrictive covenants still surface but they are not enforceable.

--Easements. These are rights extended to non-owners of the fee for ingress and egress over property usually for specific purposes, such as access to a roadway or beach. Other easements give non-owners the right to use the air over the property or subsurface rights for utility installations, soil removal, flood control or mineral deposits. Appraisers must consider the effect of an easement on the value of the property and report this effect in the appraisal report. Normally, the value estimate includes the assumption that the property is free and clear of all easements. If this is not the case, the appraiser must take special care to evaluate and report the nature and effect of any easements so that the report will not be misleading.

--Encroachments. Two types of encroachments exist. Either the improvement may extend over the property line onto abutting properties or the improvements on abutting properties may encroach onto the subject site. The appraiser is not expected to make a survey to determine if there are any encroachments. Normally, a statement in the "limiting conditions" section of the report declares that the assumption is that there are no encroachments. However, as with easements, if an encroachment is encroachment is evident, it must be reported in the appraisal and care must be taken not to mislead a potential user of the appraisal as to the effect of such encroachment.

--Party Wall Agreements. A party wall exists when improvements are so erected that one common wall is used by two abutting property owners. Many party walls exist without any written agreement. When such an agreement is part of a deed, the appraiser should ascertain whether it imposes any unusual requirements upon the owner of the property being appraised and include this in the report.

--Environmental Restrictions. Controls on land use are becoming more common and more important to appraisers. Like zoning regulations, they appear to be based on the police power of government, although some of the laws are still being tested in the courts. Appraisers must be familiar with current environmental developments that affect value, including wetland controls, flood hazard area designations and other land use restrictions.

--Riparian Rights. These deal with the rights of owners whose land abuts a body of water (lake, river, stream, ocean) with respect to the use of the water. These rights may include the right to construct piers, boathouses and other improvements over the water or may be for use of the body of water for fishing and recreational purposes or for irrigation. Riparian rights may have a substantial effect upon the value of the land and must be carefully considered where they apply.

-- Zoning. Zoning is part of the police power of the government. Zoning gives the public the right to control the uses of private property for the benefit of the entire community. Zoning as it is known today did not exist during the 19th century, which was the major development period for most American cities. As a result of this lack of control and planning, cities developed with congested streets, overcrowed buildings, poor light and air, and a mixture of uses, each negatively affecting the others. From this disorganization came the deteriorated commercial areas, slums and urban blight of today. Uncontrolled social pressures increased the population density still further, resulting in the construction of large apartment houses that were built to the boundaries of their lots. People with enough money fled the cities into newly developing suburbs. As city redevelopment continues, this trend has reversed. There is a national trend to move back into the cities.

In the early 1900's, Los Angeles and Boston passed laws that controlled the use of land. In 1916, New York City passed the first truly comprehensive zoning law. Included in it were use districts, control of building heights and area coverage regulations. Shortly thereafter other cities passed zoning ordinances that stood up against many court challenges. By the middle of the 1920's the constitutionality of zoning laws, based upon the government's right to use its police power to regulate private property, was well established in legal precedent.

The zoning regulations of the 1920's were primarily concerned with height regulations and front, side and rear yard requirements, to ensure that the population had adequate light and air. By the late 1920's, zoning regulations began to emphasize the separation of residential neighborhoods from commercial and industrial uses. Also, high density apartments were segregated from low density single family areas.

Since World War II a new thrust in city zoning has occurred. These newer zoning regulations emphasize direct control of development and design in an effort to prevent further spread of urban congestion and decay. Zoning often restricts the use of a site that would be physically possible and economically feasible. In such cases, a change in zoning to permit such uses would change the highest and best use of the site. The highest and best use must always be a use that is legally permitted (see Chapter 9), but an appraiser must be alert to potential zoning changes. If there is a reasonable probability that the applicable zoning may be changed in the near future, the appraiser must consider how the market will react. Care must be taken not to anticipate changes that are only speculative. Residential properties are often bought and sold subject to the success of an application for zone change, such as from residential to more intensive apartment use or from residential to industrial or business use. The potential re-zoning of nearby property may have a substantial effect on the value of the property being appraised.

Some suburban communities have attempted to use zoning as a method of preventing further growth, which is accomplished by increasing the minimum lot requirements to sizes greater than necessary for orderly growth. Other requirements making it economically impossible to develop vacant land have been imposed in some areas, but growing social and legal pressures are being applied to stop the use of punitive (or "exclusionary") zoning to restrict community growth.

Ideally, zoning should be used to regulate and promote orderly and consistent development but should not be used to stop expansion. Good zoning fosters sound values, sufficient municipal services such as schools and parks and a climate of orderly growth without the stagnation of highly restrictive regulation.

A new type of zoning classification increasing in popularity is the planned unit development (PUD). Residences are grouped in clusters, with part of the land dedicated to open space for use by everyone. Ownership in the common land may be held by an owners' association or by the community. In its most advanced form, the PUD can actually be an entire city, where some of the non-residential land is reserved for commercial and industrial development as well as recreational and open space use.

Not every community has resorted to zoning to control its development. There are vast areas of the country that are not governed by zoning regulations. Many of these areas are rural or sparsely populated. However, one of the best anti-zoning arguments in the country is the metropolitan center of Houston, Texas. Without zoning, Houston has developed into one of our most modern, exciting cities. The citizens of Houston have voted several times to remain an unzoned community.

The key to Houston's orderly development has been the use of deed restrictions and the enforcement of a rigid building code that includes control of density. By a special act of the Texas legislature, the enforcement of deed restrictions is the responsibility of the city attorney rather than the individual property owner. Deed restrictions are also enforced by the local lending institutions, which refuse to loan money for purposes that violate deed restrictions. In addition, Houston's civic clubs help enforce and police deed restrictions. There are problems, of course. Federal funds for urban renewal were withheld for a time, and in many areas the mixture of uses has caused severe losses in value for adjoining properties. Older residential areas tend to be hastened through the last phase of their life cycle. Still, advocates of non-zoning make a strong case that land values and land uses should depend on the natural highest and best use of property, and not on the misguided whims or outright self-interest of local political appointees.

Any reasonable probability of a zoning change must be considered. If the highest and best use of a site requires a zoning change, an appraiser investigates the probability of such a change. An appraiser may obtain pertinent information by interviewing planning and zoning staff or elected officials. An appraiser may also consult a study of patterns of zoning changes to draw conclusions about the likelihood of a change in a particular instance. If a highest and best use recommendation relies on the probability of a zoning change, that probability must be supported by three elements. These are physical practicality, economic feasibility, and political probability.

ASSESSMENT AND TAXES

Traditionally, a substantial portion of the funds needed by a community to provide services to its citizens is raised by taxes levied on real estate, based on the value of the property, hence the term "ad valorem" taxation.

Taxes are intended to pay for services that make ownership more desirable, but net benefit is obviously decreased when taxes are out of proportion for those benefits. Therefore, the appraiser compares the tax status (assessed values, tax rates, and tax burdens) of the appraised site with that of competitive or comparable sites. In some communities the assessed value of land for tax purposes bears a reasonable relation to market value, particularly when a recent reassessment has been made; but in other communities the assessed value does not have a realistic relation to value.

The first step the appraiser takes in considering taxation is to report the actual assessment and tax rate of the community as it applies to the appraised property. The assessment is often divided between the land and the improvements. Sometimes the site improvements are assessed separately. There may be a single tax rate or a series of separate tax rates to provide segregated funding for education, utilities, etc.

Usually the assessment is supposed to represent some percentage of market value. In communities with efficient assessors and frequent revaluations there is a good relationship between assessments and values. In many communities, however, where the assessor is unqualified, understaffed or not motivated, or where revaluations are infrequent, there may be little relationship between assessments and market values.

Two longstanding traditions exist in the assessment and taxation process. One is that assessments are often a percentage of market value; the second is that the tax rate is expressed in mills rather than as a percentage of assessment. A mill is a tenth of a cent. The "mill rate" is the number of mills per dollar of assessed value. For example:

Assessment	$1.00
Mill Rate	100 ($1.00 x .100)
Taxes	$ .10

Assessment	$1,000
Mill Rate	90
Taxes	$90

This system is confusing to both the public and the appraiser because it is difficult to readily compare the taxes in one community with those in another. For example, a lot that has a value of $8,000 might be assessed at 70% in one community with a tax rate of 40 mills. Taxes would be calculated as follows:

Market Value $8,000

Assessment ratio   70% (.70 x $8,000 = $5,600)

Assessment $5,600

Tax rate   40 Mills

Taxes $ 224 (.040 x $5,600)

A similar lot valued at $8,000 in another community might be assessed at 35% with a tax rate of 80 mills.

Market Value $8,000

Assessment ratio   35% (.35 x $8,000 = $2,800)

Assessment $2,800

Tax rate   80 Mills

Taxes $ 224 (.080 x $2,800)

In some states, tax rates are expressed in terms of dollars per $100 of assessed value. The above example for this system is:

Assessment $2,800

Tax rate $ 8

Taxes $ 224 (28 x 8)

Widely varying assessment ratios and mill rates can produce the same tax burden on a property, depending on their combined influence. However, far too often a community's supposed assessment ratio (for example, 60% of market value) is actually not in effect. Although legally set at 60%, actual relationship of the assessed value to market value may be markedly different among similar properties or among different classifications of property.

The second step the appraiser takes is to compare the tax burden on the appraised property to that on competitive properties both in the subject community and in competing communities. One way to accomplish this is to compare the dollars of taxes directly with the market value. This is done by dividing the actual dollar amount of the tax burden on a property by the market value of the property, to give an "effective rate" of taxes.

Market Value $8,000

Taxes $ 224

Tax rate   .028 or 2.8% ($224 : $8,000)

By using this direct comparison method, the appraiser determines how consistent the taxes within a community are and also how taxation in one community compares with that of competitive communities.

Unit-foot depth and corner premium tables are often used to establish uniformity between assessments in valuations made by assessors for tax purposes. The purpose of such tables is to express equivalent values for one foot of frontage applicable to sites of varying depth. The standard area of land represented has one foot of frontage, in a uniform lot width, and a specified depth. For a lot of any stated type or location, a standard depth is established. (It originally was fixed in most localities at 100 feet). For example, if the adopted standard depth is 100 feet, a lot 50 by 100 feet worth $2,175 would have unit-front-foot value of $43.50. Another lot, 50 feet wide and 150 feet deep, might be worth $2,500, or $50 per front foot, with the same unit-front-foot value of $43.50--that is, it would be equivalent in value to $43.50 per front foot for a depth of 100 feet, multiplied by a depth factor of 115%. The percentages are designed to provide a uniform system of measuring the additional value that accrues because of added depth.

One of the first depth rules was the 4-3-2-1 rule, which described a system where the front quarter of a lot contributed 40% of the value; the second quarter, 30%; the third quarter, 20%; and the fourth quarter, 10%. Because this left too wide a margin for assessment purposes, the deficiency usually has been overcome by the establishment if more specific depth tables expressed in percentages for every foot, or at least for every 10 feet of depth, to reflect the conditions applicable in a certain locality or for certain types of property (residential, business, industrial, commercial).

Similarly, corner influence (premium) tables have been developed for "ad valorem" tax purposes, to establish the amount by which the market value per unit foot of an inside lot is increased for a lot with a corner location. Such tables are also related to the localities and types of land for which they are prepared.

Appraisers should excercise extreme caution in using any standard depth or corner influence (premium) table. The use of such tables is a major cause of non-uniform assessments. To apply a table established for one neighborhood or community to another area is not good appraisal practice. The only depth tables that might be useful would be those specifically constructed for the community and neighborhood in which the appraised property is located. Assessors are required in some communities to use them to provide equalizations.

SPECIAL ASSESSMENTS

These are levied by a specific district taxing authority for a definite period of time, usually for a public improvement such as sewers, street paving, sidewalk construction, etc. Usually the assessment is based on the benefits derived by the property from the improvement, rather than the cost of providing the improvement to a specific property. For example, it might cost $3,000 to provide sewers for one lot, and $1,000 to provide sewers for another lot in the same project area. The amount of the special assessment, however, may well be equal, based on the assumption that the lots would be equally enhanced in value.

When a property is sold subject to a special assessment, adjustment must be made if comparable properties are not subject to the same special assessment. When a property is subject to special assessments that are greater than the value of the benefits derived, the property is reduced in value by the special assessment burden.

PHYSICAL CHARACTERISTICS

Every appraisal must contain an accurate, physical description of the site being appraised. Although much of the data can be obtained easily, some of it may prove to be more difficult to find or be totally unavailable. The appraisal report must state the assumptions that have been made about the nature of the property or site in the absence of precise information. For example, in the case of an unimproved lot, a soil test is usually desirable. In the absence of such a test, the appraiser should carefully point out that assumptions have been made as to the physical characteristics of the soil, and that the value estimate as given may be substantially different if these assumptions do not reflect the actual conditions of the site.

SIZE AND SHAPE

--**Width and Frontage.** Although width and frontage are often used synonymously, they have two distinct meanings. Width is the distance between the side lines of a lot. When a lot is irregular in shape, the term "average width" is often used. Another important measurement is width at the building line. Many zoning regulations specify a minimum width at this point, which is required in order to permit the use of the site for construction of a particular type of improvement. "Frontage" refers to the length of boundaries that abut a thoroughfare or accessway. In the valuation of residential lots, "front feet" are often used as units of comparison, but the importance of frontage appears to vary from one location to another. Care must be exercised in using front footage as the unit of comparison for residential lots. Once a lot meets the standard size acceptable in the neighborhood, excess frontage does not always add proportionately to the value of the lot.

--**Depth.** Depth is always considered together with the width and frontage of a lot. Most residential neighborhoods have a standard acceptable lot depth so that lots with less depth sell for less, and lots with excess depth sell at a premium. The penalty or premium paid for depth consideration, however, is rarely directly proportionate to the actual footage involved.

The problem of varying and disproportionate increases or decreases in value relative to changes in depth may be analyzed by constructing a table to reflect these value changes. These depth tables are popular with assessors and other mass appraisers who staunchly defend their use, claiming that the tables can be constructed and adjusted to work in different neighborhoods. Theoretically, this may be possible; nevertheless, depth tables have been so widely misused and misunderstood that most professional appraisers avoid using them altogether, unless absolutely convinced that a particular table truly applies to the neighborhood of the property being appraised. Some rules do apply to many residential lots, which the appraiser should know about when considering the influence of depth:

1. As the depth of a lot decreases from that of the typical lot in the neighborhood, its value per front foot decreases, but its value per square foot or per acre increases.

2. As the depth of a lot increases beyond that of the typical lot in the neighborhood, the value per front foot increases, but its value per square foot or per acre decreases.

--Shape. The shape of a lot affects the value of the lot differently from one neighborhood to another. In some areas, irregularity of shape may decrease value; in other areas, as long as the lot is suitable for a house, little difference appears to exist between the value of regularly and irregularly shaped lots. If the irregular lot shape results in increased construction costs, however, it would probably decrease the value of the lot. The value of irregularly shaped parcels is usually indicated in dollars per square foot of area or in dollars per acre.

--Size. If value were directly related only to size, the unit of comparison (such as square feet or acre) for lot values would always be value per square foot or value per acre. However, frontage, width, depth and shape interplay with size to affect value.

PLOTTAGE

"Plottage value" is the increase in unit value resulting from improved utility when small plots are combined to form a larger one. To accommodate a substantial building development, small plots may be assembled, often from different owners. This procedure usually entails extra costs, and key parcels may need to be purchased for more than their individual land value, either because they are already improved or because of a negotiating disadvantage.

After assembly, the project must support the excess costs of the land in addition to other capital costs involved. It is not the cost of assembly that creates plottage value. Size itself is no guarantee of a plottage increment in value. For plottage value to be realized, there must be the potential of a higher and more profitable use. Otherwise, the whole could not be worth more than the sum of its parts, as is the case with plottage.

The area of a lot can also be divided into its effective area and its excess land. Usually the excess land (particularly if it cannot be used) is worth substantially less per unit of measurement than that part of the lot within the effective (usable) area.

CORNER INFLUENCE

--Corner and Cul-de-Sac Influences. Historically, because a corner location provides more light and air and may afford more prominence on a particular street, it was thought to have more value. However, a corner lot also has less privacy and often is taxed at a higher rate. It also may be subjected to more noise and more passing traffic. The appraiser must make a judgment, based on the specific lot and its market, if a corner location adds or detracts from the value when the property is compared with other lots in the neighborhood. Lots located at the end of dead-end streets that have cul-de-sacs for turnarounds also may have different values from similar lots without the cul-de-sac influence. Again, no universal rule applies, and the appraiser must look to the market for evidence of the effects of a specific location on value.

--Contour and Topography. Probably the most desirable residential lot is one that slopes up gently from the street to where the house is located, and then slopes downward steeply enough so that there can be a walkout basement door leading directly to the rear yard recreation area. Again, what is true for one neighborhood is not necessarily the case for other areas. Sites tend to have lower value if they are costly to improve because of extreme topographical conditions. A lot higher or lower than the abutting street level may create additional costs to correct poor drainage, erosion, or accessibility problems. Frequently however, difficult conditions are offset by advantages recognized in the market, such as a scenic view or extra privacy. Another factor to be considered is the amount of site work required to make the site buildable. If there is bedrock, excess excavation costs may be incurred. In some cases a site may require fill, or it may have excess fill that can be sold.

SURFACE AND SUBSOIL

--Surface Soil. In many areas the soil's ability to support a lawn and landscaping is an important factor in the marketability of the property. An appraiser should note whether the soil appears to be suitable and typical of the surrounding neighborhood. When appraising a new subdivision, the appraiser should determine if the natural surface soil (topsoil) will be replaced at the end of the construction process or whether it is being stripped during site preparation. A trend today among developers is to disturb as little as possible the natural growth and topsoil during the building process. A naturally sandy or rocky soil may require the extra expense of purchased topsoil to support future lawns and landscaping.

--Subsoil. The character of subsoil definitely affects the cost of preparing a site for building; it can also influence the design of the structure that can be erected on the site. If bedrock must be blasted, or if the soil is unstable, the cost of improvements is increased. Soil conditions are usually determined by an engineering study of the bearing quality of the soil and its suitability for foundations. Extra expense is incurred for foundation walls and the sinking of pilings if a site must be filled in. Underground tunnels can present a hazard in mining districts. The appraiser must include a consideration of such possibilities in a thorough site analysis.

LANDSCAPING

--Value of Landscaping. Natural trees and shrubs are usually considered part of the land itself. Landscaping is treated separately by most appraisers as a site improvement. Lawns, shrubbery, gardens and plantings in general improve the appearance and desirability of residential properties. However, because plantings are a matter of individual taste and will deteriorate rapidly without good care, typical buyers are inclined to discount the cost of replacing such plantings especially if they are very elaborate. Although such improvements are usually regarded as an asset, their contribution to the value of a property will vary with location and character.

DRAINAGE

--Surface and Storm Water Disposal. Some method must be provided to drain the site of surface and storm water. It may be a simple swale that channels the water off the surface of the lot to the street or into some natural drainage. When the lot is level or slopes away from the water disposal area, storm sewers must be constructed. In some areas, the leaders or downspouts that collect rain falling on the house may be connected into the storm water disposal pipes. When a house has a basement, footing drains are needed to carry the water from under the basement to prevent leaks from developing. When the house is built on a slope, special care must be taken to keep the surface water away from the sides of the house.

UTILITIES

--Water. Every house requires an adequate supply of water of acceptable quality. Water can be obtained from a municipal or private company or from a well. Common sense and the FHA Minimum Property Standards require that when a public water supply is available, it should be used. Some houses still obtain water directly from rivers, streams, lakes and even rain water collected from the roof and stored in tanks. None of these systems is considered satisfactory, since they will not consistently supply an adequate quantity of safe water. When water is supplied by a public or publicly regulated company, the appraiser usually need only check on its availability at the site, including whether there is sufficient pressure. When the water is supplied by a smaller, unregulated company, this must be reported and the dependability of the supply must be analyzed. Wells, either artesian or shallow, should be capable of delivering sustained flow of five gallons per minute. The water should meet the standard bacteriological and chemical requirements of the local health authorities.

When appraising vacant land not on a public water supply, appraiser should check surrounding properties where wells have been dug to determine the probability of an adequate water supply being found for the property being appraised.

--Sewers. Few will argue the substantial advantage of being connected to a municipal sewer system. It is estimated, however, that almost 50 million people in 15 million homes depend on septic systems for their waste disposal and that 25% of new houses being constructed do not connect to municipal systems. If no public sewer exists, a percolation test must be made to determine if the soil can absorb the runoff from a septic system.

--Installation of Public Utilities to the Site. Included in the value of a site is the cost of bringing water, electricity, gas, telephone, and storm and sanitary sewers to the site. A recent addition to this list is cable television. The site may have additional value because of the availability of these utilities even if they are not connected to the subject house. It is not unusual to find a house still using a well or septic system even where public water and sanitary sewers are available.

ACCESS

--Streets and Alleys. A site cannot be used unless there is some type of usable access. It may be a right-of-way over abutting property or a private driveway or street. Access may also take the form of a public street or alley. When access is not by public street, special attention should be given to who maintains the street and if lending institutions servicing the neighborhood will make mortgages on houses without public access.

--Street Improvements. The description of a site should also include information about street improvements, such as the width of the street, how it is paved, and the condition of the pavement. In some areas, lenders require substantial details about private streets when they represent the only access to a property. Also reported are details about the sidewalks, curbs, gutters and street lighting.

SITE IMPROVEMENTS

--Other site improvements. In addition to utility connections, which are sometimes classified as site improvements, a variety of other site improvements are typically found on an improved residential lot. These include fences, walls, sidewalks and driveways, pools and patios, tennis courts and other recreational faciltes. These all must be described in the appraisal report, and an analysis must be made as to their contribution to the value of the property.

VIEW'S AFFECT ON VALUE

--**The view** enjoyed from a property may substantially affect its value. Lots in the same neighborhood identical in all respects except location and orientation, have markedly different values which are directly attributable to the effect of superior views. The most popular views are of water, mountains and valleys. Conversely, a poor view reduces value.

HAZARDS AND NUISANCES

--**Hazards.** Sometimes hazards exist in the neighborhood that reduce the value of a property. The most common hazard is heavy traffic, and the market will definitely recognize and penalize this problem. The awareness of flood hazards has become quite important in many parts of the country now that most lenders cannot issue a mortgage in a flood hazard area without flood insurance. An appraiser must learn whether the site is in an identified flood hazard area, and if so, if flood insurance is available and at what cost. The effect on value must also be considered and reported in the appraisal. Other hazards that should be investigated include potential slides, earthquakes, dangerous ravines and bodies of water, or any unusual fire danger.

--**Nuisances.** A variety of services contribute to the value of a site when they are in the neighborhood but detract from value when they are too close. For example, a fire house, public school, stores, restaurants, hospital, medical offices and gas stations are desirable nearby but not immediately adjacent to residential property. Industries, large commercial buildings and offices, noisy highways, utility poles and high tension wires, motels and hotels, funeral parlors and vacant houses all generally detract from property values when they are located in a residential neighborhood.

ENVIRONMENT

--**Climatic or Meteorological Conditions.** Generally, climate affects the whole region or community and should be reported and analyzed in that section of the appraisal report. Sometimes these conditions specifically affect the value of the site being appraised. In some regions there may be an increase in the value of lots that face a certain direction. For example, if prevailing winds are consistent, lots may be favorably or adversely affected by their relation to the direction of the wind.

EXCESS LAND

The portion of land area that provides a typical land-to-building ratio with the existing improvements may be considered an economic unit. Excess land is the portion of a property that is not necessary to serve existing improvements. Assuming that the excess land is marketable or has value for future use, its market value as vacant land constitutes an addition to the estimated value of the economic entity. Therefore, excess land is typically valued separately.

RELATIONSHIP TO SURROUNDINGS

Because the location of a site is fixed, its surroundings have a significant effect on value. Much of this location effect has been covered in the region, community and neighborhood analysis. To be considered here is the relationship of the specific site to its immediate environment.

CONSIDERATIONS

--Use of Nearby Lots. The use of the immediately adjacent lots is of great importance to the value of a property. The principle of conformity states that to obtain maximum value, the improvements of the property being appraised should reasonably conform to those on surrounding lots. For example, if neighboring lots are improved with medium-value, colonial-style, multi-story houses, the appraiser might seriously question the appropriateness of plans for construction of a high-priced, extremely contemporary, split-level on the site being appraised. However, it is not always necessary to conform to obtain maximum value.

--Orientation of Improvements. Again, the principle of conformity applies in the orientation of the improvements. If the abutting houses are set back 75 feet from the street and face out towards it, it will probably be difficult to orient the house on the subject lot differently, even if such orientation (such as with the living/social zones facing towards the rear yard) would seem preferable.

--Abutting and Nearby Streets and Traffic Flow. Abutting and nearby streets may be in the older grid pattern or the newer style of dead-end or limited-access streets. Some streets in a neighborhood will become thoroughfares and suffer from heavy traffic flow. Access by a back alley or a special service road may add to or detract from value, depending on the market.

--Public Transportation. The value of a residential lot is affected by the availability of public transportation. Most important is the availability of such transportation to places of work and shopping, and to recreational areas. Changes in the availability of public transportation can affect the value of property. New systems, such as San Francisco's BART rapid transit system, increase values in the area but deteriorating systems tend to decrease values. The quality and quantity of public highways leading from the property being appraised to places of work, shopping and recreation also have an effect on property values.

--Access by Car. Automobile access to work, shopping and recreation areas substantially affects value. Lots that slope steeply upward towards the street are less desirable than level lots or lots that slope downwards. It is dangerous to have to back into traffic or be forced to enter on a curve or hill where visibility from oncoming cars is limited and the market will penalize a site for these problems.

--Safety of Children from Traffic. The sheer volume of traffic is not the only safety consideration of parents with smaller children. Traffic and speed controls and sidewalks from the site to places such as schools and parks are also important factors. Another important point is the availability of places away from the streets for children to play.

ECONOMIC FACTORS

Many economic factors have already been discussed in the regional, community and neighborhood analyses. Some economic factors apply specifically to the individual site under appraisal rather than to larger areas.

CONSIDERATIONS

--Prices of nearby lots. The price of nearby lots offered for sale has at least a short-term effect on the value of a site. The principle of substitution would limit the price paid for the lot being appraised to that paid for similar lots in the neighborhood at least until the supply was exhausted.

--Tax burden compared to competitive lots. If assessments are not uniform, lots with excessive tax burdens are depressed in value, at least temporarily, by the excess levy. The reverse would also be true; lots that are underassessed might be expected to bring a premium.

--Utility costs. If location necessitates incurring extra costs to bring utilities to a site, the market may recognize a parallel decrease in the value of the lot.

--Service costs. Some lots are not eligible for municipal services such as garbage collection because they are not on public streets. These services must be purchased privately, which would decrease the value of the site, if competitive sites had such municipal services.

SUMMARY

The site data and analysis portion of the appraisal should first positively identify and describe the property being appraised. A deed description and survey, together with a neighborhood and community map, is the ideal way. Other shortcut methods are acceptable only if the property being appraised is positively identified.

Data is gathered and organized into four categories: (1) title and record data; (2) on-site physical characteristics; (3) relationship to surroundings; and (4) economic factors.

All of the data is carefully considered and analyzed in relation to the appraised site. Relevant material is reconciled and processed for use in the highest and best use analysis, which forms the basis of the appraisal.

2½ STORIES

CLAPBOARD ON ADDITIONS

UNSUPPORTED HOOD OVER FRONT DOOR

PENT ROOF

GRAY LEDGE STONE WALLS

Colonial American

PENNSYLVANIA DUTCH COLONIAL OR PENNSYLVANIA GERMAN FARM HOUSE (Penn Dut - 110)

CENTRAL ENTRANCE · SHINGLES · GAMBREL ROOF · 1½ STORIES · SHUTTERS

Colonial American

CAPE ANN COLONIAL (Cape Ann - 105)

9 Highest and Best Use

This chapter discusses that highest and best use analysis of the two major elements of a residential property - the site and the improvements thereon. Appraisal theory has long supported the concept of the highest and best use of the site. Only relatively recently has the concept been developed of the highest and best use of improvements on the site - the house, apartment or other major buildings "as improved".

For a site to have value, it must have utility and be in demand. In highest and best use analysis, the appraiser considers that use, among all options that most fully develops a site's potential utility. Highest and best use analysis forms the base on which the appraiser builds the three traditional approaches to value.

DEFINITION

"**Highest and best use**" is defined as "that reasonable and probable use that will support the highest present value, as defined, as of the effective date of the appraisal." Alternatively, it is "that use, from among reasonable, probable and legal alternative uses, found to be physically possible, appropriately supported, financially feasible, and which results in highest land value." Simply stated, the highest and best use of a site is "the perfect improvement that can be constructed on the site which will produce the maximum rate of return on the capital invested."[1]

The second definition applies specifically to the highest and best use of land or sites as though vacant. When a site contains improvements, the highest and best use may be determined to be different from the existing use. The existing use will continue unless and until land value in its highest and best use exceeds the value of the entire property in its existing use plus the cost to remove the improvements.

The determination of highest and best use takes into account the contribution of a specific use to community development goals as well as the benefits to individual property owners. The determination of highest and best use results from the appraiser's judgment and analytical skill - that is, that the use determined from analysis represents an opinion, not a fact. In appraisal practice, highest and best use is the premise upon which value is based. In the context of most probable selling price (market value), another term for highest and best use would be "most probable use". In the context of investment value, an alternative term would be "most profitable use".

---

[1]Henry S. Harrison, *The Residential Appraiser*, Highest and Best Use Analysis of a Single Family House, The Real Estate Appraiser, Mar./Aprl. 1975, pp. 48-49.

The definitions of highest and best use indicate that there are two types of highest and best use. The first type is highest and best use of land or a site as though vacant. The second is highest and best use of a property as improved. Each type requires a separate analysis. Moreover, in each case, the existing use may or may not be different from the site's highest and best use.

Any determination of highest and best use includes identifying the motivations of probable purchasers. These motivations are based on perceptions of the benefits that accrue to property ownership. Different motivations influence highest and best use and are significant to an appraiser's conclusions about the highest and best uses of any parcel of real estate.

When potential buyers contemplate purchasing real estate for personal use or occupancy, their principal motivations are such user benefits as enjoyment, prestige, or security. Such motivations are particularly evident in the purchase of residential properties. User benefits also apply to commercial and industrial property ownership. Benefits to the owner-occupant include assured occupancy, low management costs, control and potential enhancement as well as future value.

The benefits of investment properties that are not owner-occupied relate to net income potential and to eventual resale or refinancing. The highest and best use decision for investment property is often influenced by tax implications and inflation-hedge aspects of the existing or proposed improvements. Determination of the type and intensity of the improvements which will be the highest and best use of an investor's land requires an "after-tax return" analysis of all reasonable alternatives.

Land or improved property that has resale profit as its principal potential benefit is purely speculative land. The price such land commands in the market reflects the real motivation of the typical purchaser -- speculation.

HIGHEST AND BEST USE OF LAND OR A SITE AS THOUGH VACANT

Highest and best use analysis is always done in two steps. First the site is analyzed as if vacant.

For purposes of this analysis, it is assumed that the site has no building improvement. In other words, the problem the appraiser solves is if the site was vacant what would the best potential use of the site be. What improvements would return the maximum in terms of money and amenities. The appraiser should describe the type of building or buildings and other improvements (if any) which should be constructed on the land if it were vacant.

Not every parcel of land (even those already improved) are economically ready to be developed. In fact, the majority of vacant land falls into this category. In these cases, the correct conclusion is that the highest and best use is to leave the parcel vacant until some time in the future, when it may become economically feasible to develop it.

If the conclusion is that the site is economically feasible to develop, the appraiser must conclude which type of improvement with which characteristics should be constructed.

The prevailing use on the site may not be the highest and best use. The land may be suitable for a much highest (more intense) use than the existing use. For instance, the highest and best use of the land as though vacant may be a 10-story office building, whereas the current office building contains only three stories.

HIGHEST AND BEST USE OF PROPERTY AS IMPROVED

The second step is to analyze the property as improved. The appraiser considers the use that should be made of the property as it exists. Should the 100 year old home be maintained as it is, renovated, expanded, partly demolished, or any combination of these? Or should it be replaced with a use different in type or intensity?

In this context, the use that maximizes the investment property's net operating income (NOI) on a long-term basis is its highest and best use. For uses that require no capital expenditures for remodeling, the net operating incomes estimated for various uses can be compared directly. However, for uses that would require capital expenditures to convert the structure from its existing use to another use, a rate of return must be calculated for the total investment in the property, including capital expenditures. This rate of return can then be compared with rates of return for uses that do not require capital expenditures.

An appraiser's conclusions regarding highest and best use for owner-occupied properties also reflect consideration of rehabilitation or modernization that is consistent with owner-occupant motivations. For example, highest and best use conclusions for a luxury residence would include the amount and type of rehabilitation required for maximum enjoyment of the property.

PURPOSE OF HIGHEST AND BEST USE ANALYSIS

The purpose of highest and best use analysis is different for each type of highest and best use. An appraiser should clearly separate the two types in the appraisal analysis. An appraiser's report should clearly identify, explain, and justify the purpose and conclusion for each type.

HIGHEST AND BEST USE OF LAND AS THOUGH VACANT

The value of land is always estimated as though vacant.[1] For land that is, in fact, vacant, the reasoning is obvious: an appraiser values the land as it exists. For land that is not vacant, land value is dependent on the uses to which it can be put. Therefore, highest and best use of land, as though vacant, must be considered in relation to a variety of uses, including its existing and all potential future uses.

An an example of land value being determined by potential rather than actual use, consider a valuable high density residential site, in an excellent location, that currently has a small single-family house on it. A purchaser may pay a price for the property for an apartment house use that includes no value (or even negative value) for the existing improvements. The potential use, not existing one, usually governs the price that will be paid.

Any existing building can be demolished. The fact that most buildings are not demolished does not negate the possibility. This possibility is the premise for the

---

[1]One exception to this rule concerns legally non-conforming improvements, which are discussed later in this chapter.

concept of highest and best use of land as though vacant. Land values are never penalized because of deficiencies in existing buildings. Buildings can be changed; the basic characteristics of sites cannot.

A trend away from demolition and towards preservation of existing structures became clearly evident in the early 1980s. The effect of the trend has been to decrease significantly the number of instances in which the highest and best use of a site is the demolition of its building or buildings. Historic-district zoning controls that make demolition permits difficult or impossible to obtain have resulted from the preservationist trend. In addition, the special tax incentives available to older buildings can substantially enhance their value and thus alter their highest and best use in many cases.

The purpose of estimating the highest and best use for land or a site is to identify the uses that cause the land to have value. Several appraisal techniques require a separate estimate of land value; therefore, the identification of the land's highest and best use is necessary for estimating its value. The highest and best use of comparable properties should be the same as, or similar to, that of the subject property. Thus, there are two reasons for identifying the highest and best use of land as though vacant in an appraisal.

HIGHEST AND BEST USE OF PROPERTY AS IMPROVED

There also are two reasons for analyzing the highest and best use of a property as improved. The first is to identify the use of property that is expected to produce the highest overall return per dollar of invested capital. If the property is currently being used as rental apartments, will that use continue to provide the maximum level of benefits? Or would the rate of return be increased by converting the property to an apartment hotel? The value of the property would be different under those two use assumptions, and the use providing the highest present value would reflect the highest and best use.

The second reason is to help in identifying comparable properties. Just as the highest and best use of land as though vacant of the comparable properties should be the same as that of the subject property's, the reverse is true. For example, using a comparable property that has a highest and best use as offices in appraising a subject property that has a highest and best use as a hotel would be an inappropriate appraisal technique.

RELATION TO ECONOMIC THEORY

Although modern economists have rejected the idea that land or real estate is less entitled to a return than other agents in production, the residual analysis implied by classical economic theory still prevails in highest and best use analysis. Although land may be as entitled to a return as the other agents in production the fact that buildings can be changed while the essential characteristics of sites cannot means that the income potential of any particular site is dependent on the use decision. From an overall, or economic, point of view, the fact that one site can be substituted for another means that their returns are established in the general market for sites. For a particular site, however, land value is a function of the income that remains after improvement costs are compensated.

Highest and best use of land as though vacant is an old concept that is derived from classical economic theory. Highest and best use of a property as improved is a much newer concept. It has evolved since the 1960s to answer two important questions that the older concept does not address. How should the property as improved be used? Should the existing improvement be continued in use, or should it be demolished and a new improvement constructed. The older concept of highest and best use of land as though vacant addresses only the question of how the land should be used if it were vacant; it is primarily a tool for land valuation.

ELEMENTS IN HIGHEST AND BEST USE ANALYSIS

To estimate the highest and best use of a site, the appraiser utilizes four tests. The projected use must meet all four of these tests:

1. Legally permitted.
2. Physically possible.
3. Economically feasible.
4. Most profitable.

Each potential use of a property is considered by the appraiser in terms of these four tests. If a proposed use fails to meet any of the tests, it is discarded and another use is reviewed. The highest and best use meets all four tests.

LEGALLY PERMITTED

Each use must be tested first to see if it is legally permitted on the site. Public legal restrictions consist of zoning regulations, building codes, environmental regulations and other applicable ordinances. Private restrictions are limitations that run with the land and are passed from owner to owner. Generally, they are imposed by the developer of the tract who attempts to preserve the value of the entire development by restricting what can be done with individual lots. Easements, encroachments, party wall agreements and the like also restrict the development of a site.

A gasoline station, for example, may appear to be the highest and best use for a level corner lot at the intersection of two major traffic arteries. The appraiser cannot consider this to be the highest and best use of this site unless it is legally permitted by the zoning regulations currently in effect or there is a high degree of probability that existing zoning can be changed within the near future to permit such development.

Occasionally a site is clearly not being utilized to its highest and best use, not because of any lack of market demand or physical suitability, but solely due to legal restrictions. Since the land is usually zoned according to a political/social scheme, rather than an economic one, zoning frequently does not conform to current market requirements. In such cases, the land remains economically under-utilized until the prescribed limitations are lifted. When the land manifests more valuable potential use than allowed by law and if there is reasonable probability that a change in use will be permitted at some point in the near future, this must be considered by the appraiser.

In such a situation, the appraiser must be extremely careful that the value estimate is not speculative, but rather that the market would widely recognize the strong possibility of a zoning change, and that a high degree of probability (exists) that the zoning can be changed within the very near future.

PHYSICALLY POSSIBLE (SUITABLE)

The use of a site must be physically possible. Uses might be limited by the physical characteristics of a site, such as size, frontage, topography, soil and subsoil conditions and climate conditions. Despite the need for single-family residential housing, an area of severe terrain with poor subsoil characteristics cannot be considered appropriate for such development. For example, sites along earthquake fault lines in California are not considered safe for house construction. Flood plains are also considered unsuitable for house construction. A corridor in the Palm Springs, California, area is considered undesirable because prevailing winds from the coast carry smog and fog.

ECONOMICALLY FEASIBLE

A realistic assessment of market demand for a proposed use is a critical factor. For example, acreage may be available that is zoned for single family residential use of a certain concentration, served by all utilities and with good proximity and access; however, similar subdivisions already in the market have remained unsold for some time. There is no need for the addition of such lots and so even though the property meets the first two tests, it fails economic feasibility. Thus, market demand acts to create highest and best use. In reviewing alternative uses, the appraiser must consider the demand for each use and the other available competitive land suitable for that use, which constitutes the supply. These factors must be weighed in the economic analysis. All physically possible and legal uses that fail to meet the test of economic feasibility are discarded. The remaining uses produce some net return to the property.

MOST PROFITABLE

The fourth test is essentially a test for maximum return. The appraiser is seeking the most profitable among all legally permitted, physically suitable, and economically feasible uses.

Because change is constantly occurring, the existing use of land is often no longer the highest and best use. If the land alone has a higher value under an alternate physically suitable, legally permitted use than the whole property as currently improved and utilized, the proposed use becomes the highest and best use. The existing improvement is at the end of its economic life but it still will be the highest and best use during the transition period. For example:

Market value of site zoned for commercial use
(highest and best use, as if vacant) $230,000

Market value of property as currently improved
for residential use $200,000

Contribution of improvement   None

The highest and best use of this property is no longer the existing use, except during the transition period.

TESTING HIGHEST AND BEST USE

To test highest and best use for the land as though vacant or for a property as improved, an appraiser analyzes all logical, feasible alternatives. Usually, the appraiser can reduce the number of such alternatives to three or four uses. Alternative uses must first meet the tests for physical possibility and legal permissibility. The number of uses meeting the first two tests can then be analyzed logically to limit the number of financially feasible alternatives that must be analyzed. For example, a market analysis might indicate need for a large office building in a community. However, if the site being analyzed is surrounded by modern single-family residential developments, a large multi-story office building probably would not be logical even if legally permitted. Similarly, development of housing for the elderly might be permissible for a site, but if most residents of the area are under 40 years old, such development might not be logical and probably would not satisfy the criterion of financial feasibility.

TESTING HIGHEST AND BEST USE OF LAND AS THOUGH VACANT

The following examples illustrate the testing of highest and best use for land as though vacant.

Example #1: Single Family Residence

Once the decision has been made that single family residential use is the highest and best use of a property, the appraiser must describe the "perfect" improvement that should be built on the site. Such a house would take advantage of all the factors analyzed in the community, neighborhood and site sections of the appraisal report. Also considered are the structural type and architectural style of this "ideal" house, its size, number of rooms, layout, quality of construction, kinds of material, mechanical systems and special features.

The principle of conformity tends to set the size, price range and other characteristics of the ideal improvement since houses that are similar to others in the neighborhood will normally have the highest ratio of value to cost. Once the house size has been determined, the structure type should be considered. Generally, single family houses can be classified into one of eight major types. These include 1-story; 1-1/2 story; 2-story; 2-1/2 story; 3 or more stories; bi-level or split-entry (raised ranch) houses, split-levels and mansions. Two and three-story houses were popular before 1900 but are not as common today as the split-entry or one-story house.

Once the ideal size and type of house have been chosen, the architectural style should be decided The neighborhood may call for a traditional colonial look, or one of the popular French or English styles, with special window treatments and exposed half-timbering. In Santa Fe, New Mexico, modern homes in some neighborhoods conform to the highest and best use only if they are built in the accepted pueblo or adobe style. In general, good design produces maximum value, regardless of whether the structural configuration or architectural style of a house is traditional or contemporary.

The next step in highest and best use analysis is to consider the market preferences for interior design. The number of bedrooms, baths and types and sizes of various auxiliary rooms in the ideal improvement vary greatly from neighborhood to neighborhood.

By completing this type of detailed improvement analysis, the appraiser describes the perfect improvement that should be constructed on the site, if it were vacant. If the appraisal is of a piece of unimproved residential land, this would conclude the highest and best use analysis.

Once these decisions have been made the appraiser might finally have to decide how big a house to build. It is determined that the cost to construct the proposed house is as follows:

> 2,000 Sq. ft. version $48.00 per Sq. ft. $ 96,000
> 2,250 Sq. ft. version $46.00 per Sq. ft. $103,500
> 2,500 Sq. ft. version $44.00 per Sq. ft. $110,000

The value of the site is estimated to be $35,000.

It is estimated that the sale prices of the houses will be as follows:

> 2,000 Sq. ft. version $140,000
> 2,250 Sq. ft. version $155,000
> 2,500 Sq. ft. version $160,000

The calculations to test which proposed house is the highest and best use are shown below:

	2,000 Sq. ft. House	2,250 Sq. ft. House	2,500 Sq. ft. House
Market Value	$140,000	$155,000	$160,000
Cost to Construct	- 96,000	-103,500	-110,000
Site Value	- 35,000	- 35,000	- 35,000
Anticipated Profit	$ 9,000	$ 16,500	$ 15,000

It appears that the 2,250 Sq. ft. house is the highest and best use among the alternatives considered. By constructing the 2,250 Sq. ft. house, the maximum potential profit can be realized. Both the bigger and small houses will potentially produce less profit.

Another consideration the appraiser must take into account is whether the total profit on the investment is high enough to warrant the risk that is incurred whenever one builds new houses on speculation. In this example, the builder must invest $138,000 ($35,000 site plus $103,000 construction costs) to earn $17,000. This is a return on the investment of 12.3% ($17,000 ÷ $138,000). If higher rates of return are available with similar risks than the proposed development is not the highest and best use.

Example #2: Small Income Property

Unlike the above example, where the highest and best use is a single family house, and the site value is known, in this example where the highest and best use is an income producing property, the value of the site is unknown. Often as in this example, the purpose of conducting the highest and best use analysis is to estimate the land value. Thus, various permitted uses must be tested to determine which will produce the most residual income after deducting income allocated to improvements for total NOI under each use.

In this example, there is a half acre site zoned residential, multiple family. It is located in a neighborhood with an active rental market. Investigation of the rental market develops the following comparable rental data.

      600 Sq. ft. 1 Bedroom apartments rent for $500 per month
      800 Sq. ft. 2 Bedroom apartments rent for $650 per month
   1100 Sq. ft. 3 Bedroom apartments rent for $725 per month

It will cost the following to construct the buildings:

      600 Sq. ft. 1 Bedroom apartment $45 per Sq. ft.
      800 Sq. ft. 2 Bedroom apartment $40 per Sq. ft.
   1100 Sq. ft. 3 Bedroom apartment $35 per Sq. ft.

In this market it is estimated that all expenses (fixed, operating and reserves) are 40% of gross rental income. There is enough parking on the site for 12 cars. Zoning requires one space per bedroom. The following are three configurations to be tested to determine which is the highest and best use.

The appraiser reduces the choices to some logical alternatives and then assembles data on construction costs, market rates of return and income that can be expected for each alternative use. These costs and incomes are shown in the following example, along with the market capitalization rate for the improvements.

Uses

	12 One Bedroom Apartments	6 Two Bedroom Apartments	4 Three Bedroom Apartments
Cost to Construct	$324,000 (600 Sq. ft. x $45 per Sq. ft. x 12 apartments)	$192,000 (800 Sq. ft. x $40 per Sq. ft x 6 apartments)	$154,000 (1100 Sq. ft. x $35 per Sq. ft. x 4 apartments)
Gross Income Potential	72,000 (500 per month x 12 months x 12 apartments)	46,800 (650 per month x 12 months x 6 apartments)	34,800 (725 per month x 12 months x 4 apartments)
Estimated Expenses	- 28,800 (72,000 x 40%)	- 18,720 (46,800 x 40%)	- 13,920 (34,800 x 40%)
NOI	$ 43,200	$ 28,080	$ 20,880
Return to Improvements (12%)	- 38,880	- 23,040	- 18,480
Return to Land	$ 4,320	$ 5,040	$ 2,400
Indicated Land Value (at 10%)	$ 43,200	$ 50,040	$ 24,000

According to this analysis, it appears that the 6 two bedroom apartment development is the highest and best use (it is possible that a mixed use building would produce a higher rate of return to the land. With the use of a computer program such as Lotus 1-2-3® all of the possible combinations could easily be tested).

In addition, the calculations indicate that highest and best use is not determined by any single item, such as cost, size, total income, or rate of return. Highest and best use is the relationship among these items that determines the income remaining to the land after the other agents in production contained in the building are allocated their market-determined value. These items are compensated before land. The tendency is for rents to be lower and expenses to be higher in an older building than in a new building. Thus, the older building would not be replicated on the site if it were vacant. It is only in the case of a new or nearly new building that the residual income to land would be maximized.

TESTING HIGHEST AND BEST USE OF A PROPERTY AS IMPROVED

An analysis of the property as improved should be made to determine if its current use is the highest and best use, or if alternate uses would produce a greater rate of return. When an alternate use produces a higher NOI, it does not automatically mean that this use will produce a higher value. The element of risk must also be considered.

Sometimes an alternate use can be accomplished with little or no capital expenditures. Other alternate uses may require substantial capital expenditures, such as proposed rehabilitation or remodeling.

Example #3:   No Capital Expenditures

In a college town, many of the property owners are converting their multiple family units from unfurnished apartments rented with one and two year leases, to faculty and others not connected to the college, to furnished apartments rented to students on an eight month lease. Usually these apartments remain vacant for the balance of the year. Furniture is rented from a local furniture store for $1,200 per year per apartment.   The store assumes the risk of loss or damage to the furniture. Experience has shown that expenses run 40% of gross income. The vacancy and collection loss is estimated to be 5% for the unfurnished apartments and 10% for the furnished apartments. The six apartments in the building being appraised now rent for $400 per month which is estimated to be their market rent. It is estimated that the market rent of the apartments rented furnished to students will be $800 per month. The following calculations show how to calculate which use is the highest and best use of the property.

	6 Unfurnished apartments 12 month rentals	6 Furnished apartments 8 month rentals
Gross Income	$28,800 ($400 per month x 12 months x 6 units)	$38,400 ($800 per month x 8 months x 6 units)
Vacancy & Collection Loss	1,440 (5% Gross Income)	3,840 (10% Gross Income)
Effective Gross Income	$27,360	$34,560
Furniture Rental	-0-	- 7,200
Operating Expenses	-11,520 (28,800 x 40%)	-15,360 (38,400 x 40%)
Net Operating Income	$15,840	$12,000

Thus, it appears from these calculations, that the highest and best use of the property as improved, is to continue to rent it as unfurnished apartments.

Example #4:   Capital Expenditure Required

A four-family house (each unit has two bedrooms) is located in an area that has been rezoned for high-density multiple dwellings. The owner feels that he should add a wing to the house. The architect has suggested two plans that meet the new zoning requirement. Addition A will create four additional two bedroom units. Plan B will create six additional one bedroom units. Estimates from local builders indicate that addition A could be constructed for $150,000 and that addition B would cost $200,000. The property "as is" has an appraised value of $160,000. Vacancy and collection losses are estimated to be 5% in this neighborhood for both one bedroom and two bedroom units. Operating expenses including reserves are 40% of gross income. Two bedroom units rent for $550 per month and one bedroom units for $400 per month. The following calculations show how to calculate which use is the highest and best use of the property.

	Present Use	Addition A	Addition B
	4 Family House	4 Family House and 4 two-bedroom apartment addition	4 Family House and 6 one-bedroom apartment addition
Gross Income	$ 26,400	$ 26,400	$ 26,400
Existing House	($550 per month x 12 months x 4 units)		
Proposed Addition	N/A	26,400 ($550 per month x 12 months x 4 units)	28,800 ($400 per month x 12 months x 6 units)
Gross Income	$ 26,400	$ 52,800	$ 55,200
Vacancy & Collection Losses (5%)	-1,320	-2,640	-2,760
Effective Gross Income	$ 25,080	$ 50,160	$ 52,440
Expenses (40%)	-10,032	-20,064	-20,976
Net Operating Income	$ 15,048	$ 29,520	$ 31,464
Capital Invested, 4 Family House	$160,000	$160,000	$160,000
Addition	N/A	150,000	200,000
Total Investment	$160,000	$310,000 (RD)	$360,000 (RD)
Return on Investment	9.40%	9.52%	8.74%

Thus, it appears from these calculations that the highest and best use of the property as improved, is to build the four, two bedroom apartment addition.

TYPICAL HIGHEST AND BEST USE STATEMENTS

All appraisal reports should contain summary statements that describe the analyses and conclusions for highest and best use of land or a site as though vacant, or of a property as improved, or both if a separate land valuation is included. When the highest and best use conclusion is the primary objective of an evaluation report, the income and return calculations and reasoning should be included. If the conclusion of the highest and best use of an improved property is different from the existing use, similar justification should be included in a market value appraisal report. Whenever the highest and best use conclusions are based on application of techniques to discover the highest and best use among two or more potential uses, the full analysis is included.

In appraisals in which land value is estimated separately, it is appropriate to discuss in the report the highest and best use of the land as though vacant as well as the highest and best use of the property as improved. When land value is not estimated separately and a condition of the appraisal is continued use of the property as improved, the appraiser typically discusses only the highest and best use of the property as improved.

Each parcel of real estate may have one highest and best use of the land or site as though vacant and a different highest and best use of the property as improved. In cases in which an appraiser comments on both highest and best use of the land as though vacant and the property as improved, each highest and best use must be identified separately in the highest and best use section of the appraisal report. First, the highest and best use of the land or site is presented, along with a statement that the determination was made under the theoretical presumption that the land is vacant and available for development. Second, the highest and best use of the property as improved is given, along with a statement that the determination was made according to the future potential of the land and improvements as existing.

If the land is already improved to its highest and best use, the two statements may be combined. But the report should state specifically that the determination is the same for both the land as though vacant and the property as improved, or that the land is improved to its highest and best use.

The report also should identify the highest and best uses, both vacant and improved, of the comparable sales. If the improved comparables have different highest and best uses of the land if theoretically vacant and of the improved property as existing, this must also be explained. The difference could affect value, especially in the sales comparison approach.

The following examples, two for a single family residence and two for an income-producing property, illustrate highest and best use statements. Obviously, the actual statements for any particular appraisal would be tailored to the situation.

Example #5: Single Family Residence - Highest and Best Use of Land as Though Vacant

This type of highest and best use is employed to estimate the value of land separately from improvements. It recognizes that any significant elements of accrued depreciation would not be replicated if the land were vacant and a new building were constructed on the site. It is also helpful in identifying comparable properties, which is why it is used in this appraisal.

The existing structure is not the highest and best use of the land as though vacant. The house was constructed approximately 10 years ago and contains measurable elements of physical deterioration and functional obsolescence, as do most structures after they are two or three years old. If the site were vacant, a new single family residence would be its highest and best use. The new house would be more architecturally compatible with other houses in the neighborhood. It would contain approximately 2,000 square feet and would include three bedrooms and two baths. The living room would be larger. The house would have more electrical outlets. All elements of physical deterioration would be eliminated.

Example #6: Single Family Residence - Highest and Best Use of Property as Improved

This type of highest and best use recognizes that existing improvements should be continued in use until it becomes financially advantageous to demolish the structure and build a new one or to remodel the existing one. The existing use of the property as a single family residence is its highest and best use of the property as improved. No other use of the property would be so beneficial or profitable. The existing structure is well maintained and is in good repair. It has an effective age of about 8 years and a remaining economic life of approximately 50. The structure fits well in the neighborhood, which is zoned for single family residential occupancy only. The structure was designed as a single family residence, and no other use would be legally or financially feasible.

Example #7: Income-Producing Property - Highest and Best Use of Land as Though Vacant

The existing structure is not the highest and best use of the land as though vacant. This type of highest and best use recognizes that any significant elements of accrued depreciation would not be replicated if the site were vacant and a new building were constructed. The income allocated to the land under highest and best use is capitalized to estimate the value of the land separately from the improvements. (At this point, an appraiser might state: This valuation procedure is shown in the section entitled Land Valuation.)

If the site were vacant, a new apartment building would be its highest and best use. It would contain 12 apartments (the maximum number permitted by zoning for this site). Each apartment will contain a living room, dining room, kitchen, bathroom, lavatory and 2 bedrooms. Each apartment will be 1,025 sq. ft. The building will be cement block construction with brick veneer exterior walls, frame subfloors, and flat, built-up roof. The building will be two stories with 6 apartments on each floor. It will be set in the middle of the site allowing for an attractive front yard, parking on both sides for 30 cars and a rear yard with recreational facilities for children. All physical deterioration would be eliminated in a new building, and its functional layout and design would be consistent with modern apartments of this type.

Example #8: Income-Producing Property - Highest and Best Use of Property as Improved

The existing use of the property as rental units should be eliminated and the building should be converted into 10 condominium dwelling units. The property currently contains 10 apartments that have a high vacancy rate during the past five years. The units require renovation and remodeling to remain competitive in the local housing market. However, the amount of money necessary to make these renovations and remodeling will make the property uneconomical to maintain as rental units as the rent that would be required is above what can be obtained for this type of property in this market.

The following calculations show the existing capital investment and additional capital investment required for the existing use and for conversion into condominiums. It shows the return estimated for the current use and the profit anticipated from a condominium conversion.

Type of Use	Present Use	Proposed Conversion
	10 Rental Units	10 Condominiums
Present Capital Investment	$300,000	$300,000
Renovation and Modernization	250,000	325,000
Total Capital Investment	$550,000	$625,000
Net Operating Income	40,000	N/A
Overall Return	7.3%	N/A
Selling Costs & Legal Expenses	20,000	75,000
Total Investment	$320,000	$700,000
Estimated Selling Price	$275,000	$800,000 (10 units @ $80,000)
Profit (Loss)	($ 45,000)	$100,000

Thus, the figures indicate that continuing the use of the property as rental units would not produce a satisfactory return on the investment, with the needed renovation and remodeling costs. Conversion into a condominium project would produce an estimated $100,000 profit which is considered satisfactory, for this type of project.

SPECIAL SITUATIONS IN HIGHEST AND BEST USE ANALYSIS

The basic premises of highest and best use analysis that have been discussed in the preceding pages are fundamental to all studies of the uses to which vacant land and sites or improved properties may be put. However, unique considerations in identifying and testing highest and best uses are necessitated by single use properties, interim uses, legally nonconforming uses, nonhighest and best uses, multiple uses, special purpose uses, speculative uses, and excess land. The special requirements for highest and best use analysis, in each of these situations, are discussed in the following sections.

SINGLE-USE SITUATIONS

The highest and best uses of land or sites as though vacant and properties as improved are generally consistent with and similar to surrounding uses. For example, single family residential use is usually not appropriate in an industrial neighborhood. Nevertheless, highest and best use may be an unusual or even a unique use. For example, demand may be adequate to support one large multi-story office building in a community, but inadequate to support more than one. A special purpose property, such as a museum, may be unique and highly beneficial to the site but not justifiable for surrounding land uses or comparable properties. The land value will be based on its highest and best use.

INTERIM USES

Often the appraisal is of an existing house that has not reached, but appears to be reaching, the end of its economic life. It may be an older house, in an established neighborhood of older homes, conforming substantially to the houses in the neighborhood. As with the analysis of the site as if vacant, the appraiser must determine what the perfect improvement for the site is. However, the appraisal must consider utilization of the existing improvements to obtain the maximum profit. If there is a house on the site, the appraiser must estimate what can be done to make it the most profitable use of the site. Any improvement that will add more value than the cost to produce it should be considered in the analysis. These improvements might range from simple repairs to major remodeling, modernization or rehabilitation.

An existing use may be nearing the end of its economic life but still be the highest and best use of the site at this point in time. If the existing house still contributes to the overall value of the total property, it continues to have utility. For example:

Market value of property as currently improved for residential use	$26,000
Market value of a site zoned for commercial use (highest and best use, as if vacant)	23,000
Contribution of the structure	$ 3,000

Although the highest and best use of this property as if vacant is different from the existing use, the old residential structure continues to add to the total value of the property. Thus, the existing residential use is the best use of the site for the remaining economic life of the structure.

Frequently, a site is improved with a building that is at the extreme end of its economic life. Such use is often an "interim use", a temporary use of the property until the time when the ultimate highest and best use can be attained. A downtown property utilized as a residence may not appear to be the highest and best use of the land, but it may still contribute enough additional income to the owner to justify its continuation as a "tax payer" while plans and financing arrangements are completed for more profitable development in the future. In an area where demand has not created an active market, an interim use may be necessary to hold the property until a more favorable market response is noted. A parcel of land suitable for a residential subdivision, for example, may be marginally farmed, until such time as the residential housing market will support the cost of its conversion to several new building lots.

LEGAL NON-CONFORMING USES[1]

A legal non-conforming use is a use that was lawfully established and maintained, but no longer conforms to the use regulations of the zone where it is located. This kind of use frequently results from subsequent zoning or a change in the zoning ordinances. Zoning changes may create underimproved or overimproved properties. A single-family residence located in an area that is subsequently zoned for commercial use is an underimprovement. In this case, the residence will most likely be removed so that the site can be improved to its highest and best use, or the house will be considered an interim use until converted to commercial use.

Non-conforming, overimproved property results when zoning changes reduce the permitted intensity of property use. For example, an old country store may be included in a neighborhood that is zoned for low-density residential use. Non-conforming uses may also result from changes in the permitted density of development and changes in development standards that affect features such as landscaping, parking, setbacks, and access. Zoning ordinances vary with the jurisdiction; they usually permit a pre-existing use to continue, but prohibit expansion or major alterations that support the non-conforming use. When the non-conforming use is discontinued or terminated, it usually cannot be re-established.

When valuing land with a legal non-conforming use, an appraiser must recognize that the current use may be producing more income, and thus have more value, than the property could produce with a conforming use. It may also produce more income and have a higher value than comparable properties that conform to the zoning. Therefore, to estimate the value of a non-conforming property by comparing it with similar, competitive properties in the sales comparison approach, the appraiser should make an adjustment to reflect the higher intensity of use allowed for the subject property.

In most non-conforming use situations, the property value estimate reflects the non-conforming use. Land value, however, is based on the legally permissible use, assuming that the land is vacant and its value can be deducted from the total property value. The remaining value reflects the contribution of the existing improvements and possible bonus for non-conforming use. The appraiser may find it helpful to allocate value separately to the non-conforming improvements and the bonus created by the non-conforming use.

Usually, any bonus resulting from a non-conforming improvement and use is directly related to the existing improvements. Therefore, the extra income or benefit should be capitalized over a time period that is consistent with the economic life of those improvements.

Often, legal non-conforming uses that correspond to the highest and best use of the property as improved are easily recognizable. Sometimes, however, it is not clear whether an existing non-conforming use is the site's highest and best use. The question can only be answered by carefully analyzing the income produced by the non-conforming use and the incomes that would be produced by alternative uses if the property were brought into conformity with existing regulations. Some jurisdictions specify a time period for phasing out legal non-conforming uses. In

---

[1]*Appraising Real Estate*, 9th Edition, American Institute of Real Estate Appraisers, Chicago, IL 1988.

most jurisdictions, a non-conforming use must be eliminated if the property suffers major damage.

Uses That Are Not Highest and Best

The theory of consistent use is basic to appraisal practice and highest and best use analysis. A property nearing transition to a new use cannot be valued on the basis of one use for land and another for improvements. The improvements must add to the value of the land in order to have value attributed to them.

The land is always valued first, and as if vacant. If the buildings existing on the site add to the value of the overall property, even if their presence restricts it to a less intensive use, the existing use continues to be (potentially) the highest and best use. Only when no value may be attributed to such improvements or they represent a negative value (burden) to the property, does an alternative use become the highest and best use.

An illustration of the violation of the consistent use theory in valuing a site is shown in the following example. A turn-of-the-century house is located on a corner lot, where both main thoroughfares are moving to nonresidential uses. Recent rezoning permits business use and the corner being considered is classified to permit the construction of a gasoline service station. The house (converted to apartments) is still being used. An uninformed appraiser learns from the market that such corners have been selling as service station sites for $70,000. Then, in violation of the consistent use theory, the appraiser adds to site value a value for the existing building of $30,000 for a total of $100,000. The correct consideration is to accept the $70,000 for the site "as if vacant". To make it vacant, demolition costs of $5,000 are estimated. The market value of the site in its highest and best use, therefore, is $65,000 ($70,000 - $5,000).

Multiple Uses

Highest and best use often includes more than one use for a parcel of land or for a building. A larger tract of land may be suitable for a planned unit development, with a shopping center in front, condominium units around a golf course, and single family residential sites on the remaining portions of the land. Industrial parks often have sites for retail stores in front and warehouse and light manufacturing structures in the rear. Farms often have family homes, storage areas for crops and equipment, and facilities for raising animals and crops.

Moreover, the same land may serve multiple functions. Lands for timber or pasture may also provide space for hunting, recreation, and mineral exploration. Land that serves as a right-of-way for power lines can double as open space or a park.

Buildings can have multiple uses. A hotel may contain a restaurant, a bar, and retail shops as well as guest rooms. A multi-story building may contain offices, apartments, and retail stores. An office building may contain retail stores and a restaurant, as well as offices. A single family, owner-occupied home may contain an apartment upstairs, or a professional office.

An appraiser can often estimate the contributory value of each use on a multiple use site or in a multiple use building. For example, if the market value of a timber tract that can be leased for hunting is compared on a unit basis with another timber tract that cannot, the difference should be the value of the hunting rights. In oil-producing areas, a common problem for appraisers is to segregate the value of mineral rights from the value of other uses of the land. Certain properties may have mineral rights value; others may not. In all such appraisals, an appraiser must make sure that the sum of the values of the separate uses does not exceed the value of the total property.

SPECIAL PURPOSE USES

Special purpose properties are appropriate for one use or for a very limited number of uses. Thus, an appraiser may encounter practical problems of specifying the highest and best uses of such properties. The highest and best use of a special purpose property as improved is probably its current use. For example, the highest and best use of a plant currently used for heavy manufacturing is usually to continue in heavy manufacturing. The highest and best use of a grain elevator probably is to continue as a grain elevator.

In certain cases, if the existing uses of special purpose properties are physically or functionally obsolete and no alternative uses are feasible, the highest and best use of the property as improved may be scrap or salvage.

Sometimes an appraiser needs to make two appraisals of the same special purpose property: one on the basis that a purchaser could be found who would use the property for its existing use, and the other on the basis that a purchaser would use the property for an alternate purpose. This type of analysis may be required because the owner of a large, special purpose property decides to abandon the property to consolidate operations. In such cases, it is usually not possible to determine, in advance, whether a purchaser can be found who has a need for the special purpose features of the improvements.

SPECULATIVE USES

Land that is held primarily for future sale may be regarded as speculative land. The purchaser or owner may believe that the value of the land will appreciate, but there may be considerable risk that the expected appreciation will not occur within the time the speculator intends to hold the land. Nevertheless, the current value of the land is a function of its future highest and best use. In such cases, an appraiser should discuss potential future highest and best uses. The exact future highest and best use may not be predictable, but often the future type of highest and best use (such as a shopping center or industrial park) is known or predictable because of zoning or surrounding land use patterns. In addition, there may be several potential highest and best uses, such as single family or multifamily residential developments. Appraisers usually cannot identify future highest and best uses with much specificity, but they can discuss logical alternatives and general levels of projected incomes and expenses.

As noted previously, interim uses may be the current highest and best uses of properties, for which highest and best uses are expected to change in the foreseeable future. Such properties may derive the greatest value contribution from the future highest and best use. Nevertheless, the interim use may also contribute to present value.

EXCESS LAND

Many parcels of land are too large for their principal highest and best uses. Land, in addition to that which is necessary to accommodate a site's highest and best use, is called excess land. Such parcels may have, in effect, two highest and best uses; the primary highest and best use and the highest and best use of the remaining, or excess land. In many cases, the highest and best use of excess land is for open space, or non-development. In other cases, the highest and best use may be for some less intensive use. In any event, an appraiser should treat parcels having excess land as two separate parcels. The land that supports the site's primary highest and best use usually has a higher unit value than the excess land, which is valued separately.

Land that is required to support the primary use, such as a parking lot for an office building or a playground for a school, is not excess land. Only land beyond the normal needs of a particular use, as determined in the market, can be considered excess land. Some atypically large sites cannot be considered as having excess land because the acreage that is beyond the normal needs of the particular use cannot be separately used. For instance, the overly large lot in an area that is 100% built up, or a site that cannot be divided because of the location of its buildings, are not considered to have excess land. An appraiser should clearly identify any land that is considered excess and indicate a separate unit value. The appraiser should than add the value of the excess land to the value of the primary parcel to obtain the value of

SUMMARY

To determine highest and best use, the appraiser first analyzes the site as if vacant and determines what the perfect improvement for such a site would be. Four tests are applied to the proposed uses. Only the use that meets all four tests (legally permitted physically possible, economically feasible and most profitable) is the highest and best use.

Next the appraiser analyzes the property as improved. If the value of the site and its improvements, maintained in its present use, is less than the value of the site if vacant and available for alternative use, the present improvements are no longer the highest and best use. If the present improvement, in its existing program of utilization, produces a higher value for the property than if the site were vacant, the current use is potentially the highest and best use.

The appraiser must analyze the existing improvements to see what rehabilitation, modernization or remodeling is needed to produce the maximum profit (see Chapter 10). The improvements, when renovated, would be the highest and best use of the property, "as improved".

Finally, several special situations may necessitate unique considerations when identifying and testing highest and best use. These include single use situations, interim uses, legal non-conforming uses, uses that are not highest and best, multiple uses, special purpose uses, speculative uses, and excess land.

EAVES FLARE
OUTWARD

OFF-CENTER CHIMNEY

CENTRAL
ENTRANCE

DUTCH DOOR

GAMBREL ROOF

2 OR 2½ STORIES

SMALL PANE
WINDOWS

Colonial American

DUTCH COLONIAL (Dutch Co - 108)

WHITE CLAPBOARD

STEEP, PITCHED ROOF

SIMPLE BOX SHAPE

Colonial American

NEW ENGLAND FARM HOUSE (N E Farm - 102)

10 Site Valuation

PURPOSE OF SEPARATE SITE VALUATION

It has been argued that once the site is improved with a house or multifamily dwelling, a separate site valuation is difficult, if not impossible and unnecessary. The claim is that only a total property valuation is possible in such cases and that the two units are inseparable. In spite of the theoretical merits of this argument, there are many practical reasons for making separate site valuations even when the property is already improved.

Separate site valuations are required by statute in most states for "ad valorem" (real estate) tax purposes. The assessed value is almost universally split between the land (or site) and the improvements. Special assessments for public improvements, such as streets, water lines, and sewers are often based on their estimated effect on land or site values. Income tax preparation also requires that the cost of a property be split between the improvements and the site. The first step of the cost approach is to estimate a separate market value of the site. Separate site value estimates are also commonly used for establishing condemnation awards, adjusting casualty losses, deciding whether to raze existing improvements to free the site for a new use, or establishing site rentals.

No single accepted manner exists in which to organize and present the necessary data; the following example groups the four categories of material in the order they would normally be collected.

1. Title and record data.
2. On-site physical characteristics.
3. Relationship to surroundings.
4. Economic factors.

SOURCES OF DATA

The sources of market data are varied. They differ by community and the character and location of specific properties. The most direct and thorough approach is to interview the parties involved in the transaction -- the seller, buyer, and broker. By talking directly to individuals, the appraiser can gain information about conditions surrounding the sale that may have influenced the transaction. A good deal of information may be revealed in the recorded instruments of conveyance and other public records on file with the local record office. Such records may identify the buyer, seller, mortgagee and trust deed holder and provide an accurate and complete legal description. Other data, such as sales price, encumbrances and approximate date of sale is also available. In some circumstances, deed restrictions and other limitations on the use of the property are found as part of these records.

Often real estate professionals other than appraisers can provide valuable background material as well as market data. Bankers, savings and loan executives, real estate brokers and mortgage bankers may be able to provide a clear picture of local real estate market activity and can contribute information reflecting the conditions surrounding specific sales which have been chosen for use in the direct sales comparison approach.

A large number of publications and professional information services are available, which serve as another excellent data source. Multiple listing systems (MLS), for example, usually contain records of all the activities of members in a local real estate board. Valid information on listings, offers and final sales prices is available from most MLS services. Certain government agencies (FHA, VA) often maintain records of the prices, conditions, sizes and other pertinent information about the housing stock and sales in their jurisdiction.

PROCEDURES FOR ESTIMATING VALUE

Five basic procedures for estimating market value of individual residential sites are:

1. Sales Comparison Approach.
2. The Allocation Procedure.
3. Extraction Method.
4. Capitalization of Ground Rental.
5. Land Residual Technique.

SALES COMPARISON APPROACH

The Sales Comparison Approach is based on comparing and contrasting pertinent data on comparable sites that have actually sold, with the site being appraised. It is the most popular and practical site valuation procedure. The appraiser may also consider offering and listing prices and other market information, but primary attention is given to actual sales of like sites, consummated under typical market conditions as close to the date of the appraisal as possible. Sellers may offer a property at any price they choose, and potential purchasers may bid any price they like; but the actual selling price of a site (a figure acceptable to both buyer and seller) best reflects market conditions.

As discussed in Chapter 3, market value is intended to describe the results of the interaction of buyers and sellers operating in an open market, all parties being knowledgeable, willing and able. Thus, having exposed the real estate in the open market for a reasonable period of time, the result is an agreed-upon price that is recognized as market value. The Sales Comparison Approach results in the development of market values of sites by converting sales prices for comparable sites (and sometimes other evidence) into market value for the site being appraised.

Appraisers are cautioned to consider and, if possible, adjust for any unusual pressures present in sales being used as market data. Obviously, the threat of foreclosure, the need to sell or buy rapidly or changes in local zoning regulations resulting in different potential uses all have a strong effect on selling price. Also, prices paid by federal or local governments usually are not acceptable as open market transactions because of the possibility that compulsion was involved, which eliminates the willing buyer-willing seller concept.

CLASSIFICATION AND ANALYSIS OF DATA

All pertinent market data regarding comparables should be organized so that it can be retrieved quickly in a format that promotes easy and accurate comparison with the residential lot being appraised. To qualify as a acceptable comparable sale, the details of each transaction must be verified. Hearsay evidence is not sufficient since the bona fide nature of each comparable must be clearly established The use of key-sort record cards is a practical and efficient technique. A more expensive method is the computer which provides instant and comprehensive recall of all stored facts. Many professional appraisal organizations are moving toward the development and use of elaborate computer systems.

The process of comparing the property being appraised with others in the market always involves two components - elements of comparison and units of comparison. A standard format is recommended to better organize the comparison process.

ELEMENTS OF COMPARISON

Appraisers use six elements of comparison when considering the comparability of sites. These are:

1. Financing Terms.
2. Conditions of Sale.
3. Market Conditions (Time).
4. Location.
5. Physical Characteristics.
6. Income Characteristics.

Financing Terms

The sale prices of similar properties may differ because financing arrangements vary. If conventional financing is typical for the type of site in question, comparables with 100% financing, conditional sales contracts or with financing other than conventional, require special analysis and judgment. If such special conditions produce a price different from that which would have been paid with conventional financing, an adjustment must be made. The conditions of financing, which include the amount of interest charged, the length of the mortgage and the ratio of loan to value, must be analyzed for every sale. When there are substantial differences between the comparables and the property being appraised, either a percentage or dollar adjustment must be made. This must be extracted from the market and requires thorough and complete analysis of the circumstances involved.

Conditions of Sale

This element of comparison is probably the most difficult to extract from the market and to make adjustment for. It refers to the circumstances under which both buyer and seller make their decisions to purchase and sell a specific residential site. By definition, market value requires a willing, informed and able purchaser and a willing and informed seller. Quite often, however, and probably more frequently than is generally realized, there are more than normal compulsions to buy or sell. An obvious situation of unusual pressure is bankruptcy.

The conditions of sale element is often difficult to prove in the market. Even if certain conditions are recognized, it may be difficult to apply an appropriate or justifiable dollar or percentage adjustment for the differences between the property being appraised and the comparable in the market. Some professional appraisers feel strongly that if the conditions of sale are different from those applying to the property being appraised, the comparable should not be used. Others feel that if reasonable adjustments can be made for conditions of sale, it is permissible to use the comparable to reach an indication of the market value of the subject site.

Market Conditions (Time)

The process of comparing the date of the appraisal with the date of sale of the comparables recognizes that market conditions do change from time to time. This process determines if the comparable sale took place under the same or similar market conditions. Sometimes market conditions remain relatively stable for a year or more; at other times they may change within a three- to six-month period, or even less.[1] The interaction of demand and supply affects prices; if one or the other or both change, prices adjust accordingly. In either a sellers' market or a buyers' market, price changes occur. This is the type of phenomenon that the appraiser must investigate, identify and compensate for.

Judgments regarding the element of time of sale are made by a close study of market conditions at the time of the appraisal, compared and contrasted with those at the time of the sale of the comparable. If the comparable was sold in a market similar to that prevailing at the time of the appraisal, no adjustment need be made. If, however, the appraiser recognizes that market conditions varied considerably between the two dates, an adjustment must be made.

The simplest example is that of a residential site which sold one year ago in an open market situation after a reasonable listing period. Then, for justifiable reasons, it sold again just two months ago for $1,200 more than the earlier price. This illustrates a singular example of the change in the market between two time periods, as expressed by the difference in two sales prices. It also illustrates the kind of process the appraiser must apply to identify dollar or percentage adjustments between markets. An intimate knowledge of the market is necessary to establish the amount of

---

[1]In the process of analyzing the differences in the market from the time of the appraisal to the time of the sale, strange phenomena may be encountered. One may tend to think that market prices and costs are even and steady in their change -- that is, going up 4% per year, or remaining the same throughout the year, or declining 2% per year. This, however, may not be realistic. Markets are known for their erratic activity in short periods of time; such activity may be cyclical, seasonal or a combination of both. There may be short periods of time in an annual market period that will have very erratic activity, but the average for the whole year would not identify them For example, average increase for the last calendar year may be 6%; however, closer scrutiny reveals that all of this was experienced in the last quarter of the year. Use of sales data from the first three quarters would have to be adjusted accordingly. Thus the monthly average increase is not 1/2% nor is each quarterly average increase 1-1/2%.

the adjustment. Continuous collection and storing of such data are essential to help appraisers reach defensible conclusions.

Location

The fourth element of comparison is that of location. Much emphasis has already been made of the importance of neighborhood influence on marketability of sites. Chapter 6 outlined in detail the physical, social, economic, and governmental factors to be considered in analyzing neighborhoods.

If a comparable site is in the same neighborhood as the appraised site, then there is a likelihood that no neighborhood adjustment would be made. In rare instances, if it were on the edge of a neighborhood and subject to either some beneficial or undesirable elements, neither of which affected the site being appraised, an adjustment would be made. If the neighborhood has been properly identified, it is unlikely that differences in schools, parks, and other kinds of important neighborhood considerations will be found.

In the event that a site being considered as a comparable is located in a different neighborhood from the property being appraised, a more thorough analysis must be made of possible differences between the two neighborhoods. Two separate neighborhoods may be very similar in all respects and no adjustments will need to be made.   On the other hand, if there are major differences between the two neighborhoods, appropriate adjustments must be calculated.

For example, the neighborhood of the appraised site may be served by excellent schools in close proximity to the site. In contrast, the comparable may be located in a neighborhood with less desirable schools much farther away. The market typically would recognize both factors and pay accordingly. To estimate the difference in price for these two variations, the matched pair system can be used again. That is, the comparable in a different neighborhood is compared with an identical site that has sold in the subject's neighborhood. If the former has a lower sale price, this is an indication of the difference the market recognizes in the two neighborhoods because of the school situation.

Many other kinds of neighborhood differences, such as variations in deed restrictions, zoning and building codes must be considered and if they are recognized by the market, an adjustment must be made.

Physical Characteristics

In this comparison process only major physical similarities and differences are identified and considered. A physical inspection of each comparable is desirable. The appraiser must be reasonably well-informed about the basic soil conditions and physical characteristics of the comparable sites so that justifiable adjustments can be made between them and the property being appraised.

If a great number of physical differences exist between the properties, the sale probably should not be used as a comparable. If there are none or only a few such differences, it may be a justifiable and usable comparable.

The same procedure is followed for determining the amount of adjustment for differences in physical characteristics as for the other elements of comparison.

Professional appraisers rely heavily on the local, active market from which to extract dollar (or percentage) adjustments. The "matched pair" technique may be used.

If there are two lots which are comparable in all respects except depth, one lot having 20 extra feet of depth, which sold for $250 more than the other lot, it is reasonable to conclude that the market paid $250 more for the extra depth of 20 feet. Such conclusions, however, should be supported by more than one pair of sales. The greater the number of sales to support dollar (or percentage) adjustment figures, the more convincing the appraiser's conclusions.

When necessary, pairs of sales can be used to extract adjustments from the market even when there are two or more differences between the sales. One sale is selected as a base sale and all known differences between it and the other sale are adjusted for. The remaining difference is then attributed to any remaining unadjusted difference between sales.

Among other items to be considered are such thing as:

1. Inside lot compared to a corner lot.

2. A rectangular lot compared with an odd-shaped lot (five or six sided).

3. Difference in storm water disposal (one area has no facilities, another is well-drained by storm sewer; the market probably would recognize this difference).

4. Difference between a lot which is flat and relatively easy to build on and one which drops 20 feet below the street level.

Income Characteristics

There are a few markets where there is an active residential land rental market. The largest probably is Hawaii. When sites that are in such a market are analyzed, it is appropriate to make comparisons and adjustments based on the property's income characteristics.

TECHNIQUES OF MAKING ADJUSTMENTS

In the past there have been a variety of techniques for making adjustments. Now the URAR has become universally accepted so most appraisers make adjustments according to the instructions which are printed on the URAR. It states: "The undersigned has recited three recent sales of properties most similar and proximate to subject and has considered these in the market analysis. The description includes a dollar adjustment, reflecting market reaction to those items of significant variation between the subject and comparable properties. If a significant item in the comparable property is superior to, or more favorable than, the subject property, a minus (-) adjustment is made, thus reducing the indicated value of subject; if a significant item in the comparable is inferior to, or less favorable than, the subject property, a plus (+) adjustment is made, thus increasing the indicated value of the subject."

For example, a lot being appraised is considered to be $500 better than Comparable A because of physical terrain. If Comparable A sold for $6,000 the adjustment would be made as follows: The comparable sale is poorer than the subject lot therefore, a plus adjustment of $500 is made to the comparable sales price of $6,000 giving an indicated value for the lot being appraised of $6,500 ($6,000 + $500). It is necessary to remember that an unfavorable element of the comparable property becomes a plus adjustment in the comparison process.

It is essential to remember that adjustments are being made to the comparable for the justifiable difference between the comparable and the property being appraised. In this manner, the comparable is being made as much like the property being appraised as possible.

SEQUENCE OF ADJUSTMENTS

A sequence for making adjustments is required whenever percentage adjustments are used, either solely or in combination with dollar adjustments. An appraiser obtains intermediate price figures and applies succeeding adjustments to each prior adjusted figure. The sequence, which includes all percentage adjustments, appears below:

Element of Comparison	Adjustment	Adjusted Price
Sale Price		$100,000
Special Financing	- 5%	-5,000
Adjusted Price		$95,000
Special Conditions	+10%	+9,500
Adjusted Price		$104,500
Market Conditions	+10%	+10,450
Adjusted Price		$114,950
Location	+ 5%	+5,745
Physical Characteristics	-10%	-11,495
Indicated Value of Subject Property		$109,200

The first adjustment is for special financing which is applied to the transaction price. The adjustment reduces the price for which the property would have sold under normal market financing.

Next any adjustment for special conditions of sale is made. The appraiser should indicate they have considered conditions of sale even when no adjustment is required by entering a zero in the appropriate place. The resulting adjusted price at this stage in the sequence reflects the amount for which the property would have sold under normal financing and sale conditions.

Next, the appraiser adjusts for market conditions. Presumably, the market conditions adjustment has been derived from properties that sold under normal financing and similar conditions of sale. The adjustment would be distorted if applied to an actual transaction price that includes non-market considerations. The adjustment for market conditions results in a figure that represents what the comparable would sell for at the appraisal date under normal financing and conditions of sale.

Next, the appraiser applies adjustments for location and physical characteristics to the time-adjusted normal price. These adjustments account for the differences between the comparable and the subject property. They are applied to the price of the comparable that would pertain at the date of the appraisal under normal financing terms and sale conditions. After all adjustments are made for locational and physical characteristics, the resulting figure is called the adjusted sale price. It is the price that as realistically and accurately as possible reflects the price for which the comparable property would sell on the date of the appraisal if it were exactly like the subject property. It is thus a value indication for the subject property.

Note in the above example that if the percentage adjustments were added together and the resulting percentage was applied to the transaction price, the adjusted sales price would be $115,000; that is, +25% -15% = +10%. This procedure would result in an error of almost $800 or almost 1%. Obviously, errors could be larger or smaller in situations in which a sequence is not used.

Although a sequence is not required when only dollar adjustments are made, its use is recommended in all applications of the sales comparison approach.

In deriving and applying adjustments, appraisers should always state the percentage relationship of the subject to the comparable. For example, the appraiser should state that the subject property's location is 10% better than that of the comparable, or that the quality of construction of the subject is 5% inferior to that of the comparable. The price of comparable is known; the price or value of the subject property is not. It is incorrect to state a percentage relationship in terms of the unknown.

UNITS OF COMPARISON

Adjustments for differences between the site being appraised and the comparables may be made in dollars or in percentages (see Figures 9-2 and 9-3). If dollar adjustments are used, they may be based on either the total price of the whole property or on the other units of comparison, such as price per square foot, price per front foot (designated F/F), price per acre or per dwelling unit permitted by zoning on the site. Depending on local custom and practice, units of comparison may be used rather than total price of the whole site. A reference to $100 per F/F for a site is more specific and understandable than $10,000 for the site. It is sometimes easier to make adjustments using units of comparison than the whole price of a lot.

A front-foot unit of comparison can be used appropriately even if the front footage of the site being appraised and that of the comparable are not identical. This system automatically takes care of the difference as long as the two lots have basically the same utility. In circumstances where major frontage differences exist, the square-foot unit of comparison may be preferable. Another unit of comparison for residential lots is an acreage unit for larger estate-type sites.

Percentage as well as dollar adjustments may be used. Like dollar adjustments, percentages may be used to recognize differences in market conditions from one time to another. If it is evident from empirical evidence that single family lot prices increased by 10% from last year to this year, a 10% adjustment is applicable to the lot being appraised in comparison with the sale of a year ago.

Typically, adjustments are made on a plus or minus basis. In Figure 9-3, the sales price of the comparable lot would be adjusted upward by 10%. Other adjustments might result in minus percentages.

RECONCILIATION OF ADJUSTED SITE SALES PRICES

The next step is to reconcile all the adjusted comparable sales prices into an indicated value of the site being appraised. Use of a simple arithmetic average of the value indications is not acceptable appraisal practice. Averaging small groups of numbers produces a meaningless measure of central tendency, which may or may not reflect actual market value. The accepted procedure is to review each sale and judge its comparability to the property being appraised. The final value is based on all the information available to the appraiser.

When a unit of comparison is used, two extra steps are needed. First, the adjusted unit sales prices are reconciled into a single (or range of) adjusted sale prices per unit. Then the number of units in the site being appraised is multiplied by the value (or range of values) per unit to give an indicated value (or range of values) of the site.

For example, assume the indicated value of the site being appraised is $100 per F/F, based on the reconciled adjusted sales prices of comparable sites. If the site being appraised has 75 front feet, its total value is $7,500 (75 F/F x $100 per F/F). If the indicated value of the site was $.10 per square foot and the site has 80,000 square feet, its indicated value is $8,000 ($80,000 sq. ft. x $.10 per sq. ft.).

For both dollar and percentage adjustments, the amount of adjustment should be extracted from the market in a valid manner. In some instances, adjustment amounts may not be available from the market. If so, either a logical judgment must be made regarding the amount of the adjustment or the sale must not be used as a comparable.

THE ALLOCATION PROCEDURE

A relationship exists between the application of the agents of production and the market value of a site. This is confirmed by the application of the principles of balance, contribution, surplus productivity and increasing and decreasing returns. Therefore, site value can be estimated by allocating the total sales price of a comparable between its two utilitarian and productive parts--the lot and the improvements. The appraiser determines what portion of a property's sales price typically may be allocated between the lot and the improvements, estimating the market value of the house and other improvements first. The balance (residual) is allocated to the site.[2]

Statistics shown in the U.S. Census reports demonstrate the relationship between sale price and site value of residential properties. The statistics are presented on a national and regional average. The older the improvements, the higher the ratio of

---

[2]The National Association of Home Builders reports that land cost, which was about 11% of the cost of a new home just after World War II, has risen to 35% today.

land value to total value. The typical ratio can be affected by a lot of unusual size or characteristics, and by building costs.

To estimate the value of unimproved property in an area where vacant land sales are lacking, the appraiser can allocate from the total sales price of a comparative property the part that could reasonably be assigned as building value. The remainder, except for intangibles, is the site value.

For example, assume that a property with a 1,500 square foot house sold for $175,000. The appraiser estimates the depreciated cost of the house at $100 per square foot, or $100,000. The remainder ($75,000) is the residual price of the site, assuming that the house represents typical or highest and best land use and that no extraneous considerations were involved in the transaction.

EXTRACTION METHOD

The extraction method also involves an analysis of improved properties. The contribution of the improvements is estimated and deducted from the total sales price to arrive at a sales price for the land. This technique works best when the contribution of the improvements to the total price is small.

CAPITALIZATION OF GROUND RENTAL

The ground rental attributable to a property can be capitalized into an indication of the value of a site. This procedure is useful when comparable rents, rates, and factors can be developed from an analysis of sales of leased land.

LAND RESIDUAL TECHNIQUE

In the land residual technique, the site is assumed to be improved to its highest and best use, and the net operating income, attributable to the site, is capitalized by the land capitalization rate into an indication of land value.

VARIATIONS IN THE PROBLEM: VALUE FACTORS

The same fundamental principles underlie all site valuation procedures; however, the key factors that influence the utility and value of a given site vary with the type of property being appraised. For example, heavy pedestrian traffic would tend to increase value in a retail business site but might lower value in a residential area. The aesthetic considerations and amenities that are important in establishing the value of a residential site might have little relevance to the value of a commercial site.

Value factors differ according to the type of land use. For instance, in a residential area the primary value factors may include convenient location to schools and shopping, amenities available in the neighborhood, or the beauty of the site. In an industrial development, the key value factors may be availability of raw materials, zoning regulation or proximity to transportation.

SUBDIVISIONS

Special Techniques are used to estimate the value of land that is suitable for subdivision into individual lots.

STEPS OF SUBDIVISION ANALYSIS

Subdivision development analysis consists of five steps.

1. Estimate the size and number of the subdivided lots.

2. Estimate the value of the finished lots by sales comparison.

3. Estimate the development costs, the development schedule, the anticipated selling period, and a reasonable entrepreneurial profit.

4 Subtract all development costs and the entrepreneurial profit from the anticipated gross sales price to derive the net proceeds of sale after development is complete and the individual lots have been sold.

5. Select a discount rate that reflects the risk incurred during the anticipated development and selling period. Discount the net sales proceeds over this period to obtain the present value of the raw land.

Determine the Number and Size of the Lots

All physical, legal, and economic factors must be considered. Legal limitations are imposed by subdivisions and zoning regulations. Projected lots must conform to requirements concerning size, frontage, topography, soil quality, and site improvements such as water facilities, drainage, sewage, and streets and curbs. The physical advantages and disadvantages of the subdivision site can be ascertained with the help of a survey and engineering studies. A reasonable estimate of the size and number of lots can sometimes be deduced from zoning and subdivision ordinances, or from the number of lots created in subdivisions with similar zoning. Most importantly, the size and arrangement of the lots should conform to market standards.

Estimate the Value of the Finished Lots

By analyzing appropriate comparables from existing, competitive subdivisions that have recently been developed, an appraiser can obtain an indication of the value of the finished lots.

Estimate All Development Costs.

All costs associated with the development and sale of the improved lots must be calculated. These include the engineering expenses to clear, grade, and finish the land; to build streets, roads, and sidewalks; and to install utilities. There are also carrying charges for taxes, insurance premiums, and inspection fees and expenses for sales commissions and advertising.

The development and selling period must then be projected. The longer a property stays on the market, the greater the costs and risks to the developer.

Estimate the entrepreneurial profit that will be realized by the developer if the project is successful. This is included among the costs to develop the land.

Deduct Development Costs

Subtract from the estimated value of the finished lot all the development costs including interest during the holding period, selling costs and entrepreneurial profit.

Discount Income Stream

The income stream that results from the sale of the lots must be discounted to present value.

Select an Appropriate Discount Rate

The income stream from the sale of the lots is discounted to present value. The rate should be high enough to reflect the high risk of land subdivisions.

FIG. 10-1 EXAMPLES OF A SUBDIVISION ANALYSIS

A developer is planning to subdivide an eight-acre tract and develop 32 residential lots. The anticipated gross sales price of the finished lots is $800,000 ($25,000 x 32 lots). The following development and absorption costs will be incurred.

Site development costs for grading, clearing, paving, and curbing; sewage and water lines; and design engineering	$300,000
Management and supervision	20,000
Contractor's overhead and profit	100,000
Sales expenses	30,000
Carrying charges (e.g., taxes, insurance)	20,000
Entrepreneurial profit	60,000
Total Costs	$530,000

It is estimated that the developer will sell on the average of one lot per month and therefore receive $25,000 per month. This is discounted to present value at an interest rate of 12%. The present worth of the income stream of $25,000 per month for 32 months discounted at 12 % is: $742,000 (RD)

The estimated value of the undeveloped land is: $212,000

SUMMARY

Of the two procedures for site valuation, the comparative process is basic. If the comparative sale is typical, the appraiser compares it with the site being appraised in terms of time, location, physical characteristics and conditions of sale. Adjustments are made to develop an indicated market value for the site being appraised.

Other procedures can be used when comparable sales data are lacking or when circumstances limit their application. The allocation procedure is helpful in existing neighborhoods and as an aid to the comparative process. The development procedure can be used in estimating the value of land available for improvement, usually in large tracts.

The highest and best use of the land or site determines the crucial value factors for consideration in each individual case.

Techniques for making adjustments for differences between the site being appraised and comparables, illustrated in this chapter, show that adequate support from the marketplace is essential in developing such dollar or percentage figures.

Subdivision analysis requires special techniques. It is incorrect to base the value of vacant land directly on the value of the projected finished lots without deducting all the costs of subdivision including entrepreneurial profit. The income stream must also be discounted to present value.

LOOKS LIKE OLD MISSION CHURCH

ARCH-SHAPED DOORS AND WINDOWS

PYRAMID-SHAPED ROOF

PARAPET

TILE ROOF

STUCCO WALLS

Nineteenth Century American

MISSION (Mission - 717)

11 Specific Data Collection and Preliminary Analysis

The entire appraisal process is dependent upon the collection and analysis of data from the market. All three approaches to value are really market approaches and depend upon market data.

This chapter presents methods by which Specific Data is collected, screened and analyzed. The final analysis of the data takes place in the improvement description and analysis and in the three approaches to value portions of the appraisal.

Specific Data is the basis of the three approaches to value. The process of extracting relevant material from the vast array of available market data helps an appraiser to develop a perception of the market. The validity of the final estimate of value depends on the extent to which it can be supported by data.

Specific Data is analyzed through the process of comparison. The key to comparison is locating data that provides the information needed to apply the correct techniques in each of the approaches. A number of different data sets may be needed to extract all information pertinent to the appraisal problem. For example, if the subject property is an apartment building of three-bedroom units, the appraiser may be able to base adjustments for time of sale, location and physical characteristics on information from comparable sales of similar apartment buildings. However, it may be necessary to analyze data on competitive properties that have <u>not</u> sold recently to obtain adequate rental rates and expenses for apartment buildings in the area.

INVESTIGATION OF MARKET TRANSACTIONS

A study is made to find those comparable sales and listings whose costs, income and expense information are similar to the property being appraised. Generally, the more current the comparable data and the more similar it is to the property being appraised, the better it will be as an indicator of the value of the property being appraised. Often more sales and listings and other data are considered than are finally used in the appraisal.

COLLECTING DATA

The accuracy of the value indication via the sales comparison approach depends upon the quantity and quality of sales, offerings and listings data for competitive properties.

The selection of the appropriate data first depends upon a detailed description and classification of the subject property's characteristics and components. The information obtained in the land and building analysis help the appraiser select the data to be used in the sales comparison, income and cost approaches.

It is only after a complete analysis of the property being appraised that an appraiser can select the data that are most similar to the subject property.

In selecting market transactions for analysis, an appraiser eliminates transactions that are not pertinent to the specific market for the subject property. For example, when an appraiser considers a 10-year-old single family residence that has three bedrooms, two baths, and 1,800 square feet of livable area, he or she usually eliminates two-and four-bedroom houses if there is sufficient data concerning three-bedroom house sales. The appraiser would also probably ignore the sales of 25- or 30-year-old houses, and possibly the sales of new homes. If sufficient sales remained, sales of houses smaller than 1,600 square feet or larger than 2,000 square feet might be rejected. The first determinant of the data that are ultimately used is the quantity of data that is available.

When comparable sales data in the area are limited, an appraiser may have to extend the data search to adjacent neighborhoods and communities that are similar to that of the subject property. When the selection of data is still limited to an unacceptably narrow sample of current market activity, the appraiser may decide to use sales that are less current and to interview brokers, buyers, sellers, owners, and tenants of similar properties in the area to discover evidence of potential market activity - that is, listings of offers to sell and offers to purchase. These may also be used as comparables if the proper adjustments are made.

An appraiser learns broad information about the market from the pattern of sales. Important information can be revealed by the:

1. Number of sales.
2. Period of time covered by the sales.
3. Availability of property for sale.
4. Rate of absorption.
5. Rate of turnover (volume of sales, level of activity).
6. Characteristics and motivations of buyers and sellers.
7. Terms and conditions of sale.
8. Use of property before and after the sale.
9. Other significant characteristics.

In analyzing available data for the selection of comparable sales, an appraiser begins to form certain conclusions about the general market, the subject property, and the possible relationships between the data and the subject property. The appraiser begins to ascertain market strengths and weaknesses; the probable supply of, demand for, and marketability of properties most similar to the property being appraised; and the variations and characteristics that are likely to have the greatest impact on the value of properties in the market. Thus, an appraiser does not analyze market data in a vacuum. He or she analyzes data against a background of information about the specific area and the specific type of property, as well as the current market.

LOCATION OF SALES DATA

Through a sound collection program, a large bank of market data can be accumulated in the appraiser's own files and organized to serve the appraiser's needs most effectively. Only some of the data may be immediately pertinent; the remainder may be collected, filed and cross indexed for future use. Records should carry the address, a file number, and additional salient information. Sales information is often collected and recorded on a standardized sheet. As the system grows, an indexing system must be devised to facilitate data retrieval. Many offices are using computers for data storage, retrieval and analysis.

--Public records. An appraiser searches public records to acquire a copy of the property deed. Deeds provide important information about the property and the sales transaction. The full names of parties to a transaction and the transaction date are cited on the deed. A legal description of the property is provided, as are the property rights included in the transaction, as well as any outstanding liens on the title.

Occasionally, full names give clues as to unusual motivations for the sale. For example, a sale from John Smith to Mary S. Jones may be a transfer to a daughter, or a sale from John Smith, William Jones, and Harold Long to the SJL Corporation may not be an arms-length transaction.

Statutes in some states require that the consideration paid upon transfer of title be shown on the deed. However, it is not always dependable as a reflection of the sales price because some purchasers deduct the estimated value of personal property (e.g. in motels or apartments) from the true consideration in order to reduce transfer taxes. These personal property values are sometimes inflated, making the recorded consideration for the real property less than the true consideration. Occasionally, the indicated consideration will be overstated in order to obtain a loan higher than actually justifiable, or understated in order to justify a low property tax assessment. Although some states require that the true and actual consideration be reported on the deed, other states allow the consideration to be reported as "$1.00 and other valuable consideration."

Records of the local tax assessor may include property cards for both the subject property and comparables, with land and building sketches, areas, sale prices, and so forth. In some localities, legal or private publishing services issue information about revenue stamps and other pertinent facts about current transfers.

--Real Estate Newspapers. Real estate newspapers concentrate on people making real estate news, major sales and leases and new construction; they often have information about subdivisions, condominiums and other developments that would be difficult to obtain elsewhere.

--Commercial Publications. In some areas, special commercial publications give sales and rental information along with other business news. Although they usually report only the information available from the recorded deeds and leases, they are an excellent source for locating comparable sales.

--General Circulation Newspapers. Daily newspapers often publish information pertaining to real estate transfers as well as proposed developments, zoning changes and other general real estate news. Many weekend papers carry special real estate supplements or sections. The classified advertisements are a good source of information about properties for rent and for sale.

--Realtors and real estate brokers provide a good source of data. Especially in areas where other sources are not available, the appraiser may elect to use the files of individual brokers, which are often elaborate and accurate. Brokers are a particularly good source of rental data and information about listings and unsold houses.

--Sharing sales data is traditional among appraisers. Working with other professionals saves considerable duplication of effort and increases the quality of everyone's work. Some appraisers charge each other for exchanged sales data. Exchanges of data should not be viewed as a substitute for personal research.

--Property managers and bankers often have information about real estate transactions and may give leads to important facts.

--Multiple Listing Services. These can be a bountiful source of information because they often require a detailed description of the listed property. There can be pitfalls in using this information however. Adjectives used by brokers and sales people to describe property conditions are sometimes different from those used by appraisers. "Average" to an appraiser should mean a house that is typical of its market, one whose effective age is approximately the same as its actual age (see Chapter 12). A broker or sales person might describe the condition of the same house as "good" or "very good". They may say a substandard house is "fair", and one that is not even habitable may be called "poor". Houses rated by an appraiser as "above average" may be called "like new", "excellent" or "A-1" on the MLS card. Another problem with MLS information is that functional and economic obsolescence is rarely accurately described. Square foot measurements, if shown, may prove to be inaccurate or may not be the gross living area figure used by appraisers. Finally, conditions of sale are rarely indicated. Once the MLS is used to locate a sale, the property should be personally viewed by the appraiser to obtain needed information.

--Deeds are a traditional source of sales information but their main contribution is in reflecting the existence of a sale. They usually contain only the address of the property, a legal description (this is part of a good positive identification), names of grantors and grantees, and the date of title transfer (which is sometimes a substantially different date from the actual date of the closing). In some areas, deed records also show the sales price (or have tax stamps affixed, which indicate the sales price) and the terms of the financing, but it is imprudent to rely upon this data alone as comparable sales data.

--SREA Market Data Center. The Data Center is an independent nonprofit organization, sponsored by the Society of Real Estate Appraisers. It is a good source of data particularly when it represents a sufficient percentage of the sales in the market. Data is collected on a standardized form (primarily from lending institution appraisers), processed through a central computer and displayed in printouts prepared at regular intervals. Because input is made by appraisers, the description of condition is in appraisal terminology, with at least some functional and economic obsolescence identified. There may be an indication of unusual conditions of sale. This service assists appraisers in identifying potential comparable sales. When a sale is selected, it should be inspected and the data verified by the appraiser.

--Listing and offers. Whenever possible, an appraiser should accumulate information on listings of other properties offered for sale. The appraiser can request that his or her name be added to the mailing lists of banks, brokers, and others offering properties for sale. Classified ads also provide information on properties being offered for sale. In addition to providing asking prices, the ads give some measure of the strength or weakness of the local market for a particular type of property. Offers to purchase are also useful information which may be obtained from brokers or managers. Listings are generally higher than the eventual transaction price; offers are generally somewhat lower.

--Government, FHA, VA and Private Mortgage Insurers. The FHA and some private mortgage insurers are good sources of data. Like lending institutions, they often have appraisals in their files for recent sales, which contain good, accurate information.

--Mortgage Loan Records. An excellent source of information, often overlooked by appraisers, are the records of lending institutions. They usually include appraisals of nearly every property for which a loan application has been made. Many lending institutions make this information available to bona fide appraisers.

--Title Companies. Title company data ranges from complete descriptions of houses to information similar to that found on deeds. Even companies that have nothing more than deed information may be helpful, if they file information by street rather than chronologically, as is done in most deed recording offices.

--Assessment Records. A cooperative, knowledgeable assessor with up-to-date records can be a major asset for the appraiser. A good set of assessor's records contains an accurate description of the property. Many assessors, however, inspect properties at intervals of 10 years, and the descriptions may not include recent improvements. Many assessor's measurements are quite accurate. Although they may not use gross living area calculations, their measurements can usually be converted to such figures. Appraisers must resist the temptation, however, to depend on the assessor's description and measurements without personally viewing the property.

--Atlases and Survey Maps. These give data on lot size, relate legal descriptions to street numbers and frequently show building locations and dimensions to scale.

--Transfer Tax Records. Some communities keep separate records of transfer taxes. The main advantage of this information is its accuracy and ease of use, particularly if it is filed by street.

VERIFICATION OF SALES DATA

Each sale used as a comparable in an appraisal report should be personally inspected and the data confirmed with the buyer, seller or broker. The appraiser must be assured that all depreciation has been considered, the measurements are correct and the reported price and terms are accurate.

Verification and inspection processes do more than confirm the accuracy of the data gathered. They also provide for exploration of the motivating forces involved in a sale. Were both buyer and seller acting without financial pressure? Was the sale an "arms-length" transaction, or were the parties related in some way? Were both buyer and seller knowledgeable about the property and market in which the sale took place? Did the seller have reasonable time to sell and the buyer to buy? Were there any special concessions granted by either party? Was financing typical of the market, or was there a purchase money mortgage, second mortgage, assumed mortgage or other unusual situation? Were there any other special sale conditions such as inclusion of personal property in the sale (furniture, above-ground pools, boats, automobiles, sports equipment, etc.)? Was there any special government program involving a subsidy, attractive financing terms or guarantee of payment?

Sometimes an owner sells for less than expected if allowed to continue to occupy the property for a substantial period of time after the transfer of title. Sometimes a sale is the result of an option granted in the past when different market conditions prevailed, resulting in a sales price that may not be typical of the current market. These are only some of the possible conditions that might make the reported sales price different from the market value. Only by personally interviewing the buyer and seller or broker can the appraiser gain knowledge about such conditions.

FILING SALES DATA

A common characteristic among successful appraisers is a filing system where they collect comparable data as it becomes available and store it in an organized manner until such time as they need it for an appraisal assignment. The method of storing this data ranges from index cards to modern computer data banks.

Most of the stored data falls into two broad categories:

1. Data obtained from published records, MLS services and other sources which provide information about properties which have not been inspected by the appraiser.

2. Data developed as part of the process of making appraisal reports which contain detailed information about properties that have been inspected.

File Storage System Office

How the data is indexed depends on the type of practice the appraiser has and the volume of data being stored.

An appraiser who specializes in small residential properties and who collects large amounts of data may first divide the data by community and then by type of residential property. An appraiser with less extensive data may elect to put all the residential property together, making the initial division by property category.

One such classification of residential property is as follows:

> Single Family Residences
> Small Income Properties (2 to 12 family)
> Apartments (over 12 families)
> > Garden type
> > High Rise
> Individual Condominium
> Condominium Projects
> Cooperatives
> Mobile Homes
> Timeshare Units
> Residences on Leased Land
> Resort and Recreation Houses
> Housing for the Elderly

Farm and Ranch Houses
Mansions
Historic Homes
Experimental Houses
Solar Houses

It is appropriate to cross reference data on some properties. For example, a single family solar home would be filed both under single family residences and solar houses.

Appraisers who have practices that include other types of properties would establish similar filing systems for commercial, industrial, agricultural and special purpose properties.

INVESTIGATION OF ADDITIONAL MARKET DATA

The investigation of the market extends beyond the determination of available comparable sale properties. Useful specific data is obtained by investigating properties that are similar to and competitive with the subject property, even though such properties have not sold recently. Information used in applying the cost and income capitalization approaches must often be sought from market sources other than sales. Such information may also be useful in refining adjustments made in the sales comparison approach. In the investigation of general and neighborhood data, an appraiser learns significant information on trends regarding such items as construction costs, lease terms, typical expenses, and vacancy rates. Investigation of these trends provides additional specific data needed to derive value indications through the three approaches.

IMPROVEMENT COST DATA

Several reliable sources for obtaining cost data exist.

--Cost Data File. The use of square foot cost estimates involves assembling, analyzing and cataloging data on actual house costs. An appraiser should have comprehensive current cost information for the types of houses and other improvements, including data on current material and labor costs. A system of grading quality of construction may also be used to refine the data further. This data can often be obtained from local builders, lenders, material suppliers and trade associations.

A file of this kind provides a check against costs of reproducing or replacing an existing residence as well as against known or projected costs for existing or proposed houses of varying grades of construction. It also provides a check against the probable cost of different components of a house.

--Cost Services. Several recognized cost reporting services are also available to the appraiser. Some include illustrations of typical structures and provide adjustments to tailor the standard example to differently shaped or equipped residences. Some provide adjustment for individual cities or areas. Some show cubic foot costs, some square foot costs, and some are designed for unit-in-place information. (A listing of some of these cost services appears in Appendix H).

--**Cost Indices.** A cost index service reflecting the relative cost of construction over a period of years is also useful. When the actual cost of a residence constructed some years ago is known, application of the index will indicate the present construction cost (provided the actual cost was a typical figure). For example, assume that a house cost $53,000 to build in January 1955 and that a 1955 cost index, from a national service, as 284.4 The April 1977 cost index was 596.3. Based upon this data, in April 1977 the building cost 2.097 times its January 1955 cost (596.3 divided by 284.4), or an indicated cost of $111,141.

INCOME AND EXPENSE DATA

In deriving pertinent income and expense data, an appraiser investigates comparable sales and rentals, as well as information on competitive income-producing properties in the same market. Current gross income estimates should be reviewed in light of average rent levels for several successive years. Vacancy rates, collection losses and operating expenses typical for this type of property help an appraiser to refine the forecasts of income and expenses for an income-producing property.

The published information on property values for several consecutive years suggests the rate of appreciation or depreciation that is evident for various property types. Interviews with owners and tenants in the area can provide lease and expense data. Lenders are a useful source of information on current terms of available financing.

An appraiser attempts to obtain all the income and expense data for income property comparables. These figures should be derived and tabulated in reconstructed operating statement format (see Chapter 18), and filed by property type.

Rental information is often difficult to obtain. Therefore, an appraiser should take every opportunity to add rents to the data plant. Long-term leases are usually a matter of public record. A separate county index of leases may be available, which lists the parties to recorded leases and refers to the volume and page of the recorded lease. Sometimes this information is listed among the deeds and mortgages, but it is normally coded so that a lease may be spotted fairly easily. In certain cities, abstracts of recorded leases are printed by a private publishing service. Classified ads are also a source of rental information. Many appraisers regularly check for advertised rentals and post them to rent comparable cards for a particular property type or area. The final actual rental is usually much closer to the asking rental then is the case for asking prices. Rental data should be filed by property type and area according to the same classifications used for sales data.

The income and expense comparables should be filed chronologically and by property type. They can thus be retrieved easily to help estimate the expenses for a similar type of property. Income and expenses should be converted to units for comparison and analysis. Income may be reported in terms of rent per apartment unit, per room, per hospital bed, per square foot, and so forth. Expenses, such as insurance, taxes, painting, decorating, and other maintenance charges, can be expressed in any of the units of comparison used for income, but they may also by expressed as a percent of the effective gross rent. Any unit comparison must be used consistently throughout the analysis.

The data for a rented property may show the actual vacancy rate and operating expenses as a percentage of the effective gross rent. These data are essential in the valuation of income-producing properties. Other important information includes the age and type of construction and any utilities that are provided by the owner.

CAPITALIZATION RATES

Market capitalization rates are also an essential type of market data. When income, expense, and mortgage data are available for sale properties, these indications may be used to calculate the overall capitalization rate and the equity dividend rate associated with the sale. Whenever possible, an appraiser should derive the overall and equity dividend rates of return, which are indicated by sales of comparable properties, and file the information for future reference. In the sales comparison, these rates would be analyzed according to the similarly of the comparable property's characteristics to those of the subject property.

Overall and equity dividend capitalization rates derived from sales may also be used as bases from which other rates could be derived. Therefore, it is important that appraisers consider these rate indications whenever information on sales is adequate for their derivation.

ORGANIZATION OF DATA

Before undertaking any analysis, an appraiser organizes all specific data accumulated during the market investigation. A spreadsheet that is carefully constructed provides a tabular representation of market data organized into useful and ultimately measurable categories. Depending on the complexity of the information that must be analyzed, an appraiser may have to design several spreadsheets to isolate and study specific data. On the initial spreadsheet, the appraiser lists each characteristic of the subject and comparable properties that can be isolated at that time.

The spreadsheet should include the total sales price for each comparable and the date of each sale, which can be expressed in relation to the date of valuation of the subject property (for example, on month or 16 months ago). The spreadsheet also includes information about financial arrangements and any unusual motivation that resulted in a negotiating advantage for either the buyer or the seller, such as the desire to liquidate for inheritance tax or the desire to acquire a particular property for expansion. Financial arrangements and unusual motivations can significantly influence selling price and thus must be carefully examined.

The spreadsheet often also contains other market data that may be significant for other appraisal assignments. Examples of such data are reproduction costs for building and land improvements, development costs, amount of accrued depreciation, indicated economic life attributed to improvements similar to those on the subject property, rates of return, percent of land value appreciation evident in the area, and average value of commodities produced on or services rendered by properties similar to the one being appraised.

The initial spreadsheet can include all characteristics of the subject and comparable properties, sales transactions, and pertinent market data from sources other than sales. However, an appraiser may decide to use one spreadsheet for comparable sales information and others for information derived from sources other than sales. This tabulation of data allows the appraiser to isolate aspects of both individual sales and the total market that may be significant in the valuation problem.

The isolation of specific data provides an initial indication of the information an appraiser will be able to derive from the collected information, and it identifies variations among properties that may be significant to their value and suitability as comparables.

An analysis of the initial spreadsheet may indicate that certain data are not pertinent and thus will not be useful in the application of the approaches. An appraiser may also find that additional data is required. The analysis may point to the need to create other spreadsheets to include additional information or to isolate data required for specific approaches. Appraisers should view the analysis of data as a developing process and the spreadsheet as a tool that helps advance that process and leads to valid indications of a property's value.

SALES COMPARISON APPROACH: ANALYZING AND COMPARING THE DATA

Comparison of sales, offers and listings provides a basis for estimating the market value of the property being appraised. When comparable properties are similar to the property being appraised; have sold very recently; and have few if any physical, locational and conditions of sale adjustments, such information is helpful to the appraiser in reaching a market value figure. On most assignments, however, the appraiser recognizes substantial differences between the appraised property and the comparable sales. As described in Chapter 14, two analytical tools are used by appraisers: elements of comparison and units of comparison. Each element of comparison (financing terms, conditions of sale, market conditions (time), location physical characteristics and income characteristics) must be considered; the units of comparison provide a means for making these considerations.

The initial step of the analysis is to determine the appropriate unit of comparison. For a single family house appraisal, it is usually either the total property price including the site and site improvements or the sales price per square foot of gross living area of the house.

Either of the units may also be used when appraising small income properties. Other appropriate units of comparison are price per square foot of total building area (price per square foot of gross living area is usually used only for single family residences), price per bedroom, price per room, price per square foot of livable area and potential or effective gross rent multiplier.

Units of comparison are used in data analysis in all three approaches. In the sales comparison approach, the selling price may be divided by the unit of comparison. In the cost approach, the total cost to construct and the total accrued depreciation are divided by the unit of comparison. In the income capitalization approach, the income and expense items and the net operating income may be similarly divided by the chosen unit of comparison. In all approaches, several different units of comparison may be used, depending on the information the appraiser needs and the focus of the analysis. However, the same unit must be applied to both the subject property and all comparable sales in any single analysis.

Different units of comparison are typically used with different types of property. Comparisons can be made on the basis of the price, cost, income, and expenses per unit, depending on the approach by which the comparable property is being analyzed.

INCOME CAPITALIZATION APPROACH: DATA ANALYSIS

Data from comparable sales, leases, and income and expense statements provide a variety of information that is useful in applying income capitalization approach techniques. Much of the data for this approach is derived from interviews with individuals who are familiar with the subject property or comparable sale properties. An appraiser also interviews owners and managers of similar properties for information on typical rents and other lease terms, vacancy rates, management fees, and other operating expenses.

If all necessary data are not reflected in comparable sales, an appraiser can use data gathered from other market sources. In the income capitalization approach, an appraiser should particularly have market indications of average income and expenses on a unit basis, as well as indications of the various types of relationships between income and value. These trends provide support for the net income and rates that are projected for the subject property.

When the data provides an appraiser with adequate knowledge of the income, expenses, and mortgage associated with each sale, he or she can derive an estimate of the net operating income and equity dividend for each sale property. The overall capitalization rate and equity dividend rate that are reflected in each sale can then be determined by dividing the net operating income by the sale price for the overall capitalization rate and dividing the equity dividend by the equity investment for the equity dividend rate. This data analysis technique provides meaningful information only if an appraiser uses the same income and expense categories to derive net operating incomes from comparable sales and to project the net operating income for the subject property. For example, if an allowance for replacement is made in the expense statement for one comparable property and not in the others, the rate derived by dividing that property's net operating income by its sale price would not be comparable to those derived from other properties.

COST APPROACH: DATA ANALYSIS

The application of the cost approach requires two types of data, plus the information needed to develop the value of the site.

The first is construction cost information which is used to estimate the reproduction cost or replacement cost of the improvements. The best cost data is obtained locally from builders and others who have first hand information about costs in the local area. The problem is that it is difficult to obtain this information in a form that will make it useful.

In developing cost estimates by analyzing data obtained through observation and interviews, an appraiser must ascertain precisely what the reported expenditure represents in relation to the total actual cost of building. Quoted costs for improvements may not reflect the owner's related risk, labor and equipment costs, financial charges, costs of land preparation, engineering cost, or other indirect expenses.

The appraiser must also be aware that cost estimates for reproduction or replacement of improvements as of the appraisal date, which are developed in this type of investigation, may not reflect any profit realized by the current owner because of a change in the property. Of course, final cost estimates should take such profit into consideration if it is evident in the market.

One of the best ways to obtain overall cost data is to extract it directly from the sale of a new residence. This data becomes particularly useful if by interview and analysis, the appraiser is able to obtain a good estimate of site value and developer's profit.

For example, an appraiser locates the sale of a new 10 unit apartment containing 11,000 square feet that sold for $900,000. The developer reports to the appraiser and lender that the profit was a typical 15%. The appraiser develops from good market data that apartment sites in this area are selling for $10,000 per permitted apartment unit and therefore this site has a value of $100,000.

Based on this data, the following analysis provides a good indication of the reproduction cost of apartment houses (including a typical builder's profit).

FIG. 11-1   REPRODUCTION COST BASED ON BUILDER SUPPLIED DATA

Total Sales Price	$900,000
Site Value based on market data	-100,000
Reproduction Cost of the Improvements	$800,000

Reproduction Cost per Units of Comparison

Total Sales PRice Sq. Ft. of Improvements ($800,000 ÷ 11,000 sq. ft.)	=	$72.73 per sq. ft.
Number of Apartments ($400,000 ÷ 10 units)	-	$80,000 per apartment

SUMMARY

The valuation process divides data selection and collection into general data and specific data. Specific data includes information about the property being appraised and information about comparable sales rentals, costs, expenses and other relevant data. The ability to collect and analyze specific data has a direct bearing on the validity of the final value estimate.

The first step is a detailed description of the property being appraised. It is only after a complete analysis of the subject property that data most relevant to the appraisal of the subject property can be selected from the market.

Some sources of market data are real estate newspapers, commercial publications, general circulation newspapers, Realtors®, property mangers, other appraisers, lenders, multiple listing services, deed records, SREA Market Data Centers, government and private mortgage insurers, mortgage loan records, title companies, assessment records, atlases and survey maps, and tax transfer records.

Improvement cost data can be obtained directly from the market and from published cost services. It can be adjusted for time with the use of cost indices.

The market is also the source of income and expense data used in the Income Approach and to develop capitalization rates.

The data is analyzed and applied to the three approaches to value. In the Direct Sales Comparison Approach it is used to establish the amount of the adjustments needed to compensate for differences between the comparable sales the property being appraised.

For the Cost Approach, it is used to develop the value of the site, the reproduction or replacement cost of the improvements and the amount of depreciation.

Data from the market is used to develop appropriate income and expense estimates and capitalization rates for analysis by income capitalization techniques.

Further analysis of the data takes place in the Improvement Description and Analysis, Sales Comparison Approach, Cost Approach and Income Approach section of the appraisal.

PROJECTING
UPPER STORIES

UNIQUE LOOKING

MULTI-STORY

TURRETS

BAY WINDOWS

BIG CHIMNEYS

VARIETY OF
SURFACE TEXTURES

VARIOUS FORMS
OF WINDOWS

IRREGULAR SHAPE

MANY
SMALL
DETAILS

Nineteenth Century American

QUEEN ANNE (Q Anne - 712)

12 Improvement Description and Analysis

Every appraisal must contain an accurate and adequate description of the improvements. It is also customary to include photographs of the property and a building sketch. This description is based on a physical inspection of the property by the appraiser.

This chapter presents details on residential construction and components to guide the appraiser in making the inspection. The assumption is that the appraiser makes a complete inspection of the exterior and interior of the property. If this is not done, the appraisal report must prominently state that complete inspection was not made by the appraiser and cite the reasons for this omission, and how the information about the property was obtained.

There are a variety of ways to organize a property description and analysis. The following outline works well for many residential properties:

1. Site improvements.
2. Placement of improvements on site.
3. Classification (CTS System).
4. Size of residence.
5. Number of rooms.
6. Car storage.
7. Description of exterior construction.
8. Description of interior construction.
9. Mechanical systems and equipment.
10. Items requiring immediate repair.
11. Deferred maintenance items.
12. Overall condition and age of improvements.
13. Interior design and layout (functional utility).
14. Renovation: rehabilitation, modernization and remodeling.

This chapter also includes information about graphic aides, sketches, photographs and How To Read A House Plan.

SITE IMPROVEMENTS

In the chapter on site data and analysis, it was noted that the term "land" implies no improvements of any kind and that "site" is land plus those improvements which make it ready for use. In the typical appraisal some of these improvements are included as part of the site value and other improvements are valued separately. Because there is no universally accepted way to treat site improvements, the appraiser must be familiar with local customs. The appraisal report must indicate clearly which items are included in the site value and which are treated as site improvements.

The following allocation of improvements between the site value and site improvement is common in many areas:

Improvements Included in the Site Valuation:

1. Clearing.
2. Grading.
3. Draining.
4. Landscaping (often valued separately).
5. Installation of public utilities to the site.
6. Access (streets and alleys).
7. Lighting.
8. Sidewalks and curbs (often valued separately).

Site Improvements Valued Separately:

1. Septic system (often included in site valuation).
2. Utility connections.
3. Well (often included in site valuation).
4. Driveways and parking spaces.
5. Patios.
6. Pools and courts.
7. Fences and walls.
8. On-site lights and poles.

It is customary on the URAR and other appraisal forms to skip the step of estimating the reproduction cost of the site improvements. Instead the appraiser estimates directly how much they contribute to the value of the property.

PLACEMENT OF IMPROVEMENTS ON SITE

A lot, like a house, should be divided into zones for good planning. There are three zones: the public zone, the private zone and the service zone.

The public zone is the area visible from the street. The service zone consists of sidewalks and driveways plus trash storage and clothes drying areas. The private zone is where the children play, the patio or family porch is located, and the vegetable gardens grow.

As well-designed house takes advantage of the fact that during the summer the sun rises in the northeast, travels in a high arc across the sky and sets in the northwest. In the colder winter months, it rises southeast, travels in a low arc and sets in the southwest. As a result, the south side of the house, when protected by a large roof overhang, will receive much more sun in the winter than in the summer. The opposite is true of the east and west sides of such a house. All other factors being equal, such as street location, topography and view, the best direction in which to face a house is with the broad side containing large windows towards the south.

CLASSIFICATION (CTS SYSTEM)

The Realtors National Marketing Institute of the National Association of Realtors® developed a standard method of describing residences known at the CTS System (Class, Type, Style). This system is described and illustrated in detail in my book <u>Houses: The Illustrated Guide To Construction, Design and Systems</u>. The following material and illustrations which describes the CTS System are taken from my book.

Figure 12-1 is a chart that summarizes the CTS System. Figure 12-2 shows illustrations of the most common house types. Next is a brief history of architectural styles in the USA and pictures of the most common styles. In addition to the common national types and styles there are many others found mostly locally in one part of the country or another.

FIG. 12-1 CTS SYSTEM

^ THE CTS SYSTEM
(CLASS, TYPE, STYLE)
A UNIFORM METHOD FOR DESCRIBING HOUSES

# CODE	DESCRIPTION	ABBREVIATION
	CLASS	
1	One-family, detached	1 FAM D
2	Two-family, detached	2 FAM D
3	Three-family, detached	3 FAM D
4	Four-family, detached	4 FAM D
5	One-family, party wall	1 FAM PW
6	Two-family, party wall	2 FAM PW
7	Three-family, party wall	3 FAM PW
8	Four-family, party wall	4 FAM PW
9	Other	OTHER
	TYPE	
1	One-story	1 STORY
2	One-and-a-half story	1½ STORY
3	Two-story	2 STORY
4	Two-and-a-half story	2½ STORY
5	Three-or-more Stories	3 STORY
6	Bi-level	BI-LEVEL
6	Raised ranch	R RANCH
6	Split entry	SPLT ENT
7	Split-level	SPLT LEV
8	Mansion	MANSION
9	Other	OTHER
	STYLE	
100	COLONIAL AMERICAN	COL AMER
101	Federal	FEDERAL
102	New England Farm House	N E FARM
103	Adams	ADAMS CO
104	Cape Cod	CAPE COD
105	Cape Ann	CAPE ANN
106	Garrison Colonial	GARR CO
107	New England	N E COL
108	Dutch	DUTCH CO
109	Salt Box	SALT BOX
109	Catslide	CATSLIDE
110	Pennsylvania Dutch	PENN DUT
	Pennsylvania German Farm House	GER FARM
111	Classic	CLASSIC
112	Greek Revival	GREEK
113	Southern Colonial	SOUTH CO
114	Front Gable New England	F GAB NE
114	Charleston	CHARLES
114	English Colonial	ENG COL
115	Log Cabin	LOG CAB
200	ENGLISH	ENGLISH
201	Cotswold Cottage	COTSCOT
202	Elizabethan	ELIZ
202	Half Timber	HALFTIM
203	Tudor	TUDOR
204	Williamsburg	WILLIAMS
204	Early Georgian	E. GEORG
205	Regency	REGENCY
206	Georgian	GEORGE

# CODE	DESCRIPTION	ABBREVIATION
300	FRENCH	FRENCH
301	French Farm House	FR FARM
302	French Provincial	FR PROV
303	French Normandy	FR NORM
304	Creole	CREOLE
304	Louisiana	LOUISIA
304	New Orleans	NEW OR
400	SWISS	SWISS
401	Swiss Chalet	SWISS CH
500	LATIN	LATIN
501	Spanish Villa	SP VILLA
501	Italian Villa	IT VILLA
600	ORIENTAL	ORIENT
601	Japanese	JAPAN
700	19th CENTURY AMERICAN	19th CTY
701	Early Gothic Revival	E GOTH
702	Egyptian Revival	EGYPT
703	Roman Tuscan Mode	RO TUSC
704	Octagon House	OCTAGON
705	High Victorian Gothic	HI GOTH
706	High Victorian Italianate	VIC ITAL
707	American Mansard	MANSARD
707	Second Empire	2nd EMP
708	Stick Style	STICK
708	Carpenter Gothic	C GOTH
709	Eastlake	EAST L
710	Shingle Style	SHINGLE
711	Romanesque	ROMAN
712	Queen Anne	Q ANNE
713	Brownstone	BROWN S
713	Brick Row House	BR ROW
713	Eastern Townhouse	E TOWN
714	Western Row House	WEST ROW
714	Western-Townhouse	W TOWN
715	Monterey	MONTEREY
716	Western Stick	W STICK
717	Mission Style	MISSION
800	EARLY 20th CENTURY AMERICAN	EARLY20C
801	Prairie House	PRAIRIE
802	Bungalow	BUNGALOW
803	Pueblo	PUEBLO
	Adobe	ADOBE
804	International Style	INTERNAT
805	California Bungalow	CAL BUNG
900	POST WORLD WAR II AMERICAN	POST WW2
901	California Ranch	C RANCH
902	Northwestern	NORTH W
902	Pudget Sound	P SOUND
903	Functional Modern	FUN MOD
903	Contemporary	CONTEMP
904	Solar House	SOLAR
905	"A" Frame	A FRAME
906	Mobile Home	MOBILE
907	Plastic House	PLASTIC

FIG. 12-2 HOUSE TYPES

One-Story, Ranch, Rambler (1 Story - 1)

Three or More Stories (3 Story - 5)

Two and One-Half Story (2½ Story - 4)

Bi-Level, Raised Ranch, Split Entry, Split Foyer
(Bi Lev or R Ranch or Splt Ent or Splt Foy-6)

Two-Story (2 Story - 3)

Split Levels — Side To Side, Back To Front, Front To Back (Splt Lev - 7)

One and One-Half Story (1½ Story - 2)

Mansion (Mansion - 8)

FIG. 12-2 HOUSE TYPES

SPLIT LEVEL — BACK TO FRONT

Cellar

SPLIT LEVEL — FRONT TO BACK

Cliff side house

The Hillside Ranch

Townhouse w/Eng. bsmt.

39

FIG. 12-3 HOUSE STYLES - COLONIAL AMERICAN

SOUTHERN COLONIAL

CAPE ANN COLONIAL STYLE

NEW ENGLAND FARM HOUSE STYLE

DUTCH COLONIAL STYLE

ENGLISH COLONIAL STYLE

LOG CABIN

CLASSIC COLONIAL STYLE

GREEK REVIVAL STYLE

GARRISON COLONIAL STYLE

ADAMS COLONIAL STYLE

PENNSYLVANIA DUTCH COLONIAL STYLE

CAPE COD COLONIAL STYLE

NEW ENGLAND COLONIAL STYLE

SALTBOX COLONIAL STYLE

FEDERAL STYLE

FIG. 12-4 HOUSE STYLES - ENGLISH, FRENCH, SWISS, LATIN, ORIENTAL

COTSWOLD COTTAGE

ELIZABETHAN STYLE

TUDOR STYLE

WILLIAMSBURG GEORGIAN

REGENCY STYLE

GEORGIAN STYLE

FRENCH FARM HOUSE STYLE

FRENCH PROVINCIAL STYLE

CREOLE

SWISS CHALET

SPANISH VILLA STYLE

FRENCH NORMANDY STYLE

JAPANESE HOUSE

ITALIAN STYLE VILLA

FIG. 12-5 HOUSE STYLES - NINTEENTH CENTURY AMERICAN

EARLY GOTHIC REVIVAL STYLE

EGYPTIAN REVIVAL STYLE

ROMAN TUSCAN MODE

OCTAGON HOUSE

HIGH VICTORIAN GOTHIC STYLE

HIGH VICTORIAN ITALIANATE STYLE

CARPENTER GOTHIC STYLE

SHINGLE STYLE

EASTLAKE STYLE

MONTEREY STYLE

QUEEN ANNE STYLE

BROWNSTONE

WESTERN ROW HOUSE

ROMANESQUE STYLE

MISSION STYLE

AMERICAN MANSARD STYLE

WESTERN STICK STYLE

FIG. 12-6 HOUSE STYLES - EARLY TWENTIETH CENTURY AMERICAN, POST WORLD WAR II AMERICAN

PRAIRIE HOUSE

BUNGALOW

PUEBLO STYLE

INTERNATIONAL STYLE

CALIFORNIA BUNGALOW STYLE

PLASTIC HOUSE

CALIFORNIA RANCH STYLE

NORTHWESTERN STYLE

CONTEMPORARY STYLE

SOLAR HOUSE

"A" FRAME STYLE

MOBILE HOME

BRIEF HISTORY OF ARCHITECTURAL STYLES

In December, 1620, 102 Pilgrims landed at Plymouth. In spite of cold weather, they immediately started to build their first house. Shortly after it was completed, the house burned down forcing the Pilgrims to live much of that first winter in holes in the ground that were covered with timbers, canvas and sod.

By the middle 1660's there were thousands of houses in the Colonies. They ranged in type and style from small wood, thatched roof cottages to large stone, brick and frame houses. Many of these houses were constructed by craftsmen who formerly built houses in the large European cities. With this imported expertise and some imported materials they were able to construct houses that were equal in quality to those being built in Europe. Many of the colonial styles developed in this early period of our history. At the same time the fad of copying styles from builders' handbooks and architectural design books was developing. At first, only portions of the exterior designs were taken from the books. Then, whole houses were constructed exactly like their European counterparts, built from designs in the same books.

Different styles developed in different regions of the country. Many of the early colonists copied styles from their homelands. Others copied the classic Gothic, Greek and Roman designs while yet others developed truly indigenous American styles.

SIZE OF THE RESIDENCE

It is only recently that standard methods of measuring residential properties were required by Fannie Mae and Freddie Mac. These standard methods unfortunately are still not used by Realtors® and assessors. Therefore, whenever an appraiser uses size figures supplied by other sources there is a high probability that had the appraiser measured the property him or her self, a different size figure would result.

SINGLE FAMILY RESIDENCES

The standard method for measuring single family residences is to calculate the Gross Living Area.

Gross Living Area (GLA)

The following are the rules for determining The Gross Living Area (GLA):

1. Measure around the outside of the house above the foundation to determine the GLA per floor.
2. In multi-floor houses count each floor above grade.
3. Include all of the above grade habitable living area.
4. Do not include the basement (even when finished and heated). Do not include any basement area unless it is 100% above grade.
5. Garages are never included in the GLA.
6. Porches are included only when they are heated and finished in a manner similar to the rest of the house.
7. Upper stories are divided into two areas.
   a. Attic – unfinished or having low cielings (below 5 feet) – does not count in GLA.

   b. Habitable area – finished and heated substantially like the rest of the
       house with normal ceiling height – is included in GLA.

The Fannie Mae guidelines recognize that these Gross Living Area rules will not work
for all houses in all markets. When the appraiser elects to deviate from this system
the appraisal should clearly spell out what system is used.

INDIVIDUAL CONDOMINIUM AND COOPERATIVE UNITS

How to measure a condominium is carefully spelled out by Fannie Mae. Their system
seems to be acceptable to Freddie Mac too.

The rules are the same as the Gross Living Area rules with one exception for
condominiums, that the **interior perimeter unit dimensions are used** rather than
the exterior dimensions.

Only rooms that are 100% above-grade are included regardless of the quality of their
finish. **Garages and basements (including those that are partially above-grade)
should not be included.**

Fannie Mae says, "However, if the Appraiser needs to deviate from this approach
because of the style of the subject property or on any of the comparables, he or she
must explain the reasons for the deviation and clearly describe the comparisons that
are being made."

Residential Valuation Magazine interviewed Mark Simpson of Fannie Mae who
confirmed that the best way to obtain the necessary interior dimensions for a
condominium unit is from their plans which are often available to the Appraiser.

Of course, the plans should be field checked to be sure that they appear to conform
with the actual unit being appraised.

SMALL INCOME PROPERTIES (2-12 FAMILIES)

The rules established by Fannie Mae are acceptable to Freddie Mac for measuring
Gross Building Area (GBA) and are substantially the same as the rules for calculating
Gross Living Area (GLA).

However, some appraisers interpret them to mean that common hallways are not
included in the GBA.

APARTMENT BUILDINGS

Most appraisers first calculate the Total Gross Area of the building by measuring
around the outside and including everything above grade. They also include living
units that are in the basement. They usually do not include unfinished basement
area.

Often they also include the measurements of individual units. These are measured
the same way as individual condominium or cooperative units.

HELPFUL HINTS ON HOW TO MEASURE

A house is measured by attaching the end of the tape measure to one exterior corner of the residence, measuring the distance to the next corner, and then repeating this process until all exterior walls have been covered. After noting the measurements on a rough diagram of the house, the appraiser checks to see whether the measurements of parallel sides of the structure are equivalent. This procedure is known as *squaring the house.* The total front building measurements should equal the total rear measurements; the total left-side measurements should equal the total right-side measurements. Minor discrepancies may suggest that the corners of the structure are not perfect right angles; greater discrepancies may be attributable to errors in measuring or rounding inconsistencies.

If there are attachments to the house or the house has an irregular shape, the appraiser sketches the shape of the house and measures each side. Once all the measurements have been verified, the appraiser divides the figure drawn into smaller geometric units, calculates the area of each, and adds the areas together. Areas are not normally considered part of the gross living area, such as attached garages and entry-ways must be excluded from the calculations. Computer programs are available for calculating areas, but the appraiser must still "square" the property from the measurements.

Current Fannie Mae and Freddie Mac guidelines suggest that the appraiser provide a sketch showing all the dimensions used in the area calculations together with the actual calculations based on these measurements. They should be presented in a format that will permit a reviewer with a calculator to check the appraiser's calculations.

NUMBER OF ROOMS

The HUD/FHA March 1987 guidelines state "room design and count should reflect local custom". Since the reader of the appraisal may not be familiar with local custom, the appraisal should contain information about which rooms are included and excluded from the reported room count.

The HUD/FHA guidelines go on to say, "A dining area built as an L-shape off the kitchen may or may not be a room depending upon the size. A simple test which may be used to determine whether one or two rooms should be counted is to hypothetically insert a wall to separate the two areas which have been built as one. If the residents can utilize the resulting two rooms with the same or more utility and without increased inconvenience, the room should be two. If the existence of the hypothetical wall would result in a lack of utility and increased inconvenience, the room count should be one."

CAR STORAGE

A majority of families owning houses also own two or more cars. Americans like their cars and they like to keep them under cover in garages and in carports. Their desire to do this varies from area to area. In many northern parts of the country any house without a two-car garage is substandard. In parts of the West and South the demand for garages and carports is more flexible and often a one-car carport with an additional parking area for the second or third car is acceptable.

The garage that is built to Minimum Property Standards (FHA- MPS) standards serves only to shelter the car. These standards call for a one-car garage or carport to be 10 feet wide and 20 feet long, measured from the inside of the studs and door to the edge of the opposite wall, stair platform or any obstruction, whichever is the narrowest dimension. To build a garage to these minimum standards is false economy. For only a small additional amount of money, the garage can be built about 3 feet longer and wider. It then becomes a truly functional area of the house. Here is the cheapest and most convenient place to store all of the paraphernalia of outdoor living. If built even bigger, it can house the laundry and drying equipment and also serve as a workshop and a place for the children to play on cold or wet days.

The choice between a carport or a garage is mainly influenced by local custom and climate. Some carports are so elaborate that they cost almost as much as a garage. Others are very simple and consist only of a roof extended from the house supported on a few columns or a simple wall. A carport is a good choice when it fits into the neighborhood and the prime purpose will be to shelter the automobile from the sun and rain. It is also desirable when the house is so located on the site that a garage would tend to block the breeze or appear to crowd the house.

DESCRIPTION OF EXTERIOR CONSTRUCTION

A detailed description of the exterior includes information about the major construction details, including:

1. Footings and foundation walls.
2. Framing.
3. Insulation.
4. Ventilation.
5. Exterior wall coverings.
6. Masonry walls.
7. Windows.
8. Storm doors and windows.
9. Weatherstripping.
10. Screens.
11. Gutters and downspouts.
12. Roofs.
13. Flashing.
14. Chimneys.

The condition of these items and any needed repairs or modernization should also be reported in this section of the report.

CONSTRUCTION DETAILS

Footings and Foundation Walls

The objective of the footing is to provide support for the building without excessive differential or overall settlement or movement. It is the perimetric base of concrete on top of which all foundation walls are poured or laid. Block foundations walls must be properly laid and well-mortared, then filled with concrete and made watertight with cement plaster or other waterproofing compounds.

FIG. 12-7 FOOTINGS AND FOUNDATION WALLS

FOOTING AND FOUNDATION

STRUCTURAL SLAB ON GRADE

The three basic design types are slab-on-ground, basement and crawl space. Slabs are constructed by first building footings for support, although some slabs (known as "floating slabs") are built without them. The excavation is then covered with gravel, and a vapor barrier and insulation are installed around the edge. A basement floor is constructed similarly to a slab. Crawl spaces are constructed similarly to basements except that the distance from the floor to the joists is 3 to 4 feet. They provide flooding protection and also a convenient place to run heating ducts, plumbing pipes and wires that must be accessible for repairs.

Framing

Most houses built in the United States are of wood frame construction. This includes many homes that have brick veneer siding. Platform frame construction is the most common type. Balloon framing was popular for multi-story brick veneer houses, but because of poor fire resistance it does not comply with many building codes. Plank and beam framing was used for barns and colonial houses; it is used today for contemporary designs where the framing members are left exposed (as in exposed beam ceilings). Panelized construction, a new method of framing, is becoming more popular.

Most multi-family buildings are now being constructed of masonry especially in the South and West. It is becoming difficult to construct a frame multi family building that will comply with the building and fire codes.

It is harder to spot poor construction in a new building. After a building ages, visible defects become more apparent.

Bulging exterior walls can often be detected. Window sills that are not level are a sign of settling, defective framing or original sloppy carpentry. A careful inspection should include opening and closing windows. Sticking windows may be sign of settling or defects in framing. Doors should be checked, including a look at their bottoms to detect if they have been resawed. Sagging and sloping floors may be detected visually or by putting a marble on the floor and watching if it rolls. Other signs of defective framing include large cracks developing on the outside of the house between the chimney and exterior wall or cracks running outward at an angle from the upper corners of window and door frames.

Cracks in the walls other than these may be cause for concern but in themselves are not conclusive evidence of a serious problem. All buildings settle unless built upon solid rock; it is a rare building that doesn't develop some wall and ceiling cracks. If defects are suspected, professional consultants may be called in to confirm this opinion.

Insulation

Any building without adequate insulation is substandard today. Insulation is as important in warm climates to keep the heat out as it is in cold climates to keep heat in. Prior to World War II, many buildings were constructed without insulation. Many of these homes have since been insulated. Insulation falls into the following five categories: loose, blanket and bat, sprayed-on, foil and wallboard.

The two primary benefits of insulation are fuel economy and occupancy comfort. Its secondary benefits are the reduction of noise transmission and of fire hazard since insulation will impede fire from spreading. The difference between fuel costs for an uninsulated building and for an otherwise identical one with storm windows and doors and good insulation can be 50%. The standard measurement for the effectiveness of insulation is its R value (resistance to heat flow). The higher the R value the better the insulation. Over-the-ceiling or under-the-roof insulation should have an R rating from R-20 to R-24 or higher.

Exterior wall insulation ranges from R-8 to R-11. Floor insulation should be at least R-9 and preferably R-13.

FIG. 12-8 BASIC TYPES OF FRAMING

BALLOON FRAMING

- CEILING JOIST
- TOP PLATE
- RAFTER
- STUDS (CONTINUOUS)
- SUBFLOORING
- FIRE STOPPING
- JOIST
- RIBBON (1 X 4)
- 2ND FLR. JOIST
- CORNER POST (BUILT-UP)
- SUBFLOORING
- JOIST
- 1ST FLR. JOIST
- SILL PLATE
- FOUNDATION WALL

WESTERN PLATFORM FRAMING

- CEILING JOIST
- TOP PLATE
- RAFTER
- STUDS
- SUBFLOORING
- SOLE PLATE
- 2ND FLR. JOISTS
- CAP PLATE
- STUDS
- CORNER POST (BUILT-UP)
- SUBFLOORING
- SOLE PLATE
- 1ST FLR. JOISTS
- SILL PLATE
- FOUNDATION WALL

The main difference between platform framing and balloon framing is that in platform framing the studs do not extend through the joists as they do in balloon framing (note circles).

- ROOF PLANK (TONGUE AND GROOVE)
- ROOF BEAMS
- RIDGE BEAM
- POST
- PLANK FLOORING
- POST
- STUD WALL
- FLOOR BEAM
- STUD POST
- BLOCK
- SILL PLATE
- SOLE PLATE
- BAND
- PLANK FLOORING (TONGUE AND GROOVE)

PLANK AND BEAM FRAMING

Ventilation

To prevent water condensation, a flow of air is necessary in the attic, behind the wall covering and through the basement or crawl space. When water condensation collects in unventilated spaces, it promotes rot and decay. This air flow will also reduce attic heat in the summer. Ventilation can be accomplished by providing holes ranging in size from one inch to several feet in diameter; these holes should always be covered with screen to keep out vermin. The use of attic, basement, kitchen and bathroom fans also is part of the ventilation system.

Exterior Wall Covering

The construction of an exterior wall on a frame building starts with the attachment of sheathing to the wall framing studs. Next the sheathing is covered with waterproof sheathing paper (often asphalt-saturated felt). A wide variety of wall finishes and exterior wall covering exists; many buildings have more than one type of siding.

A masonry veneer is built by attaching the masonry (clay or concrete bricks, split blocks or stone) to the sheathing. In buildings with masonry veneer walls, all the structural functions of the walls are performed by the framing and not by the masonry. When the walls are constructed, three-quarters to one-inch air spaces are left between the masonry and the sheathing, and weep holes are installed at the base to let moisture escape.

A variety of other types of siding materials are available, including aluminum, stone, hardboard, gypsum board, fiberglass and metals.

Masonry Walls

Masonry walls are either solid or hollow. Solid masonry walls, if well constructed, are durable and easily maintained. They should be insulated and require a larger foundation than a wood frame wall. Such walls can be either one or two units thick. Single-unit masonry walls are constructed of either two layers of brick, tile or cement block or of a combination of materials, with the higher grade material on the outside and the cheaper unit as the back-up.

Hollow masonry walls have two wall units separated by a two to four-inch air space and bonded together with metal ties for joint reinforcement. These cavity walls are used mainly in northern sections of the United States for protection against severe outside temperature and storms. Masonry bonded walls are similar to cavity walls. Although they are economical to construct, their insulation qualities are inferior to cavity walls and they are used primarily in the Southwest.

Windows

Among window types commonly found are single and double hung windows, casement windows, horizontal sliding (traverse) windows and jalousie windows.

During the inspection, dust streaks or water stains around the windows may be noticed, which can be evidence of leakage. Missing locks and window lifts or counter balance weights also may be discovered.

Weatherstripping

The purpose of weatherstripping on windows and doors is to provide a seal against drafts and dust. A common kind of weatherstripping used today is the "spring tension" type made of bronze, aluminum, rigid vinyl, stainless or galvanized steel or rigid plastic steel. Other types are woven felt, compression sash guides and compression bulbs.

Storm Doors and Windows

These serve as a means of insulation and may provide a fuel savings of between 10% and 20%. Today they are often made of aluminum and permanently installed, together with screens. The wooden type, which are removed and stored during the summer, are becoming obsolete.

Screens

Screens are needed in almost every part of the country. The old-fashioned wood frame is becoming obsolete. Most screens today have aluminum frames and screening material and are combined with storm windows.

Gutters and Downspouts

These provide the means for controlling water run off from the roof to prevent property damage and unsightly exterior wall stains where roof overhangs are not provided. Gutters or eve troughs carry rainwater off the roof to downspouts or leaders. Metal gutters of aluminum, copper or galvanized iron, which are attached with various types of metal hangers, are the most common type of gutter now in use. Built-in gutters are made of metal and set into the deeply notched rafter a short distance up the roof from the eaves. Pole gutters consist of a wooden strip nailed perpendicular to the roof and covered with sheet metal.

Downspouts or leaders are vertical pipes that carry the water from the gutter to the ground and into sewers or dry wells. The junction of the gutter and downspout should be covered with a basket strainer to hold back leaves and twigs.

Roofs

The roof must be constructed to support its own weight, plus that of snow, ice and wind, and also act as a base for the application of the roof finishing materials. The most common systems of roof construction found are trusses, joists and rafters, joists alone, plank and beam roofs and panelized construction.

Roof sheathing provides support for roof loads and a backing for the attachment of roofing materials.

A majority of house roofs consist of shingles and shakes made of wood, asphalt, asbestos, cement, slate or tile. Metal, clay tile and built-up or membrane roofs can also be found. Many multi-family buildings have flat built-up roofing systems. Since the roof covering rarely lasts to the end of the building's economic life, the appraiser carefully observes the roof and reports its condition, age and estimated remaining life.

Water may leak through the roof for a variety of reasons. Asphalt shingle roofs may leak in a high wind if light-grade shingles are used. As these shingles get older, they curl, tear and become pierced with holes. Wood shingles may curl, split, loosen, break and fall off the roof, and asbestos shingles may crack and break. Metal roofs can rust, become bent and pierced with holes. Rolled and built-up roofs may loosen, tear, and become patched and worn through.

--Flashing. Flashing is needed whenever a roof is intersected by two different roof slopes, adjoining walls or projections through the surface by chimneys, pipes or vents. Flashing is a process by which metal stripes, impregnated felt or a combination of both are nailed across or under the intersecting point; a waterproofing compound or cement is then applied and finally the roofing or siding materials are applied over the edges to hold the flashing in place permanently.

--Chimneys. The efficiency of any heating system (except electric) depends upon the chimney or vent. A good chimney is safe, durable and smoke tight. Defective chimneys and vents may constitute serious fire hazards. A chimney may be a simple flue or an intricate masonry construction consisting of heater flues, ash pits, incinerators, ash chutes, fireplaces and fireplace flues. Whatever its construction, the chimney must be supported by its own concrete footings, which must be designed so that it will not settle faster than the rest of the building. Masonry chimney walls should be eight inches thick when they are exposed, and must be separated from combustible construction. A two-inch air space must extend at least two feet above any part of the roof, roof ridge or parapet wall within 10 feet of the chimney.

The heart of the chimney is the vertical open shaft, called a flue, through which smoke and gas pass to the outside air. A rough surface retards this outward flow of smoke or warm air; a flue lining will overcome this problem. The flue should extend out a few inches above the top of the chimney wall, (which should be capped with concrete, metal, stone or some other noncombustible waterproof material,) sloped from the flue to the outside edge.

The furnace and hot water heater are connected to the chimney by a smoke pipe, which, for fire safety, should be at least 10 inches below the floor joists. The joists should be further protected with plaster or a shield of metal or asbestos.

Prefabricated chimneys that are assembled off the premises are now available. Many of these units consist of a flue liner encased in a concrete wall.

FIG. 12-9 ROOF CONSTRUCTION AND COVERING

SLOPED ROOF JOISTS

JOIST-AND-RAFTER

TRUSS

ROOF FRAMING SYSTEMS

SHINGLE ROOFING

CLAY TILE ROOFING

PLYWOOD

DIAGONAL BOARD

HORIZONTAL BOARD

SPACED BOARD
(FOR WOOD SHINGLE ROOFING)

ROOF SHEATHING

DESCRIPTION OF INTERIOR CONSTRUCTION

The description of the interior rooms should provide information about their location, individual size, number of closets, and floor, wall, and ceiling coverings or finishes. Special features should also be described and any needed repairs or modernization should be reported. Typical items included in a description of the general interior construction (exclusive of the mechanical systems and equipment, which are described separately) are:

1. Basement construction and finishing.
2. Main bearing beam and columns.
3. Subflooring.
4. Floor covering.
5. Interior walls and ceilings.
6. Stairs.
7. Doors.
8. Molding and trim.
9. Cabinets.
10. Fireplaces.
11. Termite protection.

The condition of these items and any needed repairs or modernization should be reported in this section of the report.

CONSTRUCTION DETAILS

--Basement Construction and Finishing. The basic construction of the basement consists of the footings and foundation walls previously described; a basement floor, which usually is poured concrete over a vapor barrier and gravel; and the ceiling, which often is the unfinished underside of the first floor subflooring. Dirt floors are obsolete.

Basements can be finished in a variety of ways. There is a trend to raise the basement part way out of the ground to provide better natural light and ventilation and direct access to the outside. In raised ranch and hillside ranch-type houses the basement often is finished so as to be an integral part of the house.

A main problem with basements is dampness, which may be caused by poor foundation wall construction, excess ground water not properly carried away by ground tiles, poorly fitted windows or hatch, a poorly vented clothes dryer, gutters and downspouts spilling water too near the foundation wall or a rising ground water table. A basement that is wet or damp only part of the year can usually be detected any time by the presence of a powder-white mineral deposit a few inches off the floor. Stains along the lower edge of the walls and columns and on the furnace and hot water heater are indications of excessive dampness, as is mildew odor.

--Main Bearing Beam and Columns. Most buildings are too large for the floor joists to span between the foundation walls. Bearing beams resting on columns are used for support. Steel beams, because of their high strength, can span greater distances than wood beams of the same size. Most beams are supported by wood posts, brick or block piers or metal Lally columns, which are concrete-filled steel cylinders.

--Subflooring and Bridging. Subflooring provides safe support of floor loads without excessive deflection and adequate underlayment for the support and attachment of finish flooring materials. Plywood is the most common material now being used for residential subflooring. Bridging is used to stiffen the joists and prevent them from deflecting sideways.

--Floor Covering. Flooring made of strips of hardwood was the residential standard in many markets for over 50 years. Before that time planks of hard and soft woods were used.

Carpeting, installed over either finished flooring or subflooring, is rapidly gaining in popularity. Carpeting, however, tends to depreciate very rapidly and often does not add value equal to its cost, especially when it is laid over another floor covering. Ceramic tile is still popular for bathrooms and lavatories, and quarry tile is becoming more common in kitchens.

Concrete slabs may be used for floor covering with no further treatment, painted with special concrete paint or covered with other flooring materials. Resilient tile, glued with special adhesives, must not be installed directly over a board or plank subfloor; a suitable underlayment must first be installed. Terrazzo flooring is made of colored marble chips mixed into cement; it is ground to a smooth surface after being laid.

--Interior Walls and Ceiling. Most interior walls are made of wood studs or metal studs, covered with a variety of materials. The materials most commonly used include plaster, gypsum, plywood, hardboard, fiberboard, ceramic tile and wood paneling.

Gypsum and other wood composition walls are installed directly onto studs or masonry, eliminating the drying time needed for plaster walls. Ceramic tile walls are installed similarly to ceramic tile floors, either by cement plaster or special adhesives.

--Stairs. A well-planned stairway provides safe ascent, adequate headroom and enough space for moving furniture and equipment. A simple check for adequate design includes noting: headroom, width clear between handrails, run, rise, winders, landings, handrail and railings. Railings should be installed around the open sides of all interior stairwells including those in the attic and basement.

--Doors. There are seven basic types of doors: batten, sliding glass, folding, flush solid, flush solid core, flush hollow core, and stile and rail doors. Batten doors, consisting of boards nailed together in various ways, are used where appearance is not important, such as for cellar and shed doors. Flush solid core doors are made with smooth face panels glued to a core that is made of either a composition material, glued-together wood blocks or glued-together wood pieces. Solid doors are often used as exterior doors. Flush hollow core doors are also perfectly flat. They have a core that consists mainly of crossed wooden slats. These doors are light and are used for interior doors. Stile and rail doors consist of a framework of vertical boards (stiles) and horizontal boards (rails). The hanging of doors is difficult. If the door is improperly hung, it will stick. Pre-hung doors are now available.

--Molding and Trim. Molding is made from a variety of hard and soft woods that are cut, planed and sanded into desired shapes. A general rule is; the thicker the molding, and the more intricate the design, the more expensive it is.

--Cabinets. Prior to World War II most cabinets were made of wood. Factory-made metal cabinets are often used today. Drawers, adjustable shelves, back, sides and fronts are of enameled pressed steel sheets. Doors are usually hollow steel.

--Fireplaces. In most American homes a fireplace is an amenity rather than a primary source of heat. There is no rule of thumb as to how much value one adds, and it is a mistake to assume, without market evidence, that it adds value equal to its cost.

Fireplaces are usually constructed of masonry, but metal ones are becoming common. They must be well-designed and constructed to work properly. Many fireplaces allow smoke to back up into the house, especially when it is windy outside. For fire safety, the hearth should extend at least 16 inches from the front and eight inches beyond each side of the opening.

--Termite Protection. The subterranean termite (see Fig. 12-10) is becoming common in most parts of the United States. Termites live in the moist earth, not in wood; they travel from the ground into the wood only to feed. They do not like light and will travel above ground through cracks in masonry foundations, through wood or in mud tunnels they construct on masonry surfaces.

Termite protection is provided by (1) controlling the moisture content of the wood used; (2) providing effective termite barriers and (3) using naturally durable or treated wood. Most appraisers are not qualified to make a complete termite inspection; however, they can make a preliminary examination which should report the following:

1. Wood that is not at least six inches above ground.
    (Joists, sills and girders should have even more clearance.)
2. Soft wood that may be termite infested.
3. Cracks in masonry that could be termite pathways.
4. Mud termite tubes that are signs of termites.
5. Insects that appear to be termites.
6. Termite shields and other special termite protection.

If there is _any_ sign of termites, inspection by a professional termite inspector should be recommended in the appraisal report.

FIG. 12-10 TERMITES AND ANTS

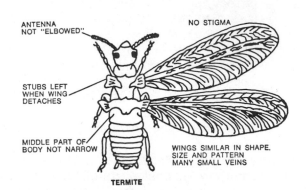

**DIFFERENCES BETWEEN WINGED ADULT
ANTS AND TERMITES**

MECHANICAL SYSTEMS AND EQUIPMENT

A building does not function satisfactorily unless its mechanical systems are in good working order. Each system must be inspected by the appraiser and described in the appraisal report. There is no standard way to categorize the mechanical systems and equipment; the following is a summary of the major systems described in this chapter:

1. Heating system.
2. Cooling system.
3. Plumbing system.
4. Hot water system.
5. Electrical system.
6. Miscellaneous systems.

Heating Systems

Heating systems are based on warm air, water, steam or electricity. Warm (or hot) air heating systems utilize either the natural force of gravity or some type of pressure blower to push heated air through the ducts. Filters can be installed to clean the air and a humidifier is often added to increase the moisture content. All the air systems distribute the heated air into the rooms through registers. Most gravity systems are old and obsolete and ready for replacement; however, gravity floor furnaces are still being installed in small houses. A space heater is another type of low-quality gravity system.

FIG. 12-11 HEATING SYSTEMS

ONE-PIPE SERIES CONNECTED HOT WATER SYSTEM

This system may be identified by looking up at the part of the basement ceiling that is directly under the first floor radiators. In a one-pipe series connected hot water system, one wide-diameter pipe will be seen going in and out of each radiator. There will be no small-diameter feeder pipes.

SINGLE PIPE INDIVIDUAL TAKE-OFF HOT WATER SYSTEM

Looking up at the area of the basement ceiling that is directly under the first floor radiators, one wide-diameter pipe will be seen under each radiator. Each of these pipes will be connected to its radiator by two smaller feeder pipes.

TWO-PIPE REVERSE RETURN HOT WATER SYSTEM

Looking up at the part of the basement ceiling that is directly under the first floor radiators, two wide-diameter pipes will be seen under each radiator. Each will be connected to its radiator by a smaller feeder pipe.

ONE-PIPE RETURN TEE FITTING

TWO-PIPE STEAM — CAST IRON RADIATOR

BASEBOARD CONVECTOR

TWO-PIPE HOT WATER SYSTEM — CAST IRON RADIATOR

ONE-PIPE STEAM — CAST IRON RADIATOR

FIG. 12-11 HEATING SYSTEMS

PERIMETER LOOP
WARM AIR SYSTEM

EXTENDED PLENUM
SYSTEM

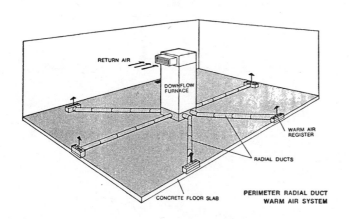

PERIMETER RADIAL DUCT
WARM AIR SYSTEM

GRAVITY HOT AIR SYSTEM

WALL REGISTER

BASE BOARD REGISTER

RETURN REGISTER

FLOOR REGISTER

CEILING REGISTER

AIR REGISTERS

--**Hot water systems** (also known as hydronic systems) hold heated water in a cast iron or steel boiler. Some old systems depend on gravity to circulate the water through the radiators. Most modern systems use one or more electric circulators to pump the heated water through pipes into either baseboard panels or convectors, radiators or tubes embedded in the floors, walls or ceilings. These units depend on both convection (air being warmed as it passes over the heated metal and then circulated into the room) and radiation (heat waves being transferred directly from the heated metal to the object being heated by radiant energy). There are also combination systems in which the heat is brought to the radiator by warm water. A fan in the radiator blows air over the radiator fins, heating the room by convection.

--**Steam heat** is produced by a furnace that is a boiler with a firebox underneath it. As the water boils, steam is created that is forced by its pressure through pipes into radiators.

--**Electricity** may be considered as either a fuel to heat air or water in a furnace or a source of heat itself. Its use with resistance elements produces heat at the immediate area to be heated. These resistance elements, which convert electricity into heat, are embedded in the floors, walls and ceilings to provide radiant heat. The advantages claimed for electric radiant heat are the lack of visible radiators or grilles and its ability to maintain adequate air humidity levels. Electric heat also provides the advantage of individual room temperature control.

--**Electric heating panels**, also with individual resistance elements, are often used for auxiliary heat.

Type of Fuel

The type of fuel used in any heating system must be considered as world fuel markets and prices change from day to day. Fuel needs and supplies have become a major factor in international economics and politics. Each fuel has its own significant advantages and disadvantages which change from time to time and differ from one region to another. Coal was once the most popular fuel but most coal systems are now obsolete; however, new systems are again being manufactured as a return to coal from oil and gas is being suggested.

--**Fuel oil** is still the least expensive fuel in the Northeast and Northwest sections of the United States and is competitively priced in many other areas as well.

--**Natural gas** offers the convenience of continuous delivery via pipeline without the necessity of storage tanks. In most areas of the country (the major exceptions being the Northeast and Northwest), gas has been the most economical fuel. Liquid petroleum gas is used in many rural areas. It requires on-premises storage tanks and is usually more expensive than natural pipeline gas. In other respects it is similar to natural gas.

--**Electricity** appears to be the fuel of the future. Electric systems are the least expensive to install since they require no furnace, furnace room, ducts, flue or plumbing. They do require, however, a much larger electric service into the house and wiring to each unit. To date, in spite of advertising to the contrary, electric heat costs remain high, except in lower-cost power areas.

--**Solar** is the least developed source of heat to date comes directly from the sun. Solar heat is still in the experimental stages. A variety of solar heating systems are on the market today and appraisers will have to stay current on solar heat developments to appraise a house with solar heating.

Cooling Systems

Until the late 1940's, most cooling was done with fans. In some areas of the West, where the humidity is low even in periods of high heat, a simple system which blows air across wet excelsior or some other water-absorbing material is used to cool the air. Most buildings being currently built have some type of air conditioning system.

--**Window (or sleeve) air conditioning units** are sold by the millions each year. Small 4,000- to 5,000-BTU units usually can be self-installed and plug into a regular duplex outlet. New units gaining popularity are those no longer requiring a sleeve or window mounting. The unit is split into two parts; the compressor hangs or stands on the outside and the fan is hung on the interior wall. Only a small hole in the wall is needed for the connecting tube and wire. The appraiser must determine whether by custom or law air conditioners are classified as real or personal property, and the appraisal report should clearly indicate which case applies.

--**Ducted central air-conditioning systems** may be custom made or pre-wired, pre-charged, factory-assembled packages that are connected at the home site. The condenser portion is set outside the house or on the roof. It is connected by pipe to the evaporator air-handling unit inside the house. The air-handling unit, consisting of the evaporator and a fan, is connected to a system of ducts that distributes cool air to areas of the house to be cooled. If the house has a warm forced-air heating system, the air-conditioning system can use the same fan, filter and duct work. However, the ducts may not be suitable for air conditioning because cooling generally requires double the duct size of heating, and the cooling system works much better if the registers are high on the wall or are the type that direct air steeply upward.

--**Heat pumps** are another device for both heating and cooling. The heat pump is actually a reversible refrigeration unit. In the winter it takes heat from the outside air or ground or well water and distributes it inside. Its efficiency decreases when it is very cold outside and it must be supplemented with resistance heating. In the summer the system cools be extracting heat from the inside of the house like a typical air-conditioning unit. Heat pumps constitute only a small percentage of systems being installed.

Plumbing Systems

The plumbing system is an integral part of any building; the materials used for this system determine its ability to supply adequate clean water and remove wastes over a long period of time. The pipes carrying clean water should work without leaking, making noise, reducing pressure or imparting any color or taste to the water. Brass was used for many years, but is now expensive. Older brass pipes tend to crystalize and become coated inside in areas where the water is corrosive. Galvanized steel is used in some areas; like brass, it is easy to work and is connected with threaded joints and fittings, but it easily attacked by corrosive water. Galvanized wrought iron is similar to steel but more resistant to corrosion. Copper and lead are also used; lead is still used for the pipe from the water main to the house. Plastic is the newest material for pipes. Although plastic piping is gaining acceptance, it is still not permitted in many cities.

FIG. 12-12 PLUMBING SYSTEM

PLUMBING SYSTEM

--**Water pipes** must be strong to withstand the pressure necessary for water to flow through them. Because there is no pressure in a waste drain line, the pipes must be slanted so that waste will flow from each fixture through the main lines into the sewer or sewage disposal system. Pipes for the drainage system are made of cast iron, copper, plastic, tile, brass, lead or fiber. Special fittings are often used, especially on cast iron pipes, to aid the flow of sewage.

--**Standard bathroom fixtures** consist of lavatories (wash basins), bathtubs, showers, and toilets (water closets). The best material for lavatories is cast iron covered with acid-resistant vitreous enamel. Newer ones are made of fiberglass. Bathtubs are the most expensive bathroom fixture. The most common materials are ceramic tile, steel or cast iron covered with vitreous enamel or fiberglass. Standard size is 5 1/2 feet long by 16 inches deep. Many tubs also have a shower unit because they are less expensive to build than a separate tub and shower stall. Separate shower stalls are often prefabricated steel or fiberglass units.

--**Residential toilets** mostly consist of a bowl and a tank that stores sufficient water to create proper flushing action. The toilet can be rated by its self-cleaning properties, its flushing action, the amount of noise during flushing, and the ease of cleaning around the exterior.

--**Kitchen plumbing fixtures** include a single or double sink, generally installed in a counter. The sink drain should have a removable crumb cup or combination crumb cup and stopper. Kitchen sinks may be made of acid-resistant enameled cast iron, enameled steel, stainless steel or Monel metal. A garbage disposal unit and/or a dishwasher may be connected to kitchen plumbing.

--**Bathroom and kitchen fittings** both include a series of faucets, spigots and drains, which require occasional repair or replacement. The most common type of faucet arrangement has two separate valves, one each for hot and cold water. Most faucets now being installed feed into a single spout and a further refinement is a single control valve that controls both the water temperature and volume. A shower should have an automatic diverter control that switches the flow of water back to the tub after each shower so that the next user will not accidentally get wet or scalded. Most modern kitchen sinks have a combination faucet with a swing spout. A separate spray on a flexible tube is also common. Another attachment now available for a kitchen sink provides boiling water instantly.

--**Specialized plumbing fixtures,** such as laundry tubs or a wet bar, may also be found in laundry and family recreation rooms.

Domestic Hot Water System

An adequate supply of hot water is essential. Buildings with inadequate hot water systems suffer from functional obsolescence. The supply is usually generated in a hot water heater, with optional storage tanks as a supplement. The heater may be powered by electricity, gas or oil as a separate unit; or hot water may be supplied from furnace heat. The latter system supplies only a small amount of hot water, which may be exhausted too quickly; another disadvantage is the need to run the furnace all year.

The recovery rate (the time it takes to heat water) determines the size tank needed. Standard gas hot water tanks range from 30 to 80 gallons. Because the recovery rate of an oil hot water heater is faster than gas or electricity, a 30-gallon tank provides enough hot water. They are not popular, however, because of the initial high cost and installation, especially if no flue or oil storage tank is already available.

In many areas of the country, large amounts of minerals such as calcium, magnesium, sulfates, bicarbonates, iron or sulphur are often found in the water. These minerals react unfavorably with soap, forming a curd-like substance which is difficult to rinse from clothing, hair and skin. A water softening system can be installed to eliminate these mineral deposits.

Electrical System

Most electrical services begins at a "service entrance" which brings power from outside utility wires through an electric meter to a distribution panel. The service entrance may be designed to bring in 30, 60, 100, 150, 200, 300, or 400 amperes of electricity. In smaller and older houses 30 or 60 ampere service may still be found. A 100-ampere service is the standard today for each dwelling unit that do not have electric heat or central air conditioning. It provides 23,000 watts of power. A typical panel box has 12 to 16 fuses or circuit breakers. In larger units, and where electric heat, central air conditioning or a large number of appliances are used, 150 to 400 ampere service is needed.

--The distribution box has a switch that cuts off all electric service in the house when manually pulled in the event of an emergency. It also must contain either a master fuse or circuit breaker that will automatically disconnect the entire system if the system overloads. A fuse is a piece of wire that will melt when more than the prescribed amount of electricity flows through it. A circuit breaker is a special type of automatic switch that switches off when excess electricity passes through it. The distribution box divides the incoming electric service into separate branch circuits. Each individual circuit must also be protected by a fuse or a circuit breaker. If an overload or short circuit occurs on the line, it automatically shuts off without tripping the main fuse or circuit breaker.

--Wiring comes in a variety of types. The most preferred type of wiring is through rigid steel pipe, which looks like water pipe. It is also the most expensive method. Wires are pulled through the pipe after it is installed. A less expensive system that has code approval in most cities makes use of armored (BX) cable which consists of insulted wires wrapped in heavy paper and encased in a flexible, galvanized steel covering wound in a spiral fashion. Surface raceways made of metal or plastic are sometimes used. Flexible steel conduit is constructed like BX cable except that it is installed without the wire, which is drawn through the conduit after installation.

--Nonmetallic cable is made of wire which is wrapped with a paper tape and then encased in a heavy water and fire resistant fabric. A similar system has cable with a thermoplastic insulation and jacket; the cables are attached to the joists and studs with staples. A now obsolete system involves running two parallel exposed wires from the panel box to outlets and fixtures. The wires are attached to the house with white porcelain insulators, called "knobs." When the wire passes through a wall or joist, it is placed through a white porcelain tube—hence the name "knob and tube wiring." This type of system should be replaced.

FIG. 12-13 ELECTRICAL SYSTEM

SERVICE FROM STREET UTILITY WIRES

WEATHER CAP

CONDUIT

METER

MAIN SWITCH

ON
OFF

CIRCUIT BREAKERS

BRANCH CIRCUITS

GROUND TO WATER PIPE OR GROUND ROD

BRANCH CIRCUITS

DISTRIBUTION PANEL

Here is the usual relationship between ampere service, number of circuit breakers and maximum number of watts:

Size of Service	No. of Branch Circuits (fuses or circuit breakers)	Maximum No. of Watts
30 ampere	4	6,900
60 ampere	6 to 8	13,800
100 ampere	12 to 16	23,000
150 or more amperes	20 or more	30,000 or more

ELECTRIC SERVICE ENTRANCE

--**Telephones and doorbells** use low voltage wiring that does not present a safety hazard and therefore can be run loose throughout the walls and along the joists. Intercommunication, central music and burglar alarm systems also use low voltage, hazard-free wiring.

--**The duplex receptacle** was until 1960 the most common type household outlet used. It accepts a two-prong plug, the type most often found on lamps and small appliances. In 1960 the National Electric Code required that all receptacles be of the grounding type, designed to accept a three-prong plug, to reduce shock hazard. Special waterproof receptacles with caps for outside use and other special purpose outlets are available.

--**Wall switches** control permanently installed light fixtures and wall outlets. The simplest and most common switch is a two-way snap switch. Three-way switches are used to control a fixture or outlet from different locations, which is useful, for example, for a light in a stairwell.

--**Low-voltage switching systems** are used for control in some buildings. Instead of the switch directly opening and closing the circuit, it controls a relay, which in turn, operates the switch. The advantage of this system is that many lights and outlets can be controlled from one place.

--**Adequate switching arrangements** allow one to walk anywhere in a building, turning on a path of light and then being able to turn it off without having to retrace steps or walk in the dark.

Sewers, Septic Tanks and Cesspools

Few will argue the substantial advantage of being connected to a municipal sewer system by a single outlet or separately into the sanitary and storm water disposal system. Freddie Mac and Fannie Mae require that, when available, the municipal sewer system be used. With increasing awareness of the damaging effects of pollution on our environment, rapid improvement and expansion of these systems can be expected in the near future. Health experts estimate that 50 percent of the septic systems now in use are not working properly. Still, it is estimated that almost 50 million people in 15 million homes, especially in the suburbs and rural areas, depend upon a septic system for their waste disposal and that 25 percent of new houses being constructed do not connect to municipal systems.

--**A septic system** typically consists of a large concrete tank with a capacity of 900 gallons (about 8' by 4' by 4') buried in the ground. One end accepts the waste material from the house drain line. Once inside the tank, the waste tends to separate into three parts. The solid waste materials (only about 1 percent of the total volume) sink to the bottom. The grease (also less than 1 percent of the total volume) rises to the top. The rest is liquid. Bacteria in the tank decompose the solid wastes and grease and a relatively clear liquid flows from the opposite end through the drain line either into a distribution box that directs the liquid into a network of buried perforated pipes called a leaching field or into a seepage pit. From here the liquid runs off into the ground to be absorbed.

FIG. 12-14 SEPTIC SYSTEM

DETAIL — ABSORPTION TRENCH

EARTH BACKFILL MIN. 12"

DRAIN TILE LAID WITH OPEN JOINTS

2"
6"
3' MAX.

GRAVEL, CRUSHED STONE OR SLAG MATERIAL

PROVIDE SEPARATION FROM BACKFILL BY COVERING WITH STRAW OR BUILDING PAPER

DISTRIBUTION BOX

ABSORPTION FIELD TRENCH (SEE DETAIL)

SEPTIC TANK (SEE DETAIL)

MANHOLE COVER
HANDHOLE COVER

MIN. 16"

LIQUID LEVEL

INLET
SANITARY TEE

INLET LEVEL

1" MIN.

OUTLET

SANITARY TEE

DETAIL — SEPTIC TANK

SEPTIC TANK AND ABSORPTION FIELD SYSTEM

The required capacity of the tank depends upon the size of the house and usage. The size of the leaching field depends on the soil's capacity to absorb water. The rate at which the soil will absorb water can be measured by making a percolation test. A hole at least 12 inches deep is dug in the ground and filled with water. Each hour the depth of the water is measured. Anything less than an inch decrease in depth each 30 minutes is substandard. This test should be carried out in the wettest season of the year and preferably by an expert. Usually the local health department will make the test at no cost or for a nominal charge. Also, it is likely that the local health authorities will have previous knowledge of the individual system.

--Septic tanks must be checked frequently to make sure they are not clogged and that the bacterial action is working properly. Chemicals must be used with care as they can kill bacteria. Often the tank must be pumped out and the cycle started anew.

--A cesspool is similar to a septic system except that instead of a tank there is a covered cistern of stone, brick or concrete. The liquid seeps out through the walls directly into the ground rather than into a leaching field or seepage pit. It is important to learn about a house's particular system, including the location of the clean-out main, which is often buried in an unmarked spot, so that inspections and repairs can be made as required. A properly working system should produce no odor which is one of the first signs of trouble. Learning the location of the clean-out main from the current owner saves a lot of digging and searching if it is buried

Anyone wishing to gain information on septic systems should find out how often the system has to be pumped out. In many towns the local health officer is very knowledgeable about many systems in the jurisdiction and of problems in a particular neighborhood.

--Septic system problems may sometimes be corrected by simply pumping out the tank. Sometimes new leaching fields are required. Unfortunately, there are situations when the soil absorption rate is poor or the water table is close to the surface and little can be done to make the system function properly.

MISCELLANEOUS SYSTEMS AND EQUIPMENT

A variety of mechanical systems and special equipment is being installed today. Many reflect fads or the special interests of the owner. They include such items as intercommunication and sound systems, burglar and fire alarms, automatic doors, elevators, incinerators, laundry chutes, and central vacuum cleaners. The appraiser must judge each situation to determine how much value these specialized items add. A further consideration in some cases is whether the items are realty or personalty.

ITEMS REQUIRING IMMEDIATE REPAIR

Except for buildings in an exceptional state of maintenance, there will almost always be items needing repair as of the date of the appraisal. The repair of these normal maintenance items should add more value to the property than the cost. In the cost approach, these items fall under "physical deterioration-curable." The repair list should include conditions observed by the appraiser that constitute a fire or safety hazard. Many clients request that these items be listed separately in the report. Sometimes the appraiser is requested to estimate the cost of each repair (cost to cure). Some of the most commonly found items of immediate repair are:

1. Touching up exterior paint.
2. Minor carpentry repairs to stairs, molding, siding, trim, floors, porches.
3. Redecorating interior rooms.
4. Fixing plumbing leaks and noisy plumbing.
5. Freeing stuck doors and windows.
6. Repairing holes in screens and replacing broken windows or other glass.
7. Re-hanging loose gutters and leaders.
8. Replacing missing roof shingles and tiles.
9. Fixing cracks in pavements.
10. Making minor electrical repairs.
11. Replacing rotted floor boards.
12. Exterminating vermin.
13. Fixing cracked or loose bathroom and kitchen tiles.
14. Repairing septic system.
15. Eliminating all fire and safety hazards.

DEFERRED MAINTENANCE ITEMS

Although the paint, roof, wallpaper, etc., may show some signs of wear and tear, it may not be ready for replacement on the date of the appraisal. The test is whether its repair or replacement will add more value to the property than its cost. For example, if a building has an exterior paint job that is three years old in an area where this type of paint lasts five years, the paint has suffered some depreciation. Repainting, however, probably would not add value to the property equal to its cost if it were done at the end of three years.

The following items normally have to be repaired or replaced before the end of the economic life of the building. They are known as short-lived items:

1. Interior paint and wallpaper.
2. Exterior paint.
3. Floor finishes.
4. Shades, screens and blinds.

5. Waterproofing and weatherstripping.
6. Gutters and leaders.
7. Storm windows.
8. Roof covering and flashing.
9. Hot and cold water pipes.
10. Plumbing fixtures.
11. Domestic hot water heater.
12. Electric service entrance.
13. Electric wiring.
14. Electric switches and outlets.
15. Electric fixtures.
16. Furnace.
17. Ducts and radiators.
18. Air conditioning equipment.
19. Carpeting.
20. Kitchen appliances.
21. Kitchen counters and cabinets.
22. Well pump.
23. Water softener system.
24. Laundry appliances.
25. Ventilating fans.
26. Fences and other site improvements.

The appraiser should note any of these or other short-lived items whose condition is better or worse than the overall condition of the building of which they are a part.

Overall Condition of Improvements

This section of the report is substantially completed when all items requiring immediate repair and all deferred maintenance are described. One last step, however, is to report the condition of items that should last the normal economic life of the building. Their condition is affected by abnormal wear and tear, and they can be damaged accidentally. They also may have been poorly made or installed. It would be a very unusual property where all the long-lived items were in exactly the same condition. For example, the clapboard siding may show signs of warping because of a roof leak; the condition may not be bad enough to warrant replacing the siding now. This case is a form of "physical deterioration-incurable."

INTERIOR DESIGN AND LAYOUT (FUNCTIONAL UTILITY)

The perfect residence is one that is the exact size, shape and design to produce the maximum profit. It would be the theoretical highest and best use of the site. Most residences are not the perfect or ideal improvements for their neighborhood. Room sizes, their number and type, and the design and layout differ from the idealized highest and best use. In fact, many things could be improved in the design and layout of a typical building. The appraiser is not on a quest for the perfect building but is trying to identify design elements that adversely affect value. These items constitute "functional obsolescence" in the cost approach.

Since most appraisers have little or no training in design, they tend to rely on their own likes and dislikes as a basis for making design judgments, an inappropriate basis on which to rely. It is better to learn what is generally accepted in the market as good design.

House Zones

A good way to consider the interior layout of a house it to divide it into zones. The private/sleeping zone contains the bedrooms, bathrooms and dressing rooms. The living/social zone consists of the living room, dining room, recreation room, den and enclosed porch. The working/service zone consists of the kitchen, laundry, pantry and other work areas. In addition to these three zones, are circulation areas consisting of halls and stairs plus guest and family entrances (see Fig. 12-15).

The three zones should be separated from one another so that activities in one zone do not interfere with those in another. The private/sleeping zone should be located so that it is insulated from noise in the other two zones, and it should be possible to move from the bedrooms to the bathrooms in this zone without being seen from the other areas of the house. The working/service zone is the nerve center of the house; from here the household activities are directed. From the kitchen, it should be possible to control both guest and family entrances, activities in the private/sleeping zone and living/social zone, plus activities in the porch, patio and backyard areas.

FIG. 12-15 ZONING ONE STORY HOUSE

ZONING: ONE-STORY HOUSE

The guest entrance should lead into the center of the house. From here there should be direct access to the living areas, guest closet and guest lavatory. A noise and visibility barrier should exist between the guest entrance and the private/sleeping zone.

Ideally the family entrance should be from the garage, carport, or breezeway into the kitchen or from a circulation area directly connecting to the kitchen. Traffic from this entrance should not have to pass through the work triangle of the kitchen to enter the other rooms of the house. Circulation should be such that one may move from working/service zone to the private/sleeping zone without going through the living/social zone.

If the house has a basement, it may have a separate outside entrance. The inside basement entrance should lead into a circulation area that has access to the private/sleeping zone, the living social zone and both the guest and family entrances, without going through the living room or the kitchen work triangle.

Common Floor Plan Deficiencies

According to a national survey of homeowners, some of the most common floor plan deficiencies include the following items. These will vary depending on the geographic region and the size and value of the residence.

1. Front door entering directly into the living room.
2. No front hall closet.
3. No direct access from front door to kitchen, bath or bedroom without passing through other rooms.
4. Rear door not convenient to kitchen and difficult to reach from the street, driveway and garage.
5. No comfortable area in or near the kitchen for family to eat.
6. A separate dining area or room not easily accessible from the kitchen.
7. Stairways off a room rather than in a hallway or foyer.
8. Bedrooms and baths that are visible from the living room or foyer.
9. Recreation or family room poorly located (not visible from kitchen).
10. No access to the basement from outside the house.
11. Walls between bedrooms not soundproof (separation by a bathroom or closet accomplish soundproofing).
12. Outdoor living areas not accessible and/or not visible from kitchen.

Living Room

Until World War II, the living room was the living center of the house. In the past several decades, the status of the living room has undergone a change. Today, the family room, patio and kitchen are more likely to be the locations for relaxing, socializing and entertaining. As these areas have grown and developed, the size and the importance of the living room has diminished.

The location of the living room may be in the traditional front of the house or, if view or access to outdoor living area is better, in the back or on a side of the house. The room should be positioned to supplement the dining and outdoor entertainment areas in the house. Often one end of the living room is the dining area, so it must have good juxtaposition with the kitchen/service areas as well. The living room should not be a traffic-way between other rooms. The following are some guidelines for judging the size of the living room compared with the rest of the house.

In a three-room house, the living room should have minimum dimensions of 11 by 16 feet, or at least 170 square feet. The recommended dimensions are 12 by 18 feet. If a dining area is at one end of the room, dimensions may go up to 16 by 26 feet or more. A maximum width of 14 feet is recommended for proper furniture arrangements around the room. Where traffic is necessary through the room, a width of 15 or 16 feet could conceivably be used to advantage by routing the traffic outside the conversation circle created by the furniture (see Fig. 12-16).

FIG. 12-16 LIVING ROOM CONVERSATION CIRCLE

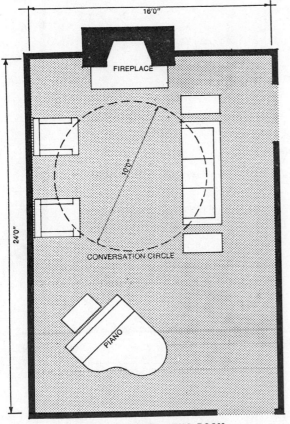

LONG AND WIDE LIVING ROOM

MINIMUM SIZE LIVING ROOM

Kitchen

Traditionally, the kitchen was located at the back of the house. Today it can be located wherever it best fits into the overall design and a current trend is to locate it at the front of the house. The kitchen should not be a main thoroughfare.

The size of the kitchen depends on the space available, the number of people in the family, the kind of equipment desired and what activities other than those directly associated with food preparation are carried on there. The minimum size for a kitchen in a small house is 8 by 10 feet. Better sizes are 10 by 10 and 10 by 12 feet.

Ten percent or more of the cost of a new home is spent on the kitchen. A functional kitchen should have adequate storage space, appliance space, counter and activity space, all arranged for maximum efficiency. The term triangle has become fashionable to describe the essential work zone of the kitchen, since there are three key work areas of use and activity: the refrigerator areas, sink/wash/preparation area and range/serving area. They can be arranged in any logical way, determined by the space available and the personal preference for one particular center over another (see Fig. 12-17).

FIG. 12-17 KITCHEN LAYOUTS

The total of the three sides of the Work Triangle should not exceed 22 feet.

However the kitchen is arranged, work should flow in a normal sequence from one center to another. Ideally, no traffic should move through the triangle in the main kitchen work area. Properly establishing the location of windows and doors will help to ensure a traffic pattern that does not interfere with efficient use of the kitchen. Most building standards require that the window area should equal at least 10% of the floor area of the room. At least one section of a work counter should have a window over it with provision for controlling direct sunlight. Many people prefer to have a window located over the sink. (For reasons of both safety and good housekeeping, the range should never be located under a window.)

Many kitchens suffer from one or more of the following inadequacies (listed in order of most common occurrence):

1. Insufficient base cabinet storage.
2. Insufficient wall cabinet storage.
3. Insufficient counter space.
4. No counter beside the refrigerator.
5. Not enough window area.
6. Poorly placed doors that waste wall space.
7. Traffic through the work triangle.
8. Too little counter space on either side of the sink.
9. No counter beside the range.
10. Insufficient space in front of cabinets.
11. Distance between sink, range and refrigerator too great.
12. Range under a window.

Dining Rooms and Dining Areas

A dining room was included in most pre-World War II homes. Now many houses have dining areas that are part of another room. The traditional space requirements for dining rooms probably no longer apply to many markets. A minimum size dining room is 9 by 11 feet, with 12 by 12 being preferable. In some markets an acceptable alternative to the dining room or area is an extra large "eat-in" kitchen. The appraiser must determine what the market wants and judge if the appraised house meets the requirements.

Bedrooms

The number of bedrooms in a house is an important design consideration. Three bedrooms is most common today. Houses with only two bedrooms are often constructed at the direction of an owner who does not need the third room; however, many markets do not accept only two bedrooms without a substantial discount. A fourth bedroom is appealing to many families, but in many markets the additional price a four-bedroom house brings is not as great as the cost of the extra bedroom. Of course, luxury homes may have five or more bedrooms. One bedroom homes are usually substandard in any market, except for recreational homes.

Two key factors in the location of bedrooms are that they be isolated from the noise generated in the rest of the house, and that one should be able to get from each bedroom to a bathroom without being seen from the living/social zone of the house. The minimum size bedroom for a single bed is 8 by 10 feet; this size is satisfactory only if the layout is good and no space is wasted. The minimum size room for a double bed is 10 by 11-1/2 feet. Some markets expect bedrooms to be more than minimum size; other markets will not pay the extra cost for the larger space.

Each bedroom should have at least one closet with a minimum depth of two feet, a width of three feet and a height sufficient to allow five feet clear hanging space. It should also have a shelf not over 74 inches above the floor of the room with at least eight inches clear space over the shelf.

Bathrooms and Lavatories

Houses with only one bathroom are obsolete in many markets; 1-1/2 baths is becoming a minimum standard, except in low-priced and recreation homes. The older minimum standard for two-story houses of one bath upstairs and a lavatory downstairs is being replaced in many markets with a standard of two baths. The minimum size for a bathroom containing a five-foot tub/shower combination, basin and toilet is 5 by 7 feet. This allows for the toilet to be on the wall opposite the tub rather than between the tub and basin, which is unsatisfactory; it also allows the door to swing in without hitting a fixture (see Fig. 12-18). A bathroom should not be located between two bedrooms with a door leading directly into the bathroom from each bedroom. (This is, however, a common feature of many Victorian homes).

The terminology used to describe bathrooms and lavatories varies around the country. In most areas a full bath consists of a room with a toilet (also known as a water closet), wash basin (also known as a sink, lavatory or vanity) and a tub. A 3/4 bathroom has a toilet, wash basin and stall shower (called a full bath in some areas). A half-bath (also known as a lavatory, lavette, or powder room) has a toilet and washbasin.

FIG. 12-18 BATHROOM LAYOUT

BATHROOM WITH TWO LAVATORIES

MINIMUM SIZE BATHROOM

BATHROOM WITH CLOSETS AS SOUND BARRIERS

BATHROOM — COMPARTMENTED

MINIMUM SIZE LAVATORY

The bathroom requires the most heat and the best ventilation of any room in the house.   A bathroom or lavatory with or without a window is equally acceptable, but ventilation of an interior bathroom or lavatory is essential. A ventilation fan, ducted to the outside, should be wired to the light switch so that it goes on automatically when the room is in use and turns off automatically when the lights are turned off.

Family and Recreation Rooms

Before World War II attics, dens and finished basements generally were used as additional recreation space. Today the family room is used as a den, study, guest room, nursery, library, TV room, or hobby entertainment center. The key to the successful location of this room is to have it visible from and easily accessible to the kitchen. It also should be accessible to the outdoor living area, such as the backyard or patio. A good size for the recreation room in a small house is 12 by 16 feet. Appraisers should remember that many family or recreation rooms are overimproved or too large for a particular market.

Patios and Porches

In some areas patios are very elaborate and an integral part of the house. They can be described as part of the improvements rather than a site improvement. Porches have been decreasing in popularity and importance for many years except in a few areas of the country. The exceptions seem to be sun and side porches on more expensive homes, the Hawaiian "lanai" (a covered or open porch) and screened-in porches in beach and summer homes. Some styles have special porch features, such as the Victorian wrap-around porch, which will usually add value.

Laundry Rooms and Storage Areas

A growing trend has been to bring the washing machine and clothes dryer out of the basement. These appliances are being installed in the kitchen, a separate laundry or utility room, the garage, or even in hallways or closets on the first or second floors. Anyone who has lived in a house with a basement finds it hard to understand why they are not more universally accepted. A house without a basement may suffer from a lack of adequate storage space, which will be penalized by the market. Alternate acceptable storage areas are attics, closets, storage rooms, garages, storage sheds, etc.

RENOVATION: REHABILITATION, MODERNIZATION AND REMODELING

Often the appraiser finds that substantial renovations are necessary if the existing improvement is to achieve the highest and best use of the site. These alterations and improvements go beyond the normal curable physical deterioration and functional obsolescence. The owner of the property may have come to a similar conclusion before the appraisal and may already have done some or all of the work.

These substantial changes can be described by the terms rehabilitation, modernization and remodeling. Each term has a specific meaning with which the appraiser should be familiar:

--Rehabilitation. The restoration of a property to satisfactory condition without changing the plan, form or style of a structure. In urban renewal, the restoration to good condition of deteriorated structures, neighborhoods, and public facilities. Neighborhood rehabilitation encompasses structural rehabilitation and in addition may extend to street improvements and a provision of such amenities as parks and playgrounds.

--Modernization. Taking corrective measures to bring a property into conformity with changes in style, whether exterior or interior or additions necessary to meet standards of current demand. It normally involves replacing parts of the structure or mechanical equipment with modern replacements of the same kind.

--Remodeling. Changing the plan, form or style of a structure to correct functional or economical deficiencies.

Rehabilitation

A growing trend in many cities throughout the country is the restoration of older neighborhoods and homes. People are moving back into city neighborhoods, and older homes in center city locations are now attracting young professionals, business people and white-collar workers. Some older homes are not much more than four good walls and sturdy ceilings; more often the interior floors and walls are usable. The woodwork can be restored and although the mechanical systems usually have to be replaced, some parts of the original systems may be usable. The appraisal of this type of property often requires the appraiser to help plan the rehabilitation.

Modernization

Modernization implies replacement or remodeling specifically designed to offset the effect of obsolescence or making additions necessary to meet current design standards. The replacement of old radiators and lighting or plumbing fixtures with new items of fundamentally the same type, is nothing more than improving the condition of the old installation. However, the substitution of convectors for cast-iron radiators, of built-in bathtubs for tubs on legs, or of modern lighting fixtures for old-fashioned types would not necessarily reflect on the physical condition of the items being replaced and therefore would constitute an improvement of the property. These expenditures offset obsolescence and may be classified as modernization. Modernization may cost more than simple renewal but can be economically justified where it offsets the obsolescence inherent in the older equipment.

Modernization usually extends the economic life of property. To be justified, a modernization is done because the owner desires the convenience it creates. The installation of a modern kitchen at a cost of $10,000 may add only $5,000 in value. This is an example of a superadequacy or overimprovement.

Remodeling

Remodeling becomes practical when the use of part of the house can be changed. Common examples are finishing a basement or attic or adding a bathroom to an existing room. Considerable remodeling is often done to suit the needs of a specific owner without much thought given what the market in general expects and will pay for. The expenditure of $6,000 to finish a basement playroom may add only $3,000 to the property value in some markets.

RENOVATION COSTS

It is much more difficult to estimate renovation or rehabilitation costs than that of new construction. Unit-in-place costs for new work, plus an additional allowance for the normally higher cost of repair work, aid in making renovation estimates difficult. Rehabilitation estimates frequently may be based upon actual recent costs for the same or equivalent work performed in the property or in similar properties. Management records may even include bids for specific rehabilitation items that have not been accomplished, such as exterior painting, roof repair, or interior decorating.

The cost of some rehabilitation work may approximate that for similar work in new construction. However, the cost of modernization or remodeling work is almost invariably higher than that for new construction, for several reasons. Although the quantity of materials may be the same as for new work, more labor is involved and the conditions are different. The alteration of a structure usually involves tearing out old work and performing small portions of new work under conditions not conducive to the degree of efficiency attainable on new construction. If the estimate made by the contractor is on a flat-fee basis, the charge may be substantially higher than the cost of identical work in new construction, so the contractor can be protected against complications that may develop as the remodeling progresses. Such unforeseen complications may involve the placement of existing conduits, pipes, and structural loadbearing members.

Other costs to be considered are those that may be incurred by the owner rather than the contractor. These include the architect's fee, the owner's cost of supervision and loss of use of the house while the work is being done.

FEASIBILITY OF RENOVATION

Whether rehabilitation, modernization or remodeling is involved, the justification for any renovation program depends on what constitutes the highest and best use of the property. The study that the appraiser gives to this question produces the cost estimates necessary for a program to achieve such use, which in turn provide the basis for a decision as to its economic justification.

If the property is old but in sufficiently sound condition for remodeling, if the neighborhood standards and trends are materially higher than the property's present status, and if the prospective value increase is substantial, a comprehensive program may be feasible. A wide range of potential programs may justify consideration, but there is only one satisfactory way to select the final plan. This is to explore the alternatives, estimate the cost and potential value increases and then be guided by the results of a comparison of the data.

Assume that a brownstone townhouse is available in a neighborhood going through a period of redevelopment. The house can be purchased for $60,000. It is estimated that it will take about $40,000 to rehabilitate the house to meet the minimum code requirements. The estimated value when the rehabilitation is completed is $120,000. Based on these figures, the rehabilitation to meet minimum standards is feasible. A second possibility is to restore the house to its original historical appearance and do a much more elaborate renovation. The estimated cost of this renovation would be $120,000, but the final value would be $240,000.

Renovation Example 1:

Acquisition price	$60,000
Rehabilitation cost	$40,000
Total Cost	$100,000
Estimated value after renovation	$120,000

	Estimated profit	$20,000
Renovation Example 2:	Acquisition price	$60,000
	Renovation cost	$120,000
	Total cost	$180,000
	Estimated value after renovation	$240,000
	Estimated profit	$60,000

Both the above programs are feasible. However, Example 2 represents the highest and best use of the property, since it produces the maximum profit. In some cases where the profit potential, due to a program of rehabilitation, modernization and modeling is substantial, the "as is" value estimate for the property being appraised should be modified upward. In many cities properties have been purchased at relatively low prices by imaginative investors who have undertaken programs of selective modernization, sometimes involving new exterior ("skin") treatment and other major expenditures. Modernized and attractive properties thus created have become marketable at levels substantially higher than the investments involved. Whether this is practical in any specific situation can be ascertained only by completion of a before-and-after feasibility analysis.

In the final analysis, the appraiser's estimate of a renovation program is part of the process used to arrive at a value estimate for the property. Whether or not the owner actually carries out such a program, the value of the property in its existing state may be influenced by its potential for increased value under a feasible renovation program.

GRAPHIC AIDS

PHOTOGRAPHY

Use of photographs has become an important part of the appraisal report. Out-of-focus, over or under-exposed amateur photos are no long acceptable as part of a professional appraisal report. Instant photography methods are acceptable to some clients. Others require more professional pictures taken with a conventional camera. A 35mm camera is the choice of many experienced appraisers, because of the rectangular shape of the photographs, the versatility of the equipment, the availability of film and low cost for color reproduction. The use of color photographs has become standard.

There is no absolute rule as to what the photographs should include. However, at a minimum, photographs of all sides of the improvements and any major site improvements, plus a shot of the street in both directions showing the subject in the foreground, may be required. When the assignment warrants the extra expense, photographs of construction details and of the interior may also be included.

PLOT PLAN

A plot plan shows the lot boundaries, important topographical features and the location of the improvements. A well-drawn plot plan is made to scale, with lot dimensions indicated on the boundary lines. In addition to the house and garage or carport, it should show the position of sidewalks, driveways, patios, pools, etc. Any abutting rights-of-way, known easements or apparent encroachments should also be shown. An appraiser is not expected to be a professional draftsperson but the plot plan should be neat and carefully drawn.

SKETCH OF THE BUILDINGS

Often a simple sketch of the exterior walls of the buildings (and garage or carport, if any) or a more complete drawing showing the location of doors, windows and interior walls is included as part of the report. Many appraisers take special pride in their ability to produce professionally drawn sketches. Such drawings are not required for a typical appraisal; a simple, neatly drawn sketch to approximate scale, showing the important dimensions, will usually suffice. The dimensions that appear on the sketch should be the same ones used to calculate the gross living area.

READING A HOUSE PLAN

The appraiser who is appraising a house planned for construction, under construction or being considered for a program of renovation must be able to read the plans that detail the proposed construction. Architects use orthographic projections to picture the proposed work rather than perspective drawings. An orthographic projection permits proportional reduction of the drawing while maintaining the size and spatial relationships of the completed house. Lines drawn parallel in an orthographic projection represents walls that are parallel in the finished house.

A complete set of house plans consists of:

1. Orthographic projections of each floor and the basement.
2. Electric plans.
3. Plumbing plans.
4. Wall sections.
5. Elevations of all sides.
6. Plot plan.
7. Door and window schedules.
8. Specifications.

The dimensions of an actual house may not appear to agree with those indicated on the house plans. It is impossible to tell from looking at the plans what the actual points of measurement are. An actual measurement read on the tape may be from one inch to more than five inches less than the dimension indicated on the plan. Architects seldom indicate dimensions from one wall surface to another. On drawings of frame houses, they prefer to indicate the dimensions between the surface of the studs of opposite walls or from the center of the opposite wall studs. When stud-surface-to-stud-surface is used, the actual tape measurements are about one inch less than the indicated dimension line measurement, which is the thickness of the sheetrock. When the center of the stud is used as the point of measurement, the tape reading is about five inches less, since half the thickness of the stud is usually two inches plus the thickness of the sheetrock.

The techniques for dimensioning masonry construction are different from those for frame construction. Dimension lines on masonry construction plans usually run from one masonry surface to another, rather than to the surface of the sheetrock or other wall coverings.

To read house plans, it is necessary to know the many symbols architects use to represent the materials, electric switches and outlets, plumbing fixtures and pipes, some of which appear on the following pages.

SUMMARY

The description of the improvements is an important part of the appraisal report. It provides the information used in the three approaches to value. It includes a description of all the improvements to the site as well as a complete description of the residence and any ancillary improvements. Information about all the physical components including their design, quality and condition is included. A list of items requiring immediate repair, plus a list of items that will require repair in the near future, should also be given. When appropriate, any feasible renovations should be specified.

SHINGLE COVERED
GABLE ROOF

PARTS
RESEMBLE
FURNITURE
LEGS

TOWER OR
TURRET

OPEN
FRONT
PORCH

ROWS OF
SPINDLES

Nineteenth Century American

EASTLAKE (East L - 709)

13 Cost Approach

The Cost Approach like the other two approaches to value is based on the assumption that the cost to produce a building plus the cost to acquire and improve the site to make it suitable for building is a good indication of what a property is worth.

Every real estate parcel is different, so that location is a very important component of value. Unlike other commodities where suitable substitutes are easily found, the cost of a property is not as perfect an indication of its value as it is for these other commodities, i.e., automobiles, diamonds, gold, etc.

There are some appraisers and some important buyers of appraisals who do not believe the Cost Approach is useful in residential appraising. The Employee Relocation Council has eliminated it from its required relocation form (see Addenda K). Others (including the author) believe it works well on residences, especially if the reproduction cost is obtained from a computerized cost service and the depreciation is taken from the market by the abstraction process which is explained later in this chapter.

Cost is not necessarily or automatically the equivalent of market value. The procedure for developing the estimated value of the improvements requires the conversion of "cost to construct" figures to market value figures. The process of making such a conversion requires care, caution and skill.

A separate valuation of the improvements is needed for a variety of reasons, and the Cost Approach is one of the ways to obtain it. These reasons include tax purposes (where ad valorem tax laws dictate this separation in value), accounting (where it is used to report the depreciation of buildings) and to obtain the value of the land by the land residual method. The cost approach is especially useful when estimating the value of special purpose properties where there is no market.

STEPS OF THE COST APPROACH

1. Estimate the value of the site and site improvements (this technique is described elsewhere in this text).

2. Estimate the Reproduction Cost of the improvements (some appraisers use Replacement Cost; when Replacement Cost is used it should be noted in the comments section).

3. Estimate the amount of depreciation from all causes and categorize it into the three major types of depreciation: Physical Deterioration, Functional Obsolescence and External Obsolescence.

4. Deduct the total estimated depreciation from the reproduction or replacement cost of the improvements to derive the amount of value the improvements contribute to the property.

5. Add together the value of the site, the value contributed by the site improvements and landscaping, and the cost of all the improvements less the applicable depreciation.

ESTIMATE THE VALUE OF THE SITE

The value of the site is normally estimated assuming it is unimproved and ready to be used for its highest and best use.

"Under certain circumstances, the appraisal of a property may require that the site be considered in terms other than its highest and best use. In appraisal to estimate the use value or legal, nonconforming use value of an improved site, an appraiser may often need to value the site according to its specified use or the existing improvements, not its highest and best use. In this case, the appraiser should value the site both in terms of its highest and best use and its conditional use."[1]

In the past the estimate of site value was part of the Cost Approach in the Valuation Process. Now it is considered to be a separate step. It is covered in Chapter 10 "Site Valuation" in this text.

ESTIMATE THE COST NEW OF THE IMPROVEMENTS

REPRODUCTION COST VERSUS REPLACEMENT COST

Reproduction cost is the dollar amount required to construct an exact duplicate of the subject building, at current prices.

Replacement cost is the cost of creating a residence and other improvements having the same or equivalent utility, using current standards of material and design, based on current prices for labor and materials.

Theoretically, reproduction cost is easier to use but as a matter of practicality it becomes quite difficult to estimate for older buildings, because identical materials are not always available and construction methods and design are constantly changing. The use of replacement cost provides a practical alternative. It represents the funds required to build an equally desirable substitute building, not necessarily with identical materials or to the same specifications.

For example, reproduction cost for an older house erected with solid brick walls would be computed on the basis of identical construction today. On the other hand, an estimate of replacement cost would not necessarily imply a structure with solid brick walls.   Quite possibly current design and construction standards in the neighborhood for a house of this type, style and value would be frame construction with brick veneer walls. Accordingly, by using replacement cost instead of

---

[1]*Appraisal of Real Estate*, 9th Edition, American Institute of Real Estate Appraisers, Chicago, IL.

reproduction cost, some of the obsolescence or "inutility" present in the house with solid masonry walls would be eliminated from the estimate before deductions for accrued depreciation are made.

Care must be exercised not to take double depreciation. In the above example, the solid masonry walls have already been treated by using replacement cost of a frame house with brick veneer walls. A penalty should not again be deducted under functional obsolescence.

TYPES OF COSTS

For both reproduction cost and replacement cost estimates, costs can be broken down into direct or hard costs and indirect or soft costs. To these are added the developer's entrepreneurial profit.

Direct (Hard) Costs

These are costs of labor, materials, and contractors and subcontractors overhead and profit. It does not include the profit hoped to be made by the developer (who may or may not be the contractor).

Typically direct costs consist of the following:

1. Labor.
2. Materials.
3. Equipment.
4. Contractor profit and overhead.
5. Security during construction.
6. Temporary construction building.
7. Temporary fencing and walls.
8. Utilities used during construction.
9. Storage of materials during construction.
10. Contractor's performance bond.

Indirect (Soft) Costs

These are all the other costs associated with the construction of a building not included in the direct costs.

Typical indirect (soft) costs consist of the following:

1. Professional services.
   a. Architect's fees.
   b. Engineer's fees.
   c. Surveyor's fees.
   d. Legal fees and expenses.
   E. Appraisal fees.
2. Developer's overhead.
3. Building permits and licenses.
4. Insurance premiums.
5. Interest.
6. Taxes.
7. Selling expenses (commissions, advertising, promotion).
8. Carrying costs from time of completion to sale or occupancy.

Entrepreneurial Profit

Many appraisers feel that an additional amount should be added to the direct and indirect cost to represent entrepreneurial profit. Since not all developers make a profit, this figure should represent the typical anticipated developer profit.

ESTIMATING REPRODUCTION OR REPLACEMENT COST

There are three methods for estimating the reproduction or replacement cost of a building:

1. **Square foot method,** in which the cost per square foot of a recently built comparable structure is multiplied by the number of square feet in the subject property.

2. **Unit-in-place method,** in which the construction cost per square foot of each component part of the subject building (including material, labor, overhead, and builder's profit) is multiplied by the number of square feet of that component part in the subject building.

3. **Quantity survey method,** in which the cost of erecting or installing all of the component parts of a new building are added. Indirect costs (building permit, land survey, overhead expenses such as insurance and payroll taxes, and builder's profit) are totaled, as well as direct costs (site preparation and all phases of building construction, including fixtures).

The quantity survey method is the one generally used by cost estimators, contractors, and builders. Of the three methods, the quantity survey method results in the most accurate cost estimate, since all of the building's components are analyzed. The square foot and unit-in-place methods are generalized cost figures for either comparable building type (square foot method) or specific buildings components (unit-in-place method). Of the two methods, the unit-in-place method is more exact, since it allows for more variables in the subject building.

Square Foot Method

To begin the square foot method of estimating reproduction cost, the appraiser must find the dimensions of the subject building to compute the number of square feet of ground area the building covers. In collecting cost data to use in the square foot method, the appraiser must find the cost of a comparable new building. Since a comparable new building may not be available, the appraiser usually relies on cost manuals for basic construction prices.

A page from a typical cost manual appears in Fig. 13-1. The type of building is specified and construction features are itemized, with utilities (mechanical features) listed separately. If the closest example in the cost manual still has significant differences from the subject building, a cost differential could be added to (or subtracted from) the cost per square foot given in the cost manual. Computer services are available which also produce cost data for appraisers. (See Fig. 13-2).

FIG. 13-1 PAGE FROM A COST MANUAL

Square Foot Method
Average Quality
TOWN HOUSES AND DUPLEXES

Average Quality Town Houses and Duplexes are usually constructed to local building code and will exceed the minimum requirements of mortgage insuring agencies. Overall architectural design is simple with attention given only to the front elevation to distinguish one unit from another. The overall quality of materials and workmanship is average.

FOUNDATION .... Concrete perimeter foundation with continuous foundation under interior bearing walls, based on a moderate climate. Use Square Foot Adjustments for mild or extreme climate foundations, dividing by number of stories.

FLOOR STRUCTURE...... Wood structure and subfloor on first and upper story floors. For concrete slab on grade, deduct using Square Foot Adjustment per square foot of slab area.

FLOOR COVER .... Floor cover is not included in the basic residence cost. Floor covering includes carpet, hardwood and asphalt or vinyl composition tile or sheet. The floor cover allowance is a weighting of those typically found at this quality, and can be used if floor cover is not itemized.

EXTERIOR WALL .... Adequate fenestration using standard grade sash. The basic cost is wood frame with stucco. For other wall types, use percentage adjustments provided below the cost table.

ROOF .... Wood structure with lightweight composition shingles or built-up with small rock. Use Square Foot Adjustments for other types of roofing, dividing by number of stories.

INTERIOR FINISH .... Interior walls are taped and painted drywall. Ceilings are usually sprayed drywall with some enamel paint in kitchen and bath. Adequate wardrobe type bedroom, guest, and shelved linen closets. Cabinets in kitchen are hardwood veneer or paint grade wood. The cabinet tops are laminated plastic or ceramic tile with splash. Interior doors are stock, hollow core or flat panel, with standard grade hardware.

HEATING/COOLING ..... The basic residence cost includes a forced air heating system with adequate output and ductwork. Use Square Foot Adjustments for other types of Heating and/or Cooling.

ENERGY PACKAGE ...... The energy package in the base cost includes those insulation, framing and glazing items typically found in a moderate climate, as outlined in the Introduction to the Square Foot Method. Square Foot Adjustments should be made for deviations from the moderate climate base.

ELECTRICAL .... Adequate number of outlets and standard grade fixtures.

PLUMBING .... Seven competitively priced white plumbing fixtures and one plumbing rough-in are included in the base cost. The fixtures can include any of the following: water heater, toilet, lavatory, tub, tub with shower over, tile or fiberglass stall shower, or kitchen sink. Use Lump Sum Adjustments for deviations from seven fixtures and one plumbing rough-in.

BUILT-IN APPLIANCES ... None are included in the base residence cost. The built-in appliance allowance is a weighting of those typically found at this quality level, and can be used when appliances are not itemized.

PORCHES/BALCONIES .. Similar to the base residence in both quality of materials and workmanship, porches and balconies are priced per square foot of floor area.

BASEMENT, UNFINISHED Costs are inclusive of poured concrete or concrete block walls, concrete slab, floor drains, the necessary columns and beams to support the living area above, and an adequate number of electrical outlets.

BASEMENT, FINISH ...... As an additive cost to an unfinished basement, costs are provided for two degrees of finish: minimal and partitioned. The minimal finish is typical of game rooms and the partitioned finish is somewhat similar in both quality of materials and workmanship to that of the base residence.

GARAGES................ Garage costs include a reinforced concrete slab floor, an overhead door and electrical lighting, all of which conform to the residence in both quality and construction.

For Bi-level construction, price as a one story with basement and add partitioned basement finish. For two and one half story residences with a finished upper level, enter the two story cost column at the total floor area of all three levels, and multiply that cost by .956.

3/88
page A-142

TOWN HOUSES AND DUPLEXES
Square Foot Costs
Average Quality

FRAME AND STUCCO COSTS PER UNIT:

Sq. Ft. Floor Area	END ROW				INSIDE ROW			
	1 Story	1-1/2 Story	2 Story	Split level	1 Story	1-1/2 Story	2 Story	Split level
700	$36.79	$32.97	$35.37	$35.92	$34.71	$31.11	$33.31	$33.89
800	35.78	32.06	34.40	34.93	33.75	30.25	32.39	32.95
900	34.91	31.27	33.56	34.08	32.93	29.51	31.60	32.15
1000	34.14	30.59	32.83	33.33	32.21	28.87	30.91	31.45
1100	33.47	29.99	32.18	32.68	31.57	28.29	30.30	30.82
1200	32.86	29.45	31.60	32.09	31.00	27.78	29.75	30.27
1400	31.82	28.51	30.60	31.07	30.01	26.90	28.81	29.30
1600	30.94	27.72	29.75	30.21	29.18	26.16	28.02	28.49
1800	30.19	27.05	29.03	29.47	28.47	25.52	27.33	27.80
2000	29.53	26.46	28.40	28.83	27.85	24.96	26.74	27.19
2200	28.94	25.93	27.84	28.26	27.30	24.47	26.21	26.65
2400	28.42	25.47	27.33	27.75	26.80	24.02	25.74	26.17

FRAME: Plywood/Hardboard, − 2%; Siding/Shingle, + 1%; Masonry Veneer, + 8%; **MASONRY:** Common Brick, + 12%; Concrete Block, + 4%

SQUARE FOOT ADJUSTMENTS:

ROOFING: (Divide by number of stories)
Comp. shingle/B.U. rock....	(base)
Wood shingle	+ $ .76
Wood shake	+ .92
Concrete tile	+ 2.05
Composition roll	− .49

SUBFLOOR:
Wood subfloor	(base)
Concrete slab..............	− $1.69

FLOOR COVER:
Allowance (if not itemized)	+ $1.51
Hardwood	+ 3.82
Carpet	+ 1.48
Resilient floor cover	+ 1.39
Lt. wt. concrete	+ .53

PLASTER INTERIOR: .... + $ .78

LUMP SUM ADJUSTMENTS PER UNIT:
PLUMBING: 7 fixtures + rough-in
Per fixture .... + or −	$530
Rough-in .... + or −	215

FIREPLACES:
Single, 1 story....	$1,100 - $1,575
Single, 2 story.	1,450 - 1,950
Single, 3 story.	1,800 - 2,325

BASEMENT: Outside entrance: $695

HEATING/COOLING:
Forced air	(base)
Oil fired	+ $ .56
Floor or wall furnace	− .96
Gravity furnace	− .08
Electric, radiant	− .05
Baseboard or panel	− .13
Hot water, baseboard......	+ .91
Warm & cooled air	+ 1.28
Heat pump, packaged......	+ 1.38

ENERGY ADJ.: Moderate climate (base)
Mild climate	− $ .91
Extreme climate...........	+ 1.19

FOUNDATION: (Divide by no. of stories)
Moderate climate...........	(base)
Mild climate	− $ .94
Extreme climate...........	+ .94

BUILT-IN APPLIANCES:
Allowance (if not itemized)	+ $1,290
Range & oven.............	+ 595
Hood & Fan..............	+ 140
Dishwasher	+ 385
Garbage disposer	+ 140
Exhaust fan or bath heater .	+ 90
Wall air cond., 3/4 ton	+ 465

Unfinished, basement:	End Row				Inside Row			
	200	400	800	1600	200	400	800	1600
Concrete walls	$16.16	$11.91	$ 8.78	$ 6.47	$14.94	$11.01	$ 8.12	$ 5.98
Concrete block walls	14.11	10.40	7.66	5.65	13.05	9.62	7.09	5.22
	Minimal Finish				Partitioned Finish			
Add for finish	$ 3.61	$ 3.26	$ 2.95	$ 2.68	$15.66	$13.51	$11.65	$10.06

PORCH/BALCONY: Exterior stairways per flight: Wood: $555, Cement comp.: $935

Area	Floor Structure:				Wall Enclosure:		Add For Roof	Add For Ceiling
	Open Slab	Open W/Steps	Wood Deck	Cement Comp. Deck	Screen Only	Knee Wall W/Glass		
25	$ 3.31	$ 8.22	$10.49	$12.19	$ 6.62	$32.78	$ 5.88	$ 1.79
50	2.83	7.30	9.44	10.97	4.63	22.93	5.32	1.62
100	2.43	6.48	8.51	9.88	3.25	16.04	4.82	1.47
300	1.90	5.36	7.21	8.36	1.85	9.10	4.11	1.25

GARAGE:

	Area	Plywood or Hardboard	Stucco	Siding or Shingle	Masonry Veneer	Common Brick	Concrete Block	Add For Finish
Attached	200	$12.95	$13.24	$13.33	$14.50	$15.54	$13.74	$ 2.58
	400	11.34	11.60	11.67	12.70	13.48	12.01	2.40
Detached	200	$18.47	$18.90	$19.10	$21.70	$23.78	$19.86	$ 3.29
	400	14.10	14.43	14.56	16.30	17.60	15.08	2.75
Built-in	200	$ 9.30	$ 9.57	$ 9.46	$10.31	$11.00	$ 9.67	$ .70
	400	7.90	8.13	8.17	8.71	9.20	8.14	.53

Basement Garages, add lump sum to unfin. bsmt. costs: Single: $ 960, Double: $1,295
Carports: Shed or Flat roof: $5.75, Gable roof: $6.70

FIG. 13-2   COMPUTER PRODUCED COST ESTIMATE

REPRODUCTION COST

The reproduction cost of the house was obtained by using the Marshall and Swift cost service. Information about the suject house was inputed into an office computer using the Marshall and Swift software. The cost calculations were printed on our printer as shown below:

```
City, State, ZIP: Bloomville, IL, 60611
Surveyed by    : Henry S. Harrison
Date of Survey : March 12, 198

Single Family Residence          Floor Area: 1,888 square feet
Effective Age: 30 years          Quality: Average
Cost as of 3/8                   Condition: Average

              Style:  One Story
   Heating & Cooling:  Baseboard, Hot Water
       Exterior Wall:  Face Brick
             Roofing:  Composition Shingle
     Floor Structure:  Wood Subfloor
         Floor Cover:  Standard Allowance
            Plumbing:  Standard Allowance
           Appliances: Standard Allowance
      Other Features:  Single Fireplace

                                  Units     Cost      Total
                                  ---------------------------
Basic Structure Cost...........   1,888    53.35    100,721
                                  ---------------------------
Garage:
  Attached Garage..............     506    16.15      8,170
                                  ---------------------------
Extras:
  Roofed Porch w/Steps.........     144    13.44      1,935
  Domestic Solar Hot Water Unit.                      3,500
  Subtotal.....................                       5,435
                                  ---------------------------
Replacement Cost New.:.........   1,888    60.55    114,326
                                  ---------------------------
Less Depreciation:
  Physical Depreciation.........  <40.0%>            <45,730>
  Functional Depreciation.......   <7.9%>             <9,000>
  Locational Depreciation.......   <5.0%>             <5,716>
  Subtotal.....................   <52.9%>           <60,446>
Depreciated Cost...............   1,888    28.54     53,880
                                  ---------------------------
Miscellaneous:
  Land.........................                      20,000
  Site Improvements............                       3,000
  Subtotal.....................                      23,000
                                  ---------------------------
Total..........................   1,888    40.72     76,880
                                  ---------------------------
Cost data by MARSHALL and SWIFT
```

Unit-In-Place Method

The unit-in-place method is also called the segregated-cost method. It employs unit costs for various building components as they are normally installed.

A unit-in-place cost estimate is made by breaking up a building into components and estimating the cost of the material and labor required to install that unit into the building that is being built, theoretically, on the date of the appraisal.

Unit-in-place cost estimates are made in terms of standard costs for each of the building components as installed.

Many contractors use numerous subcontractors, who have special expertise in certain areas and often can do the work better and cheaper than a general contractor. Typically, general contractors who use a substantial number of subcontractors figure the cost of a building by breaking it down into components corresponding to the work done by the various subcontractors. Popular cost services also use this technique, calling it the segregated cost method. It is based on the use of unit prices for the various building components, using workable units such as square foot or linear foot or some other appropriate basic unit.

In Fig. 13-3 a typical list of house construction components is given. The cost estimates for these components are made in terms of standardized unit costs for installation. Providing that the units accurately reflect costs, this estimate is a short cut to an actual quantity survey. The resulting figure should correspond in accuracy with that derived from a quantity survey.

Based on the summary in Fig. 13-3 an appraiser would estimate the reproduction cost new at $160,000. Note that this example is not in itself a complete quantity survey breakdown but represents a recapitulation of the cost estimator's quantity survey analysis.

FIG. 13-3 EXAMPLE OF A COST BREAKDOWN FOR A SINGLE FAMILY HOUSE*

Component	% of Total	Cost
Survey & Financing	1/2	$ 200
Plans & Plan Checking	1/2	800
Site Preparation	1/2	800
Excavation	1	1,600
Footings & Foundation	4	6,400
Basement	6	9,600
Framing	7-1/2	12,000
Interior Walls & Ceiling	3-1/2	5,600
Exterior Siding	3	4,800
Roof Covering & Flashing	5	8,000
Insulation	2	3,200
Fireplaces & Chimneys (no fireplace)	2	3,200
Leaders & Gutters	1	1,600
Exterior & Interior Stairs	1	1,600
Doors, Windows & Shutters	2	3,200
Storm Windows, Doors & Screens	1	1,600
Main Floor Covering (Carpeting)	3	4,800
Kitchen Flooring	1/2	800
Bathroom & Lavatory Floors	1/2	800
Hardware	1/2	800
Water Supply	1	1,600
Waste Disposal	1	1,600
Heating	4	6,400
Cooling (no central air conditioning)	-	-
Domestic Hot Water	1	1,600
Piping	4	6,400
Plumbing Fixtures	3	4,800
Kitchen Cabinets & Counters	3	4,800
Built-In Appliances	1-1/2	2,400
Shower Doors	1/2	800
Bathroom Accessories	1/2	800
Vanities, Medicine Cabinets & Counters	1/2	800
Electric Service	2	3,200
Electric Wires & Outlets	2	3,200
Lighting Fixtures	1	1,600
Painting & Decorating	4	6,400
Porches (none)	-	-
Patios	1/2	800
Finish Grading	1/2	800
Landscaping	1	1,600
Garages & Carports	5	8,000
Clean Up	1/2	800
Interest, Taxes & Insurance	1	1,600
Contractor's Overhead & Temporary Facilities	4	6,400
Professional Services, Permits & Licenses	1	1,600
Selling Expenses, Carrying Costs	5	8,000
Contractor's Profit	7-1/2	12,000
TOTAL COST	100	$160,000

Quantity Survey Method

This comprehensive method used by many contractors requires preparation of a detailed inventory of all the materials and equipment used to build the house. To this list is applied the cost of each item as of the date of appraisal. Also estimated is the amount of labor in hours needed to install each item, using current labor rates. Finally the indirect costs, overhead and profit items are added to the cost of material, equipment and labor.

An example of a section of a contractor's cost breakdown for a typical house is shown in Fig. 13-4.

FIG. 13-4 SECTION OF CONTRACTOR'S COST BREAKDOWN

		Material			Labor		Total
Item	Units	Price	Total	Hours	Rate	Total	Cost
Cabinet work base-finised w/formica top	16	$ 88	$ 704	14	$14.60	$204.40	$ 908.40
Plumbing 60-gal. hot	1	$1,300	$1,300	30	$30.80	$924.00	$2,224.00

To prepare this breakdown using the quantity survey method, the contractor first lists all the material and equipment and estimates the amount of labor required to install each item. Then the material, equipment and labor are priced out per unit and extended to give the total cost of installing each item.

Except for an unusual appraisal, this type of breakdown is beyond the scope normally required. When such a breakdown is required, the services of a trained cost estimator should be obtained.

Appraisers often use a summary of the contractor's cost breakdown; Fig. 13-5 shows a typical cost breakdown for a house. The specifications and general description of the house used for this example are as follows:

General Description: One-family, one-story, ranch-style, seven rooms (living room, family room, dining room, kitchen, three bedrooms, two full baths), full unfinished basement. No porches. Gross living area: 1,422 square feet. Two-car, attached garage.

General Construction: Concrete footings and foundation walls. Exterior walls: cedar shingles. Roof covering: cedar shingles. Wood, double-hung windows, combination aluminum storm windows and screens, aluminum gutters and downspouts, Batt type insulation. Wood platform framing, plywood subfloors, oak floors, except kitchen (vinyl asbestos) and bathrooms (ceramic tile wainscot).

Mechanical Systems: Plumbing: copper water and waste pipes connected to municipal services in street. Electric 60-gal. domestic hot water heater. One double, stainless steel kitchen sink. Each bathroom has standard water closet, lavatory and tub with shower. Laundry tub in basement and washer/dryer hook-up. Heating: Oil-fired, hot water furnace; two circulators; baseboard radiators. Electrical: 10-ampere service; 16 circuits protected with circuit breakers; BX cable; adequate outlets and features. Built-in Appliances: gas oven and range, hood with exhaust fan in kitchen.

service; 16 circuits protected with circuit breakers; BX cable; adequate outlets and features. Built-in Appliances: gas oven and range, hood with exhaust fan in kitchen.

General Quality: House is average quality throughout and meets FHA minimum standards.

FIG. 13-5 ESTIMATE COSTS OF HOUSE CONSTRUCTION COMPONENTS*

Component	Unit	Quantity	Unit Cost	Total
General expense (engineering, plans, survey, site)	sq. ft./GLA	1,442 sq. ft.	$ 2.76	$ 4,000
Foundation	sq. ft./GLA	1,442 sq. ft.	4.44	6,400
Basement	sq. ft./GLA	1.442 sq. ft.	6.64	9,600
Floors	sq. ft./GLA	1,442 sq. ft.	7.52	10,400
Exterior walls & insulation (including windows & exterior doors)	lin. ft./wall	1,450 lin. ft.	12.96	18,800
Roof	sq. ft./GLA	1,442 sq. ft.	8.32	12,000
Roof dormers	lin. ft across face	None	-	-
Interior walls, ceilings, doors, cabinets, trim and accessories	sq. ft./GLA	1,442 sq. ft.	13.04	18,800
Stairways	each	2 outside	800.	1,600
Attic finish	sq. ft./fin. area	None	-	-
Heating	sq. ft./GLA	1,442 sq. ft.	4.44	6,400
Cooling				
Electric System	sq. ft./GLA	1,442 sq. ft.	5.56	8,000
Plumbing system	sq. ft./GLA	1,442 sq. ft.	11.08	16,000
Fireplaces & chimneys	each	1 chimney	3,200	3,200
Built-in appliances	each	2	1,200	2,400
Porches	sq. ft./porch	none	-	-
Patios	sq. ft./patio	144 sq. ft.	5.56	800
Other	doors & windows	22	72.72	1,600
Site improvements (not included in land value)	each lump sum	-	2,400	2,400
Garage	sq. ft./garage	460 sq. ft.	24.36	8,000
Indirect costs**	sq. ft./GLA	1,442 sq. ft.	2,052	29,600
TOTAL				$160,000

*These are not actual costs but an illustration of how costs might be approximately allocated in a $160,000 house.
**May be added to each component (rather than shown separately, as in this example).

The square foot unit cost varies inversely with the size of the house. It reflects the fact that plumbing, heating systems, doors, windows and similar items do not necessarily cost proportionately more in a large house than in a small one. If a similar cost is spread over a larger area, the unit cost is obviously less.

The apparent simplicity of the square foot comparison method can be misleading. Dependable square foot cost figures require the exercise of care and judgment in the process of comparison with similar or standard houses for which actual costs are known. Inaccuracies may result from selection of a square foot cost that is not properly related to the house under appraisal. However, correct application of this procedure will provide estimates of reproduction or replacement cost that are reasonably accurate and entirely acceptable in appraisal practice.

SOURCES OF COST FIGURES

Several reliable sources for obtaining cost data exist.

--Cost Data File. The use of square foot cost estimates involves assembling, analyzing and cataloging data on actual house costs. An appraiser should have available comprehensive current cost information for various types of houses and other improvements, including data on current material and labor costs. A system of grading quality of construction may also be used to refine the data further. This data can often be obtained from local builders, lenders, material suppliers and trade associations.

A file of this kind provides a check against costs of reproducing or replacing an existing residence, as well as against known or projected costs for existing or proposed houses of varying grades of construction. It also provides a check against the probable cost of different components of a house and of the various trades or work involved.

--Cost Services. Several recognized cost reporting services are also available to the appraiser. Some include illustrations of typical structures and provide adjustments to tailor the standard example to differently shaped or equipped residences. Some provide adjustment for individual cities or areas. Some show cubic foot or square foot costs, and some are designed for unit-in-place information.

--Cost Indices. A cost index service reflecting the relative cost of construction over a period of years is also useful. When the actual cost of a residence constructed some years ago is known, application of the index will indicate the present construction cost (provided the actual cost was typical figure). For example, assume that a house cost $53,000 to build in January 1955 and that a 1955 cost index, from a national service, was 284.4. The April 1989 cost index was 863.2. Based upon this data, in 1989 the building cost 3.035 times its January 1955 cost (863.2 + 284.4), or an indicated cost of $160,863.

BUILDING COST ESTIMATES

Building cost estimates should include all materials, equipment and labor. The contractor's overhead and profit, architect's fees and other outside professional services, taxes, insurance, administration and interest on borrowed funds during the period of construction may or may not be included. Some appraisers elect to allocate these costs proportionately across the direct costs; others estimate and report them separately. Some appraisers also add developer's profit.

For example, assume as a benchmark house a two-story, brick residence costs $150,000 to build, exclusive of detached garage or other site improvements. The quality of construction is roughly comparable to that of an average mass-produced home with asphalt shingle roofing, 1/2-inch drywall, good average finish and equipment with combination forced-air heat and air conditioning, plus a dishwasher, disposal and fireplace. Included are three bedrooms, 2-1/2 baths and full basement. This residence contains 1,496 square feet, thus costing approximately $100.000 per square foot of gross living area.

Assume that the appraiser is preparing a cost estimate for a house roughly comparable to the above example. In contrast to the benchmark house, the house being appraised has a concrete block foundation in lieu of poured concrete, no fireplace and a good grade of wood siding instead of brick exterior walls. The appraiser makes downward adjustments for these differences: $5,000 for wood siding; $1,000 for the block foundation; and $3,000 for lack of fireplace. The adjusted unit cost is now $91.00 per square foot. If indirect costs are not included in these unit cost adjustments, their total may be increased by an additional 15% to 20%.

DEPRECIATION

A simple definition of depreciation is "the difference between the cost of an improvement on the date of the appraisal and the value of the improvement."

More formally, it has been defined as:
> A loss of utility and hence value from any cause. An effect caused by deterioration and/or obsolescence. Deterioration or physical depreciation is evidenced by wear and tear, decay, dry rot, cracks, encrustations, or structural defects. Obsolescence is divisible into two parts, functional and external. Functional obsolescence may be due to poor plan, mechanical inadequacy or overadequacy, functional inadequacy or overadequacy due to size, style, age, etc. It is evidenced by conditions within the property. External obsolescence is caused by changes external to the property.

Depreciation begins upon construction of the improvements; they immediately begin to age physically and to suffer from functional obsolescence in their design. Negative environmental forces cause immediate external obsolescence.

When the improvements are constructed their economic life begins. During this period, they should contribute value to the property. If they are the "perfect improvement", the amount of value they contribute would be their total cost. Since few, if any, perfect improvements are constructed, a difference exists between their total cost and their value, which represents some form of depreciation. At the point when an improvement cannot be profitably utilized, or when it no longer contributes to the value of the property, it is at the end of its economic life and depreciation has reached 100%.

Generally, if the house is of average condition and design and conforms to the other houses in a neighborhood that is not subject to unusual economic influences, its effective age and chronological age will be about the same. If the house has had better than average maintenance, rehabilitation or modernization, its effective age probably will be less than its chronological age. If it is in poorer condition than typical houses of the same age or has not been modernized or rehabilitated as other similar houses in the neighborhood, or if some off-site economic or environmental factor is negatively affecting the value, the effective age will be greater than the chronological age.

TECHNIQUES FOR ESTIMATING ACCRUED DEPRECIATION

Accrued depreciation may be estimated directly through observation and analysis of the components of depreciation affecting the property or through use of a formula based on physical or economic age-life factors. It may also be estimated indirectly by use of the income or market data approaches.

Three techniques are used by appraiser to measure depreciation:

1. The breakdown method separates charges in the basis of origin for cause of loss (physical deterioration, curable and incurable; functional obsolescence, curable and incurable; and external obsolescence). Each component is estimated separately, using the engineering method or observation techniques.

2. The age-life method is accomplished by estimating the typical economic life of the improvements and their effective age.

3. The abstraction or market method extracts depreciation directly from the market.

THE BREAKDOWN METHOD

The breakdown method is accomplished by dividing depreciation into its three separate components: physical deterioration, functional obsolescence and external (environmental) obsolescence. Physical deterioration and functional obsolescence may be further broken down into curable and incurable types. A grasp of these underlying principles is essential to an overall understanding of depreciation.

--Physical Deterioration-Curable. These are all the items of maintenance that a prudent owner would accomplish on the date of appraisal to maximize the profit (or minimize the loss) if the property were sold. Almost any item of physical deterioration can be corrected at a price. However, to be classified as curable, the cure normally must contribute more value than it costs. Items of normal maintenance usually fall into the category, including paint touch-ups and minor carpentry, plumbing and electric repairs (leaking faucets, squeaking or tight doors and windows, etc.). Interior and exterior painting and redecorating may also be included.

The ultimate test is whether the market will recognize as additional value at least the cost of the repair. Realtors® have long recognized that minor repairs do add value equal to or in excess of their cost and they try to have an owner make these repairs before a house is offered for sale. The measure of physical deterioration-curable is the cost to cure. Many appraisal clients require that an itemized list of the curable items be part of the report together with an estimate of the cost to cure.

--Physical Deterioration-Incurable. As soon as a house is constructed, it begins to age and suffer from wear and tear. Physical deterioration-incurable is based on the physical condition of the components of the house. The total physical life of the house would equal its total economic life if other forms of depreciation were not present. One of the practical problems in estimating the percentage of physical deterioration-incurable is estimating the physical life of the components. There is a tendency to assign too much depreciation to physical deterioration-incurable by using estimates of 50 to 100 years for items such as footings, foundations, framing, wall and ceiling coverings, etc; some of these items may last hundreds of years.

To measure physical deterioration-incurable, items are divided into two categories: long-lived and short-lived. Long-lived items, such a footings, foundations, etc. can be depreciated as a group by making an estimate of their effective age and remaining physical life based on their condition. The engineering method, in which items are separately listed and their reproduction cost estimated, can also be used (see Fig. 13.6). By observation a percentage of depreciation is estimated and extended into a dollar estimate for each component. Indirect costs must be either allocated proportionately to each component or listed separately, and depreciation for them also estimated.

FIG. 13-6 COMPONENT PHYSICAL LIFE (ENGINEERING METHOD)

House Component	Reproduction Cost New		Estimated % Deterioration		Accrued Depreciation
Survey & engineering	$ 800	x	20%	=	$ 160
Foundation	3,200	x	20%	=	640
Plumbing	4,000	x	30%	=	1,200
Electrical system	8,000	x	35%	=	2,800
TOTAL	$160,000				$88,000

Short-lived items are components whose remaining physical life is shorter than the total estimated remaining economic life of the house. Typically they include roof, gutters and downspouts, kitchen cabinets and counters, painting and decorating. Sometimes these items are classified as physical deterioration-curable-deferred.

Again, the technique for estimating depreciation is to make a list of components, estimating the reproduction cost of each as well as a percentage of depreciation, based on the appraiser's observations. These estimates are extended into a dollar estimate for each component and totaled. The process may be shortened by estimating a total reproduction cost of all the short-lived items and using an average percentage of depreciation; this may decrease the accuracy of the estimate.

--Functional Obsolescence-Curable. Most functional obsolescence-curable in residential properties is caused by some kind of deficiency. In other types of properties some superadequacies would also be considered curable but they are rare in residential properties. Typical items that fall into this category are kitchens that need new counters, cabinets, fixtures and floor coverings; inadequate electrical service and hot water systems; and need of an additional bath or powder room where adequate space exists. Again, the test is whether the value added by correcting the obsolescence is greater than the cost to cure as indicated in the market.

The measure of functional obsolescence-curable is the difference between what is would cost on the date of appraisal to reproduce the house with the curable item included and to reproduce the house on the same date without it. Only the excess cost of adding the item to the existing structure above the cost of incorporating the item as part of a total house construction process represents the measure of accrued depreciation. It is neither proper nor logical to deduct accrued depreciation from reproduction cost of an item that has not been included in the reproduction cost estimate for the existing house.

For example, assume that in light of current market expectations, the house being appraised lacks a second bath where room exists to install one. The estimated cost to include this bath as part of the total house construction program as of the date of appraisal is $8,000. The estimated cost to do it as a separate job as of the same date would be more because it generally costs more to build parts of a house separately as compared to building the whole house at one time. If it would cost $10,000 to build the extra bath as a separate job, the measure of depreciation would be the $2,000 excess cost.

--Functional Obsolescence-Incurable.   These items can be divided into two categories: loss in value caused by a deficiency or by an excess or superadequacy. Deficiences are caused by exterior or interior design that does not meet current market expectations. This can be measured by the rent loss attributable to the deficiency multiplied by the gross monthly rent multiplier applicable to the property (See Fig. 13.7).

FIG. 13-7 ESTIMATING INCURABLE FUNCTIONAL OBSOLESCENCE BY CAPITALIZING RENT LOSS

Monthly rental, House A with 3 bedrooms	$1,140
Monthly rental, House B with 2 bedrooms	1,060
Difference	$ 80
GMRM for neighborhood	130
Difference in value between A and B ($80 monthly rent loss x 130 GMRM)	$10,400

--Functional Obsolescence-Superadequacy. The second type of incurable functional obsolesence is caused by superadequacy. Probably only a small percentage of houses exist that do not have some such obsolescence. The number of superadequacies tends to increase as a house gets older and the occupants improve it with features suited for their individual living sytle. Superadequacies are not only improvements made after construction but also anything initially built into the hosue that does not add value at least equal to its cost. For example, a builder elects to install in a new house an intercom system, central air conditioning, stainless steel kitchen sink and vinyl kitchen floor, the cost of which might be $20,000 total. If they only add $16,000 value to the house, the lost $4,000 would be functional obsolescence-superadequacy, assuming no other forms of depreciation existed.

Another example is a master bedroom, 16 by 18 feet, which cost $2,000 more to build than a bedroom 14 by 16 feet. If the extra size only adds $1,200 value, the lost $800 is functional obsolescence, superadequacy (again, assuming there are no other forms of depreciation).

Almost all superadequacies are incurable in houses. (In commercial and investment properties sometimes it pays to remove them because of excess operating costs). For example, a new house suffering from no physical deterioration or external obsolescence has a swimming pool that cost $40,000 to install. It adds only $25,000 value, so $15,000 is functional obsolescence-superadequacy.

Superadequacies are measured in the same manner as deficiencies, by finding a matched pair of sales from the market. If a rent differential can be attributed to the superadequacy, it can be capitalized to indicate the value of the superadequacy. The difference between this value and the cost of the item, less other forms of depreciation, would be classified as functional obsolescence-superadequacy.

--External Obsolescence. Also called locational or environmental obsolescence by some appraisers, it is the loss of value caused by factors outside the property boundaries. It is unique to real estate, caused by its fixed location. The value of a house is directly affected by the neighborhood, community and region in which it is located. In analyzing the location and environment of the property, the appraiser must consider government actions, economic forces, employment, transportation, recreation, education services, taxes, etc.

Consideration must also be given to factors in the immediate vicinity that detract from value. Unattractive natural features such as swamps, polluted waterways, and obstructed views are examples of items that will detract from value. Poorly maintained non-conforming houses, and uncollected junk in nearby yards are indications of possible economic obsolescence. Although facilities such as fire stations, schools, stores, restaurants, hospitals, and gas stations are advantageous nearby, if they are too close to the house, they may detract from its value. Nearby industry, highways and airports may be another type of nuisance, especially if they are unattractive, noisy or smoke and odor-emitting. External obsolescence can also be caused by factors that affect the supply or demand (such as an unusual number of houses for sale) of houses competitive with the house being appraised.

The list of factors causing economic obsolescence is almost endless and the appraiser should carefully search for and evaluate anything off the property that detracts from the value of the house.

External obsolescence like functional obsolescence can also be measured by the rent loss attributable to the factor causing the obsolescence. However, a different method is used because part of the rent loss caused by economic obsolescence often is allocated to the land For example, the market indicated that houses next to gasoline stations rent for $40 less than other houses. The GMRM for the neighborhood is 130. The land-to-improvement ratio in this neighborhood typically is land, 15%, improvements, 85%. Some of the rent loss must be allocated to the land, which in this case is 15% (see Fig. 13-8).

FIG. 13-8 ESTIMATING ECONOMIC OBSOLESCENCE USING RENT LOSS METHOD

Total rent loss	$ 40.00
Loss allocated to land ($40 x 15%)	<u>6.00</u>
Loss allocated to improvement	$ 34.00
Economic obsolescence ($34.00 x GMRM 130)	$ 4,420

External obsolescence can also be calculated by finding matched pairs of sales. The pair must consist of one sale that is affected by the influence causing economic obsolescence and another sale that is not so affected. First, all other differences are adjusted for and any remaining difference is attributed to economic obsolescence. For example, House E is a new, one-story, ranch-style house with a two-car garage. It is two blocks from the local school. House F is very similar to House E except that it has a one-car garage and is next door to the school. House E sold for $192,000. House F sold for $178,000. Two-car garages in this market add $12,000 value to houses in this neighborhood and one-car garages add $4,000 value. Lots in this neighborhood are about 20% of total value of typical property (see Fig. 13-9).

FIG. 13-9 ESTIMATING ECONOMIC OBSOLESCENCE USING MATCHED SALES

Sale price, House E with 2-car garage, away from school	$192,000
Sale price, House F with 1-car garage, next to school	<u>-178,000</u>
Difference	$ 14,000
Difference between value of 2-car garage and 1-car garage	<u>-8,000</u>
Indicated difference in value cased by school	$ 6,000
Value loss allocated to improvements ($6,000 x 80%)	$ 4,800
Percent of depreciation caused by location next to school ($4,800 + $192,000 = .0250 or 2.5%)	2.5%

AGE LIFE METHOD

Definition of Terms

Economic life is the time period over which a house may be profitably utilized. It is the total period of time that the improvements contribute value to the property. As soon as the site alone is worth as much as the site and the improvements combined, the improvements have reached the end of their economic life.

Physical life is the time period during which the house may be expected to remain physically in existence. Since over 90% of the houses ever built in the United States are still in existence and since houses in Europe have lasted hundreds of years, it is almost impossible to forecast the estimated physical life of a house. Caution must be exercised in the use of tables that purport to estimate the total physical life of different types of houses. They are of limited use to the appraiser.

Effective age is how old the house appears to be, based on observation, considering its condition, design and the economic forces that affect its value. To paraphrase an old saying, "If it has the physical condition and design of a 13-year-old house, then for appraisal purposes it should be treated as a 13-year-old house, (effective age: 13

years), even if it is 10 or 20 years old." The chronological age of the house should be noted in the appraisal (if known) but it normally has little use in the value estimation.

Remaining economic life is the period of time from the date of the appraisal to the end of the houses's economic life. It is that period of time the house will continue to contribute value to the property. This is the period the appraiser attempts to estimate. The assumption should not always be that the property will continue to deteriorate at its present rate. Often rehabilitation, modernization or remodeling will extend the life of the property; lack of nomal maintenance will shorten the economic life. Changing economic conditions and public tastes will also affect the remaining economic lfie. The estimate must be based on the assumption there will be no significant changes in the house or neighborhood, and be qualified to recognize that any changes may extend or shorten the remaining economic life.

The relationships between effective age, remaining economic life and total economic life are shown in Fig. 13-10.

FIG. 13-10 LIFE SPAN OF A HOUSE

*MAY BE EXTENDED BY REHABILITATION, REMODELING OR MODERNIZATION OR CHANGING CONDITIONS.
**MAY ALSO BE GREATER THAN ACTUAL AGE.

ABSTRACTION METHOD

This method involves the use of market data to obtain an indication of the amount of depreciation existing in the property being appraised. An analysis of current sales indicates the amount of depreciation with which the market has penalized each sale. By analyzing sales of residential properties similar to and in the same neighborhood as that being appraised, the amount and annual rate of depreciation can be calculated. The assumption is that residential properties of similar age, construction, size, condition and location depreciate at the same annual rate.

The following steps are used to analyze the sales of comparable houses to obtain an indication of depreciation:

1. Select recently sold houses that are comparable to the one being appraised and obtain all the data necessary to estimate their reproduction cost.

2. Estimate the value of the site (land) for each comparable. Use the market comparison approach if sales data is available.

3. Deduct the site (land) value from the comparable sales price and obtain an indicated depreciated value of the improvements.

4. Estimate the reproduction cost new of each comparable sale as of the date of the appraisal. Use any of the appropriate techniques described in the first part of this chapter.

5. To obtain the total amount of depreciation indicated for each of the sold properties, subtract the depreciated value of the improvements (Step 3) from the reproduction cost of the improvements (Step 4).

6. Estimate the effective age of the comparable property.

7. To obtain the average annual amount of depreciation indicated by each of the sold properties, divide the total depreciation by the effective age.

8. To obtain the average annual rate of depreciation, divide the annual amount of depreciation by the reproduction cost of the improvements.

9. Convert the rate to a percentage (multiply by 100 and add a percent sign).

The process outlined above should be performed for several comparable sales in the neighborhood. As with the market data approach, the more sales that are used and the closer they are in similarity to the property being appraised, the more accurate the estimate of depreciation will be. Fig. 13-11 is a more specific example. Assume a 20-year-old (actual and effective age), two-story colonial style house, with 2,200 sq. ft. of gross living area, including living room, dining room, kitchen, recreation room, four bedrooms and two full baths. There is also a two-car garage with an estimated reproduction cost of $9,900 and site improvements with an estimated cost of $3,600. Lots are estimated to be worth $27,000 from market data available. The estimated reproduction cost of the house is $81.75 per sq. ft. of gross living area. The house sold for $136,500.

FIG. 13-11 ESTIMATING ACCRUED DEPRECIATION BY ABSTRACTION— EXAMPLE A

Step 1:   Select a house that has sold and obtain
the needed data to estimate its
reproduction cost new. Sales Price: $165,000

Step 2:   Estimate the value of the site (land) from
the market. Less site (land) value: -36,000

Step 3:   Depreciated value of improvements: $129,000

Step 4:   Reproduction cost of comparable sale
as of date of appraisal: $207,000

Step 5:   Less depreciated value of improvements   -129,000

Total amount of depreciation indicated
by the market $ 78,000

Step 6:   Estimated effective age   13 years

Step 7: $\dfrac{\text{Depreciation (from Step 5)}}{\text{Effective age (from Step 6)}}$ = $\dfrac{\$\ 78{,}000}{13}$

Average annual amount of depreciation   = $6,000

Step 8: $\dfrac{\text{Annual depreciation (from Step 7)}}{\text{Reproduction cost (from Step 4)}}$ = $\dfrac{\$\ 6{,}000}{\$207{,}000}$

Average annual rate of depreciation   =   .0289

Step 9:   Averge annual percentage of depreciation   =   2.89%
(.0289 x 100)

FIG. 13-12 ESTIMATING ACCRUED DEPRECIATION BY ABSTRACTION— EXAMPLE B

Step1:	Sales Price	$136,500
Step 2:	Less site (land) value (from market)	-27,000
Step 3:	Depreciated value of the house and other improvements	$109,000

Step 4: Reproduction cost

House (2,200 sq. ft. x $81.75)	179,850
Garage	9,900
Site improvements	3,600
Total Reproduction cost	$193,350

Step 5:	Less depreciated value of improvements	-109,500
	Total depreciation indicated by market	$83,850
Step 6:	Effective age	20 years

Step 7:

$$\frac{\text{Total depreciation}}{\text{Effective age}} = \frac{\$ 83,850}{20}$$

$$\text{Annual amount of depreciation} = \$ 4,192$$

Step 8:

$$\frac{\text{Annual depreciation}}{\text{Reproduction cost}} = \frac{\$ 4,192}{\$193,350}$$

.0217	Average annual rate of depreciation =	.0217
Step 9:	Average annual percentage of depreciation = (.0217 x 100)	2.17%

In this example the reproduction or replacement cost of the site improvements, such as stone walls, fences, driveways, landscaping, etc., is difficult to estimate. Under these circumstances an alternate acceptable method is to deduct the estimate value these items contribute to the sale price first and then proceed to abstract the depreciation of the improvements (see Fig. 13-13).

FIG. 13-13 ESTIMATING ACCRUED DEPRECIATION BY ABSTRACTION— EXAMPLE C

Step1:	Sales Price		$180,000
Step 2:	Site value		45,000
	Contribution of site improvements		13,500
	Value of site and improvements		-$58,500
Step 3:	Depreciated value of the house and other improvements	=	$121,500
Step 4:	Reproduction cost		
	House (3,000 sq. ft. x $87.00)		$261,000
	Garage		18,000
	Total reproduction cost		$279,000
Step 5:	Less depreciated value of improvements		-121,500
	Total of depreciation	=	$157,500
Step 6:	Effective age		15 years
Step 7:	Total depreciation	=	$157,500
	Effective age		15
	Annual amount of depreciation		$ 10,500
Step 8:	Annual depreciation	=	$ 10,500
	Reproduction cost		$279,000
	Average annual rate of depreciation	=	.0376
Step 9:	Average annual percentage of depreciation (.0376 x 100)	=	3.76%

A single type of depreciation can also be calculated by the abstraction method. This is done by first calculating the total depreciation as in the above examples. Then two of the three forms of depreciation (physical, functional and economic) are estimated by observation and subtracted from the total depreciation; what remains is the amount attributed to the remaining form of depreciation.

Total Accrued Depreciation by Abstraction
Less: Physical Deterioration and Functional Obsolescence
Gives: Economic Obsolescence

Total Accrued Depreciation by Abstraction
Less: Functional and Economic Obsolescence
Gives: Physical Deterioration

Total Accrued Depreciation by Abstraction
Less: Physical Deterioration and Economic Obsolescence
Gives: Functional Obsolescence

To estimate Economic Obsolescence, follow this example:

Total depreciation estimated by abstraction	$83,850
Estimated physical deterioration	49,500
Estimated functional obsolescence	21,900
Total physical deterioration and functional obsolescence	-$71,400
Depreciation attributable to economic obsolescence =	$12,450

This technique is limited by the accuracy of the observed estimates of physical deterioration and functional obsolescence. Care must be taken not to attribute to economic obsolescence what is actually an error in estimating physical and functional obsolescence, land value or cost new. The possiblity of error is reduced when a number of properties is used.

AGE LIFE METHOD

This method of estimating depreciation is based primarily upon observation. The basis is that the percentage effective age represents of the typical economic life is the same percentage the accumulated depreciation represents of total reproduction cost. Both of these figures are as of the date of the appraisal. This concept can be stated as a formula:

$$\frac{\text{Depreciation}}{\text{Reproducion Cost}} = \frac{\text{Effective Age}}{\text{Typical Economic Life}}$$

An example of this formula is as follows:

$$\frac{20\% \text{ Depreciation}}{100\% \text{ Reproduction Cost}} = \frac{10 \text{ Years Effective Age}}{50 \text{ Years Typical Economic Life}}$$

The formula can also be expressed as follows:

$$\frac{\text{Effective Age}}{\text{Typical Economic Life}} = \text{\% Depreciation of Reproducion Cost}$$

Some appraisers prefer to use the following ratios to estimate the depreciatoin:

$$\frac{\text{Actual Age}}{\text{Actual Age + Remaining Economic Life}}$$

or

$$\frac{\text{Effective Age}}{\text{Effective Age + Remaining Economic Life}}$$

No matter which technique is used, if the estimates are correct and the assumptions are the same, the estimate of depreciation will be valid.

The age-life method can be used to estimate either depreciation from all causes or a single form of depreciation. Care must be taken to define clearly in the appraisal what is being estimated. The following examples show how the estimates are made.

A house has an estimated typical economic life of 50 years. Its chronological age is 20 years. Its effective age, based on its condition, design, and environment, is 25 years because it is in poor condition and is located near a gasoline service station.

$$\frac{25 \text{ years (effective age)}}{50 \text{ years (Typical Economic Life)}} = .50 \text{ or } 50\% \text{ depreciated}$$

Another house in the same neighborhood also has an estimated typical economic life of 50 years. Its chronological age is also 20 years. Its effective age, based on its condition, design and environment, is 20 years because it is in average condition and there are not unusual adverse environmental influences.

$$\frac{20 \text{ years (Effective Age)}}{50 \text{ years (Typical Economic Life)}} = .40 \text{ or } 40\% \text{ depreciated}$$

Still another house in the same neighborhood has an estimated economic life of 60 years. This longer economic life is forecast because it is of superior design and construction. Its chronological age is 20 years. Its effective age, based on its superior construction, modernization and lack of negative environmetnal influences, is 12 years.

$$\frac{12 \text{ years (Effective Age)}}{60 \text{ years (Typical Economic Life)}} = .20 \text{ or } 20\% \text{ depreciated}$$

These examples show how three houses in the same neighborhood, all the same chronological age, can suffer from substantially different amounts of depreciation. All of these estimates considered the effect of all three forms of depreciation.

When the estimate of effective age considers only one form of depreciation–say, physical deterioration–then the result is the amount of depreciation caused by physical deterioration. For example, a house has an estimated typical physical life of 75 years. The effective age, based only on the physical condition of the house, is 25 years.

$$\frac{25 \text{ years (Effective Age)}}{75 \text{ years (Typical Economic Life)}} = .333 \text{ or } 33.3\% \text{ depreciated physically depreciated}$$

The age-life method is an easy-to-understand, simple-to-use method based primarily upon the appraiser's observations, research and judgment. Therefore, its accuracy is heavily dependent upon the appraiser's knowledge and experience. It is an effective way to estimate the depreciation accumulated to the date of the appraisal but has proved to be a very poor way to estimate the rate of depreciation the property will suffer in the future.

For example, if by the age-life method it is estimated that a 25-year old residence has depreciated at the rate of 2% per year and is now 50% depreciated, it is incorrect to say that the remaining economic life is 25 years. This will only be true if:

1. The present rate of depreciation continues into the future on a straight line basis.

2. There are no changes in the forces that affect the value of the property.

3. There is no modernization, rehabilitation or remodeling.

4. The property is "normally" maintained through its remainig economic life.

A forecast that is based on a series of assumptions that most likely will not all be true serves a limited purpose. This kind of forecast has been misused by lenders to limit the term of mortgages. If an estimate of remaining economic life is required, it must be made considering all the above factors and it must be noted that any changes may extend or shorten the remaining economic life.

SUMMARY

The cost approach is based on the principle of substitution. It holds that value tends to be set by the cost of a reasonable substitute improvement that could be built without undue delay. The steps of the cost approach are:

1. Estimate the value of the site (land) in its highest and best use as if vacant.

2. Estimate the reproduction cost (or replacement cost) new of all the improvements.

3. Estimate accrued depreciation from all sources.

4. Deduct the accrued depreciation (from all causes) from the cost new of the improvements to derive the depreciated value of the improvements.

5. Add the site (land) value to the depreciated value of the improvements to derive an indicated value of the property by the cost approach.

Site (land) value is estimated in its highest and best use as if vacant from data found in the market.

Reproduction cost is the cost of creating a replica of the house and other improvements. Replacement cost is the cost of certain improvements with the same or equivalent utility using current design and materials. Estimating reproduction cost can be done using the quantity survey, unit-in-place or comparative methods.

Accrued depreciation is the difference between reproduction cost new of the improvements and their value as of the date of appraisal. It is the loss of value from all cases, which may be broken down into physical deterioration, functional obsolescence and external obsolescence. There are three principal methods used to measure accrued depreciation. The abstraction method uses sales from the market to indicate the depreciated value of the improvements. The age-life method is based on observation, in which estimates of economic life and effective age are converted into percentages of depreciation. The breakdown method divides depreciation into three categories (physical deterioration, functional obsolescence and external obsolescence). Each one is estimated by whatever technique is most applicable to the property being appraised.

The accuracy of the cost approach depends on the appraiser's accuracy in estimating the value of the land, as of the date of the appraisal, reproduction cost new of all the improvements and all forms of depreciation. Without market data to make these estimates, the possibility of significant error is great.

Extreme caution should be practiced when the cost approach is used alone or as the most significant indicator value. The report should contain valid justification as to why the appraiser has elected to do so.

CORNICE WITH DENTILS

CHIMNEY AT EACH END

SMALL PANE, DOUBLE-HUNG WINDOWS

GABLE ROOF

2½ STORIES

WING

SIDE LIGHTS

WORKING WOOD SHUTTERS

Colonial American

NEW ENGLAND COLONIAL (N E Col - 107)

CHIMNEYS AT ENDS

SHINGLE COVERED GABLE ROOF

UNFINISHED LOGS

Colonial American

LOG CABIN (Log Cab - 115)

14 Sales Comparison Approach

The sales comparison approach, which used to be called the market date approach, involves making a direct comparison between the property being appraised and other properties that have been sold (or listed for sale). All three approaches to value are based on market data, but the cost and income approaches depend on a less direct comparison than does the sales comparison approach.

When carefully collected, analyzed, verified and reconciled, market data usually provides the best indication of market value for a property. The price that a typical buyer pays is often the result of a shopping process, in which many properties are examined and evaluated. Buyers often base their value conclusions primarily on properties that are being offered for sale. Appraisers use this information plus information about properties that have sold and rented.

The principle of substitution states that when several commodities or services with substantially the same utility are available, the one with the lowest price attracts the greatest demand and the widest distribution. It is important to understand how this principle specifically applies to the theoretical framework of the market data approach. In single family residential markets, this means that when a residence is replaceable in the market (which it usually is), its value tends to be set by the cost of acquiring an equally desirable substitute residence. The assumption is that there will be no costly delay encountered in making the substitution. Experienced real estate brokers know that most buyers will accept more than one house in the market in which they are shopping and will accept only a short delay in negotiating the purchase of any specific house.

A popular myth is that one can sell a house at almost any price if one is willing to wait long enough for the one buyer who wants only that particular house and will pay substantially above its market value to obtain it. Houses that are listed substantially above market value generally remain unsold no matter how long they are offered for sale. The principle of substitution provides the basis for the premise that the market value of a house is the value indicated by active and informed buyers in the market for comparable houses offering a similar quality of shelter, amenities and other considerations characteristic of that market.

Individual sales often deviate from the market norm because of individual motivations, knowledge and/or conditions of sale; but in sufficient numbers, they tend to reflect market patterns. When information is available on a sufficient number of comparable sales, offerings and listings in the current market, the resulting pattern is the best indication of market value.

The principle of substitution also applies to income properties. A typical informed buyer compares income properties being offered for sale. The buyer also considers alternate forms of investment. Investment buyers are comparing return _of_ their investment, return _on_ their investment, tax shelter, the burden of management and many other factors.

STEPS IN THE SALES COMPARISON APPROACH

In applying the sales comparison approach, the appraiser takes five steps:

1. Studies the market and selects the sales and listings of properties most comparable to the residence being appraised. Generally, the most current and similar comparable sales prove to be the best indicators of the value of the subject.

2. Collects and verifies data on each selected property's selling and listing prices, dates of transaction, physical and locational characteristics and any special conditions.

3. Analyzes and compares each property with the subject as to time of sale, location, physical characteristics and conditions of sale.

4. Adjusts the sales or listing price of each comparable for dissimilarities between it and the subject. Adjustments are derived from the market whenever possible, using "matched pairs", regression analysis and other adjustment techniques.

5. Reconciles the adjusted prices of the comparable properties into an indicated value of the appraised residence.

STUDYING THE MARKET

A market study is made to find those comparable sales and listings that are similar to the property being appraised. Generally, the more current the comparable sale and the more similar it is to the property being appraised, the better it will be as an indicator of the value of the property being appraised. More sales and listings are usually analyzed than are finally used in the appraisal. The best comparables are used in the final calculations and value estimate.

COLLECTING THE DATA

Accuracy of the value indication from the sales comparison approach depends heavily upon the quantity and quality of sales, offerings and listings of competitive properties.

Through a sound collection program, a large bank of market data can be accumulated in the appraiser's own files and should be organized to serve the appraiser's needs most effectively. Only some of the data may be immediately pertinent; the remainer may be collected,filed and cross-indexed for future use. Records should carry the address, a file number, and additional salient information. Sales information often is collected and recorded on a standardized sheet, or in a computer data base.

VERIFYING THE DATA

Each sale used as a comparable in an appraisal report should be personally inspected and the data confirmed with the buyer, seller or broker. The appraiser must be assured of the facts--that is, that all depreciation has been considered, the measurements are correct and the reported price and terms are accurate.

Verification and inspection processes do more than confirm the accuracy of the data gathered. They also provide for exploration of motivating forces involved in a sale, such as: Were both buyer and seller acting without financial pressure? Was the sale an "arms-length" transaction, or were the parties related in some way? Were both buyer and seller knowledgeable about the property and market in which the sale took place? Did the seller have a reasonable time to sell and the buyer to buy? Were there any special concessions granted by either party? Was financing typical of the market, or was there a purchase money mortgage, second mortgage, assumed mortgage or other unusual situations? Were there any special sale conditions such as inclusion of personal property in the sale (furniture, above-ground pools, boats, automobiles, sports equipment, etc.)? Was there any special government program involving a subsidy, attractive financing terms or guarantee of payment?

Sometimes an owner sells for less than expected if allowed to occupy the property for a substantial period of time after the transfer of title. Sometimes a sale is the result of an option granted in the past when different market conditions prevailed, resulting in a sales price that may not be typical of the current market. These are only some of the possible conditions that might make the reported sales price different from the market value. Only by personally interviewing the buyer and seller or broker can the appraiser gain knowledge about such conditions.

ANALYZING AND COMPARING THE DATA

Comparison of sales, offers and listings provides a basis for estimating the market value of the property being appraised. When comparable properties are similar to the property being appraised; have sold very recently; and have few if any physical, locational and conditions of sale adjustments, such information is helpful to the appraiser in reaching a market value estimate. On most assignments, however, the appriaser recognizes substantial diferences between the appraised property and the comparable sales. Two analytical tools used by appraisers are elements of comparison and units of comparison. Each element of comparison (date of sale, physical characteristics, location, and conditions of sale) *must* be considered. The units of comparison provide a means for making these considerations.

ADJUSTING THE COMPARABLES

Once all of the elements of comparison between the comparable sales and property being appraised are described in the appraisal report, they must be analyzed and adjustments must be made to reflect the dollar or percentage value of the dissimilarities noted.

MATCHED PAIRS OF SALES

In the past many adjustments were based on nothing more than educated guesses. Good appraisal practice requires that adjustments be supported with data from the market. The best technique is to extract the amount of the adjustment from the market by using "matched pairs." This is often the only technique acceptable to many sophisticated purchasers of apprialsals. It involves the selection of two sales in the market, one having the item for which the adjustment is sought, and the other not. The theory behind this technique is that if this is the only difference between the two sales, the difference in sales price can be attributed to the item. Although generally reliable where only one diference is present, the technique may be less reliable where there are several differences.

The following is an example of an adjustment based on only one difference between matched pairs. Each of the comparable sales used in these illustrations is assumed to be very similar to the house being appraised and to each other, except as noted. They are also assumed to have sold recently so that no time adjustments are needed.

Comparable 1
1-acre lot
1-car attached garage
Sold recently for $114,000

Comparable 2
1-acre lot
2-car attached garage
Sold recently for <u>$120,000</u>

Difference attributable to extra garage $6,000

The only significant difference between these sales is the garage size. From this information, it appears that the market recognizes a $6,000 difference between one- and two-car garages. The indicated adjustment for this item is $6,000.

Usually more than one difference exists between two sales. In such cases, adjustments can be made for each of the differences. Any remaining difference in sales price, after all other adjustments have been made, is attributed to the item for which adjustment is being sought. Continuing the above example:

Comparable 3
1-acre lot
1-car attached garage
Next to gasoline service station
Sold recently for $105,000

This sale can be directly paired with Comparable 1. The $9,000 difference in sale price between 1 and 3 can be attributed to the gasoline service station.

Comparable 3 could also be paired with 2. There is a $15,000 difference between the sale prices of Comparables 2 and 3 of which $6,000 is caused by the difference in value between a one-car and two-car garage (based on pairing Comparable 1 with Comparable 2).

When there are two or more differences between the matched pairs, the differences may affect the sales in the same or opposite ways. In this example, they both affect the sales in the same way. Comparable 3 is $15,000 less valuable than Comparable 2 because it has a smaller garage and is affected by the gasoline service station next door.

Because it is difficult to tell if the difference affects the sales in the same way or opposite ways just by looking at them, it is necessary to estimate the effect from the market. This is done by designating one sale as the base sale and then first adjusting the other sale for all the differences between it and the base sale, except for the one being sought. When all the adjustments have been made, the remaining difference between the base sale and the other sale can be attributed to the one difference left between them.

Pairing Comparable 2 and 3 illustrates how this process works.

Comparable 2 (Base)
1-acre lot
2-car attached garage
Sold recently for $120,000

Comparable 3
1-acre lot
1-car attached garage
Adverse influence from nearby gasoline service station
Sold recently for $105,000

Adjustment of Comparable 3 to Base Sale 2 to reflect
difference between 1-car and 2-car garage   +$6,000
Adjusted Sales Price 3 $111,000

Abstraction for remaining difference attributable to adverse influence of nearby gasoline service station:

Comparable 2 (Base) $120,000
Adjusted Sales Price 3   -111,000
Amount attributable to adverse influence
of location near gasoline service station $ 9,000

This process can be extended still further. Comparable Sale 4 is also similar to the other sales and sold recently for $135,000.

Comparable 4
2-acre lot
2-car garage
Adverse influence from nearby gasoline service station
Sold recently for $135,000

This sale cannot be compared directly with any of the other sales to extract an adjustment for the two-acre lot. In each case, there is at least one other difference:

Comparable 1: 1-acre lot, 1-car garage, away from gasoline service station.
Comparable 2: 1-acre lot, away from gasoline service station.
Comparable 3: 1-arcre lot, 1-car garage.

Even though there is more than one difference in each matched pair, Comparable 4 can be paired with each of the others by first adjusting for the other differences.

Pairing Comparable Sale 4 with 1 works out as follows:

Comparable 1 (Base)
1-acre lot
1-car garage
Sold recently for $114,000

Comparable 4
2-acre lot
2-car garage
Adverse influence from nearby gasoline service station
Sold recently for $135,000

Adjustment of 4 to Base Sale 1 to reflect the difference
between 1-car and 2-car garage
(based on comparing 1 with 2)   -6,000

Adjustment of 4 to Base Sale 1 to reflect adverse influence
of gasoline service station
(based on comparing 3 with 1 and 2)   +9,000

Adjusted Sales Price 4 $138,000

Abstraction for remaining difference attributable to lot size:

Adjusted Sales Price 4 $138,000
Sales Price 1 (base)   -114,000
Amount attributable to difference between 1-acre
and 2-acre lot $ 24,000

Pairing Comparable Sales 4 and 3 works out as follows:

Comparable 3 (Base)
1-acre lot
1-car attached garage
Adverse influence from nearby gasoline service station
Sold recently for $105,000

Comparable 4
2-acre lot
2-car garage
Adverse influence from nearby gasoline service station
Sold recently for $135,000

Adjustment of 4 to Base Sale 3 to reflect the difference
between 1-car and 2-car garage
(based on comparing 1 with 2)   -6,000

Adjusted Sales Price 4 $129,000

Abstraction for remaining difference attributable to lot size:

Adjusted Sales Price 4	$129,000
Sales Price 3 (base)	-105,000
Amount attributable to difference between 1-acre and 2-acre lot	$ 24,000

Fig. 14-1 summarizes the data analyzed in the preceeding example.

FIG. 14-1 COMPARABLE SALES GRID

Item	Appraised House	Comp. Sale 1	Comp. Sale 2	Comp. Sale 3	Comp. Sale 4
Sale Price	–	$135,000	$114,000	$120,000	$105,000
Time of Sale	Date of appraisal	Recent -0-	Recent -0-	Recent -0-	Recent -0-
Physical Lot size	1-acre -0-	1-acre	1-acre -0-	1-acre -0-	2-acre -$8,000
Car storage	1-car attached	1-car attached -0-	2-car attached -$6,000	1-car attached -0-	2-car attached -$6,000
Location Adverse influences	none	none -0-	none -0-	Next to gas station +$9,000	Next to gas station +$9,000
Conditions of Sale	none	none -0-	none -0-	none -0-	none -0-
Net Adjustment	-	-0-	-$6,000	+$9,000	-$21,000
Indicated value appraised house	-	$114,000	$114,000	$114,000	$114,000

In actual sales analysis, calculations would rarely work out as precisely as in this example, due to two major factors. First, even active, informed markets produce different buyer and seller opinions of the value of each comparison item considered by the appraiser; thus for each property, there may be a range of prices considered reasonable for its market. Second, the adjustment for one item of difference may already include a partial adjustment for another item of difference.

To illustrate, in the above example, the price per acre may differ for locations near service stations. This may be true in a situation in which the market might require a larger lot to better buffer against the adverse influence, yet not pay more for the extra land. Adjustment for both adverse influence and lot size may overstate the actual difference because an adjustment for location near the service station may already include a partial adjustment for lot size.

The appraiser must be cautious to avoid the conclusion that apparent precision of adjustment processes provides a more accurate estimate of value. In many situations that accuracy may be reduced by adding more adjustment factors. Unless aided by properly applied adjustment processes such as regression analysis, the appraiser should generally make the fewest adjustments possible and should reflect the uncertainties of multiple adjustments in final reconciliation of the value estimate. This is particularly true in making multiple adjustments for physical differences.

Likewise, the appraiser should avoid the temptation to use cost estimates as a basis for market adjustments. While relationships between cost and value contributions of components may exist, they may be supported only by market data. Thus, comparison of market data should be used to support the adjustment used.

REGRESSION ANALYSIS

In recent years, attention hs been drawn to methods of analyzing market data through use of regression analysis and other mathematical techniques. Step-wise multiple regression routines, like more traditional methods, are based upon the concept that certain identifiable characteristics of residential markets (called independent variables) may each be studied for their individual and joint contributions to value. Unlike traditional methods, however, the mathematics of analyzing comparable sales is more complex and generally requires more powerful computing equipment.

A major contribution of these newer techniques has been to focus attention on the adjustment process in sales analysis. Where more than one set of matched pairs is used to extract adjustment factors, the possibility of "doubling up" on adjustments exists. This is due to the interdependence or interaction of many comparison elements (often referred to as their "co-linearity"). Traditional comparison methods have generally overlooked these relationships and do not provide a means for measuring interdependence of data.

For example, if adjustments are made for both square footage of living area and number of bedrooms, either variable is likely already to include some consideration of the other. Regression techniques (particulary step-wise) can serve to reduce this problem and provide a means of measuring where significant interdependence is present. Regression techniques also permit a measure of reliability and significance of both data used and results produced.

Another reason for the growing use of regression analysis and similar techniques is that they often allow use of more market information and provide a better analysis and understanding of markets for market value estimates than traditional methods. In simple terms, traditional application of the market approach has usually taken the mathematical form of:

1. $Yc = bX$
Where Yc means calculated value, b is a multiplier obtained for a unit of comparison, and X is measured data for the property appraised. Example: the market indicates a price of $82.14 per square foot, and appraised property has 1,738 square feet.

$Yc = (\$82.14)(1,738) = \$142,759.$

2. $Yc = bX + a + b \ldots + n$

Where $a, b, \ldots n$ are plus and minus adjustment factors. Example: In addition to data already given, the appraiser considers property appraised to be $4,500 superior as to condition but $2,250 inferior as to location:

$Yc = (\$82.14)(1,738) + \$4,500 - \$2,250 = \$145,009$ or $145,000

3. $Yc = a + b + c + \ldots n$

Where a is lump sum amount, and $b, c \ldots n$ are various adjustment factors. Example: An appraiser estimates a base market value of $142,500 before adjustments (or is dealing with a comparable which sold for that amount) and then considers the condition and location adjustments already mentioned:

$Yc = \$142,500 + \$4,500 - \$2,250 = \$144,750$ or $145,000

4. $Yc = X(a + b + \ldots n)$

Where $a, b, \ldots n$ are percentage adjustment factors that are added and subtracted; alternatively each may be applied independently to X, the base for calculations. Example: A property appraised is considered 3% superior as to condition, but 2% inferior as to location to a base of $142,500:

$Yc = \$142,500 (100\% + 3\% - 2\%) = \$143,925$ or $144,000

These basic methods and relationships have other variations in common use. Each should be understood in applying the market data approach to avoid commonly encountered abuses and errors. Particularly important is recognition that the model used for final application of market adjustments must also be used as the model for original extraction of adjustment factors from market data. It is improper to extract adjustment factors using one method and apply them using another.

Where sufficient data for analysis is available, many appraisers have found that simple linear regression analysis may provide more accurate use of available data and an analysis of more market information than traditional methods. This is particularly true in situations where a simple price-per-square-foot unit of comparison is used. To illustrate, assume that an appraiser has collected sales data for 10 nearby properties which have recently sold, as shown in Fig. 14-2.

FIG. 14-2: COMPARABLE SALES DATA SET FOR SIMPLE REGRESSION ANALYSIS

Sale No.	Sq. Ft. Gross Living Area	Total Sale Price	Sale Price per Sq. Ft. GLA
1	1,000	$87,000	$87.00
2	1,100	82,500	75.00
3	1,200	87,000	72.50
4	1,400	87,000	62.13
5	1,500	93,000	62.01
6	1,600	90,000	56.25
7	1,650	96,000	58.17
8	1,750	91,500	52.02
9	1,850	96,000	51.90
10	1,950	94,500	48.45

Several situations are found in common practice:

1. In appraising an 1,100 square foot dwelling, the appraiser might consider Sales 1, 2, and 3, which have a mean price of $78.16 per square foot, as the three prices per square foot do not form an applicable pattern.

2. In appraising a 1,500 square foot dwelling, the appraiser might consider Sales 4, 5, and 6, which have a mean price of $60.13 per square foot, as the three square foot prices again do not form a regular pattern.

3. In appraising an 1,800 square foot dwelling, the appraiser might consider Sales 7 through 10, which have a mean price of $52.64 per square foot, as the pattern is once again inconclusive.

4. In appraising any property for which these sales are considered comparable, it will be extremely difficult through traditional means of analysis to apply more than three or four of the sales in any one sales comparison process. Thus, the concept of market is reduced because of the simple mathematical inadequacies of traditional anlaysis methods.

Particularly distressing is the tendency of many brokers (and some buyers and sellers) to generalize, based on these 10 sales, the "the market indicates about $60.00 per square foot for properties in this area," (the arithmetic mean of the 10 sales is actually $62.54). Such a generalization is potentially meaningful only for sales near the middle of the group and is severely misleading for those not near the middle.

Often overlooked is the fact that any use of a simple unit of comparison such as price per square foot is an application of simple linear regression analysis. Each of the square foot prices discussed ($78.18, $59.58, $52.71 and $62.58) may be substituted for b in the relationship $Yc=bX$ where X is square footage, and a simple linear regression model is implicit with any such use of comparison units. Unfortunately, this application is an oversimplification of a more accurate form of simple linear regression which adds a constant "a" to the equation: $Yc=a+bX$

Fig. 14-3 illustrates the difficulty of applying the traditional unit of comparison relationship $Yc=bX$ and one of the advantages of the more extensive form $Yc=a +bX$. By plotting the price/square foot relationship, it can be seen that a regular pattern of price increase with increase in square footage exists. Alternatively, prices per square foot could be illustrated. If the $60 per square foot generalization is used, a 1,500 square foot dwelling would be expected to sell for $90,000. Likewise, a 0 square foot dwelling would be expected to sell for $0. While the latter is ridiculous, the expectation establishes the slope of the price expectations at any reasonable square footage. Thus, the traditional method forces a price per square foot slope of the price expectations at any reasonable square footage. Therefore, the traditional method forces a price per square foot slope to pass though the intersection of the X and Y axis (the zero intercept) regardless of the actual slope of price to square foot relationships.

FIG. 14-3 COMPARISON OF Yc=bX AND Yc=a + bX AS DESCRIPTORS OF RESIDENTIAL SALES DATA

Square Feet of Living Area

Note: the formula for a straight line is Y = a + bX

This zero intercept fallacy may be overcome by application of the $Yc=a+bX$ relationship which can be calculated by simple linear regression techniques. Figure 14-3 shows that this formula provides a much better explanation of the market data than the traditional method and allows the use of all 10 sales in this instance. While the mathematics of this calculation can be handled by even simple calculators, it is also possible to approximate the relationships by freehand drawing, on graph paper, once the basic data is plotted.

This same example also illustrates the hazard of inadvertently "doubling up" on adjustments in the traditional market approach when there is an interdependence of comparison units. Fig. 14-4 includes data for both square footage and bedrooms for each of the 10 comparable sales. Use of both comparison units is common in applying the market approach. However, analysis shows that a high interdependence between square footage and bedrooms is present in this data.

FIG. 14-4 COMPARABLE SALES DATA SET FOR SIMPLE REGRESSION ANALYSIS

Sale No.	Sq. Ft. Living Area	Bedrooms	Sales Price
1	1,000	2	$87,000
2	1,100	2	82,500
3	1,200	2	87,000
4	1,400	2	87,000
5	1,500	3	93,000
6	1,600	3	90,000
7	1,650	3	96,000
8	1,750	4	91,500
9	1,850	4	96,000
10	1,950	4	94,500

Analysis of this data through a step-wise multiple linear regression model produces the following "correlation matrix," which measures the amount of correlation among variables:

Square Feet	Bedrooms	Price
1.00000	.92768	.84687
	1.00000	.81088
		1.00000

These results indicate that over 84% of the price variance among the sales may be explained by square footage and that about 81% is explained by bedroom data. Thus either variable used alone is capable of explaining a great deal about price. The almost 93% correlation between square feet and bedrooms is particularly significant because it indicates a very high level of interaction or interdependence between the two variables.

Other analysis by the multiple regression model produces standard error of the estimate measures, which indicate the precison of regression estimates. Standard errors were calculated for square footage and bedrooms where each was used as a single independent variable and then for their combined use as joint predictors of value, with the following results:

Independent Variable(s)	Standard Error
1. Square footage only	$2,555
2. Bedrooms only	2,812
3. Square footage and bedrooms	2,709

Use of square footage alone is shown to be a better predictor of value in this instance than either bedrooms alone or a combination of both variables. Bedrooms would seldom be used alone as a unit of comparison in traditional market data methods (except in the paired sales concept), but both bedrooms and square footage would frequently be used.

This example shows that addition of the data regarding bedrooms actually reduces the capability of the units of comparison to predict value because of the high interrelationship between square footage and bedrooms. Without the multiple regression calculation, effects of this interrelationship would possibly be overlooked and a doubling of adjustments would occur. Although the dollar amount here is minimal (due to the simplicity of this example), substantial effects can often be seen in grid analysis techniques, which commonly use numerous independent variables simultaneously.

Simple examples such as these raise at least three questions about contemporary application of the market approach:

1. Can appraisers afford to continue to use only three or four comparables where more market data factually exists and is available?

2. When using only one unit of comparison, can the traditional concept of $Yc = bXa + bX$ continue to be used in favor of the linear regression concept of $Yc = a + bX$ or similar nonlinear relationships?

3. When using more than one unit of comparison, can the appraiser continue to ignore the interdependence of data that is generally present in grid analysis techniques (or to ignore the multiple problems of combining a series of adjustments extracted by the paired sales technique)?

Appraisal methodology is still in transition, but the weaknesses of many traditional methods in the market approach can be overcome by collecting more data and using study methods which analyze larger amounts of data, such as those illustrated.

Although a full exposition of regression anaalysis is beyond the scope of this discussion, these examples illustrate the complexity of market comparison processes and point out both the basis for common errors and the possibility of overcoming these errors with newer analytical techniques.

OTHER ADJUSTMENT TECHNIQUES

Another commonly used indirect technique for adjusting the comparable is to estimate the cost new, less depreciation, of the item for which adjustment is needed. The accuracy of this technique depends on the relationship of the cost less depreciation estimates and value differences in terms of market recognition. Depreciation is especially difficult to estimate, because the market may recognize only a small portion of the cost, and substantial functional obsolescence may have to be deducted to obtain the actual value contributed by a specific item.

The appraiser should be familiar with other ways of making adjustments, even though they are usually not used for residential appraisals. Percentage adjustments are based upon a percentage of value for each comparable sale. For example, the adjustment for condition might be 3%. If the comparable sales price was $120,000 this adjustment would be equivalent to $3,600.

When percentage adjustments are used, they are usually added and subtracted to give a net adjustment percentage, which is applied to the comparable sales price to yield an indication of value for the property being appraised. For example, if the time adjustment is +5%, the location adjustment is +3%, the adjustment for physical characteristics is -2%, with no adjustment for conditions of sale, the net adjustment is +6%. The comparable sales price is then increased by 6% to give indicated value for the appraised property.

In the past some appraisers felt that it was not proper to add these percentages together; it was more accurate to convert them to decimal form and multiply them by each other to get the net adjustment figure. Using the figures given in the above example, they would calculate the adjustment as follows: 1.05 X 1.03 X .98 = 1.0598. This figure, known as a "composite adjustment," would then be multiplied by the comparable sales price to give an indicated value of the appraised property. The composite adjustment derived by multiplication is generally no longer considered valid.

Up to this point adjustments have been discussed on the basis of the whole property, resulting in a comparable sales price of the property as a whole to give a dircet indication of value for the appraised property. Adjustments on a unit basis may also be applied. A good technique is to work in units, which, for single family residences, is most commonly square feet of gross living area. If this unit is used, the sales price of each comparable is converted into a price per square foot before the adjustments are applied. The adjustments are then made in unit figures. For example, the adjustment for condition might be $2.25 per square foot.

The final value indication would be value per square foot of gross living area. This figure can be converted into an indicated value for the appraised property by multiplying its number of square feet of gross living area by the adjusted value per square foot of each comparable. This procedure could be done at this point or later in the reconciliation.

In the market data approach, each comparable property is analyzed and compared to the property being appraised, based on the four elements of comparison. A comparison or rating grid may be used on which information about the appraised property and the comparable sales is displayed and adjustments for each difference between them are shown. Fig. 14-5 is an example of such a rating grid.

FIG. 14-5 COMPARISON RATING GRID

The undersigned has recited three recent sales of properties most similar and proximate to subject and has considered these in the market analysis. The description includes a dollar adjustment, reflecting market reaction to those items of significant variation between the subject and comparable properties. If a significant item in the comparable property is superior to, or more favorable than, the subject property, a minus (−) adjustment is made, thus reducing the indicated value of subject; if a significant item in the comparable is inferior to, or less favorable than, the subject property, a plus (+) adjustment is made, thus increasing the indicated value of the subject.

ITEM	SUBJECT	COMPARABLE NO. 1	+(−)$ Adjustment	COMPARABLE NO. 2	+(−)$ Adjustment	COMPARABLE NO. 3	+(−)$ Adjustment
Address	420 Gladville Bloomville, IL	341 Pine Road Bloomville, IL		413 Cedar Street Bloomville, IL		210 Hoover Road Bloomville, IL	
Proximity to Subject		1 block South		1/2 block West		7 blocks South	
Sales Price	$ 85,000	$ 70,000		$ 73,000		$ 82,000	
Price/Gross Liv. Area	$ 45.02	$ 38.46		$ 38.93		$ 43.16	
Data Source	Lender	SREA Mkt Data Center		MLS Service		Appraiser's file	
VALUE ADJUSTMENTS	DESCRIPTION	DESCRIPTION	+(−)$ Adjustment	DESCRIPTION	+(−)$ Adjustment	DESCRIPTION	+(−)$ Adjustment
Sales or Financing Concessions		None report Equal	0	None report Equal	0	None report Equal	0
Date of Sale/Time	3/1/8	2/3/8		1/3/8		1/10/8	
Location	Average	Avg./Equal		Avg./Equal		Good/Sup.	− 5,000
Site/View	Avg./Avg.	Equal/Equal		Equal/Equal		Equal/Equal	
Design and Appeal	Average	Avg./Equal		Avg./Equal		Avg./Equal	
Quality of Construction	Average	Avg./Equal		Avg./Equal		Avg./Equal	
Age (Effective)	30 yrs.	30 yrs/Equal		30 yrs/Equal		30 yrs/Equal	
Condition	Average	Avg./Equal		Avg./Equal		Avg./Equal	
Above Grade Room Count (Total/Bdrms/Baths)	7 / 3 / 2	7 / 3 / 2		7 / 3 / 2		7 / 3 / 2	
Gross Living Area	1,888 Sq. Ft.	1,820 Sq. Ft.	+ 1700	1,875 Sq. Ft.	+ 325	1900 Sq. Ft.	− 300
Basement & Finished Rooms Below Grade	Crawl space	Crawl space Equal		Crawl space Equal		Crawl space Equal	
Functional Utility	Avg/Poor St.	Equal/Equal		Equal/Equal		Equal/Equal	
Heating/Cooling	HW/2 Win AC	Equal/Equal		Equal/Equal		Equal/Equal	
Garage/Carport	2 car att.	2 car att/E		2 car att/E		2 car att/E	
Porches, Patio, Pools, etc.	144 sq. ft. open porch	No porch	+ 1000	No Porch	+ 1000	open porch /Equal	
Special Energy Efficient Items	Solar Dom.	None	+ 2500	None	+ 2500	Solar HW/ Equal	
Fireplace(s)	1 masonry	None	+ 2000	1 FP/Equal		1 FP/Equal	
Other (e.g. kitchen equip., remodeling)	No kitchen eating area	No kitchen eating/E		No kitchen eating/E		No kitchen eating/E	
Net Adj. (total)		X + □ −	$ 7,200	X + □ −	$ 3,825	□ + X −	$ 5,300
Indicated Value of Subject			$ 77,200		$ 76,825		$ 76,700

Each comparable sale is adjusted so that its sale price is converted to an indication of the market value of the appraised property. Therefore, if an element of comparison in a comparable is more valuable than those found in the appraised property, a minus adjustment must be made. For example, the only difference between the appraised property and Comparable Sale 1 is that the first has no porch and the latter has an open porch, which contributes $4,500 additional value to the comparable in this market.

	House Being Appraised	Comparable Sale 1
Sales Price		$135,000
Porch	none	− 4,500
Indicated value of appraised property		$130,500

In the following example, the property being appraised has an in-ground swimming pool and the comparable has none. In-ground swimming pools add $12,000 value in this market, making the appraised property superior to the comparable house.

	House Being Appraised	Comparable Sale 1
Sales price		$120,000
In-ground swimming pool	yes	none
		+12,000
Indicated value of appraised property		$132,000

In this example the comparable was less valuable than the property being appraised, so a plus adjustment is made.

RECONCILIATION OF SALES COMPARISON APPROACH

After the best comparable sales have been selected and each one is adjusted to give an indicated value of the appraised property, the indications must be reconciled to produce a final estimate of value via the sales comparison approach. It is not acceptable appraisal practice to use a simple arithmetic mean of the value indications. Averaging small groups of numbers produces a meaningless measure of central tendency, which may or may not reflect actual market value.

The accepted procedure is to review each sale and judge its comparability to the property being appraised. Generally, the fewer and smaller the adjustments used on a comparable sale to produce the indicated value estimate, the more weight the sale is given in the final reconciliation. However, consideration should also be given to the basis for the adjustments.

The final value selected is a judgment made by the appraiser based on all the information available. It is not always necessary to select a single figure at this point in the appraisal process; some appraisers believe that the use of a range is more helpful. The use of such a range to describe market value is becoming more common, most likely a result of greater awareness of statistical techniques on the part of appraisers.

SUMMARY

The sales comparison approach to value is generally the preferred approach to estimate the market value of residences. However for investment properties the income approach is also given heavy weight. Appraisals that depend primarily upon the cost or income approach have a strong possibility of being subject to substantial error.

The key to the sales comparison approach is market abstraction of adjustments and the use of an appropriate unit of comparison. Typically, in the appraisal of single family houses, the unit of choice is square feet of gross living area.

Each comparable sale is compared with the appraised property. Adjustments are made to the comparable sales price to reflect significant differences between them.

Traditionally, the elements of comparison are divided into the four categories of time, location, physical characteristics and conditions of sale.   Recently, special conditions and special financing have been added as elements of comparison.

In order to obtain all of the information needed to use a comparable sale, the appraiser should inspect each comparable property and verify the nature of the sale with either the buyer, seller or broker. These are the people who can tell the apraiser about the conditions of sale, special financing and the actual physical condition of the property at the time of sale.

New techniques using more sales are available as alternatives to the above techniques. They do not depend upon adjustments based on limited market information but rather on statistical treatment of many comparable sales.

When the sales comparison approach is based upon a sufficient number of carefully chosen sales similar or adjustable to the appraised property, the value indication is usually persuasive.

ASYMMETRICAL

LARGE BRICK OR
STONE CHIMNEY

GROUND-HUGGING
COTTAGE

STEEP GABLE ROOF

SMALL
DORMER
WINDOWS

CASEMENT
WINDOWS

English

COTSWOLD COTTAGE (Cotscot - 201)

15 The Gross Monthly Rent Multiplier (GMRM) Income Approach

The income approach, applied to single family residences, is also called the Gross Monthly Rent Multiplier (GMRM), Gross Rent Multiplier (GRM) or Gross Income Multiplier (GIM).

The income approach used for single family residences is based on the assumption that there is a direct relationship between what residences sell for and their monthly rent.

By custom, monthly rents are used for single family residences. Usually they are rentals for residences that are unfurnished and do not include utilities.

STEPS OF THE (GMRM) INCOME APPROACH

When sufficient data is available, the appraiser should follow these steps to derive an indication of market value from the (GMRM) income approach:

1. Calculate the Gross Monthly Rent Multiplier.

    a. Find residences that have recently sold and were rented at the time of sale that are comparable to the property being appraised in the same or similar neighborhoods.

    b. Divide the sales price of each property by this monthly rental to derive a monthly rent multiplier, known as the Gross Monthly Rent Multiplier (GMRM).

    c. Reconcile the multipliers developed above to obtain a single multiplier or a range of multipliers that are applicable to the appraised property. This is not an average; it is a judgment of comparability and applicability.

2. Estimate the market rent of the residence being appraised.

    a. Find comparable rentals in the neighborhood.

    b. Analyze each rental, comparing its features with those of the residence being appraised.

    c. Estimate the adjustments required to obtain an indicated market (economic) rent for the residence being appraised.

    d. Consider each comparable carefully, with emphasis on the need for adjustments, and formulate an opinion of the market rent of the residence being appraised, based upon the actual rents of the comparables.

3. Develop an indicated value of the residence being appraised.

    a. Multiply the estimated market rent of the residence being appraised by the estimated monthly multiplier (or range of multipliers) to obtain its indicated market value via the income approach.

The multiplier is relied on as an indicator of market value because it tends to express a constant relationship between the gross monthly rental income of a single family residence and its sale price. Practicing appraisers rely on this indicator as a direct application of market data and income information, which expresses the relationship between sale price (or market value) and rental income.

The multiplier is a whole number. The whole number is produced by dividing the monthly rental income into the sale price of a comparable property. For example, if the sale price of a residence were $120,000 and it had been rented for $1,200 a month, $120,000 is divided by $1,200 and the multiplier is found to be 100. The system is used by practicing appraisers because it is straightforward and simple. Its reliability, of course, rests on the dependability of the data used.

Most appraisers believe that no adjustments can or should be made in the development of the multiplier. They feel that if comparable sales are not reasonably similar, they should be dropped from consideration. A few appraisers still feel that under some circumstances adjustments can be made in the data collected, on the same basis as in the market data approach, using the four elements of comparison. This process is not recommended.

LIMITATIONS OF THE GMRM

The multiplier, like any other approach, can produce excellent results if the data used is reliable and appropriate. However, it can be misleading and produce indefensible conclusions if the technique used or the information applied is inappropriate. The situations under which the results are most desirable include:

1. The properties from which the multiplier is developed have common characteristics (size, age, physical condition, neighborhood, etc.) with the residence being appraised.

2. The multiplier is extracted from properties for which there is an active market. If there is not an active market (that is, many recent sales), information on which to base a conclusion will be inadequate.

3. The market information is correct and rentals have been verified. When verification develops significant special conditions or special financing the date should either not be used or given little weight.

CALCULATING A GMRM

The following example illustrates how a GMRM is derived from the market, which is based on using actual sales and dividing them by their actual rentals at the time of the sale, without making any adjustments. The multipliers in Fig. 15-1 range from 106.4 to 112.3 with 110 as most common multiplier. It is the multiplier for properties that appears to be closest to the value of the property being appraised. Therefore, 110 was selected as the appropriate multiplier.

FIG. 15-1 FINDING THE GMRM (WITHOUT ADJUSTMENTS)

Comparable Property	Verified Sale Price	Monthly Rent	Indicate Gross Monthly Rent Multiplier
1	$119,700	$1,125	106.4
2	123,600	1,150	107.8
3	127,500	1,150	110.9
4	128,850	1,200	107.3
5	132,000	1,200	110.0
6	133,500	1,250	106.8
7	133,350	1,200	111.3
8	134,700	1,200	111.2
9	132,000	1,200	110.0
10	133,500	1,200	111.2
11	132,500	1,200	110.4
12	123,600	1,100	112.3

ESTIMATING MARKET RENT OF THE APPRAISED RESIDENCE

The following represent two illustrations that show how to derive the market rent of the residence being appraised from the market. The first is based on the actual rental of the residence being appraised, which has been ascertained to be the market rent. The second is based on comparing it with other rental residences and adjusting for any differences. The adjusted comparable rentals are used as indicators of rental value for the residence being appraised.

EXAMPLE ONE - ESTIMATING MARKET RENT WITHOUT ADJUSTMENTS

If the appraised property is rented, the monthly rental can be used as an indication of the market rent. It is not acceptable appraisal practice, however, to use this contract rent without checking it against other rents in the market. In this illustration the appraised property is rented for $1,200 per month.   Based on information obtained from the owner and tenant, it appears to be an arms-length arrangement, with both parties believing the rent is what the property should be generating. This is a good indication that the market rent for such a property is $1,200. To check this rental in the market, other rented houses similar to it should be located.

Based on the array shown in Fig. 15-2, and considering the reported rent of the appraised residence, its market rent appears to be about $1,200. Some appraisers would consider this sufficient data on which to base the estimate of market rent. Other appraisers feel it is better to adjust the rental of each of the residences and then make the estimate, especially when the comparables differ to a certain extent from the property being appraised.

FIG. 15-2 ESTIMATING MARKET RENT WITHOUT ADJUSTMENTS

Comparable Property	Monthly Rent
1	$1,185
2	1,200
3	1,215
4	1,200
5	1,200
6	1,170
7	1,230
8	1,200

EXAMPLE TWO - ESTIMATING MARKET RENT WITH ADJUSTMENTS

In this example, the property being appraised has one bathroom, a one-car garage, no central air conditioning and is rented without utilities included. Some comparable rentals have two bathrooms, two-car garages, central air conditioning and/or are rented with utilities included. Adjustments may be needed to reflect the rental differences.

Because it is difficult to tell if differences affect rents in similar or opposite ways just by looking at them, the "matched pair" technique is used to abstract adjustments from the market. When more than one difference exists, one rental is designated as the base rental, which is adjusted for all known differences except the one being sought. Then it is compared with the other rental in the pair and any remaining difference in rent is attributed to the remaining element of comparison. This technique is illustrated in Fig. 15-3.

FIG. 15-3 ESTIMATING MARKET RENT WITH ADJUSTMENTS

Comparable Rental #1 - In the same neighborhood and similar to the subject property. It had one bathroom, no central air conditioning, and a one car garage: It was recently rented unfurnished and without utilities for $1,215 per month. There were no reported special conditions.

Comparable Rental #2 - The same neighborhood and similar to the subject property. It had two bathrooms, no central air conditioning, and a one car garage: It was recently rented unfurnished and without utilities for $1,275 per month. There were no reported special conditions.

Comparable Rental #3 - The same neighborhood and similar to the subject property. It had two bathrooms, no central air conditioning, and a one car garage: It was recently rented unfurnished and without utilities for $1,320 per month. There were no reported special conditions.

Comparable Rental #4 - The same neighborhood and similar to the subject property. It had two bathrooms, central air conditioning, and a two car garage: It was recently rented unfurnished and without utilities for $1,395 per month. There were no reported special conditions.

Comparable Rental #5 - The same neighborhood and similar to the subject property. It had one bathroom, no central air conditioning, and a one car garage: It was recently rented unfurnished and with owner-supplied utilities for $1,410 per month. There were no reported special conditions.

	Adjustments	Monthly Rent
BATHROOM ADJUSTMENT		
Comparable Rental #1 (base) -	one bathroom, one car garage	$1,215
Comparable Rental #2 -	two bathrooms, one car garage	1,275
Difference attributable to number of bathrooms:		$60
GARAGE ADJUSTMENT		
Comparable Rental #1 (base) -	one bathroom, one car garage	$1,215
Comparable Rental #3 -	two bathrooms, two car garage	1,320
Adjustment to Comparable Rental #3 to reflect difference in number of bathrooms based on Comparable Rentals #1 and #2		-60
Adjusted Comparable Rental #3		$1,260
Monthly rental difference attributed to size of garage: $1,215 [base Comp. #1] - $1,260 [Adjusted Comp. #3]		$45
CENTRAL AIR CONDITIONING ADJUSTMENT		
Comparable Rental #1 (base) -	one bathroom, one car garage, no central air conditioning	$1,215
Comparable Rental #4 -	two bathrooms, two car garage, central air conditioning	1,395
Adjustment to Comparable Rental #4 to reflect difference in number of bathrooms		-60

Adjustment (based on Rentals #1 and #2) to
Comparable Rental #4 to reflect difference in
garage size
(based on Comparable Rentals #1 and #3)   45

Adjusted Comparable Rental #4 $1,290

Difference attributable to central air conditioning: $75

INCLUSION OF UTILITIES ADJUSTMENT

Comparable Rental #1 (base) - one bathroom,
                               one car garage,
                               no central air,
                               no utilities $1,215

Comparable Rental #5 -   one bathroom,
                               one car garage,
                               no central air,
                               utilities paid by owner 1,410

Difference attributable to inclusion of utilities: $195

Each comparable rental is adjusted to give an indication of the market rental of the appraised property. If an element of comparison in the comparable rental results in a higher rental than what the property being appraised would rent for, a minus adjustment is made. For example, if the only difference is that the appraised property has three bedrooms and a comparable rental has four bedrooms, with the extra bedroom contributing $250 to the monthly rental, then a minus $250 adjustment is made on the comparable rental. These adjustment techniques are identical to those used in the Sales Comparison Approach.

A rating grid may be used to display information about the appraised property and the comparable rentals, along with adjustments for each difference between them (See Fig. 15-4).

FIG. 15-4 COMPARABLE RENTAL GRID

Item	Appraised House	Comp. Rental 1	Comp. Rental 2	Comp. Rental 3	Comp. Rental 4	Comp. Rental 5
Rent		$1215	$1275	$1320	$1395	$1410
Bathrooms	one	one -0-	two -$60	two -$60	two -$60	one -0-
Garage Size	one-car	one-car -0-	one-car -0-	two-car -$45	two-car -$45	one-car -0-
Central Air Conditioning	no	no	no	no	yes	no
Utilities Payment	tenant	tenant -0-	tenant -0-	tenant -0-	tenant -0-	owner -$195
Net adjustment		-0-	-$60	-$105	-$180	-$195
Indicated rent of appraised house		$1215	$1215	$1215	$1215	$1215

Actual data would rarely work out this precisely. Often both plus and minus adjustments would be made and the indicated rents for the house being appraised would vary, requiring reconciling into a final indicated rental value.

ESTIMATING THE VALUE OF THE SUBJECT PROPERTY

The third step of the income approach is to estimate the indicated market value of the residence being appraised, which is done by multiplying the estimated market rent of the residence by the GMRM selected. For example, if the GMRM selected were 110, based on market data, and the estimated market rent of the residence being appraised were $1215. per month (unfurnished and without utilities), its indicated market value is calculated as follows:

1. Estimated market rent of house being appraised $1215

2. Gross Monthly Rent Multiplier   <u>x 110</u>

3. Indicated value of the residence being appraised
   via the income approach $133,650

SUMMARY

This chapter illustrates the use of the GMRM income approach as it applies to the single family residence. It is also referred to as the Gross Monthly Rent Multiplier approach and is considered a reliable approach to estimate market value if the data used is verified and representative of the market.

There are three steps in the GMRM income approach:

1. The GMRM is selected by finding residences similar to the residence being appraised in the same or nearby neighborhoods that were rented at the time they were sold. The whole number, which is obtained by dividing the sales price by the monthly rent (usually unfurnished and without utilities included), is known as the Gross Monthly Rent Multiplier and expresses the relationship between rental income and market value.

2. The market rent of the residence being appraised is estimated. Either the actual rent of the residence is used (after confirming that it is typical of the market) or the market rent is estimated by comparing the residence to other rented, comparable properties in the market and adjusting for any significant differences.

3. The indicated value via the GMRM income approach is obtained by multiplying the GMRM selected in Step 1 by the estimated market rent of the residence being appraised (Step 2).

LARGE CENTRAL CHIMNEY

STEEP GABLE ROOF
EXTENDED TO FIRST
FLOOR IN REAR

2 OR 2½ STORIES

SQUARE OR
RECTANGULAR
SHAPE

NO WINDOWS
IN REAR

SMALL GLASS
PANES IN
DOUBLE-HUNG
WINDOWS

Colonial American

SALT BOX COLONIAL OR CATSLIDE (IN SOUTH)
(Salt Box or Catslide - 109)

EXTERIOR END CHIMNEY

STEEP, GABLE ROOF

SMALLER WINDOWS, SECOND FLOOR

SECOND STORY OVERHANG

CASEMENT WINDOWS; SMALL GLASS PANES

DROPS

Colonial American

GARRISON COLONIAL (Garr Co - 106)

16 Reconciliation and Final Value Estimate

The purpose of an appraisal is to make a supported objective opinion of value, as of a specific date, of an adequately and accurately described property.

In each step of the appraisal process, the appraiser collects and analyzes data and reconciles it. There is also a final reconciliation. In this process the appraiser considers the quantity and quality of the data collected, analyzed and displayed in the appraisal report.

In addition, the appraiser considers any other related data about which he or she has knowledge, as well as general knowledge of the market and the economy.

In the past, this process was known among appraisers as correlation. Since correlation has a different meaning in statistics and other academic disciplines, it has been replaced by the word reconciliation.

DEFINITION OF THE PROBLEM

Reconciliation starts at the very beginning of an appraisal, with the definition of the appraisal problem, the preliminary survey and the data collection program. The appraiser must ascertain the character and quantity of work to be accomplished and begin to weigh the relative significance and applicability of various data and approaches to the problem.

IDENTIFICATION OF THE REAL ESTATE

The report must provide a positive identification of the residence being appraised. Regardless of the method of identification (street name and number, metes and bounds, etc.) the location and boundaries must be specified. All significant easements, encroachments and rights-of-way must be considered. If there is an owners' association or rights to use nearby facilities are involved, these rights must be completely identified. The appraiser should be sure the identification meets the requirements of the Uniform Standards of Professional Appraisal Practice, which requires a clear and complete description of the property.

IDENTIFICATION OF THE PROPERTY RIGHTS TO BE VALUED

When the property is in fee simple, a plain statement to this effect should be sufficient. If a leasehold or a residence on leased land is involved, the terms of these leases must be described and their effect on the estimated value must be analyzed. Analysis of condominium or cooperative ownership rights requires a survey of the entire project in which the features, both good and bad, of the entire project are related to the ownership interest being appraised. A residence that has time-sharing rights requires other consideration. For example, are the rights to use the property for December and June equal to the rights to use the same property for January and July?

The ownership rights of the property being appraised must be compared to those of comparable sales and offerings. Any differences will require adjustment.

DATE OF VALUE ESTIMATE

In a stable market, the date of valuation and any time adjustments made to comparable sales, rentals, cost estimates and offerings, present few problems. However, in unstable and rapidly changing markets any time differential is reviewed. Time adjustments are often averaged over a period of time when, in reality, the market has been moving both upward and downward during the period. Such adjustments, based on average value changes in a community, may not apply to the neighborhood or the price range of the property being appraised. Large time adjustments based on one or two matched pairs may contain substantial error caused by some unknown factor.

USE OF THE APPRAISAL

If the objective of the appraisal is to estimate the market value, the appraiser asks if it accomplishes this objective. Is the potential error in the appraisal within boundaries that are satisfactory to the user of the appraisal? Would more data and better analysis reduce the possibility of potential error? Does the appraisal state the degree of potential error that exists, or is this degree of accuracy misleading?

When the objective of the appraisal is to estimate value other than market value, the data collected and analyzed must be sufficient and proper to produce the required value estimate. For example, if the value estimated is insurable value, have all the items to be excluded such as footings, underground pipes and site work been properly treated?

Finally, the most important question is whether the value estimated is a sufficiently accurate estimate of the defined value.

DEFINITION OF VALUE

It is not satisfactory to put a stock definition of value into an appraisal report without carefully understanding its meaning.

For example, market value may be defined, in part, as the highest a price the property will bring or as the most probable selling price. One definition may be more appropriate than the other after an analysis has been made of the data. Insurable value requires a definition that is acceptable in the locale or region for the type of property being appraised. Often a different definition of insurable value exists for residential and commercial properties.

A review of the definition of value should be made after all the data has been collected and analyzed to determine if it still applies or should be modified.

OTHER LIMITING CONDITIONS

For the protection of appraisers and clients it is often appropriate for the appraiser to set forth those other limiting conditions that apply to this appraisal assignment, besides the other items included in the definition of the problem which are also considered to be limiting conditions.

PRELIMINARY SURVEY AND APPRAISAL PLAN

DATA NEEDED

A step-by-step review of the preliminary survey and appraisal is made, to determine if all the necessary data has been obtained, and adequate analysis has been provided to arrive at the value estimate. Often, the initial estimate of the data needed to make the appraisal proves to be insufficient to arrive at a satisfactory value estimate. For example, the original plan may call for only the use of comparable sales. However, when the market analysis is made, it may indicate that the shifting market is being affected by the number of competitive listings available. Therefore, information about listings should be used in the market data approach.

Changing building costs and the availability of sites and new, competitive houses may indicate that a detailed application of the cost approach, based on actual costs of available sites and residences currently under construction, will provide a good value indication. The lack of current rentals and information about rented houses that have sold may require the abandonment of an original plan to include an income approach analysis.

As part of the reconciliation process, the data used in each section of the report must be carefully analyzed with emphasis on making a final judgment about whether sufficient data has been collected and which data should be used to make the final value estimate. It is poor practice to have inflexible rules about the type and amount of data used; this decision must be made separately for each appraisal problem.

DATA SOURCES

After the initial data has been collected and analyzed, the data sources should again be reviewed to determine if additional sources may be available. For example, offerings of nearby comparable properties from an MLS may not show as sales because they were sold either by another broker or by the owner after the listing expired. By tracking these particular properties in the sales records of the community, additional useful comparable sales may be found. The search for comparables may disclose sales of residences that were recently completed by a local builder. This builder now becomes the potential source of cost data to be used in the cost approach.

Brokers, lenders, and others interviewed for information often supply leads to additional data sources. All data sources should be reviewed to determine if they have been properly used.

PERSONNEL AND TIME REQUIREMENTS

The initial estimate of needed personnel should be reviewed to see if they will be·able to obtain all the necessary data within the prescribed time. If additional data is needed, extra personnel or additional time on the part of the original personnel will be required.

Often the time originally allocated to complete an assignment will have to be revised. Only when the special requirements of a specific assignment are known, can a final estimate of the time schedule be made. Other considerations such as new assignments taking priority over existing assignments, unexpected illnesses of personnel, revised requirements of the client and personal needs of the appraiser often make scheduling revisions necessary.

The completion flow chart initially serves as a guide through the appraisal process. It can consist of simple notes on how the appraisal will be made or it may be a formal chart showing the progress of the appraisal on step-by-step basis. Some appraisers use magnetic boards and movable pieces to plot the progress of each appraisal assignment. Whatever system is used, it should be reviewed to keep track of the progress of the assignment and altered to reflect the updated requirements to complete the assignment.

FEE PROPOSAL AND CONTRACT

It is good practice to have an agreement with each client about what work will be performed, when it is due and how you will be paid. This contract may be verbal or in writing.

DATA COLLECTION AND ANALYSIS

Ongoing decisions must be made on how much data will be collected and whether the quantity and quality are sufficient to complete the appraisal assignment.

GENERAL DATA

It is easy to collect masses of general data about the region, community and neighborhood in which the residence being appraised is located. It is very hard to cull from this mass of data that information which directly describes the environment and explains the forces affecting the value of the property.

This reconciliation is probably one of the most difficult to do properly and one that tends to be downplayed in importance. "Window dressing"–an appraiser's term for unnecessary (merely decorative) figures, charts and displays–is not appropriate in a professional appraisal report.

The use of demographic information is a good example. There is little justification for simply presenting population figures. Rather, a comparison of population increase with the availability of housing stock, vacancy rates and a forecast of the rate of growth of new housing is more valuable. Raw figures cannot tell the story. All information pertaining to the region, community and neighborhood must be carefully analyzed and reconciled to produce a meaningful presentation.

Economic data, used to prepare market, financial and economic base analyses and to project future trends, also tends to be available in great masses. A visit to the local Chamber of Commerce will often supply the appraiser with pounds of this type of information. Usually one source, no matter how good, will be insufficient to provide all the needed data. As the data is sorted and analyzed, it must be reconciled into a meaningful analysis that will be useful in making a value estimate of the property being appraised.

SPECIFIC DATA

Information about the property being appraised is obtained at the community record source and at the property site. The goal is to accumulate all of the needed data during one trip to each of these places. This can be accomplished by careful planning and the use of checklists and fieldnote forms. A careful review of the data collected on location is the beginning of the specific data reconciliation.

An appraiser is not expected to be a title searcher. However, it is necessary to acquire enough skill to be able to find and use the needed documents. Title papers are examined to produce a positive description of the property; they also will reveal easements, rights-of-way and any private deed restrictions. Sometimes these items have a substantial effect on the value of the property.

Another item to be checked at the record source is the tax assessment. If possible, the assessor's field card should be examined. It often contains useful descriptive information about the property that may affect the final value estimate.

Zoning information can also be obtained at the municipal record source. A preliminary reconciliation may reveal whether the property conforms or if a reasonable probability of a zoning change exists. An initial reconciliation at the data source can determine whether additional record data pertaining either to the property being appraised or comparable properties is needed. Later, when the data about the community, neighborhood, and property being appraised is reconciled, a more accurate judgment may be made.

Most of the information is usually obtained at the site. The use of checklists or fieldnote forms is helpful. Some clients will provide forms with their special informational requirements. Some clients require a complete list of all items of observed physical deterioration-curable, together with individual estimates of the cost to cure each item. These items may have to be checked even though the appraiser normally would not include them.

The final reconciliation of this information determines whether the property has been completely and accurately described and whether there is sufficient information to complete each of the three approaches to value.

HIGHEST AND BEST USE

Estimating the highest and best use starts with an analysis and reconciliation of all the general and specific information collected about the property. It is done in two parts: first the site is analyzed as if vacant, and then taking into consideration any existing improvements. The information is reconciled with the four tests of highest and best use. First zoning information and private restrictions are reconciled to indicate what uses are currently legally permitted. Then the community and neighborhood information is reconciled with economic information to determine if a reasonable probability of change in zoning exists. The information is further reconciled into an estimate of the reasonable and probable permitted legal uses. Next, the physical information about the site is reconciled to estimate which of the reasonable and probable legally permitted uses is also physically possible.

The community, neighborhood and economic data are again reconciled to estimate what uses would result in the production of a profit. Even if the legally permitted use is for a single family residence and such a residence can be built and can produce a profit, this is not sufficient to conclude that the highest and best use is for a single family residence. The type of residence, style, size, design and construction must also be determined.

If after reconciliation of the available information it is estimated that the highest and best use is for something other than a single family residence, this should be stated.

The final step is an estimate of the most profitable use. Again, all the information is reconciled. If additional information is needed, it is gathered and analyzed. Reconciliation produces a decision about what the most potentially profitable, physically and legally permitted use of the site is, assuming it were vacant.

This analysis is then repeated to estimate the highest and best use of the property as improved. The information about the region, community, neighborhood, site and existing improvements is analyzed to estimate what renovation and repairs, if any, could be made to result in a greater potential profit (or smaller loss) by the owner if the property were sold on the date of appraisal. This estimate may range from a simple list of physical and functional curable items through major renovations and proposed additional improvements to the site.

The estimation of highest and best use is based on a thorough analysis and reconciliation of all the data collected. Again, it may be necessary to collect and analyze additional data before final reconciliation as to the highest and best use can be made. For example, the preliminary reconciliation may indicate that some renovation may be needed. At this point additional information about its cost and physical feasibility is necessary before a final determination can be made; the reconciliation process is continued after the needed information is collected and analyzed.

Information about sales of comparative sites and improved properties, comparative rentals and rented properties that have sold is initially reconciled to see if it is sufficient to produce an indicated value by the three approaches to value.

The preliminary reconciliation reviews the sources of cost data which will be used to estimate reproduction or replacement costs. If a cost service is used as one source, a second source should also be developed. The cost data should be subject to a preliminary reconciliation with the description of the improvements to see if material to estimate all of the costs is available.

A decision about the method of estimating depreciation, based on the available data should be made. If the abstraction method is used, comparable sales are analyzed to see if they are sufficient in number and comparable enough to the property being appraised to produce a satisfactory depreciation estimate. If the age-life or breakdown method is used, a preliminary reconciliation is made to determine if sufficient data has been collected.

The income approach depends upon sufficient data on comparable rented residences to estimate both the market rent of the property being appraised and also to develop the GMRM. The rentals used to develop the GMRM must be of properties that have recently sold. The initial reconciliation determines if sufficient usable data has been collected to make these estimates or whether additional rentals and sales are needed. If insufficient data regarding sales of rented properties exists, the income approach may not be usable.

Since the final value estimate of most single family residential appraisals depends heavily on the market data approach, it is necessary to reconcile the comparative sales data continuously during the appraisal process. Initial reconciliations are needed to see if sufficient comparable sales data, as well as data to make necessary adjustments, has been collected to reflect the differences between the comparable sales selected and the residence being appraised.

It is not good appraisal practice to claim that insufficient data has been found to develop the market data approach unless a thorough search of the market has been conducted. If sales appear insufficient after the initial reconciliation, the search should begin again. This expanded search can be over a wider geographic area, wider price range or greater time frame. The process may be repeated several times, each time collecting and reconciling data to determine its usefulness until it is concluded either that sufficient data is collected for the market data approach or that further expansion of the search will not produce any additional useful data.

All of the reconciling done up to this point is of a preliminary nature, with the primary goal being to collect enough useful data to proceed through the three approaches to value.

APPLICATION OF THE THREE APPROACHES

The reconciliation process continues as the collected data is further analyzed for use in each of the approaches.

INCOME APPROACH (GMRM)

The Gross Monthly Rent Multiplier technique used in the appraisal of single family residences includes the following eight steps:

1. Find residences that have recently sold in the neighborhood that are comparable to the property being appraised, that were rented at the time of sale. All recent sales are reviewed and those most comparable are selected for final use. No fixed number of comparables is needed. Many appraisers try to find at least 12. If a larger number can be found, they may lend themselves to analysis by statistical techniques (see Appendix G).

2. Divide the sales price of each comparable by the monthly rental to derive the GMRM. The resulting GMRM figures should be arranged in order to determine if they fall into a useful range and if extremes should be dropped or additional data is needed.

3. Reconcile the multipliers to obtain a single multiplier or a range of multipliers that is applicable to the appraised property. If a single GMRM is selected, it should not be an average of the multipliers obtained in Step 2. It should be a result of

considering how comparable each of the properties that produced a multiplier was to the property being appraised or the result of statistical analysis of the range of multipliers.

4. Find comparable rentals in the neighborhood. Comparable rentals are reviewed and selected for final use. Again no fixed number is standard; however, less than three usually is not satisfactory. The reconciliation here emphasizes the comparability of the rental to the property being appraised and the identification of the existing significant differences for which adjustments are made.

5. Analyze each of the comparable rentals by comparing them with the corresponding features of the house being appraised. A decision must be made on an item-by-item basis about whether the differences can be adjusted for or if the rental must be rejected. If many rentals are rejected, it may be necessary to go back to the market and expand the search to find additional useful data.

6. Estimate the required adjustments of each comparable rental property to obtain an indicated rental for the appraised property. All the additional rentals needed to estimate the adjustments are analyzed. Those that will produce indications of the needed adjustments are processed. These adjustments are reconciled with the comparable sales, and data is added or eliminated as required.

7. Consider each comparable rental carefully, with emphasis on the need for adjustments, and formulate an opinion of the market (economic) rent of the property being appraised, based on the adjusted rentals of the comparables. Often the rentals are adjusted with the aid of a grid. The result is a group of adjusted rentals, each of which is an indication of the market rent of the residence being appraised. These adjusted rentals are individually compared to the property being appraised to estimate which are most comparable. Finally, a decision is made as to the estimated market rent of the property being appraised. This estimate should not be an average but is based on the results of the reconciliation.

8. Multiply the estimated market rent of the appraised property by the estimated monthly multiplier (or range of multipliers) to obtain an indicated value of the appraised residence via the income approach. This result should not be accepted without another reconciliation of all the data. The appraiser must be satisfied that the data used is of adequate quantity and quality to produce a useful estimate.

INCOME APPROACH (CAPITALIZATION METHOD)

In the appraisal of an investment property, the income capitalization method is usually the most appropriate. The appraiser considers both the quantity and quality of the rental data used to develop the Gross Income Estimate.

Expense and Replacement Reserve estimates are developed from data collected about comparable properties and the subject property.

The rental estimates and expense estimates are reconciled into an estimate of net operating income (NOI).

The final step is to develop an appropriate capitalization rate and then divide the NOI by the capitalization rate for the subject property and market.

COST APPROACH

The reconciliation process is applied to each step of this approach.

1. Estimate the market value of the site as if vacant and available for development to its highest and best use (see Chapter 9). The estimate of the site value actually requires all of the steps of the market data approach. First, the comparable sites are reconciled, comparing their use with the estimate highest and best use of the site being appraised. For example, if the site being appraised were best suited for a house in the $80,000 to $100,000 range, sites for houses of similar value would be the best comparables even if the house being appraised were in the $30,000 to $35,000 range and therefore not the highest and best use.

The best comparables are selected and individually compared to the site being appraised. Differences between the comparable sites and the site being appraised are reported. The data is further analyzed for information on which to base adjustments for all the significant differences. A decision is then made about each comparable as to whether it can be adjusted satisfactorily or must be rejected and replaced with a better comparable. If many sales are rejected, it may be necessary to go back to the market and expand the search for more comparable site sales and/or more data on which to base the adjustments.

When the appraiser is satisfied that the assembled data is adequate and all the needed adjustments have been made, the adjusted sales price of each of the comparables is analyzed and a final indicated value of the appraised site is obtained. This estimate is not an average of the adjusted sale price of the comparables; it is based on the results of the reconciliation.

2. Estimate the reproduction (or replacement) cost new of the improvements. This estimate can be based on data from construction cost services and/or from actual costs of similar residences constructed in the same market. The available data is reconciled to determine which method will be used. Both the description of the improvements and the data being used as a cost basis are analyzed to determine if everything needed to make the cost estimate has been gathered. The cost data is reconciled with the description of the improvements data to produce an estimated reproduction or replacement cost of the residence being appraised.

3. Estimate the amount of depreciation the improvements have suffered. A decision is made as to which method will be used to estimate the accrued depreciation. When the abstraction method is used, the sales selected from which to abstract the depreciation are analyzed and processed. The range of resulting amounts of depreciation or rates of depreciation are reconciled. Reconciliation considers the comparability of the data from which the amount or rate of depreciation is abstracted. The final reconciliation considers the amount of data used, the degree of variance between the rates and whether additional data is needed to produce a satisfactory estimate of depreciation.

If the age-life method is used, depreciation may be based entirely upon observation. To estimate the typical economic life of a residence, data about the region, community and neighborhood is considered, along with specific data about the residence being appraised. Each of the four great forces that affect the value and life of the residence is considered. This data is then reconciled by the appraiser, who relies heavily on personal knowledge and experience, into an estimate of typical economic life. Finally, the percentage of depreciation is calculated by dividing the effective age by the typical economic life. A final reconciliation of the results determines how good the estimate is and how much weight it will be given in the appraisal process.

The breakdown method of estimating depreciation is done in five steps that correspond to the five types of depreciation identified by this method. First, the physical deterioration-curable is estimated by making a list of all the physical deterioration that is observed. Cost to cure these items is estimated either by the appraiser or by a local contractor who can provide the needed cost information.

Most items of normal maintenance are automatically classified as physical deterioration-curable without actually proving they add value in excess of their cost. However, it may be necessary to obtain market information to justify classifying large items of maintenance as curable. The list of items to be cured and the estimated costs to do the work are reconciled into an estimate of physical deterioration-curable.

Physical deterioration-incurable is divided into two groups. One group is items that are not ready to be cured on the date of the appraisal but will need to be cured before the end of the residence's economic life. A list is prepared together with cost estimates to repair or replace the items. These items are reconciled into an estimate of physical deterioration-incurable (short-lived items). The other group of items includes those that have suffered some deterioration but will not be economically feasible to repair or replace during the remaining typical economic life of the improvements. The estimate is often made based on an engineering breakdown of the components of the residence against which percentage of depreciation estimates are applied to produce a total estimate of the physical deterioration-incurable. This estimate depends heavily on the appraiser's knowledge and judgment. All the data used should be carefully reconciled, and the reliability of the results reported.

Items of functional obsolescence are listed and analyzed to estimate if a cure is possible. If so, it is noted whether the cost to cure is less than the value added. Reconciliation of this information may require the use of additional data to support whether the value added will exceed the cost to cure. Data is also needed to estimate the cost to cure the items as part of a total construction program as well as the cost to do so separately on the date of the appraisal. The reliability of this estimate is considered in the reconciliation.

The loss from functional obsolescence-incurable may be based on comparison of recently sold or rented residences with and without the item or features causing the obsolescence.

The items off the premises that cause a loss in value (economic obsolescence) are listed, measured and estimated.

In the past, the breakdown method was a favorite method of many appraisers. However, it is a very difficult method to use in actual practice because of all the data needed. There is usually a high probability of error.

4. Deduct the depreciation from the reproduction (or replacement) cost new of the improvements to obtain the depreciated value of the improvements "as is". If depreciation has been estimated by more than one method, the results are reconciled into a depreciation estimate. When sufficient data is available, the abstraction method usually produces the most accurate estimate because it is based directly upon market data. The age-life method usually is based primarily on the appraiser's judgment, supported more heavily by general knowledge than by

specific data. Because it is easy to explain, it usually is the best method when insufficient data is available for abstraction method. The results of the breakdown method tend to be deceiving because it is broken into five parts. Because it is not primarily based on the market, there is potential for substantial error. When used, it should be carefully reconciled to eliminate as much potential error as possible.

When more than one method is used, the results should be compared. Reasons for differences should be sought and the estimates further refined, if possible, to reduce the discrepancies. The final depreciation estimate is deducted from the estimated reproduction or replacement cost to produce the depreciated value of the improvements.

5. Add the site (land) market value obtained in Step 1 to the depreciated value of the improvements to obtain an indicated value of the property. After the estimated value is obtained, it is compared with the values indicated by the other approaches. A wide variance is indicative of possible weaknesses in the data, assumptions, or application of the cost approach or its validity and applicability to the specific appraisal problem.

SALES COMPARISON APPROACH

The reconciliation process is applied to each of the five steps of the market data approach.

1. Find the sales, listings and offerings of properties that are similar to the property being appraised. When a group of sales, listings and offerings has been collected, a preliminary reconciliation is made for the purpose of deciding if enough usable data has been obtained. The setting of arbitrary numbers of sales, listings and offerings to be used--without actually considering the quality of the data--is poor appraisal practice.

2. Verify each sale with the buyer, seller or broker to confirm the selling price, data of transaction, physical and locational characteristics and conditions of sale. The only acceptable way to find out about the conditions of sale that affected a transaction is to interview the buyer, seller or broker. Only these people will know all the terms, motivations and whether the sale was bona fide in nature. The results of the interviews should be reconciled. If information indicates conditions of sale that will be difficult to adjust for, the sale should be rejected and replaced with additional data, if possible, and the reconciliation process repeated.

3. Analyze the important attributes of each comparable and compare the corresponding features of the property being appraised. Use the elements of comparison such as time of sale, location, physical and other characteristics (see Chapter 13). The analysis of the important attributes of each comparable will identify differences between the comparables and the property being appraised. The available data is then reconciled to determine if it will serve as a basis for making the needed adjustments or whether additional data will be needed. The search continues for data until a sufficient number of sales, listings and offerings is found with differences that can be adjusted for.

4. Estimate the adjustments that will be required for the sales price of each comparable to give an indicated value for the appraised property. Adjustments should be supported with data developed from the market, which is reconciled to produce an adjusted sales price for each comparable.

5. Consider each of the comparable sales and the accuracy of any and all adjustments required because of dissimilarities among these sales and the appraised property. Formulate an opinion of market value for the latter based on the comparable sales which have been analyzed. The reconciliation of the adjusted price of each comparable into a final value estimate for the appraised property is the critical step in the appraisal process because this estimate will most likely be used as the main basis for the final value estimate. The reconciliation process considers the supporting data for each adjustment. When there is a substantial spread in adjusted prices, consideration should be given to expanding the data search and repeating the whole process to obtain better results.

In the final reconciliation of the market data approach, the quantity and quality of all the data is reviewed. Generally, the older the data, the further from the property being appraised and the more physically dissimilar, the less accurate the adjusted price will be. It is particularly difficult to adjust accurately for conditions of sale and economic influences.

Again, the market value obtained in the market data approach is compared with value indications derived in the other two approaches. Wide discrepancies in indicated value usually suggest that further collection, refinement and analysis of the pertinent data is needed.

FINAL RECONCILIATION INTO ESTIMATE OF VALUE

The final step in the reconciliation is to check all data for accuracy, reliability and applicability. The purpose and objectives of the report are summarized and the characteristics of the property are reviewed. A decision is made regarding the most appropriate approach or approaches to value and the reliability of each value indication as obtained.

ADVANTAGES AND DISADVANTAGES OF EACH APPROACH

The income approach is mathematically simple and direct. It is most useful when the subject of the appraisal is located in a neighborhood where houses are frequently rented. Disadvantages of this approach are that the condition of comparables is not always reflected in rent differentials, many quality neighborhoods have few houses that are rented and subsequently sold, and a considerable volume of rental and sales data is necessary to estimate properly the market rent and appropriate multiplier for use in this approach.

The cost approach was traditionally the favorite approach to value for many appraisers. Its advantages are that it is simple to use and usually reliable for new improvements on properties developed to their highest and best use. The disadvantages are the difficulty of accurately estimating accrued depreciation when no sales are available from which to calculate the depreciation by abstraction, and that the reproduction cost estimates may not reflect actual prevailing economic and market conditions.

The market data approach is usually the preferred approach in single family residential appraising. The value indication obtained is based on actual market transactions, is easily understood by laypeople and is most applicable in court testimony. It is not particularly useful when there is a lack of recent, reliable and highly comparable sales data.

APPRAISAL REPORT

The final step of the appraisal process is the preparation of a report of the value estimated. It is poor appraisal practice to give a value estimate without a report that meets at least the minimum reporting requirements.

All the data is reconciled once again to select the material to be displayed in the appraisal report. Reports to be used for condemnation proceedings and other legal proceedings often must be very comprehensive, containing large amounts of the data used to make the value estimate. Photographs, maps, sketches, charts and other graphics are often included to help the reader understand the analysis and reasoning that led the appraiser to the final value estimate. A lender who uses the services of an appraiser on a regular basis may require only a form report that displays the highlights of the data and reasoning used to arrive at the value estimate.

SUMMARY

The accuracy of an appraisal depends on the appraiser's knowledge, experience, and judgment. Equally important are the quantity and quality of the available data that will be reconciled in the final value conclusion. A judgement is made as to the validity and reliability of each of the value indications derived from the three approaches to value. These indications are never merely averaged. To do so is to substitute arithmetic for judgment. Rather, the appraiser reconciles the value indications, analyzes the alternatives and selects from among them that indication of value which will be most defensible and truly representative of the property being appraised.

BALCONY ACROSS FRONT AT SECOND FLOOR

SHINGLE
ROOF

2 STORIES

RAIL SIMPLE
IRON OR WOOD

Nineteenth Century American

MONTEREY (Monterey - 715)

17 Residences Requiring Special Appraisal Techniques

When one thinks of appraising a residence what usually comes to mind is a free standing single family home on its own lot. About 75% of the residences in the country fit that picture. Yet, the other 25% vary in many ways. Listed below in alphabetical order are the kinds of atypical residences covered in this chapter. Each presents to the appraiser special problems which require special appraisal techniques in order to make a satisfactory appraisal.

When you examine the list you will see that many residences fit into more than one category. Many of the special appraisal techniques described for both categories will then be helpful.

FIG. 17-1 SPECIAL KINDS OF RESIDENCES

- Condominiums
- Cooperatives
- De Minimis PUD
- Colonial Reproductions
- Elderly Housing
- Energy Efficient Homes
- Experimental Houses
- Farm and Ranch Houses
- Historic Houses
- Log Cabins
- Mansions
- Manufactured Houses
- Mobile Homes
- Planned Unit Developments
- Residences on Leased Land
- Second Homes
- Ski Lodges and Homes in Skiing Areas
- Solar Houses
- Timesharing
- Waterfront Houses
- Underground Houses

When appraising a unique residence, the appraiser must possess the specialized knowledge required to make the appraisal. It is customary for appraisers who lack the necessary knowledge to seek help from someone who possesses it. If the help that is received is significant it should be acknowledged in the appraisal report.

CONDOMINIUMS

The biggest change in American home ownership since World War II is the Condominium which did not exist prior to that time.

TYPES OF CONDOMINIUMS

"Condominium" is a form of ownership that is used for a variety of different types of residences. There is no official breakdown of the different types, but the following is a general breakdown.

> In-town residences with few amenities
> Suburban residences with few amenities
> Suburban residences with recreational facilities
> Resort second homes
> Retirement housing
> Student housing
> Large projects and new towns.

Each of these types of condominiums require different data and different analysis.

The following quotation is taken from the Fannie Mae Guidelines:

January 1988 Section 502.03 Units in Condominium Projects

"A condominium project is one in which individual owners hold title to units in the project along with an undivided interest in the real estate that is designated as the common area for the project.

Appraisals for condominium units must be documented on the Appraisal Report - Individual Condominium or PUD Unit (Form 1073). The appraisal of an individual unit in a condominium project requires the appraiser to analyze the condominium project as well as the individual unit. The appraiser must pay special attention to the location of the project the location of the individual unit within the project, the project's amenities, and the amount and purpose of the owners' association assessment since the marketability and value of the individual units in a project depend on the marketability and appeal of the project itself."[1]

Condominium is a form of ownership created by special real estate laws, which permits individual dwelling unit estates to be established within a whole, larger property estate. All 50 states have enacted condominium legislation. These acts vary from state to state but many are similar because they are patterned on a uniform condominium act.

Each condominium owner owns the fee to an individual unit and a percentage of the common areas of the land and improvements (entry ways, corridors, elevators, drives,

---

[1]*Appraisal and Underwriting Guidelines.* Seller's Guide, Federal National Mortgage Association, Washington, D.C., 1988.

walks and green areas). In some instances owners may have exclusive use of some of the limited common areas, such as basement storage, patios, and parking areas; however, most condominium laws only permit the actual living area to be individually owned.

The location of each individually owned unit must be exact in terms of both the usual horizontal description found in the deed and also a vertical description. The physical horizontal boundaries of individual units for the exterior may be anywhere from the outside of the exterior wall to its inside surface and for the interior may be the wall surface, stud surface or middle of the wall. The vertical boundaries are usually the floors and ceilings within the unit.

The boundaries of the common property are described as they would be for any other type of property. Whatever is within these boundaries and not within an individual unit is common area. The exact boundaries of the common area and the individual units are also shown on a plat (also known as a plot plan) and on the architectural plans, both of which have to be publicly recorded in many states.

A condominium is formed when a master deed is recorded that complies with the requirements of the condominium laws of the state in which it is located. These documents must also establish an owners' association to control the use and maintenance of the common areas. The association (also called a condominium or homeowners' association) is governed by a board of directors, elected by the individual owners. It operates under a set of bylaws recorded by the master deed which in turn must always comply with provisions of the condominium statutes of the state. Usually a 66% or 75% majority of the owners must vote to change the bylaws. It usually takes a 100% vote to change the master deed.

Condominiums can be new units or units in existing buildings that have been converted to condominium ownership. Either new or old, they can take the form of a highrise, townhouse, small grouping of party-wall units or free-standing unit.

An in-depth study as to what people like and dislike about condominium living has been made by the Urban Land Institute.[1] Among the favorable factors cited were:

1. Building up equity.
2. Lower cost than single family housing.
3. Freedom from house and yard maintenance.
4. Better environment.
5. Recreational facilities.
6. No rent.

---

[1]Carl Norcross, *Townhouses and Condominiums: Residents' Likes and Dislikes.* Urban Land Institute: Washington, D.C., 1973.

People were found to dislike:

1. Living too close together.
2. Noisy or undesirable neighbors and children.
3. Neighbors' pets.
4. Trouble with parking.
5. Poor association management.
6. Poor construction.
7. Dishonest salespeople who sold units.
8. Negligent builders.
9. Renters in other units, rather than owners.
10. Thin party walls.
11. Long identical rows of houses, with poor visual screening between units.

In spite of the problems some condominiums have faced, this form of ownership continues to play an important role in the housing market.

SPECIAL APPRAISAL TECHNIQUES

The appraisal of an entire condominium complex is beyond the scope of this book; the following are considerations for the appraisal of individual condominium units.

The key to these appraisals is use of the market data approach, supported by the income approach if rentals exist of units similar to that being appraised. The cost approach will usually lead to the wrong value estimates. To use it, the costs (both direct and indirect) of the entire project would have to be estimated and then a portion allocated to the unit being appraised.

The best comparables are resales of similar units in the same condominium or similar condominium projects. Because many variables exist in common charges, design, recreational facilities and size, comparable sales from any but the same or very similar complexes will prove to be extremely difficult to adjust accurately. Also, because of the unusual volatility in the market, time adjustments are often difficult to make. The price of new, similar units should be considered but resale prices in some projects are substantially lower than those of comparable new units.

Many lenders (and good appraisal practice) require an analysis of the whole project in order to estimate the value of an individual unit. Special attention should be paid to the common charges and their rate of increase. Similar units in different projects may have different common changes, which affect their value significantly.

COOPERATIVES

Until recently, New York City was the location of most of the cooperatives in the United States. In the past 10 years, this form of ownership has increased in popularity for a variety of reasons. Probably the most common reason is that in some jurisdictions it is possible to convert a building into cooperative ownership without having to comply with the complex cooperative laws.

A cooperative apartment building is owned by a corporation, which sells shares to buyers who wish to occupy individual units. Along with the ownership of a cooperative share goes the exclusive right of occupancy for a portion of the space in the building and the nonexclusive right to use other areas of the property.

Technically, a share in a cooperative apartment is not a single family residence but because these shares are bought and sold in a manner similar to condominium units, the public is only vaguely aware of the difference between these ownership forms. Cooperative-owned buildings are financed with one mortgage, whereas condominiums are financed with individual mortgages on individual units. The cooperative corporation owns everything while a condominium association owns nothing.

The shareowners (stockholders) of a cooperative elect officers and directors who run the affairs of the corporation. These officers have the power to assess shareholders for operating expenses, and the shareholder's percentage of the monthly payment on the blanket mortgage.

SPECIAL APPRAISAL TECHNIQUES

The best method to use to estimate the value of an individual cooperative unit is to compare it to similar units that have resold in the same building or in a comparable building in a similar location.

In order to compare one sale with another, it is necessary to convert the selling price into the "Effective Selling Price". This is a combination of the selling price plus the unit's percentage share of the underlying blanket mortgage.

Below is an example of two cooperative apartment unit sales whose prices seem similar yet have widely varying effective sales prices:

Sale #1: A three bedroom, two bath unit in a building with 20 units and a $3,200,000 blanket mortgage sold for $80,000.

Sale #2: A three bedroom, 1-1/2 bath unit in a similar building with 30 units and a $6,000,000 blanket mortgage sold for $60,000.

It appears that Sale #2 sold for less than Sale #1; when the effective sales price is calculated it becomes apparent that the opposite is true.

Comparison of Effective Sale Price

Sale #1	Sale Price	$ 80,000
	Share of blanket mortgage ($3,200,000 ÷ 20)	160,000
	Effective Sale Price	$240,000
Sale #2	Sale Price	$ 60,000
	Share of blanket mortgage ($6,000,000 ÷ 30)	200,000
	Effective Sale Price	$260,000

In this example, it is assumed that each unit's percentage of the mortgage is determined by dividing the total number of units into 100. Often it is determined by percentage of total square footage, and therefore varies with the size of the unit to be occupied.

COLONIAL REPRODUCTIONS

Colonial reproductions are a popular group of house styles in most areas. For example, Cape Cod, Massachusetts, is filled with houses that are reproductions of the original Cape Cod style. It has been popular for almost 100 years to copy European styles when building mansions and other large houses. Many of these homes are faithful reproductions of their European ancestors. In Santa Fe, New Mexico, there are many excellent reproductions of adobe houses constructed with synthetic adobe materials. Other examples of popular reproductions of regional historic styles exist throughout the United States.

Even the builders of tract developments often decorate standard houses with style features from colonial house styles, such as bow windows or gambrel roofs.

SPECIAL APPRAISAL TECHNIQUES

Unless the house is an authentic colonial reproduction the style usually will not significantly affect the value of the house.

DE MINIMIS PUDS

A De Minimis PUD is fee simple ownership of a home with a partial interest in nearby property that is owned together with neighbors. Often the shared property is open space or recreational land. However, to be classified as De Minimis (a Latin word meaning "of little or no importance"), the joint property must contribute little additional value to the primary residence and any maintenance dues must be insignificant compared to the property value (a few hundred dollars or less per year). The homeowners' association should be loosely constituted and should not have the right to force an owner to pay dues by using special liens.

In contrast, a regular PUD is usually created by formal documents filed in the public land records. Common property does contribute additional value, because it is usually a recreational facility or a large tract of vacant land. The homeowners' association is formally constituted with duly elected officers and directors, charges significant dues and has the right to place liens or restrict the use of common property by any owner who does not pay the assessed dues.

Freddie Mac and Fannie Mae do not currently agree (this problem is supposed to be resolved in 1989) on the exact definition of what is or is not a De Minimis PUD. For example, if there is a commonly owned swimming pool it is not a De Minimis PUD according to Fannie Mae, but may be one according to Freddie Mac.

SPECIAL APPRAISAL TECHNIQUES

Both Freddie Mac and Fannie Mae allow appraisals of De Minimis PUD to be done on the URAR, the Single Family Residential Appraisal form.

The commonly owned elements should be described and an opinion rendered that they do not add significant value to the property. The association dues should also be reported.

ELDERLY HOUSING

Elderly housing composes a growing segment of the housing market. One segment of this market is composed of people in th 50 to 65 year old age group. Some of these individuals are still employed, yet they find their housing need changing as their children leave home and they become anxious to be less burdened with the care and cost of a large suburban home. Their preference shifts to smaller houses, townhouses and condominiums, and cooperatives located in affluent neighborhood often nearer their place of work and in the city, rather than the suburbs.

New federal regulations uphold the legality of restricting the sale of some property to "the elderly" without children.

Retirement communities are another form of elderly housing. Here the emphasis is in leisure activities and the accompanying leisure facilities. The ages of these owners tend to be in the 60's and 70's.

Congregate housing facilities is another alternative available to seniors. They tend to consist of relatively small individual apartments with the emphasis being on extensive public areas including a common dining room that provides one or more meals daily. Often the facility also includes a nursing home, and some facilities are marketed together with an extensive health care plan.

SPECIAL APPRAISAL TECHNIQUES

The definition of the problem takes on special importance in the appraisal of housing for the elderly. The type of ownership and special age restrictions (both public and private) must be considered. When the project has special construction and facilities designed for the elderly, it becomes difficult using the market data approach to make the necessary adjustments with sales from outside the project. Housing for the elderly often costs more per square foot than conventional housing. Such factors as higher fire ratings of materials and special equipment may raise the cost. However, housing units for the elderly tend to contain less square footage per unit than conventional housing. Market data from conventional housing is difficult to adjust in appraisals of elderly housing units. The cost approach is useful for newer units in active areas, and the income approach is also used where there are rental units in the same or similar projects.

Housing for the elderly that is subsidized during construction or where the owners or tenants receive government aid, presents unique appraisal problems. The cost and income approaches rarely produce accurate indications of value under these circumstances. Comparable sales with similar special financing history must be found even if it means looking over a wide geographic area.

ENERGY EFFICIENT HOMES

At the height of the fuel shortage the popularity of energy efficient homes reached its peak. Houses were built with extensive insulation--often double the thickness of traditional insulation. They were tightly sealed and had small windows. As fuel costs decreased so did the popularity of this type of house. Now some authorities think the lack of normal ventilation is a health hazard, and new concerns about radon have surfaced as well.

SPECIAL APPRAISAL TECHNIQUES

Owners of special energy efficient homes may apply to their lenders for credit for the value of the special energy efficient items. The appraiser may be asked by the lender to complete an "Energy Addendum Residential Appraisal Report (FHLMC Form 70A). The form provides both a method for reporting special energy efficient items and a way to calculate the value of these items when their value cannot be estimated directly from the market.

EXPERIMENTAL HOUSES

A variety of experimental houses, which use new material such as plastic, fiberglass, foams and other nonconventional building products exist in the United States.

SPECIAL APPRAISAL TECHNIQUES

Most experimental houses lose part of their cost to functional obsolescence because they violate the principle of conformity. The experiment may have been subsidized or haave created value-in-use, but often the value-in-use is greater than market value.

Market data is the best evidence of value because the cost approach usually is based on a guess about depreciation and the income approach is rarely applicable. Location is an important consideration as is status and amenity value. For example, an experimental house designed by a nationally-known architect may have more value than one designed by an unknown. In some markets unusual house designs have experienced special market reactions. The flat-roofed, modern or contemporary house appeals to a few buyers but usually not to the market as a whole. The appraiser must take special care to consider such special market reactions.

FARM AND RANCH HOUSES

The recent economic problems of the small farmer increase the need of appraisers to have special skills and experience when appraising farms and ranch houses.

SPECIAL APPRAISAL TECHNIQUES

Freddie Mac and Fannie Mae have special requirements for the appraisal of farms that are used as residences.

The appraisal of rural houses and acreage is based on the market data approach when most of the value is in the improvements, and in the cost approach when most of the value is in the land. For example, if the property being appraised consists of 50 acres of land, with a value of $5,000 per acre, plus a 1,200 square-foot , six-room, one-story, ranch-style house, with a depreciated cost of $15,000, the appraiser should look for comparable land sales and estimate the value of the land and then add $15,000 to arrive at the total value. This produces a more accurate value estimate than using as comparables current sales of houses on small lots and making an adjustment for the excess land.

If the appraisal were of an eight-room, two-story farm house with a value of about $50,000 on two acres of land, it would be best to look for comparable sales of similar farm houses and adjust for land size differences.

A careful highest and best use analysis is essential. Often excess land is present that could be separated from the part of the property that is improved with the house and outbuildings. This land could be valued separately and may have a different highest and best use.

HISTORIC HOUSES

Many houses built before the turn of the century and earlier in the United States are still in habitable condition. Some are considered to be part of the country's national heritage, because of special architectural design or other historic note, and public interest groups have formed in many parts of the country to see that such houses are preserved. When appraising an older house, the appraiser must be aware of whether it has possible historic value.

Houses designated as historic landmarks are governed by special legislation, at either the national or state level or by the local municipality. Such legislation is concerned primarily with the control of the exterior appearance of these structures. There are usually private easements and restrictions controlling the exterior appearance. Most of these regulations provide for an administrative body, which is charged with approving or disapproving any proposed exterior renovation. In the long run, these regulations and restrictions may enhance the value of such properties, although some property owners feel that they limit their ownership freedoms and thereby decrease the value-in-use of their property, and prevent modernization unfairly.

To encourage the preservation of historic homes, special tax legislation has been passed that benefits property owners who give historic easements, which restrict and control exterior and interior renovations. Most states have historic preservation organizations that are qualified to accept historic easements. The National Trust for Historic Preservation operates in the same capacity on a national level. The advantages to the property owner for granting such an historic easement are twofold. According to current Internal Revenue Service regulations, the property owner may be permitted to deduct the value of the easement as a gift for income tax purposes. Also, some communities have special provisions in their property tax laws that lower the property taxes when historic easements have been granted.

SPECIAL APPRAISAL TECHNIQUES

It is difficult to appraise historic houses. Neither the cost approach nor the income approach is applicable. Because market data is scarce in many cases, some appraisers try to apply the cost approach on the theory that historic properties should be appraised as special purpose properties. This is not good appraisal practice. The income approach is difficult to apply since there is rarely a relationship between the rental value of an historic house and its value. This leaves the market data approach, requiring that a much wider area be screened for comparable sales than is normal for non-historic houses.

Two types of comparable sales may be used: non-historic houses in the neighborhood and historic houses wherever they can be found. Location is very important in the value of historic houses. For example, there may be two reasonably similar historic houses in a community. One is in a neighborhood that is part of a redevelopment program. A neighborhood association is being formed, houses are being renovated, exterior appearances are being controlled and the sidewalks and streets are being rebuilt. The other house is in a neighborhood that is reaching the end of its economic life. The exteriors of nearby houses are in need of carpentry repairs and paint, several houses have had serious fires and are in disrepair, the area is primarily tenant-occupied, and many nearby homes are for sale although few are sold. The first house would seem to be more valuable than the latter. A house of major historical importance, however, may be less affected by its neighborhood than a non-historic house in the same neighborhood. But even houses of major historical importance cannot completely escape the effects of their neighborhood.

Estimating the value of historic easements depends on seeking and analyzing relatively scarce market data. It may be possible to find properties granted historic easements where offers were made on the property prior to date the easement was given or where the property was sold and then resold after the easement was granted.

LOG CABINS

The log cabin market has carved itself a unique niche. These homes appear all over the country, usually integrated into an area with few or no other log cabins. Some are authentic reproductions but many are contemporary in design. Most have modern heating and mechanical systems.

SPECIAL APPRAISAL TECHNIQUES

Since there are usually few, if any, sales of log cabins in the same neighborhood as the one being appraised, the appraiser must decide if the Sales Comparison Approach is applicable. It may be justified to seek comparable sales in other similar neighborhoods quite distant from the subject.

Since most log cabins are purchased from a manufacturer, it often is possible to obtain good cost information.

MANSIONS

It is a characteristic of the English language to down grade adjectives. For example, when I was a child, Shirley Temple was a "star". Now she would be a "Super Star". The same fate has befallen the word "Mansion".

Mansions or estates used to be vehicles for gracious living for those who could afford the high cost. With many extra rooms for recreation, entertaining, guests and servant quarters, they are usually individually designed to reflect the special tastes of the owner, whose goal is often to enhance family prestige. Some mansions may have historical value.

Now the term mansion is used to describe any large house. In some communities houses as small as 4,000 square feet are called mansions.

SPECIAL APPRAISAL TECHNIQUES

Old-fashioned mansions are still few in number and are sold relatively infrequently.

The highest and best use analysis is an important part of these mansion appraisals. The appraiser must consider whether the land is now best utilized or if there is excess land that can be otherwise developed. Is the main building now suitable as a single family dwelling, or can it be converted into multi-family, institutional or other use? If the highest and best use is other than a single family residence, the appraiser should apply generally used appraisal techniques, which are beyond the scope of this book.

If the highest and best use of the property continues to be as a single family residence, only the market data approach is meaningful. The cost and income approaches will lead to erroneous conclusions in most cases.

When selecting comparable mansion sales, it is often necessary to look into other neighboring communities. The location adjustment is important, but difficult to make. When the gross living area unit value is developed, some type of meaningful range of value may be produced. Often the final value estimate is expressed in terms of a range of values which emphasizes the difficulty of estimating the value of this specialized type of housing.

MANUFACTURED HOUSES

The term manufactured house means that substantial portions of the house were assembled in a factory and then delivered to the site, usually by truck.

Some units are assembled almost totally off the site. There is little difference between a small modular house and a large mobile home. Larger modular houses consist of several segments, which are shipped to the site by rail and/or truck and joined on the site. Prefabricated houses are shells that are factory-built and then shipped to the site for assembly. They usually have less mechanical equipment as part of the package than modular homes.

Modular houses and prefabs are used for a variety of reasons. The construction of single family houses has changed less than almost any other major item manufactured in this country. Theoretically, the efficiency of the assembly line and mass production methods should be applicable to housing, and the manufacturers of modular and prefabricated homes are trying to do this. Speed of construction is another reason for this system of producing housing units. The on-site assembly of a factory-produced modular or prefabricated home is often as little as a few days. Another advantage is that the owners of individual lots can see complete model houses. This is not possible if a house is to be constructed from a set of house plans unless the builder has a similar house available for inspection. Also lot owners may feel more confident they will get a house that is truly similar to the model they have seen when they buy from a large established company rather than buying from a confusing set of plans and specifications.

SPECIAL APPRAISAL TECHNIQUES

Manufactured houses can be appraised in the same manner as conventionally built homes. In most markets, there is little, if any, value difference between these houses and conventionally built houses of the same size, design and quality. The speed of construction, cost differential and other advantages (if they exist) are enjoyed by the original owner, but they usually do not affect the resale value.

MOBILE HOMES

Although not considered real estate in many states, mobile homes account for nearly 10% of all the existing single family residences in the United States. The pre-World War II trailer has evolved into today's mobile home. The most popular size is 12 feet by 60 feet, known as a "12 wide". There are also "14-wides" (which are only permitted in a few states) and "double-wides", which may run from 24 feet by 47 feet to 28 feet by 60 feet. There are also smaller units but they are rarely used for year-round housing. Mobile home owners are insulted when their homes are called "trailers". Once settled on a pad or foundation, a mobile home is rarely moved and experienced mobile home owners claim a unit should never be moved off the original location.

Mobile homes are popular because they offer substantial living space at a cost much below comparable conventional housing. There is a wide choice of mobile homes available in most parts of the country for under $75,000. This is well below the cost of other types of comparable housing. Many mobile home owners are senior citizens, young couples, students and military personnel. Studies show that a typical unit lasts about 15 years, as year-round housing. At that time, the shell still is useful and has some value. Studies also have shown that with average maintenance the typical mobile home depreciates approximately 10% the first year (based on wholesale value) and between 5% and 6% per year thereafter.

SPECIAL APPRAISAL TECHNIQUES

The best way to appraise a mobile home is to use conventional appraisal techniques with the application of all three approaches.

Many mobile home appraisals are made using a valuation book. These books are prepared by national publishers who collect sales data from mobile home dealers all over the country; they are similar to the books car and truck dealers use to appraise used vehicles. They are a useful tool but are not a satisfactory substitute for a well prepared appraisal. The problem with their use is that their figures are derived by averaging sales in many markets. The assumption is that mobile homes can be moved. Surveys show that most mobile homes are not moved when they are sold in place, especially when they are only a few years old. Therefore, like a house, their value is affected by their individual environment, and like a house, they can suffer from economic obsolescence. An appraisal based solely on a valuation book would not reflect the environmental influence.

PLANNED UNIT DEVELOPMENTS

Planned unit developments (PUDs) are a zoning alternative, not a type of housing. Houses built in PUDs can be in fee simple or condominium ownership in the form of single family residences, townhouses or multifamily buildings. PUD developments may also include commercial and industrial uses. In essence the PUD concept permits the grouping of housing units on lots smaller than usually allowed for residential construction. As a trade-off for being allowed to build on smaller lots, the developer sets aside some unused land to be dedicated to the community or to a homeowners' association. PUD developments can provide for more flexible and sensible designs for streets, landscaping and public facilities than are possible in conventional neighborhoods.

The individual single-family residences in PUD are owned in fee simple or as condominiums with joint ownership of open areas; in some areas local law requires that open areas be deeded to the city. Driveways, parking areas, and recreational facilities may also be jointly owned by the residents. An undivided interest in these common areas runs with the title to each property. Consequently, these areas must be inspected as part of the site when individual properties are appraised.

SPECIAL APPRAISAL TECHNIQUES

Freddie Mac and Fannie Mae simplified their requirements for PUD appraisals and now allow them to be made on the URAR form.

The Fannie Mae guidelines require that when the *Uniform Residential Appraisal Report* is used for a PUD the appraiser must provide the following project information:

- If the project has been completed:
    # phases _____,
    # units _____,
    # units sold _____

- If the project is incomplete:
    planned # of phases _____,
    # units _____,
    # units sold _____

- If the project is being developed in phases:
    total units in subject phase _____,
    # of completed units _____,
    # of sold units _____,
    # of rented units _____

- A description of the common elements or recreational facilities

- Owners' association fees per month for the subject unit:$_____

- The utilities that are included in the owners' association fees

- A comment about whether the association fees are reasonable in comparison to those for units in other projects of similar quality and design

- A comment about whether the project appears to be well-maintained

RESIDENCES ON LEASED LAND

With the exception of the state of Hawaii, residences on leased land are relatively scarce.

In Hawaii, residences have long been built on leased land. Leases may be for as long as 99 years or for 50 years or less. To protect the mortgage, some leases provide that the interest of the fee owner is subordinate to the interest of the mortgagee or lender. However, most leases give the mortgagee the right to take over the land rent if the mortgagor defaults. Usually the mortgagee also has the right to find a new mortgagor to continue the lease payments. When the lease expires, the improvements become the property of the landowner, who may extend the lease after modifying it to reflect current market conditions.

SPECIAL APPRAISAL TECHNIQUES

To value a residence on leased land, an appraiser uses the same techniques applied to residences subject to other forms of ownership. The value of the leasehold interest may be estimated by capitalizing the ground rent. An adjustment is usually required to reflect differences between the ground rents and lease terms of the subject property and the comparable properties. Depending on the appraisal problem it may be necessary to estimate the value of both the leased fee interest and the leasehold interest.

SECOND HOMES

Several million houses in the United States are second homes, occupied by their owners on a seasonal basis. Some of these homes are large, expensive mansions, more valuable than many primary homes. Such homes are found in communities like Newport, Rhode Island, and Palm Beach, Florida. However, the majority of second homes tend to be simpler, possibly located near a body of water or other recreation area. Prior to World War II, these houses tended to be developed individually or in small groups. After the war many large corporations went into the second home business, developing large tracts of land and many houses at the same time. Recreational facilities serving the site also were constructed.

SPECIAL APPRAISAL TECHNIQUES

The second home market can be very volatile. Economic and weather conditions, gasoline shortages, and competitive developments may have a greater effect on the value of a second home than on a primary residence. One apparent trend in many areas is that properties on or near water tend to increase in value faster than similar properties without the water amenity.

Resales are better evidence of market value than initial sales, which are often the result of heavy developer promotions. Where recreation homes are rented seasonally, a relationship may exist between rentals and value, which would make it possible to use the income approach. The cost approach may be useful when land is still available and new homes are still being built in the area.

SKI LODGES AND HOMES IN SKIING AREAS

Skiing has grown immensely in the past 25 years. The economy of whole areas and even states (i.e. Vermont, New Hampshire, Colorado and Utah) have been changed by this winter sport. Hundreds of thousands of second homes have been constructed on or near ski slopes.

SPECIAL APPRAISAL TECHNIQUES

It takes special skills to appraise ski homes. The appraiser must be intimately familiar both with the area in which the property is located and the special design and construction of ski homes. Location is critical in some areas. Even a few hundred feet can make a big difference. Prices in some Western ski resorts defy the imagination. There has been a big shake-out recently in the market for these high value lodges. Appraisers should proceed cautiously whenever appraising a ski home.

SOLAR HOUSES

Large tax write-offs, fuel shortages and environmental concerns all helped the proliferation of solar homes in the 1970's. When fuel became cheap and plentiful again and the tax write-offs were eliminated, most solar house construction also stopped.

Solar homes are still considered experimental by many people. The additional costs of design and materials may be offset by future savings, but no conclusive evidence of this possibility now exists. Even if and when successful solar application to housing is made, the results may not apply to many areas of the country.

SPECIAL APPRAISAL TECHNIQUES

The appraiser must first determine if value to be estimated is value-in-use to a special owner or actual market value. In some markets, part or all of the excess costs of a solar house may add value. Some buyers are willing to pay a premium for the privilege of living in a solar house. They want to be part of this housing experiment and feel satisfaction and status is worth the extra cost. They feel that the solar house has a special amenity value.

Resales are scarce. The builder of a solar house may create a house with some functional obsolescence that the market will recognize on resale. The appraiser must be cautious in making the value estimate.

TIMESHARING

The essence of timesharing allows one property to be purchased by several owners, each of whom has the right to use the property for a predetermined period of time. For example, 10 owners may buy a home. Each owner shares the cost of the property equally, and each has the right to use the property five weeks per year. Other devices may be used, but the goal of all of these methods is to allocate the time equally among shareholders or proportionately to what each owner pays.

SPECIAL APPRAISAL TECHNIQUES

The first step of the appraisal process--identifying the rights being appraised--has special significance in this type of appraisal. These rights are divided into the type of ownership and the rights to use the property.

The use rights (which part of the property will be allocated for use by the shareholder) also must be established; these substantially affect value.

The best way to estimate the value of timeshare units is to look for resales in the subject complex or similar complexes. They are better evidence than new sales because the latter are often the result of heavy developer promotions which would not apply to resale properties. The income approach may also be applicable, if some of the units are rented during part of the year. Research into the market may reveal a relationship between the rental value and the resale value of this type of property.

Care must be taken to divide the appraised value between the value of the real estate and the value of the large amount of personal property that is usually included in the price of a timeshare interval. (In some cases, fractional interest in all furnishings including bed linen and kitchen supplies are part of the timeshare sale).

WATERFRONT HOUSES

Waterfront property has probably increased in value at a greater rate than almost any other type of property. Unlike other recreational properties, especially ski homes, waterfront properties have held their value.

There has also been a national trend for commercial property in cities on the water to increase in value. Many city renewal programs are focused on the waterfront of the city. Often these redevelopment programs include residential units.

SPECIAL APPRAISAL TECHNIQUES

A high percentage of the total value is often in the site. Therefore the value of the site is very important. Location within a waterfront neighborhood is very significant. In some neighborhoods a high premium is paid for lots with direct frontage on the water.   This is less important in other neighborhoods. Neighborhood location adjustments are often difficult to make.

UNDERGROUND AND BERMED HOMES

People select to build houses into the ground or into a hillside for a variety of reasons ranging from energy savings to protection from nuclear fallout.

In the United States, most underground housing is found in the Central Plains states where storm protection and reduced energy costs are important concerns.

Houses built underground benefit from the fact that temperatures below grade are moderate year round. Because the heating and cooling equipment in these houses operates with less power, energy costs are significantly reduced. Earth-covered dwellings of poured concrete and concrete block are usually located on grade or "bermed" (set into a site that is partly or completely excavated).

SPECIAL APPRAISAL TECHNIQUES

Application of the sales comparison approach is difficult because sales of similar houses are scarce. Often the appraiser has no choice but to compare these special houses with houses built with more conventional construction techniques.

SUMMARY

Millions of residences are specifically designed and uniquely located to satisfy the special needs of their owners. Others are more conventionally located and designed, yet are special because of their form of ownership. Often these homes combine two or more of these special features.

Besides the traditional ownership form of fee simple, alternative ownership forms widely available include Condominium, Cooperative, De Minimis PUD, Planned Unit Development, Leased Land and Timesharing. Each of these properties presents unique appraisal problems and requires specialized knowledge about how the ownership form works and how it affects the value of the property.

Second homes are usually found in resort areas near skiing, golf and the water. These markets tend to be volatile and are affected by changing weather conditions, availability of gasoline, the health of the economy, and the tax laws. Often only a few hundred feet difference in location can have a significant effect on the value of the property, particularly relative to an amenity like waterfront or the ski slope.

Though housing in general has been slower to change than almost anything purchased by consumers, there are some changes taking place. Manufactured houses and mobile homes are becoming a significant segment of the housing market. Each requires special appraisal skills.

The demographic profile of the population continues to shift towards older age. This increases the need for housing suitable for senior citizens. Housing for the elderly ranges from condominium projects built like traditional condominiums but limited in availability to owners over a specified age, (often these projects exclude children, which is still permitted by new Federal regulations) to other types of housing for the elderly which have special features to accommodate the handicapped. Congregate housing not only provides a place to live but also meals, social activities and medical care.

Finally, there are many houses that are designed for the special tastes and needs of their owners. This broad category includes energy efficient solar houses, experimental homes and underground homes. Many of these unique residences were designed to save fuel. As fuel has again become cheap and plentiful, market resistance has developed against the extra cost of the fuel saving features. Some are even considered to be health hazards.

Mansions and large homes provide space for gracious living for those who can afford them. As the house gets bigger the market gets smaller. What is a mansion in one area may be just another large house in another community. The appraiser must research the depth of the market in which the house is located.

Farms and ranches present a whole set of unique appraisal problems, and an appraiser who does work in this area requires special education and experience.

Finally, there are houses that are old, historic, special styles, reproductions or older styles and built of special materials such as log cabins. Each of these present unique appraisal problems and may require special appraisal techniques.

EXPOSED FRAMING MEMBERS

LOTS OF "GINGERBREAD"

COMPLEX SILHOUETTE

HIGH, STEEP ROOF

ORNATE WINDOWS AND DOORS

Nineteenth Century American

STICK STYLE OR CARPENTER GOTHIC
(Stick or C Goth - 708)

18 Income Properties

People buy property for at least three reasons: use, income and amenities. Often it is for a combination of the reasons. The income approach covered in this section will focus on the income motivation and how the appraiser can analyze the income a property produces and use it as an indication of the value of the property.

The income a property produces flows to the owner in a variety of ways:

> Current Cash Flow
> Current Tax Savings
> Deferred Income from Rents
> Deferred Tax Savings from Rent
> Capital Gains from the Sale or Gift of the Property in the Future
> Tax Savings from the Gift or Trade of the Property in the Future

The definition of market value assumes the buyer and seller to be well informed. Therefore it is also assumed that the buyers and sellers consider all of the potential benefits of property ownership.

INCOME CAPITALIZATION

In the income capitalization approach, appraisers measure the present value of the future benefits of property ownership. Income streams and values of property upon resale (reversion) are capitalized (converted) into a present, lump-sum value. Basic to this approach are the formulas:

> Income ÷ Rate = Value
> Income x Factor = Value

The income capitalization approach, like the cost and sales comparison approaches, requires extensive market research. Specific areas that an appraiser investigates for this approach are the property's gross income expectancy, the expected reduction in gross income from lack of full occupancy and collection loss, the expected annual operating expenses, the pattern and duration of the property's income stream, and the anticipated value of the resale or other real property interest reversions. When accurate income and expense estimates are established, the income streams are converted into present value by the process of capitalization. The rates or factors used for capitalization are derived by the investigation of acceptable rates of return for similar properties.

Research and analysis of data for the income capitalization approach are conducted against a background of supply and demand relationships. This background provides information in trends and market anticipation that must be verified for data analysis by the income capitalization approach.

The investor in an apartment building, for example, anticipates an acceptable return on the investment in addition to return of the invested funds. The level of return necessary to attract investment capital fluctuates with changes in the money market and with the levels of return available from alternative investments. The appraiser must be alert to changing investor requirements as revealed by demand in the current market for investment properties, and to changes in the more volatile money markets that may indicate a forthcoming trend.

More books and articles have been written, and more courses and seminars taught on the income approach to value than on any other appraisal subject. It is not the purpose of this chapter to add anything new to this body of literature, but rather, to distill from what is already written, the most practical techniques of using the income approach on a day-to-day basis in an appraisal practice.

TWO SIMPLE STEPS

Many appraisers make the income approach more complex than it need be for the types of property they are appraising. New appraisers should start by using the simple process described below and then, as their assignments become more complex, apply the more advanced techniques when they feel they are necessary.

The two simple steps of the income approach produce an estimate of the anticipated Net Operating Income (NOI) of the property being appraised, which is then converted to a value estimate using the capitalization process.

INCOME ANALYSIS

NET OPERATING INCOME (NOI)

Net operating income is a word developed and used by real estate appraisers. It has special meaning to them and is not regularly used by owners, accountants, tax people, etc. Therefore, whenever you develop the NOI of a property for appraisal purposes, it is important that you define the word in your appraisal report. Net operating income (NOI) is the estimated stabilized anticipated annual net income produced by the property being appraised, after all operating expenses and reserves are deducted, but before mortgage debt service and book depreciation are deducted.

NOI is based on the assumption that the property will be rented at the market rent. It is based on what is projected for the first year after the date of the appraisal.

Estimating the NOI starts by estimating the potential gross income (PGI). It is the anticipated total market rent and other income for the first year after the date of the appraisal.

Anticipated loss due to non-occupancy, turnover and non-payment of rent by tenants (commonly called a "vacancy and collection allowance") is deducted from the PGI. This produces the effective gross income (EGI).

From the projected annual EGI all of the annual projected stabilized expenses are deducted (fixed expenses, operating expenses and reserves). The result is the projected NOI.

To develop the NOI, the appraiser creates a special reconstructed income and expense statement. Information used on this statement is obtained for a variety of sources. The information cannot simply be obtained from the owner, agent, accountant, attorney or tax person though all of these people are potential sources for some of the information that must be assembled in order to create a Reconstructed Operating Statement. This process requires the judgment and expertise of an experienced appraiser.

POTENTIAL GROSS INCOME (PGI)

The appraiser starts the reconstructed income and expense statement be estimating the total gross income the property could produce during the first year after the date of the appraisal, assuming it was vacant on the date of the appraisal and available to be rented to the typical tenant(s), in the market, looking for this type of property. Making this estimate of potential gross income (PGI) requires knowledge of the rental market in which the property being appraised is located. Other rentals in the market are compared to the subject property and adjustments are made for the differences between the subject and the comparable rentals. (This is similar to data used in the Sales Comparison Approach). The best way to make adjustments is to find matched pairs of rentals in the market. If these rentals are similar, except for one or more significant items, that adjustment can be developed from the market data.

FIG. 18-1 EXAMPLE OF EXTRACTING A RENTAL ADJUSTMENT FROM THE MARKET

	Monthly Rent
Apartment with two bedrooms, two baths, 1000 sq. ft. with air conditioning	$850
A similar apartment without air conditioning	$825
Indicated adjustment for air conditioning	$ 25

It is not practical or possible to prove every adjustment from data in the market, but an attempt should be made to do so whenever possible. Once a matched pair is developed for an adjustment in a market, it can often be used for more than one appraisal. When an adjustment cannot be supported by market data, the appraiser has no choice but to estimate the adjustment. Large, unsupported market rent adjustments are one of the major contributing factors to the lack of credibility for the Income Approach in appraisal reports.

The potential gross income estimate is the foundation upon which the income approach is built. A small error in this estimate will be mathematically compounded as it is processed in the income approach and will become a large error in the final value estimate.

It is advisable that the rents being paid by the current tenants also be considered. However, more often than not, the contract rent will not be the current market rent of the property. This is often true because the property was leased prior to the date of the appraisal. In addition, the owner or management of the property may not be typical for this property and their skills or lack of skill will produce a difference between market and contract rent. However, the appraiser should report a rental history including information on the current rents being received in the appraisal. In spite of everything, the actual rents being received for a property should be given serious consideration by the appraiser when estimating the potential gross income.

VACANCY AND COLLECTION ALLOWANCE

No matter how good a tenant is, there is a potential that some of the rent over a projected ownership period will not be collected. Since the estimate of market rent is based on the assumption that the property is vacant and ready to be rented to a typical tenant, it would not be correct to assume it was rented to a tenant who would never be a credit risk and would remain a tenant throughout the projected period. There is no standard figure for a vacancy and collection allowance. The best way to develop figures is to take properties where you can obtain a rental history over an extended period of time and see what the actual historical results were. Property management companies are good sources of this type of information.

OTHER INCOME

Besides rents from the tenants, there is often other available income to the property owner. Some typical sources of other income are the following:

> Coin-operated washers and dryers
> Other vending machines
> Parking and garage fees
> Advertising signs

EFFECTIVE GROSS INCOME (EGI)

The Effective Gross Income (EGI) is calculated by deducting from the Potential Gross Income (PGI) the estimate Vacancy and Collection Allowance and adding any projected Other Income.

EXPENSE ANALYSIS

FIXED EXPENSES

The expenses incurred by the owner of a property are divided into three groups: fixed expenses, operating expenses and reserves. Again, these are special appraisal terms used to classify expenses on the reconstructed operating statement and normally will not be available from any one source. It will be necessary to adjust the information received from a variety of sources before using it.

Fixed expenses are the property taxes and casualty insurance. They are classified as fixed expenses because they vary little (if at all) with the occupancy of the property.

Property taxes are a matter of public record. A trip to the tax collector's office will develop accurate information about the taxes. If the tax rate has not been set for the community, an estimate is made considering the current taxes and the trend in the community. In many areas, the property tax consists of more than one tax and may include school taxes, sewer taxes, special assessments, etc.

Casualty insurance is normally a combination of fire insurance, boiler insurance, general liability, worker's compensation and flood insurance. It does not include mortgage life insurance. The owner's actual cost is often misleading. Owners sometimes pay for more than one year at a time and they often do not carry the amount or all the kinds of insurance typical owners of the property would carry.

OPERATING EXPENSES

These are sometimes called variable expenses and include expenses incurred in a typical year to maintain the property, provide services for the tenants and maintain the income stream. Shown is a list of typical expenses that should be considered when making a reconstructed operating statement. It is recommended that a checklist be used so when you are gathering expense data you will not skip an item that does not appear on the operating statement provided by the owner or the management of the property. This is a list of operating expenses of a composite of many properties:

Management Fees

Utilities
 Electricity
 Gas
 Oil
 Coal
 Telephone
 Water
 Sewer Charges

Rubbish & Garbage Removal

Employee Payroll
 Janitor
 Manager
 Groundskeeper
 Bookkeeper
 Elevator Operator
 Lifeguard
 Engineer
 Security
 Telephone Operator
 Maintenance
 Cleaning
 Other

Payroll Taxes

Employee Benefits

Maintenance and Repairs

Service Contracts
    Sprinkler System
    Elevator
    Intercom & Telephone
    Lawn & Landscaping

Pool Expenses & Supplies

Painting and Decorating

Supplies - office
    cleaning
    other

Magazines and Newspapers

Snow Removal

Travel and Entertainment

Exterminating

Bank Charges

Legal Fees

Advertising

Accounting Fees

Automobile Expense

Not every property will have all the expenses on this list, and some properties will have other expenses which do not appear on this checklist.

The figures used are not the actual expenses as reported by the owner. It is a forecast of what the expenses would be for the following year, assuming it was a

For example, for a property that requires fuel oil, you obtain a 5 year history of oil consumption which is

Last year	3,200 gallons
Year before	3,300 gallons
2 years before	3,100 gallons
4 years before	3,100 gallons
5 years before	3,300 gallons

The appraiser forecasts that consumption for a typical year is 3,200 gallons and that the price of fuel next year will be $1.25. Therefore, the forecasted fuel oil expense will be $3,950 ($1.25 x 3,200).

RESERVES

Some expenses vary considerably from year to year and others occur once or twice over a period of many years. A decision must be made as to where in the reconstructed operating statement to include these expenses. Some of these expenses, such as plumbing repairs, may be included in the maintenance and repair item in the operating expenses. Even though a particular plumbing repair may occur only infrequently, as a group they appear quite regularly; and it is possible to estimate what, as a group, they would be in a typical year. Those infrequently occurring items that are not included in the operating expenses are included in the reserve section. For example, if the typical life of a refrigerator was estimated to be 20 years and the cost of a new refrigerator was $1,200, a reserve of $60 for each refrigerator in the property might be established yearly ($1,200 ÷ 20 = $60).

The use of reserves must be carefully explained in the appraisal report because the word reserve implies that the money is being put aside. Most owners do not actually set aside these monies.

Some of the items that are traditionally included in the reserve section of the reconstructed operating statement are listed below:

> Kitchen Appliances
> > Stoves and Ovens
> > Refrigerators
> > Dishwashers
> > Garbage Disposals
> > Hoods and Vent Fans
> > Microwave Ovens
>
> Furniture
>
> Carpeting
>
> Air Conditioning
>
> Laundry equipment
>
> Linens and Drapes
>
> Dishes and Flatware
>
> Short-lived Building Components
> > Roofs
> > Boilers
> > Elevators
> > Security Systems
> > Telephone Systems
>
> Pool Equipment
>
> Grounds Equipment

Again, this is a composite list from many types of properties. It is unlikely that any one property will include all of these items. Also, some properties will require reserves for items that are not on this list.

The most common mistake that appraisers make is to include the same item in both the operating expense and the reserve sections of the reconstructed operating statement and to leave out items from both sections which should have been included.

Later in this chapter, the development of capitalization rates will be discussed. Here again the fact that any operating statement used to develop a capitalization rate must include reserves, will be pointed out. If they are left out, an incorrect rate will be developed.

OTHER EXPENSES (NOT INCLUDED)

Some expenses which are a part of an income and expense statement used for tax purposes are not included in the reconstructed operating statement. This is because these items are either reflected in the capitalization rate and to include them as expenses or reserve, would have the effect of including them twice, or they are not considered to be a cost directly related to operating the property. Included in this group are:

> Mortgage Interest
> Mortgage Amortization
> Mortgage Life Insurance
> Depreciation
> Income Tax
> Corporate Taxes
> Corporate Directors' Fees
> Franchise Taxes

SUMMARY - ESTIMATING NET OPERATING INCOME (NOI)

The first step of the income approach is to estimate the Net Operating Income (NOI) of the property. This is an appraisal technique that is accomplished by making a reconstructed operating statement for the property. This statement uses information gathered by the appraiser from the owner, management, accountant, tax person and a variety of other sources. It usually cannot be obtained from a single source in the format that is required.

The Potential Gross Income (PGI) is estimated using market data and the rental history of the property being appraised. A Vacancy and Collection Allowance is deduced from this figure. Any other income is added, and the result is a projection of what the Effective Gross Income (EGI) of the property would be if it were vacant on the date of the appraisal, and were then rented to a typical tenant in the market at current rental rates.

Next, the typical expenses are projected for the coming year after being divided for clarity in Fixed Expenses, Operating Expenses and Reserves. Other expenses such as interest, amortization, depreciation and expenses, not directly related to the running of the property, are not included.

All of the fixed expenses, operating expenses and reserves are subtracted from the effective gross income (EGI), to produce the net operating income (NOI).

FIG. 18-2 EXAMPLE OF A TYPICAL RECONSTRUCTED OPERATING STATEMENT (12 UNIT APARTMENT HOUSE)

INCOME

Potential Gross Income

6 two bedroom unit w/o air conditioning @$375/mo.	=	$27,000
(375 x 12 = 4,500 x 6 = 27,000)		
2 two bedroom units w/air conditioning @$400/mo.	=	9,600
(400 x 12 = 4,800 x 2 = 9,600)		
2 three bedroom units w/o air conditioning @$500/mo..	=	12,000
(500 x 12 = 6,000 x 2 = 12,000)		
2 three bedroom units w/air conditioning @$550/mo.	=	13,200
(550 x 12 = 6,600 x 2 = 13,200)		

Total:	$61,800
Vacancy and Collection Loss (6%)	-3,708
Other Income	
Laundry Machines (Concession)	+1,200
Vending Machines	+ 625
EFFECTIVE GROSS INCOME	$67,333

EXPENSES

Fixed Expenses	
Insurance	
(Apartment Package including rents)	2,800
Flood Insurance	300
Property Tax	7,423
School District Tax	4,240
Total Fixed Expenses:	$12,252
Operating Expenses	
Management Fees	4,040
Utilities	
Electricity (Halls Only)	823
Gas	8,300
Telephone	125
Water	1,600
Sewer Charge	160
Rubbish Removal	385
Employee Payroll	
Part-time Janitor	4,000
Payroll Taxes	120

Employee Benefits	345
Worker's Compensation Insurance	120
Lawn Care	345
Maintenance Supplies	250
Maintenance & Repairs	1,200
Painting & Decorating	600
Snow Removal	120
Exterminating	240
Legal Fees	150
Accounting	300
Bank Charges	80

Total Operating Expenses: $14,420

Reserves

Kitchen Appliances	600
Lobby Furniture	100
Carpeting	1,000
Air Conditioning	300
Roof	500

Total Reserves: $2,500

Total Expenses: -$29,172

NET OPERATING INCOME PROJECTION: $38,161

CAPITALIZATION

The second step of the Income Approach is to convert the Net Operating Income (NOI) projection to an estimate of the value of the property on the date of the appraisal. The process is called Capitalization. This is usually done by dividing the NOI by the capitalization rate.

$$\frac{NOI}{Capitalization\ Rate} = Value\ of\ Property$$

Many investors and some appraisers use a capitalization process by which they estimate the value of an investment property by multiplying either the gross income, net income or some other income figure they rely upon by a multiplier to produce the value of the property. It is common, for example, to hear investors say a particular property is worth so many time its current or projected gross rental income.

This multiplier is derived by taking properties they are familiar with and dividing the sale price by the rent or net income. This relationship can be expressed in a formula as follows:

$$\frac{Sales\ Price}{Income} = Rent\ Multiplier$$

DIRECT CAPITALIZATION

There are a variety of ways to develop a capitalization rate. The simplest (and best) is to get it directly from the market using data collected in the market. If the above formula converts NOI into value, then the following formula would convert value into a capitalization rate (assuming the NOI is also known).

$$\frac{\text{NOI}}{\text{Value of Property}} = \text{Capitalization Rate}$$

The type of rate developed in this way is called an overall rate. For example, assume there is information available about a property similar to the one being appraised. It shows that the comparable property sold for $185,000 and that it had an NOI of $27,000. Using the above formula, the capitalization rate is taken from this data as follows:

$$\frac{\$27,000 \ (\text{NOI})}{\$185,000 \ (\text{Sale Price})} = .146 \ (\text{Capitalization Rate})$$

Like any other data being used in the appraisal process, the more similar the data source is to the property being appraised the better it is. Also, it is not good practice to develop a rate from just one set of data. Often, the best source of data to develop capitalization rates comes from other appraisals where the property was sold around the date of the appraisal. This is because all the calculations needed to reconstruct the operating statement have already been made. When you receive data about a building that has been sold, you will need to reconstruct its operating statement just as you would if you were appraising the property; otherwise the rate you develop from the property being sold will not work.

Unfortunately, there has been so much emphasis on other more complex, less direct methods of constructing capitalization rates that many appraisers gravitate to these methods rather than taking the time to develop the market data derived from the method explained above.

When rates are developed for a series of properties in a market, it will become apparent that an identifiable pattern develops. Generally, the better the quality of the property, the lower the rate will be.

BAND OF INVESTMENT METHOD

This is a popular way to develop an overall capitalization rate. It is derived through a synthesis of mortgage interest rates and the rate of return a typical investor would require on their invested capital. Lenders and investors consider risk, return on capital, non-liquidity and money management when they establish the rates of interest they will require. Therefore, when these interest rates are used in the band of investment method to create a capitalization rate, they reflect all of the elements that go into making up a rate.

An assumption of this method is that typical investors of income property will attempt to obtain the maximum mortgage at the lowest interest rate that is available for the property, considering their credit worthiness. The appraiser, when estimating what this mortgage will be, should forecast what mortgage a typical buyer of the property will be able to get, not what mortgage some special buyer could obtain.

A weighted average is calculated based on the percentage each mortgage represents of the total value of the property, together with what percentage of the total value is made up of investor equity (cash).

FIG 18-3 EXAMPLE OF BAND OF INVESTMENT OVERALL RATE CALCULATION

An apartment complex had a value of $850,000. A typical investor could obtain a 75% first mortgage at 12% interest, a 10% second mortgage at 15% interest and would require 16% return on the invested capital.

```
12% 1st mortgage interest times .75(% value)  = .0900
15% 2nd mortgage interest times .10(% value)  = .0150
16% Equity rate of return times .15(% value)  = .0240
                                                 .1290
```

Overall Capitalization Rate (rounded)   .13

The accuracy of this rate can be tested by comparing the NOI produced by the property against the NOI that would be required using the overall capitalization rate produced by the band of investment calculations. The formula for this test is:

$$NOI = Rate \times Value$$
$$NOI = .13 \times \$850,000 = \$110,500$$

The closer the $110,500 is to the actual NOI, the more accurate the band of investment method proves to be.

MODIFIED BAND OF INVESTMENT METHOD

The band of investment method, according to some appraisers, does not produce the correct rate because it does not take into consideration the length of the mortgage and, therefore, the rate of amortization. To overcome this deficiency, they substitute the constant mortgage payment rate for the interest rate .

Again, a weighted average is calculated based on the percentage each mortgage represents of the total value of the property, together with what percentage of the total value is made up by investor equity (cash).

FIG. 18-4 EXAMPLE OF MODIFIED BAND OF INVESTMENT OVERALL RATE CALCULATION

An apartment complex has a value of $2,925,000. A typical buyer can obtain a 70% first mortgage ($2,047,500) at 12% fixed interest for a 20 year term. The annual payment of interest and amortization is $274,116 which is, .1339 (13.39%) of the mortgage ($274,116 ÷ $2,047,500).

A second mortgage could be obtained for 10% of the value ($292,500) at 15% fixed interest for a 10 year period with annual payments of $58,281 interest and amortization which is an annual constant of .1993 (19.93%) ($58,281 ÷ $292,500).

A typical buyer will require 16% return on the invested capital.

.1339 1st mortgage constant times .70% of value = .09373
.1993 2nd mortgage constant times .15% of value = .02989
.1600 equity rate of return .15% of value   = .02400
                                                    .14762

Overall capitalization rate (rounded)   .15

The accuracy of this rate can be tested by comparing the NOI produced by the property against the NOI that would be required using the overall capitalization rate produced by the modified band of investment method.

THE BUILT-UP METHOD

This method of constructing a capitalization rate separates the rate into its component parts. It would be almost impossible to accurately construct a rate using only this method. However, once some of the components of the rate have been estimated from other sources, they can be assembled and together they can be analyzed and tested for reasonableness by using the built-up method of rate construction.

The two basic components of a capitalization rate consist of the interest rate and capital recovery rate.

The interest rate is broken down into four parts:

1. Pure Interest - The interest rate of long term United State Government Bonds. It is the safe rate money can earn over a selected period of time. The investor knows, with a high degree of certainty, that at the end of the investment period the invested capital plus any unpaid interest will be 100% returned to the investor.

2. Additional Risk - All other investments, except United States Government Bonds, have a greater degree of risk than the bonds. There is a wide range of risk differences between various available competitive investments. The greater the risk, the higher the amount of interest necessary to entice the investors with capital to take the risk.

3. Burden of Investment Management - It is a simple process to invest in United States Government Bonds. Other investments take more effort. They all require some effort to decide which one to select. The more risky and complex the investment, the more investment management is required. (Investment management is not the same as the fee received for managing real estate, which is an operating expense that is deducted from income as part of the process of determining the net operating income (NOI)).

4. Lack of Liquidity - A United States Government Bond can be sold by making one telephone call, and the proceeds of the sale will be available to the investor within a few days. They are always saleable at anytime the investor wants to sell. Other investments require more time. It may take years to sell some types of real estate, especially when the investor elects to sell in a poor market.

FIG. 18-5 EXAMPLE OF THE BUILT-UP METHOD OVERALL RATE CALCULATION

An apartment complex has an estimated value of $500,000. At the time of the appraisal 25 year United States Government Bonds are yielding a safe rate of 9.12% interest.

In the appraiser's judgment, an investor would require 2% for the additional risk of investing in an apartment complex vs. a United States Government Bond.

In addition, a typical investor would require 1.5% to compensate for the effort required to find and place their money in an apartment complex investment vs. a United States Government Bond.

Because it will take time to sell the property should the investor wish to liquidate the investment, the investor seeks an additional 1.5% return to compensate for this lack of liquidity.

The time a typical investor estimates it will take to recover their capital from this type of property is 25 years. Therefore, 4% annually is allocated to capital recovery.

Taking all these factors together, a total interest rate and overall capitalization rate may be constructed as follows:

Safe Interest Rate	.0912
Additional Interest for Risk	.0200
Burden of Money Management	.0150
Lack of Liquidity	.0150
Total Interest Rate	.1377
Capital Recovery Rate	.0400
Overall Capitalization Rate	.1777

MORTGAGE EQUITY CAPITALIZATION (ELLWOOD METHOD)

Some appraisers feel that the modified band of investment method of capitalization rate construction is also deficient as it does not take into consideration the length of time of the projected investment or appreciation or depreciation of the property during the investment period. L.W. Ellwood, MAI in 1959 introduced his formula to incorporate these factors along with those factors already included in the modified band of investment method into one formula that could be used to test or construct an overall capitalization rate. He also constructed tables to help the appraiser apply his formula without having to do all the complex mathematical calculations.[1] Another good book that simplifies and explains what Ellwood developed was written by Charles B. Akerson, MAI.[2]

---

[1]L.W. Ellwood, *Ellwood Tables for Real Estate Appraising and Financing*, 4th ed., Ballinger Publishing Co., Cambridge. MA., 1977.
[2]Charles B. Akerson, *Study Guide: Course 1-B Capitalization Theory & Techniques*, American Institute of Real Estate Appraisers, Chicago, IL 1977.

The formula Ellwood devised for the construction of an overall rate is:[3]

$$R = Y - MC + \frac{dep}{app} \; (SFF)$$

R = Overall Capitalization Rate
Y = Equity Yield Rate
M = Ratio of Mortgage to Value
C = Mortgage Coefficient*
dep = Depreciation in property value for the projection period
app = Appreciation in property value for the projection period
SFF = Sinking-fund factor at Y rate for the ownership projection period

*The appraiser may elect to calculate the mortgage coefficient by using the formula:

$$C = Y + P \; (SFF) - f$$

P = Percentage of the mortgage that is amortized over the projection period
f = Mortgage constant

With the use of the tables pre-calculated by Ellwood, it is not necessary to calculate "C". It can be looked up on Ellwood's Table "C".

How to Construct A Capitalization Rate Using Ellwood's Mortgage Equity Tables

By carefully following these step-by-step instructions, you can successfully use the Ellwood mortgage equity method of capitalization rate construction for many income properties. It is not necessary that you understand the complex algebra or logic involved in making up the tables.

--**Step 1:** Collect the following information about the property to be appraised. To do this you must make some estimates based on your knowledge of the property and the market at the time of the appraisal.

Y (Equity Yield Rate) =

The Equity Yield Rate is the true return on an investment that a typical investor expects to receive over the period of time the investor will keep the property. It includes the loss or gain (most investors plan to sell the properties they buy for more than they purchase them for) made from the sale. Keep in mind that investors know that some of the income they receive for the property will be in the form of tax shelter, and they also consider that the proceeds of the sale may be taxed as a capital gain at the end of the investment period.

The appraiser should consider what yields are available from competitive investments. A good starting place is the yield on tax free bonds. The appraiser considers why an investor selects the property being appraised as an investment rather than invest in tax free bonds. The answer usually will be that they hope to get a higher rate of return.

---

[3]*The Appraisal of Real Estate*, American Institute of Real Estate Appraisers, 7th ed., Chicago, IL., 1978.

M (Ratio of Mortgage to Value) =

The ratio of mortgage to value is the percent of the total value of the property that can be financed by a conventional first mortgage that would be available to a typical investor on the property being appraised on the date of the appraisal.

Appraisers should not consider special financing that may be available from the owner or some special source a particular buyer might have (such as a rich relative).

Typical Mortgage Term =

Also, based on the same assumption, determine what the mortgage interest rate will be. When the typical mortgage is not being written at a fixed rate of interest, you may forecast what you estimate a typical investor feels the interest rate will be during the projected holding period. If you conclude you cannot make this projection, you make the mortgage equity method of capitalization rate construction impossible to use for the property you are appraising.

Typical Holding Period =

Some people buy property and never plan to sell it. Rather, they pass it along to their heirs. However, if you study the market in your area, you will find that many investment properties are sold, traded or refinanced in identifiable typical periods of time. You should be familiar with the current tax laws. They will help you estimate how long a prudent investor will hold a property. Generally, the tax law penalizes an investor who sells a property too soon or keeps a property too long. Later, when you use Ellwood's "C" Tables, you will have a choice of 5, 10, 15 or 20 years as typical holding periods. You save yourself a lot of work if your holding period estimate is one of these four figures (enough said).

app or dep (the amount investors believe a property will increase or decrease in value during the holding period).

During my 30 year real estate career, I never met a buyer who thought the property they were buying was going to go down in value during their projected holding period. Many investors, in my experience, are willing to take little or no cash return or immediate tax shelter from a property because they estimate there will be a large capital gain in the future. Most investors in income property believe that the value of the property will continue to rise in the future (people who do not believe this do not buy the property). Many appraisers complain that the mortgage equity capitalization technique tends to produce a rate that is too high. This may be caused by their projecting the rate of appreciation too low.

--Step 2: Determine the appropriate mortgage coefficient. Start by selecting the appropriate "C" table from your Ellwood book.[4] In order to select the appropriate table, you need the following information:

---

[4]L.W. Ellwood, *Ellwood Tables for Real Estate Appraising and Financing*, 4th ed., Ballinger Publishing Co., Cambridge, MA., 1977.

Projected Amortization Period
Projected Mortgage Interest Rate
Projected Holding Period

On the top of each "C" table page is a title "Mortgage Coefficients for Computing Capitalization Rates". Directly under this line, is a line that shows the amortization period and interest rates included in the table on this page. Go through the "C" table until you find the one that matches for the projected amortization period and projected mortgage interest rate you have determined is appropriate for the property being appraised. (See Fig. 18-6- "C Table")

FIG. 18-6 C TABLE MORTGAGE COEFFICIENTS FOR COMPUTING CAPITALIZATION RATES

"C" TABLE "C"

MORTGAGE COEFFICIENTS FOR
COMPUTING CAPITALIZATION RATES

Scope:—

Mortgage Amortization Terms; 10 years to 30 years by 5 year increments.

Mortgage Interest Rates:—3¼% to 12% by ¼% increments.

Income Projection Terms; 5 years to full amortization by 5 year increments.

Equity Yields; 4% to 30% by 1% increments.

To Find Desired Coefficient:—

1. Find Amortization Term in years.

2. Turn to page with desired mortgage interest rate and income projection term.

3. Find desired equity yield rate in *proper projection term bracket*. Move across on this line to column headed by desired mortgage interest rate.

$$Y - MC = r$$

Where:—

Y = Equity Yield

M = Ratio of Mortgage to Value

C = Coefficient from this table

r = Basic Capitalization Rate

Note:—Where coefficient is in italics or followed by a minus sign the formula is:

$$Y + MC = r$$

FIG. 18-7 C TABLE - 20 YEAR AMORTIZATION 7 3/4 TO 9%

TABLE C — Mortgage Coefficients for Computing Capitalization Rates.
20 YEARS AMORTIZATION: 7¾% TO 9% — **TABLE C**

Interest Rate Annual Requirement (f) Installment f/12		7¾% .098520 .008210	8% .100440 .008370	8¼% .102360 .008530	8½% .104160 .008680	8¾% .106080 .008840	9% .108000 .009000	$\frac{1}{s\,\overline{n}}$
Projection	Balance (b)	.872128	.874844	.877600	.881140	.883981	.886863	+ Dep. – App.
	Equity Yield			Mortgage Coefficients				
	4 % .04	.034911–	.037332–	.039761–	.042215–	.044659–	.047111–	.184627
	5 % .05	.025378–	.027739–	.030208–	.032649–	.035083–	.037525–	.180974
	6 % .06	.015836–	.018237–	.020646–	.023074–	.025498–	.027930–	.177396
	7 % .07	.006284–	.008676–	.011075–	.013491–	.015905–	.018326–	.173890
	8 % .08	.003276	.000893	.001496–	.003899–	.006303–	.008715–	.170456
	9 % .09	.012846	.010472	.008092	.005700	.003305	.000904	.167092
	10 % .10	.022425	.020060	.017688	.015308	.012923	.010531	.163797
	11 % .11	.032012	.029656	.027293	.024925	.022549	.020166	.160570
	12 % .12	.041608	.039260	.036906	.034549	.032182	.029808	.157409
	13 % .13	.051212	.048873	.046528	.044181	.041823	.039458	.154314
	14 % .14	.060824	.058493	.056157	.053821	.051471	.049115	.151283
5 Years **n = 5**	15 % .15	.070445	.068122	.065793	.063468	.061127	.058779	.148315
	16 % .16	.080073	.077758	.075438	.073123	.070790	.068451	.145409
	17 % .17	.089709	.087402	.085089	.082785	.080460	.078129	.142563
	18 % .18	.099353	.097053	.094748	.092453	.090136	.087813	.139777
	19 % .19	.109004	.106712	.104414	.102129	.099820	.097505	.137050
	20 % .20	.118663	.116378	.114088	.111812	.109510	.107203	.134379
	21 % .21	.128329	.126051	.123768	.121501	.119207	.116907	.131765
	22 % .22	.138001	.135730	.133454	.131197	.128910	.126617	.129205
	23 % .23	.147681	.145417	.143148	.140899	.138619	.136334	.126700
	24 % .24	.157367	.155110	.152847	.150608	.148335	.146056	.124247
	25 % .25	.167060	.164809	.162554	.160322	.158056	.155785	.121846
	26 % .26	.176760	.174515	.172266	.170043	.167783	.165519	.119496
	27 % .27	.186466	.184227	.181984	.179769	.177516	.175259	.117195
	28 % .28	.196178	.193945	.191709	.189502	.187255	.185004	.114943
	29 % .29	.205896	.203669	.201439	.199240	.196999	.194754	.112739
	30 % .30	.215620	.213399	.211175	.208983	.206749	.204510	.110581
	Balance (b)	.683970	.688381	.692964	.699605	.704573	.709728	+ Dep. – App.
	Equity Yield			Mortgage Coefficients				
	4 % .04	.032197–	.034485–	.036786–	.039139–	.041473–	.043823–	.083290
	5 % .05	.023394–	.025664–	.027949–	.030277–	.032592–	.034922–	.079504
	6 % .06	.014543–	.016798–	.019065–	.021369–	.023666–	.025977–	.075867
	7 % .07	.005646–	.007885–	.010137–	.012418–	.014697–	.016990–	.072377
	8 % .08	.003295	.001070	.001165–	.003423–	.005686–	.007962–	.069020
	9 % .09	.012281	.010070	.007849	.005611	.003365	.001105	.065820
	10 % .10	.021309	.019112	.016905	.014688	.012456	.010213	.062745
	11 % .11	.030379	.028195	.026001	.023804	.021586	.019358	.059801
	12 % .12	.039488	.037317	.035136	.032957	.030754	.028540	.056984
	13 % .13	.048637	.046477	.044308	.042148	.039958	.037758	.054289
	14 % .14	.057823	.055674	.053517	.051374	.049197	.047010	.051713
10 Years **n = 10**	15 % .15	.067045	.064907	.062762	.060635	.058470	.056296	.049252
	16 % .16	.076302	.074175	.072040	.069928	.067775	.065614	.046901
	17 % .17	.085592	.083475	.081351	.079254	.077112	.074962	.044656
	18 % .18	.094915	.092808	.090693	.088611	.086479	.084340	.042514
	19 % .19	.104270	.102171	.100066	.097997	.095876	.093747	.040471
	20 % .20	.113654	.111564	.109467	.107412	.105300	.103182	.038522
	21 % .21	.123067	.120985	.118897	.116854	.114751	.112642	.036665
	22 % .22	.132507	.130433	.128353	.126322	.124228	.122129	.034894
	23 % .23	.141974	.139908	.137836	.135815	.133730	.131639	.033208
	24 % .24	.151467	.149407	.147342	.145333	.143256	.141173	.031602
	25 % .25	.160983	.158931	.156873	.154873	.152804	.150729	.030072
	26 % .26	.170523	.168477	.166426	.164436	.162374	.160306	.028616
	27 % .27	.180085	.178045	.176000	.174019	.171964	.169904	.027230
	28 % .28	.189668	.187634	.185595	.183623	.181575	.179521	.025911
	29 % .29	.199272	.197243	.195210	.193246	.191204	.189157	.024657
	30 % .30	.208895	.206871	.204844	.202888	.200851	.198810	.023463

Next, select the section of the "C" Table that coincides with the project holding period you have determined to be appropriate. There are four sections for each "C" Table (5, 10, 15, 20 years). Each section is identified in the left hand column of the table.

Select from this section of the "C" Table, the mortgage coefficient you will use, by first looking for the proper column with the interest rate you have selected for the first mortgage and the line that represents the equity yield you have estimated an investor will require on the cash invested. (The equity yields are in the second column from the left).

--Step 3: Select the appropriate sinking fund factor from the same section of the "C" Table as was used for Step 2. (The sinking fund factor may also be looked up on the Sinking Fund Table. Select the appropriate line by finding the yield rate in the left column and the appropriate SFF column by finding the projection in the column heading).

Again, the estimated investor's yield on cash invested is found in the second column from the left and the appropriate sinking fund factor is on this same page in the far righthand column. (The estimated investor's yield used here should be the same as that used in Step 2).

--Step 4: Calculate R (Overall Rate) using the formula

$$R = Y - MC + dep$$
$$- app \ (SFF)$$

FIG. 18-8 EXAMPLE OF HOW TO CALCULATE THE OVERALL RATE

The property being appraised is an apartment house. In this market, for this type of investment, investors require a 14% equity yield. Typical financing is 70% of appraised value for 20 years (monthly payments, 100% amortization) at 9% interest. It is projected to appreciate 50% (5% per year average) over the projected 10 year holding period.

$$Y = .14$$
$$M = .70$$
$$C = .047010 \ \{\text{Taken from "C" Table - 20 years amortization 7 3/4 to 9\%}$$
$$(14\% \ \text{yield line - 9\% interest column})\}$$
$$app = .50$$
$$SFF = .051713 \ \{\text{Taken from C" Table - 20 years amortization 7 3/4 to 9\%}$$
$$(14\% \ \text{yield line - column})\}$$

First calculate: MC =
$$= .70 \times .047010$$
$$= .032907$$

Next calculate: + dep
$$- app \ (SFF) =$$
$$= -.50 \times .051713$$
$$= -.025857$$

Finally calculate: R = Y -MC + dep
                                      - app (SFF)

$$R = .14 - .032907 - .025857$$
$$R = .081238$$
$$R = .08 \text{ Rounded}$$

FIG. 18-9 ALTERNATE EXAMPLE

An apartment complex is being appraised. Investors in this market are seeking a 12% equity yield. Typical financing for this type of property is an 80%, 20 year term, 100% amortizing mortgage at 8% annual interest. A typical investor would plan to hold the property 10 years. Because the neighborhood is declining, a typical investor would project the property to decrease in value at the rate of 1% per year (total depreciation 10%).

$$Y = .12$$
$$M = .80$$
$$C = .037317$$
$$\text{dep} = +.10$$
$$\text{SFF} = .056984$$

First calculate: MC =
$$= .80 \times .037317$$
$$= .029854$$

Next calculate: + dep
                         - app (SFF) =
$$= +.10 \times .056984$$
$$= +.0056984$$

Finally calculate: R = Y -MC + dep
                                     - app (SFF)
$$= .12 - .029854 + .0056984$$
$$= .095844$$
$$= .096 \text{ Rounded}$$

ADVANCED CAPITALIZATION TECHNIQUES

Some appraisers have become serious students of "Ellwood" and other capitalization techniques. Some feel that even the complex "Ellwood" theories do not produce the best results in all instances.

Charles B. Akerson developed procedures that substituted arithmetic formulae for the algebraic equations used by Ellwood. He also incorporated the "J" factor into his formula which provides a tool for the appraiser to incorporate changes in the income stream and property value into the rate calculations.[1]

---

[1]Charles B. Akerson, Study Guide: Course 1-B Capitalization Theory & Techniques, American Institute of Real Estate Appraisers, Chicago, IL 1977.

One of the features that has contributed to the popularity of the "Ellwood" capitalization technique, is the ability to create a graph that displays the results and shows what alternate rates would be when some of the assumptions are changed.

Readers who are interested in these and other advanced capitalization techniques can read about them in the *Appraising of Real Estate*, 9th ed., American Institute of Real Estate Appraisers, 430 North Michigan Avenue, Chicago, IL 60611, 1987. Better still, they should take an advanced capitalization course given by one of the appraisal organizations or colleges.

SUMMARY

The Income Approach is based on the proven theory that the value of income-producing property is determined by the future income the property produces for its owner.

The first step in estimating the value of a property based on its future income stream is to estimate the amount of the income stream to be obtained by the owner in the future.

The appraiser starts by estimating the potential gross income (PGI) attributable to the property, assuming it is fully rented at market rent, for the first year from the date of appraisal. From this, an estimated income loss from vacancies and uncollected rents is subtracted. Other income from the property is added and the result is the annual projected effective gross income (EGI).

The appraiser subtracts the projected annual fixed expenses, operating expenses and reserves from the effective gross income. The result is the projected annual net operating income (NOI). This term (NOI) is unique to appraising as it does not include deductions for mortgage debt service and book depreciation because they are included as part of the capitalization rate.

The second step uses the projected net operating income to estimate the value of the property by dividing it by a capitalization rate which reflects the ratio between the NOI and the value of the property being appraised.

There are many ways to project an appropriate capitalization rate. The best, most simple and direct way is to abstract an overall rate from the market when market data is available.

The formula for converting NOI into value is:

$$\frac{NOI}{Capitalization\ Rate} = Value$$

When suitable market data is not available, other techniques must be used. Another popular way to develop an overall capitalization rate is the band of investment method. It is derived by making a weighted average of the rates in the market available to a typical investor, for mortgages, on the property being appraised, with the return on equity invested that a typical investor would expect to receive.

The modified band of investment method is similar to the band of investment method except that is also takes into consideration the length of the mortgage and rate of amortization.

Another method is the built-up method of constructing an overall capitalization rate. The rate is divided into its component parts: safe interest rate, risk, burden of money management and lack of liquidity. The appraiser estimates the amount of interest required by a typical investor for each component and adds them together to make an overall capitalization rate.

A more sophisticated direct capitalization method was developed by L.W. Ellwood known as the mortgage equity capitalization method (Ellwood Method). Ellwood devised a formula for the construction of an overall rate.

$$R = Y - MC + dep$$
$$- app\ (SFF)$$

He also constructed tables to help the appraiser apply his formula. His method provides a method for appraisers to use graphs for displaying how the rate changes when some of the assumptions are changed.

There are other methods available for appraisers to estimate the value of a property based on its income, including ones that use multipliers. No one method will work for all properties, but all require knowledge and experience to be used properly.

2 TO 3 STORIES

SIMPLE EXTERIOR LINES

LARGE, HIGH CHIMNEYS

DOUBLE-HUNG WINDOWS; SMALL PANES

RECTANGULAR SHAPE

SIMPLE FRONT

English

WILLIAMSBURG GEORGIAN OR EARLY GEORGIAN
(Williams or E Georg - 204)

STOOP UP TO
FIRST FLOOR

BROWNSTONE
TRIM

4 OR 5
STORIES

COMMON WALLS   BRICK   FLAT ROOF

SIMPLE
DOUBLE-
HUNG
WINDOWS

Nineteenth Century American

BROWNSTONE OR BRICK ROW HOUSE OR EASTERN TOWNHOUSE (Brown S or Br Row or E Town - 713)

ADDENDA CONTENTS

INCOME PROPERTY
MODEL NARRATIVE APPRAISAL

On the following pages is a Model Narrative appraisal report of a 10 unit rental apartment building. The reported is based on a actual property, appraised by Barbara Kaye in Lake Shores, Florida.

The report has been substantially modified for teaching purposes. The location of the subject property and all of the comparable sales and rentals have been fictionalized. The date has been set some time in the near future 199_.

Rarely, if ever, would an appraisal contain data of the same high quality as the fictional data in this report.

Although the appraisal does not give specific dates, the reader should assume all dates are in the same year and that all months indicated in the appraisal are therefore either within one year prior to the date of the appraisal (unless otherwise specified).

Again, I wish to thank Barbara Kaye for allowing her work to be published in this text, and Richard Chamberlin and my partner Leonard D'Agostino, RM, who collected additional data and took additional photographs for this report. Thank you to Maura Gianakos, who typed the report on our Wang Word Processor in order to make appear more realistic than it would appear if it were set in type like the rest of this book. Unfortunately, during the process the Wang required 12 service calls. Maura will soon take a short leave to have her baby and the Wang Word Processor will be junked.

This model appraisal is not intended to be an example of a demonstration appraisal applicable for credit towards a designation from an appraisal organization. Each organization has their own specific demonstration appraisal requirements. Demonstration appraisals are a type of examination in which an appraiser shows the examiners his or her knowledge of the appraisal process and the organizations special reporting requirements.

This model appraisal is intended to show the type of work an appraiser would actually do for a client.

PART ONE

INTRODUCTION

<u>REAL ESTATE APPRAISAL</u>

700 DUQUESNE DRIVE
WEST PALM BEACH, FLORIDA

OWNER OF RECORD: Etak Trebmal

DATE OF APPRAISAL: December 15, 199__

THIS IS A: 10-Unit Rental Apartment
                                    Building

APPRAISED FOR: Appraisal Students Everywhere
                                    100 Main Street
                                    Typical Town, USA   00001

APPRAISED BY: Barbara J. Kaye
                                    315 Whitney Avenue
                                    New Haven, Connecticut 06511
                                    (203)562-3159

Barbara J. Kaye
315 Whitney Avenue
New Haven, Connecticut   06511
(203)562-3159

February 25, 199_

Appraisal Students Everywhere
100 Main Street
Typical Town, USA   00001

RE: 700 Duquesne Drive
      West Palm Beach, Florida

Gentlemen:

I herewith submit for your review this appraisal report of the
property known as 700 Duquesne Drive, West Palm Beach, Florida.

The purpose of the appraisal is to estimate the market value of
the fee simple estate of the property, as of December 15, 199_,
subject to the assumptions, limiting conditions, and certificate
included herein.

I personally inspected the property on December 15, 199_, and
have gathered and analyzed all the data necessary to arrive at
the value conclusion.

The subject site has 100 feet of frontage along Haden Road, an
average depth of 210 feet, and contains approximately .48 acre.
The site is improved with a two-story, masonry, ten-unit
apartment building plus miscellaneous site improvements.

Based upon my investigations and analysis of the real estate
market in the area, and after considering all of the pertinent
facts as set forth in the body of this report, the estimated
market value of the fee, as of December 15, 199_, is:

        SIX HUNDRED THOUSAND ($600,000) DOLLARS

Respectfully submitted,

Barbara J. Kaye

Barbara J. Kaye

CERTIFICATION

I, the undersigned, do hereby certify that I have personally inspected the property located at 700 Duquesne Drive, West Palm Beach, Florida

To the best of my knowledge and belief, the statements of fact contained in this report and upon which the opinions herein are based are true and correct, subject to the assumptions and limiting conditions explained in the report.

Employment in and compensation for making this appraisal are in no way contingent upon the value reported, and I certify that I have no interest, either present or contemplated, in the subject property. I have no personal interest or bias with respect to the subject matter of the appraisal report or the parties involved.

This appraisal report identifies all of the limiting conditions affecting the analyses, opinions, and conclusions contained in this report.

The analyses, opinions, and conclusions contained in this report have been developed in accordance with the standards of Professional Appraisal Practice and the Codes of Ethics of the Professional Organizations with which I am affiliated.

No one other than the undersigned prepared the analysis, opinions, or conclusions concerning real estate that are set forth in this appraisal report. I am not currently designated or certified by any appraisal organization.

In my opinion, the subject property has a value representative of market conditions on December 15, 199_ of $600,000.

Barbara J. Kaye
Barbara J. Kaye

TABLE OF CONTENTS

QUALIFICATIONS OF THE APPRAISER
BARBARA J. KAYE

Business Address: 1985 to Present
                      Vice President and Manager, Appraisal Department
                      Bank of Boston - Connecticut
                      81 West Main Street
                      Waterbury, CT 06702

General Education: Day-Prospect Hill School, New Haven, CT
                      Syracuse University, B.S., Finance and Real Estate

Appraisal Experience: 1976-1985 Commercial Real Estate
                      Appraiser with Henry S. Harrison Appraisal Company,
                      New Haven, CT

Appraisal Education

"Basic Appraisal Principles, Methods and Techniques", given by American Institute of Real Estate Appraisers, sponsored by University of Connecticut

"Capitalization Theory and Techniques", given by American Institute of Real Estate Appraisers, sponsored by the University of Georgia.

Narrative Report Seminar and R-2 Examination, given by Society of Real Estate Appraisers, sponsored by Connecticut Chapter No. 38, SREA.

"Introduction to Commercial and Investment Real Estate", given by the National Institute of Real Estate Brokers, sponsored by the Commercial and Investment Division of N.I.R.E.B.

"Real Estate Construction Costs, Estimating and House Material", given at the University of Connecticut.

"Case Studies in Real Estate Valuation and Valuation Analysis and Report Writing", given by American Institute of Real Estate Appraisers, sponsored by Indiana University.

"Standards of Professional Practice", given by A.I.R.E.A., sponsored by University of Massachusetts.

Professional and Trade Affiliation
Associate Realtor of the Greater New Haven Board of Realtors

Real Estate Experience
Licensed real estate broker. Actively engaged in the appraisal of residential, commercial, and industrial properties. Past experience in real estate sales, management, and leasing.

Court Experience
Qualified as Expert Witness, Superior Court

Articles
What is Actual Cash Value in the Appraisal Journal, American Institute of Real Estate Appraisers, Chicago, July, 1984.

Front view looking east from Baden Road (12/15/9_)

Partial front and side view looking southeast
from Baden Road (12/15/9_)

SUMMARY OF SALIENT FACTS & CONCLUSIONS

SUMMARY OF SALIENT FACTS & CONCLUSIONS

Property Address: 700 Duquesne Drive
West Palm Beach, Florida

Owner of Record: Etak Trebmal

Date of Appraisal: December 15, 199_

Property Rights Appraised: Fee Simple Estate

Purpose of Appraisal: Estimate market value of the
unencumbered fee simple estate

Land Area: 20,908 sq. ft. or .48 acre

Building Improvement: Two-story, masonry, apartment
building containing ten, one-bedroom
units, constructed in 198_ (11 years
ago).

Zoning: RH High Density Multiple Family,
2,000 square feet per unit

Highest and Best Use
as if Vacant: Property is a legal, non-conforming
use. Only three units would be
allowed if land was unimproved and
available for development.

Highest and Best Use
as Improved: Current use as a ten-unit apartment
building

Assessment & Taxes: Assessment: $461,598.00
Tax Liability: $ 7,572.56

Values Indicated:
Cost Approach to Value: $610,000

Income Approach to Value: $600,000

Direct Sales Comparison Approach: $600,000

Final Estimate of Value: Site $130,000
Improvements $470,000

Total $600,000

PART TWO

PREMISES OF THE APPRAISAL

UNDERLYING ASSUMPTIONS AND LIMITING CONDITIONS

This appraisal report has been made with the following general assumptions, and subject to the following limiting conditions.

1. No responsibility is assumed for the legal description or for matters including legal or title considerations. Title to the property is assumed to be good and marketable unless otherwise stated.

2. The property is appraised free and clear of any or all liens or encumbrances unless otherwise stated.

3. Responsible ownership and competent property management are assumed.

4. The information furnished by others is believed to be reliable. However, no warranty is given for its accuracy.

5. All engineering is assumed to be correct. The plot plans and illustrative material in this report are included only to assist the reader in visualizing the property.

6. It is assumed that there are no hidden or unapparent environmental or physical conditions of the property, subsoil, or structures that render it more or less valuable. No responsibility is assumed for such conditions or for arranging for engineering environmental studies that may be required to discover them.

7. It is assumed that there is full compliance with all applicable federal, state, and local environmental regulations and laws unless noncompliance is stated, defined, and considered in the appraisal report.

8. It is assumed that all applicable zoning and use regulations and restrictions have been complied with, unless a nonconformity has been stated, defined, and considered in the appraisal report.

9. It is assumed that all required licenses, certificates of occupancy, consents, or other legislative or administrative authority from any local, state, or national government or private entity or organization have been or can be obtained or renewed for any use on which the value estimate contained in this report is based.

10. It is assumed that the utilization of the land and improvements is within the boundaries or property lines of the property described and that there is no encroachment or trespass unless noted in the report.

11. The distribution, if any, of the total valuation in this report between land and improvements applies only under the stated program of utilization. The separate allocations for land and buildings must not be used in conjunction with any other appraisal and are invalid if so used.

12. Possession of this report, or a copy thereof, does not carry with it the right of publication.

13. The appraiser, by reason of this appraisal, is not required to give further consultation, testimony, or be in attendance in court with reference to the property in question unless arrangements have been previously made.

14. Neither all nor any part of the contents of this report (especially any conclusions as to value, the identity of the appraiser, or the firm with which the appraiser is connected) shall be disseminated to the public through advertising, public relations, news, sales, or other media without the prior written consent and approval of the appraiser.

The purpose of this appraisal is to create a teaching model to be used for training appraisers how to make an acceptable narrative apppraisal of an income producing residential property.

It is not intended to be an example of a demonstrative appraisal made by an appraiser for the purpose of obtaining a designation from an appraisal organization. Such an appraisal would have to meet the specific requirements for demonstration appraisals as specified by the organization awarding the designation.

MARKET VALUE DEFINITION AND DATE OF APPRAISAL

The "Market Value" that is estimated in this report is defined as follows:

"The most probable price in terms of money which a property should bring in competitive and open market under all conditions requisite to a fair sale, the buyer and seller, each acting prudently, knowledgeably and assuming the price is not affected by undue stimulus."

Implicit in this definition is the consummation of a sale as of a specified date and the passing of title from seller to buyer under conditions whereby:

1.   buyer and seller are typically motivated.

2.   both parties are well informed or well advised, and each acting in what they consider their own best interest.

3.   a reasonable time is allowed for exposure in the open market.

4.   payment is made in cash or its equivalent.

5.   financing is on terms generally available in the community at the specified date and typical for the property type in its locale.

6.   the price represents a normal consideration for the property sold unaffected by special financing amounts and/or terms, services, fees, costs, or credits incurred in the transactions.

Date of Value Estimate

December 15, 199_ (this year).

PROPERTY RIGHTS APPRAISED

The property rights being appraised are fee simple.

The following is a definition of Fee Simple:

"An absolute fee; a fee without limitations to any particular class of heirs or restrictions, but subject to the limitations of eminent domain, escheat, police power, and taxation. An inheritable estate."

PART THREE

PRESENTATION OF DATA

IDENTIFICATION OF THE PROPERTY

The property being appraised is located at 700 Duquesne Drive, in the municipality of West Palm Beach, County of Palm Beach, Florida.

The property is further identified as follows: Municipality 34, Range 43, Township 44, Section 8, Subdivision 6, Block 5, Lot 23.2.

The property being appraised consists of approximately 20,908 square feet of land improved with a two-story, ten-unit apartment building and miscellaneous site improvements.

IDENTIFICATION OF NON REALTY ITEMS

There were no non-realty items included in the appraisal value.

REGIONAL DATA - PALM BEACH COUNTY

Environmental Forces

Geographic Location

Palm Beach County, the largest of Florida's 67 counties, is located along the southeast coast of Florida, situated approximately 40 miles north of Miami. Palm Beach County is bounded to the east by the Atlantic Ocean and 47 miles of sandy beaches, to the north by Martin County, to the northwest by Lake Okeechobee, to the west by undeveloped Hendry County, and to the south by urbanized Broward County.

Climate

The warm climate of Palm Beach County is a major resource. The Gulf Stream flows closer to Palm Beach County than to any other area along the Eastern Seaboard, keeping temperatures at an average 65 degrees in January and 82 degrees in August.

Transportation

The County is served by two major, north/south, limited-access highways: Florida Turnpike (a toll facility) and Interstate 95. Other major, north/south arteries include Federal Highway (U.S. 1), Congress Avenue, Military Trail, and U.S. 441. East/west arteries extend from the Atlantic Ocean to I-95, the Florida Turnpike and to the Everglades area to the west.

Most major commercial bus lines provide passenger and freight service to and from Palm Beach County and have convenient schedules and stations.

The County is serviced by rail for both passengers and freight. Amtrak provides passengers with boarding locations in the county. There is only limited interstate rail passenger traffic. The Florida East Coast Railway and Seaboard Coastline Railroad move major shipments of goods and materials through their Palm Beach County terminals and branch lines.

Servicing the Palm Beaches in air travel is the new Palm Beach International Airport.

REGIONAL DATA - PALM BEACH COUNTY (continued)

Industry

The major industry in the region is tourism, employing 46% of the county's work force between the months of December and April.

Due to the seasonal nature of the major industries - tourism and agriculture - and the cyclical nature of the construction business, the County has made a concerted effort to attract new industry. Most of the recent industrial and residential development has taken place west of the Intracoastal Waterway. The Pratt & Whitney Aircraft Division of United Technologies and IBM are the major employers.

Port of Palm Beach

The Port of Palm Beach is one of Florida's major marine terminals. The Port has become the gateway to the Bahamas and other Atlantic Ocean islands, the Caribbean, and Central and South America, as well as a stopover for cargo destined for Europe and the Middle East.

Education

The Palm Beach County School District is one of the largest in the country and is growing rapidly. There are also many private and parochial schools, colleges, and universities.

Hospitals and Medical Facilities

Palm Beach County offers 14 medical/surgical facilities, including two psychiatric hospitals. All the major communities are equiped with emergency-rescue vehicles and trained paramedics.

Shopping

The Palm Beaches have an array of malls and shopping centers, including the internationally known shopping area on Worth Avenue in Palm Beach.

Social Forces

Population

The 1980 Census Summary of General Population Characteristics showed a total population in Palm Beach County of 576,863 persons of which 52.3% were female, and the median age was 40.2 years. The total households was 234,339, with 2.42 persons per household and a total of 165,847 families.

Housing

The 1980 Census Summary of General Housing Characteristics showed a total of 295,664 housing units in Palm Beach County. Of the total housing units, 234,339 were occupied (171,736 owner-occupied and 62,603 tenant-occupied). The rental vacancy rate was 8.9%.

A wide variety of housing opportunities exist in the Palm Beaches. These opportunities vary from single family detached housing to high rise condominium community living.

Rentals are available in a wide range of choice and price. Most rental units include conventional features while others offer several luxury amenities. A lease for six or 12 months is usually required.

Because the Palm Beaches enjoy a very active tourist season (October through April), a lease during this season is usually at rates higher than year-round rates.

Economic Forces

In 1980, the Standard Metropolitan Statistical Area (SMSA) of West Palm/Boca Raton topped the growth list in the state in all business areas (i.e. grocery, restaurant, furniture, cars, department stores).

The median household income, as of December 31, 1979, was $14,258, one of the highest in the state.

Palm Beach County is one of the fastest growing areas in the nation and is an important center for industry, agriculture, international banking, and commerce, with expertise and resources that are highly attractive to investors.

Government Forces

The state and local governments are working closely to provide a healthy and prosperous environment for all Floridians. The State fully supports all activities encouraging the growth of tourism and industry.

Summary

The appraised property is linked to the central business district of West Palm Beach, the largest city in the center of Palm Beach County. A vital cultural climate exists, with resident supported museums, art galleries, symphonies, and theaters.

Downtown West Palm Beach ended the 1980's in the midst of a typical evolution from a retail and social center to a concentrated center for government and financial institutions. The downtown area is now in an extremely enviable position relative to downtown areas throughout Florida and the nation, primarily due to a group of local individuals who are dedicated to the revival of the downtown area as an attractive regional center.

The appraised property is located in the heart of one of the fastest growing areas and one of the most attractive places to live in the nation.

Palm Beach County has a solid and diversified economic base. Considering the recreational and cultural activities available, the climate, the location along the Intercoastal Waterway and Atlantic Ocean, medical and educational facilities, variety and price range of housing, and employment opportunities, it is my opinion that the appraised property will benefit from the strong growth trends in the area.

COMMUNITY MAP

COMMUNITY DATA

West Palm Beach is one of the 37 municipalities comprising Palm Beach County. Greater West Palm Beach Area has a population of 225,000 persons. The influx of people into the community continues at a rate that varies from a 1% to 3% per year population increase.

Industry and Employment
The old airport was surrounded with an industrial area that housed a variety of small industrial and commercial enterprises which benefited from the close proximity to the airport. The rate of unemployment is very low in spite of a substantial increase of available workers.

Air Transportation .
The West Palm Beach airport finally outgrew its site and the new airport recently opened. This new facility should substantially increase both the amount of passenger and freight traffic.

Medical Care
There are several well staffed hospitals in the city plus numerous nursing homes.

Education
There are a variety of local and community colleges in the community. The public schools are typical for a large Florida community.

Entertainment
There are ample movie theaters, some regional legitimate theaters, Jai Alai, and a dog track.

Shopping
There are many neighborhood and community shopping areas throughout West Palm Beach and a downtown shopping area. The Palm Coast Plaza shopping center is 1 mile west of the subject property. Worth Avenue in Palm Beach is one of the most famous high price shopping areas in the USA.

Government
The local government is traditional and typical for this area.

Summary
West Palm Beach is virtually 100% built-up, with only a few unimproved parcels remaining. The town benefits from the steady growth of Palm Beach County. The commercial development is competitive with neighboring towns. The appraised property should continue to benefit from continued demand and growth in the area.

SCALE 3" = 1 MILE

NEIGHBORHOOD DATA

General Description

The subject property is located in West Palm Beach in a
neighborhood known as the West Palm Beach Canal neighborhood.
It is on the east side of Duquesne Drive. It is surrounded with
a mixture of single family and multi-family residential
buildings. Forest Hill Boulevard is the boundary on the north,
Lake Worth on the east, 10th street on the south, and Interstate
Highway 95 on the west.

Proximity to Central Business District: Five miles north of
downtown West Palm Beach.

Percentage Built-up and Trend: Virtually 100% built-up, no new
construction observed in the immediate area. New office and
retail development on Forest Hill Boulevard.

Typical Improvement and Level of Maintenance: Newer (1960 and
later) single family dwellings range in price from $120,000 to
$160,000, exhibiting a very good maintenance level. There are
very few multi-family properties, however, those that do exist
also show a high level of maintenance.

Population Characteristics: Middle income blue and white collar
families; semi-skilled and skilled labor; retirees.

Transportation:

Highway proximity:	Interstate 95 one mile west. U.S. Route 1, 3 blocks West.
Bus:	Cotran - on Forest Hills Boulevard - 2 miles.
Railroad:	Lake Worth - (limited intra state passenger service).
Air Transport:	Palm Beach International Airport - 3 miles.

Schools

Public Grammar:	South Olive Elementary
Public Junior High:	Jefferson Davis Middle
Public High:	Forest Hills High
Parochial Grammar:	Various
Parochial High:	Various
Other:	Palm Beach Junior College and others

Employment Opportunities: Excellent - blue and white collar jobs within five miles of subject property.

Access to Shopping Facilities: Very good - minutes to banks, restaurants, offices and shopping.

Hospitals: Doctor's Hospital on 10th Avenue - 1 mile; plus four other hospitals within ten miles of subject property.

Library: Summit Road - 2 miles.

Recreation: West Palm Beach municipal golf course - 3/4 mile; Palm Beach Auditorium; museums, zoos, beaches, cultural activities.

Conclusion: The subject neighborhood is centrally located within West Palm Beach and the residential properties are well maintained. The rental apartment market is very strong in terms of occupancy and rent levels. Very few new rental properties similar to the appraised property are being developed, indicating continued strong demand. It is reasonable to expect that property values will remain relatively stable, increasing with the general inflationary trends in the country.

ZONING DATA

The appraised property is located in the RM Medium Density zoning district as designated by the Town of West Palm Beach, adopted April 13, 1964, as amended and revised.

This district is designed to provide a minimum area of multiple family, relatively high population density, residential facilities to be located where access from main thoroughfares to such facilities is especially desirable. Certain non-residential uses may be allowed by Special Exception.

Permitted Uses: Two-family dwellings; multiple family dwellings; and single family dwellings.

Permitted Accessory Uses and Structures: Facilities as may be required or useful for the operation of an apartment house, or for the entertainment of guests or tenants, but all such accessory uses shall be conducted within the building or shall be entered only from within the building, and no sign on the exterior of the building shall indicate their presence.

Special Exceptions: Religious, institutional, or public buildings; professional office buildings.

Prohibited Uses: Apartment houses in excess of two stories (20 feet in height); commercial recreational facilities.

Standards for Multi-Family Dwellings:

Minimum Lot Area:	10,000 sq. ft., provided that there shall be at least 2,000 square feet of net lot area for each dwelling unit (approximately 22 units per acre).
Minimum Lot Width:	100 feet
Minimum Front Yard:	25 feet
Minimum Side Yard:	15% of average lot width, but not less than 15 feet.
Minimum Rear Yard:	15% of average lot depth, but not less than 15 feet.
Maximum Lot Coverage:	35%
Minimum Floor Area:	600 sq. ft. per dwelling unit
Minimum Off-Street Parking:	1 1/2 spaces per dwelling unit

The subject property appears to conform with the current zoning requirements and represents a conforming use of the site.

ASSESSMENT AND TAXES DATA

By law, all property in the State of Florida is required to be assessed at 100% of market value. The current assessment for the subject property is as follows:

Land	$ 82,992
Improvements	378,606
Total Assessment	$461,598

Per Unit $46,160

The following 199_ (last year) tax rates and taxes were recorded for the subject property:

Type	Rate	Taxes
General Tax	6.6689	$3,078.35
School Tax	6.9329	3,199.93
Library Tax	.3526	162.76
Municipal Tax	2.3900	1,103.19
Sub-Total (tax rate)	16.3444	$7,544.23
Maintenance Tax (flat per acre)		28.02
Total (Per Unit $757.22)		$7,572.25

Trends

Like most Florida communities, the annual budget of West Palm Beach tends to increase gradually each year. In recent years, the total Grand List has increased at a greater rate than the annual budget, therefore, the tax rates have been decreasing.

Tax Comparables

A study of the assessment and taxes on the four properties used as comparables sales within this report was made and compared to the current assessment and taxes for the appraised property. The taxes of the four comparable properties, located in three different competitive communities, ranged from $392. to $896. per·unit.

The current taxes at the subject property are $757.22 per unit. Considering the location, age and condition of the improvements, and the overall trend in West Palm Beach, the taxes paid at the subject property are similar to the comparable properties.

TAX COMPARABLES

Address	Assessment	General Tax	School Tax	Library Tax	Municipal Tax	Maintenance Tax	Total Annual Taxes	Taxes Unit	% of Taxes to Assessment
825 South St Lake Worth	$416,162	2,613.36	2,226.26	---	1,430.84	---	6,270.46	392	1.5%
2610 Gulfstream Rd West Palm Beach	472,048	4,421.42	2,525.22	166.44	---	56.04	7,169.12	896	1.5%
3713 Davis Rd West Palm Beach	481,340	4,154.38	2,372.68	156.40	---	28.02	6,711.48	838	1.4%
675 Florida Mango Road West Palm Beach	387,578	3,416.38	2,073.44	136.66	---	28.02	5,654.50	472	1.5%
SUBJECT PROPERTY 700 Duquesne Dr. West Palm Beach	461,598	3,078.34	3,200.22	162.76	1,103.22	28.02	7,572.56	758	1.6%

A30

SITE DATA

Physical Characteristics

Dimensions:	100 feet x 210 feet average depth
Total Area:	20,908 sq. ft. or .48 acre
Excess Area:	None
Shape:	Rectangular
Drainage:	Adequate - in heavy rains, a large puddle tends to form in portion of driveway near street.
Topography:	Essentially level at street grade
Corner Influence:	No
View:	Neighboring single-family dwellings
Soil:	Typical Florida sand
Mineral Deposits:	None of any commercial valuee

Utilities

Water:	Well water
Sanitary Sewers:	Septic system, 2,500 gallon tank, drainfield
Storm Sewers:	County
Electricity:	Florida Power & Light
Telephone:	Southern Bell

Site Improvements

Sprinkler system:	Underground sprinkler for yard areas
Driveway & Parking:	Parking for 15 cars; asphalt paved, approximately 5,000 square feet was recently repaird.
Fences:	100' chain link fence - rear yard
Sidewalks:	Concrete walks
Landscaping:	Lawn, trees, and shrubs
Plot Plan:	On facing page; prepared by James D. Carlton, Inc., Registered Engineers and Land Surveyors. This plot has been reduced, therefore, does not reflect the original scale of 1"=20'.

Street Improvements

Paving:	Yes
Sidewalks:	No
Curbing:	No
Lighting:	Yes
Road Surface:	Macadam
Width:	Two lanes
Maintenance by:	Town
Condition:	Good

Easements & Restrictive
Covenants: Asphalt driveway encroaches from
                                    700 Duquesne Drive Road - see
                                    Plot Plan

Nuisances and Hazards: None. There is minimal traffic
                                    on Duquesne Drive basically
                                    generated by residents and their
                                    visitors.

Functional Adequacy: Moderate parking problem as there
                                    are only 1.5 spaces per dwelling
                                    unit.

Relationship of Site to
Surroundings: The compatibility of the
                                    appraised site is good as it is
                                    surrounded by single family and
                                    multi-family residential
                                    dwellings which are considered to
                                    be a positive influence on the
                                    value of the subject property.
                                    The marketability of the site as
                                    compared with other sites in the
                                    area is very competitive.

DESCRIPTION OF THE IMPROVEMENTS

General Description:

Substructure
Foundation: 4" concrete slab on compacted
                                     earth, with moistop vapor
                                     barrier.

Footings: 12" x 24" concrete

Columns   8' x 16" concrete

Superstructure
Exterior Walls   8" concrete block

Exterior Wall Cover   Stucco

Exterior Doors   Solid wood and metal sliding
                                     glass doors

Windows: Double-hung metal with screens

Roof: Mansard style pre-fabricated
                                     engineered wood; box trusses
                                     with full 6-1/2" batt
                                     insulation. Built-up tar and
                                     gravel roof cover. Cedar
                                     shingles on roof sides.

Second Floor: 3" concrete slab with 12"
                                     pre-cast concrete joists

Special Features: Two concrete stairways (13
                                     treads each), two ground floor
                                     concrete patios, two extended
                                     second floor concrete balconies
                                     with aluminum railings, second
                                     floor covered concrete
                                     walkway/balcony.

Interior

Each apartment consists of a living room, dining area, bedroom,
walk-in kitchen, bathroom, and three closets.

Walls & Ceilings: Painted drywall

Floors:
    Kitchen: Vinyl tile
    Bedroom, Living &
    Dining Area: Wall to wall carpet over
                                     concrete

Bathroom:	Ceramic tile flooring and wainscot, porcelain tub, shower head, water closet, vanity with sink and mirrored cabinet above.
Kitchen:	Sears two-door refrigerator, Sears self-cleaning oven, stainless steel double sink, Formica counter, ample base and wall cabinets.

Floor Areas:
First Floor:	3,288 square feet
Second Floor:	3,288 square feet
Gross Floor Area:	6,576 square feet

Unit Areas: 10 units contain 625 square feet

Mechanical Equipment

Heating:	Electric; forced air ducted
Air-Conditioning:	Each apartment is centrally air conditioned by a 1.5 ton unit with roof condensors.
Hot Water:	Each apartment has a 30-gallon electric hot water heater.
Plumbing:	Copper tubing - four fixtures per apartment - 40 fixtures
Electric:	400 amps - circuit breakers - 11 meters (including house meter).
Miscellaneous:	Water softener and iron filtering system
Age & Condition:	The actual age of the building is 11 years. The property has received regular maintenance throughout the years and is in average condition. Short-lived items are replaced when needed. The property is in a condition typical of an 11 year old building in the area.

Deferred Maintenance/
Need Repairs:
Stucco covering requires painting; yard requires some cleaning up; front portion of driveway has a drainage problem after heavy rains.

Functional Utility:
The layout, room sizes, closet space, kitchen size and equipment, and bathrooms are all considered average and acceptable.

There have been septic system backup problems, although infrequent. The tanks are pumped at least once a year.

Effective Age:
The overall effective age of a property is determined by a variety of factors, including the quality of construction (materials and workmanship), condition, design, and any external factors affecting value.

The quality of construction and design of the appraised building is rated average and compares to similar buildings in the area. Maintenance is better than average. The property is a legal, non-conforming use, having a density of 20 units per acre as compared to six units per acre allowed under current zoning regulations. The above two factors tend to reflect a lower effective age. It is my opinion that the building has an effective age of 10 years.

HISTORY OF THE PROPERTY

The appraised site was purchased by Etak Trebmal from Betty and Dorothy Corral on November 19, 1981 for $29,000 (11 years ago). (Official Record Book 2954, Page 350, Warranty Deed.) In 198_, Ms. Trebmal constructed the improvements, which were ready for occupancy in January, 198_ (10 years ago).

In 198_, Ms. Trebmal sold approximately one-half of the parcel (improved with a single family residence) for $104,400. This parcel, known as 720 Duquesne Drive, is <u>not</u> included in this appraisal.

Ms. Trebmal has been renting the apartments year round (as opposed to seasonally). She stated that she does not require a lease, however, she does require a security deposit equal to one month's rent. This property has experienced virtually 100% occupancy over the years. Most of the apartment units have been recarpeted over the last few years, appliances have been reeplaced as needed, and apartments were redecorated at least once every three years. No other major capital improvements have been necessary. Current rentals are being renewed at $675 per month.

Ms. Trebmal owns two other rental buildings and her management performance is rated adequate and competent.

A written offer to purchase the property for $500,000 was made in August, 198_ (last year). However, Ms. Trebmal declined the offer, and stated she would accept an offer of $650,000.

PART FOUR

ANALYSIS OF DATA
AND
CONCLUSIONS

THE APPRAISAL PROCESS

There are three generally recognized approaches to value, which may be used in estimating the value of real estate.

COST APPROACH - That approach in appraisal analysis which is based on the proposition that the informed purchaser would pay no more than the cost of producing a substitute property with the same utility as the subject property. It is particularly applicable when the property being appraised involves relatively new improvements which represent the highest and best use of the land or when relatively unique or specialized improvements are located on the site and for which there exist no comparable properties on the market.

DIRECT SALES COMPARISON APPROACH - That approach in appraisal analysis which is based on the proposition that an informed purchaser would pay no more for a property than the cost of acquiring an existing property with the same utility. This approach is applicable when an active market provides sufficient quantities of reliable data which can be verified from authoritative sources. The Direct Sales Comparison Approach is relatively unreliable in an inactive market or in estimating the value of properties for which no real comparable sales data are available. It is also questionable when sales data cannot be verified with principals to the transaction. Also referred to as the Market Comparison or Market Data Approach.

INCOME APPROACH - That procedure in appraisal analysis which converts anticipated benefits (dollar income or amenitites) to be derived from the ownership of property into a value estimate. The Income Approach is widely applied in appraising income-producing properties. Anticipated future income and/or reversions are discounted to a present worth figure through the capitalization process.

In order to arrive at an estimate of market value for the property being appraised, it is necessary to assemble from the marketplace as much information as is considered pertinent to the appraisal problem. This information is then utilized in the three different appraisal approaches.

After arriving at an indication of value by each of the three approaches, they are reconciled into a single estimate of value based upon the approach which has the highest quantity and quality of data available, and the one in which the market participant typically has the greatest confidence.

HIGHEST AND BEST USE OF THE SITE AS THOUGH VACANT

Real estate is valued in terms of its highest and best use. The highest and best use of the land or site, if vacant and available for use, may be different from the highest and best use of the improved property. This will be true when the improvement is not an appropriate use and yet makes a contribution to total property value in excess of the value of the site.

Highest and best use may be defined as that reasonable and probable use which will support the highest present value as of the date of appraisal. Alternatively, it is the most profitable, likely use to which a property can be put; it may be measured in terms of the present worth of the highest net return that the property can be expected to produce over a stipulated long-run period of time.

The highest and best use is that use from among one or more proposed uses that has been found to be legally permissible, physically possible, appropriately supported, and financially feasible, which is expected to generate the highest rate of net return over a given income-forecast period at the time the decision is made.

The highest and best use of the site if it were vacant and ready to be built upon would be for a 10-unit apartment building.

HIGHEST AND BEST USE OF THE PROPERTY AS IMPROVED

Any determination of highest and best use includes identifying the motivations of probable purchasers. The benefits of an investment property, like the subject property, relates to net income potential and to eventual resale or refinancing. Thus, the highest and best use will be that use which maximizes the net operating income on a long-term basis. This use must meet four criteria:

    1. Physically possible

    2. Legally permissible

    3. Financially feasible

    4. Maximally productive

1. <u>Physically Possible</u>. The existing improvements are 11 years old, of above average quality construction, and are in good condition. The building can continue to be utilized for rental apartment units, or can be converted to condominiums or a motel.

2. <u>Legally Permissible</u>. The existing improvements represent a legal, pre-existing, non-conforming use, therefore, current zoning regulations are not applicable. However, a motel would not be allowed in this zoning district.

3. <u>Financially Feasible</u>. There are two potential highest and best uses: (1) continue as a rental property, (2) convert to condominiums. I have estimated a net operating income for the subject property in the Income Approach section clearly demonstrating that continued use as a rental property is feasible. It is my opinion that conversion to condominiums is not feasible as this thime. From a careful analysis of supply and demand factors in the greater West Palm Beach area, there is currently an over-supply of condominium units. The Board of Realtors estimates there are approximately 10,000 resales on the market, 5,000 new (vacant) units, and 5,000+ planned units. Furthermore, no capital expenditures are necessary for the property to continue as a rental unit. The capital investment costs of conversion for ten units is estimateed at over $100,000. This would include interior and exterior clean up, legal costs, marketing, and a profit for the developer.

4.   <u>Maximally Productive</u>. It is apparent that the current use
     as a rental property is the highest and best use.   The
     factors contributing to this conclusion are as follows:

     a.   High intensity, legal, conforming use that would
          prompt the owner to extend the economic (useful) life
          of the improvements via competent management and
          careful maintenance.

     b.   A stable (and increasing) net operating income.

     c.   Tax advantages and inflation hedge.

     d.   The strong demand for rental units, evidenced by the
          high occupancy levels and projected population growth
          of the area.

Thus, the current uses as a ten-unit apartment building
maximizes the net operating income on a long-term basis and
represents the highest and best use.

STEPS OF THE COST APPROACH INCLUDING SITE VALUATION

The following steps including site valuation were followed in order to derive a value indication via the Cost Approach:

1. Estimated the value of the site as though vacant and available to be developed. The value of the site is determined by its potential highest and best use. The value of the site has been estimated using the Sales Comparison Approach as this is the most applicable method of estimating the market value of an unimproved site.

2. Estimated the reproduction cost of the structure on the effective appraisal date.

3. Estimated the amount of accrued depreciation in the structure, categorized by three major types:

   a. physical deterioration
   b. functional obsolescence
   c. external obsolescence

4. Deducted the appropriate estimated depreciation from the reproduction cost of the structure to derive an estimate of the structure's contribution to total value.

5. Added the depreciated reproduction cost of the structure and site improvements to obtain an estimated total present value of all improvements.

6. Added the estimated total present value of all improvements to the estimated site value to arrive at an indication of value for the subject property.

COMPARABLE SITE SALE LOCATION MAP

SCALE 3" = 1 MILE

COMPARABLE SITE SALE NO. 1

SCALE
1" = 100'

200'

130'

N STREET

MAP 42-44-25 PARCEL 567.0

Address:	1805 N. Street, West Palm Beach, Florida
Location:	1/2 mile southeast of subject
Grantor:	Kurt Coral and Jackie Coral
Grantee:	John McDonnald
Date of Sale:	May 18, 199_ (this year)
Sale Price:	$100,000
Date Source/Verification:	Town Records verified by seller
Zoning/Density	RH High density residential 2,000 sq. ft. per unit. Site has room for 8 units
Special Conditions and/or Financing:	None reported
Physical Characteristics:	
Frontage:	130'
Average Depth:	200'
Size:	Almost 1/3 acre
Typography:	Level
Available Utilities:	Electricity, telephone, cable TV
Easements, Encroachments and Restrictions:	None observed
Additional Information:	Small house which needed to be demolished at estimated cost of $4,000
Sale Price per Unit:	Price per unit $13,000 (including demolition cost)

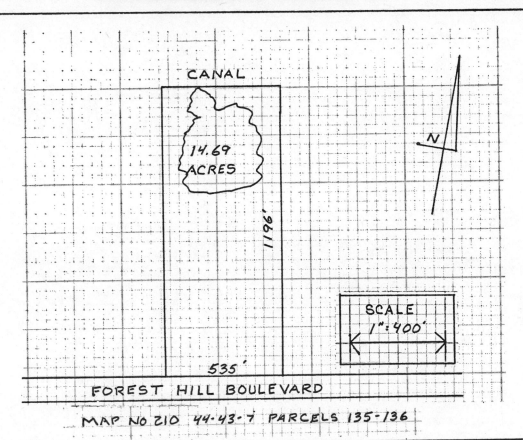

CANAL

14.69 ACRES

1196'

N

SCALE 1":400'

535'

FOREST HILL BOULEVARD

MAP NO 210 44·43·7 PARCELS 135-136

Address:	3760 Forest Hill Boulevard, West Palm Beach, Florida
Location:	1/3 mile northwest of subject
Grantor:	William Glazer and Roz Glazer
Grantee:	Donald Rump, Jr.
Date of Sale:	November 1, 199_ (this year)
Sale Price:	$1,500,000
Data Source/Verification:	Town Records verified by Broker
Zoning/Density:	RM Medium density multiple family 9,000 sq. ft. per unit. Site has room for 71 units
Special Conditions and/or Financing:	None reported
Physical Characteristics:	
Frontage:	535'
Average Depth:	1196'
Size:	14.69 acres (639,896 sq. ft.)
Typography:	Level with fresh water lake
Easements, Encroachments and Restrictions:	None reported
Additional Information:	Lake is suitable for swimming and small boats
Sale Price per Unit:	Per Unit $21,126

MAP NO 157 43-42-27 PARCEL 29-52

Address:	836 Beverly Road, West Palm Beach, Florida
Location:	1 mile northeast of subject
Grantor:	Diane Ruben and Harvey Ruben
rantee:	Binnick and Assoc.
Date of Sale:	July 22, 199_ (this year)
Sale Price:	$$810,000
Data Source/Verification:	Town Records verified by Buyers
Zoning/Density:	RH High density residential, 2,000 sq. ft. per unit. Site has room for 45 units
Special Conditions and/or Financing:	None reported
Physical Characteristics:	
Frontage:	190'
Average Depth:	458'
Size:	2 acres
Typography:	Level with some woods
Available Utilities:	Electricity, telephone, cable TV, municiple water and municiple sewers
Easements, Encroachments and Restrictions:	None reported
Sale Price per Unit:	Per Unit $18,000

FOREST HILL BOULEVARD

315'

7.67 ACRES

1055'

N

SCALE 1":400'

MAP 210 43-43-7 PARCEL 701.1

Address:	2469 Forest Hill Boulevard, West Palm Beach, Florida
Location:	1/3 mile west of subject
Grantor:	Samuel Saslafsky
Grantee:	A.H. Minnick
Date of Sale:	September 13, 199_ (this year)
Sale Price:	$800,000
Data Source/Verification:	Closing attorney
Zoning/Density:	RM Medium density multiple family 9,000 sq. ft. per unit. Site has room for 37 units
Special Conditions and/or Financing:	None reported
Physical Characteristics:	
Frontage:	315'
Average Depth:	1055'
Size:	7.63 acres
Typography:	Level
Available Utilities:	Electricity, telephone, cable TV, municiple water and municiple sanitary sewers
Easements, Encroachments and Restrictions:	None observed
Additional Information:	Was improved with a 37 one story rental apartment complex
Sale Price per Unit:	Per Unit $21,621

EXPLANATION OF SITE ADJUSTMENTS

All four site sales were in the same neighborhood and no location adjustment was needed.

All four sites were purchased within the past year. There has been significant change of values in the neighborhood within the past year. Therefore, no time adjustment was required.

There were no reported special conditions or special financing. Therefore no adjustments for them were required.

There were some some significant physical characteristic differences which required adjustment.

The subject and comparable site sales had municipal water and municipal sanitary sewers. Comparable #1 did not have either.

The subject property was zoned at a density of 2,000 sq. ft. of site per unit. Comparable Sales #2 and #4 were zoned at a lower density.

By comparing the comparable sales with each other, it was possible to derive the required adjustments directly from the market. The size differences were accounted for by using the unit price per unit.

UTILITY ADJUSTMENT

Sale # 1 and Sale #3 appear to be similar except Sale #3 has municipal water and municipal sewers and Sale #1 has neither.

        Sale #1   Sale price per unit $13,000
        Sale #3   Sale price per unit   18,000

        Difference attributable to
        availability of utilities $ 5,000 per unit

DENSITY ADJUSTMENT

Sale #3 and Sale #4 appear to be similar except for the zoning density. Sale #3 is zoned RH High density residential and Sale #4 is zoned RM Medium density.

        Sale #3   Sale price per unit $18,000
        Sale #4   Sale price per unit   21,621

        Difference attributable to
        difference in zoning density $ 3,621 per unit ($3,500 RD)

SITE SALES ADJUSTMENT GRID

SITE SALES ADJUSTMENT GRID

	Subject Property	Site Sale #1	Site Sale #2	Site Sale #3	Site Sale #4
ADDRESS	700 Duquesne Dr	1805 N Street	3760 Forest Hill Road	836 Beverly Rd	2469 Forest Hill Road
COMMUNITY	West Palm Beach,	West Palm Beach,	West Palm Beach,	West Palm Beach,	West Palm Beach,
SALE PRICE		$100,000 Plus $4,000 demolition	$1,500,000	$810,000	$800,000
PERMITTED NO. OF UNITS	10	8	71	45	37
SALE PRICE PER UNIT		$13,000	$21,126	$18,000	$21,621
DATE OF SALE	December 15, 199_ (this year)	May 18, 199_ (this year)	November 1, 199_ (this year)	July 22, 199_ (this year)	September 13, 199_ (this year)
LOCATION		Similar -0-	Similar -0-	Similar -0-	Similar -0-
DENSITY	High Density	High Density -0-	Medium Density -$3,500	High Density -0-	Medium Density -$3,500
UTILITIES	No municipal sewers or water	No municipal sewers or water	Municipal sewers and water -$5,000	Municipal sewers and water -$5,000	Municipal sewers and water -$5,000
SPECIAL CONDITIONS AND FINANCING	None reported	None reported -0-	None reported -0-	None reported -0-	None reported -0-
TOTAL ADJ.		-0-	-$8,500	-$5,000	$8,500
ADJ. SALE PRICE PER PERMITTED UNIT		$13,000	$12,626	$13,000	$13,121

SUMMARY OF SITE VALUE

All four comparable site sales were good indications of the value of the subject site.

Comparable Sale #1 did not have any significant differences from the subject property that could be identified except size. The size difference was handled by using price per permitted unit as the unit of comparison. It sold for $13,000 per unit. This was well supported by the other three sales. Comparable Sale #2 had a small lake. This did not appear to effect its value.

The subject property was zoned for 10 units. Its value was calculated as follows:

    10 units @ $13,000 per unit = $130,000

    Total Estimate Site value $130,000

Estimate of Cost New

I have utilized three of the accepted methods of estimating
replacement cost new:

1. Cost-Index Trending
2. Segregated Cost Method (Cost Service)
3. Quantity Survey Method (Professional Cost Estimator)

Cost-Index Trending

This method involves using a cost index to update a known
historical cost to a current cost estimate. I used the Marshall
Valuation Service, a nationally recognized costing service in
the appraisal field.

The owner stated his total cost to build the appraised apartment
building 11 years ago was approximately $280,000.

The comparable cost multiplier from Marshall Valuation Service,
Section 98, Page 10, Eastern, Class C, January, 199_ is 2.232.
This multiplier is then modified by a monthly correcting factor
from Section 99, Page 44 to bring the multiplier current to
December, 199_. This factor is 1.009.

Then: 2.232 x 1.009 x $280,000 = $630,584

Segregated Cost Method

This method involves using a cost service to derive a cost
estimate in terms of dollars per square foot based on known
costs of similar structures and adjusted for time and physical
differences. I have the Marshall Valuation Service.
Information about the appraised property was input from my
office terminal via time sharing into the Marshall Valuation
Service computer in California. The cost printout can be found
on the following pages.

This method indicated a replacement cost new of $644,354.

COST SERVICE ESTIMATE

COST ESTIMATE FOR: Barbara Kaye
PROPERTY OWNER: Etak L. Trebmal
ADDRESS: 700 Duouesne Drive, West Palm Beach, FL
SURVEYED BY: Barbara J. Kaye
DATE OF SURVEY: December 15, 199_

OCCUPANCY: MULTIPLE DWELLING

CLASS: C Masonry   COST RANK: 3.0 Above Average
EFFECTIVE AGE: 10 Years   CONDITION: 4.0 Good
NUMBER OF STORIES: 2.0   AVERAGE STORY HEIGHT: 8.9
FLOOR AREA: 6,576 Sq. Ft.   COST AS OF: 12/9_

COMPONENT	UNITS	COST	REPLACEMENT COST NEW
EXCAVATION & SITE PREPARATION:			
Site Preparation	20,900	0.24	5,016
FOUNDATION			
Column Footings	24	70.76	1,698
FRAME:			
Concrete Frame Members	427	26.50	11,316
FLOOR STRUCTURE:			
Concrete on Ground	3,228	3.84	12,396
Concrete, Elevated Slab	3,228	10.76	34,733
Waterproofing	3,228	0.64	2,066
SUBTOTAL			49,195
FLOOR COVER:			
Carpet and Pad	5,590	3.82	21,354
Tile, Ceramic	460	11.08	5,097
Vinyl Sheet	526	4.10	2,157
SUBTOTAL			28,607
CEILING:			
Gypsum Board, Taped & Painted	6,576	1.68	11,048
INTERIOR CONSTRUCTION:			
Interior Construction, Frame	6,576	17.82	117,184
PLUMBING:			
Plumbing	6,576	7.74	50,898
HEATING AND COOLING:			
Electric	6,576	3.20	21,043
Refrigerated Cooling	6,576	4.60	30,250
SUBTOTAL			51,293
ELECTRICAL:			
Electrical	6,576	5.86	38,535
EXTERIOR WALL:			
Concrete Block	5,283	18.30	96,679
WALL ORNAMENTATION:			
Stucco on Masonry	5,283	2.44	12,891
ROOF STRUCTURE:			
Wood joists, Wood deck	3,288	6.50	21,372
ROOF COVER:			
Wood Shingles	891	3.04	2,709
Insulation	3,288	1.20	3,946
Built-Up Composition	3,288	1.86	6,116
SUBTOTAL			12,770

QUANTITY SURVEY ESTIMATE

<u>Quantity Survey Method</u>

This method is considered the most comprehensive and accurate method of cost estimating. It is a repetition of the contractor's original method of developing a bid figure.

I obtained a cost breakdown from a reputable local general contractor, Steve Martin, of Sharpestimator, Inc. Contractor's Licence No. I0UI0I4. Mr. Martin's summary of his breakdown, as submitted to me, is on the following page.

This method indicated a replacement cost new of $626,800.

QUANTITY SURVEY ESTIMATE

SHARPESTIMATOR, INC
299 PONCE DeLEON
WEST PALM BEACH, FL 33411

OWNER   Etak L. Trebmal
CONTRACTOR   SHARPESTIMATOR, INC.
JOB LOCATION   700 Duouensne Drive, West Palm Beach, FL

```
 1 Earthwork & Exc.                 $5,000
 2 Soil Poisoning                      600
 3 Concrete Labor & Mat.            32,000
 4 Masonry Labor & Mat.             20,000
 5 Metal Windows & Doors            13,000
 6 Alum. Rails                       9,200
 7 Roof Trusses                     15,000
 8 Roofing & Sheet Metal            16,000
 9 Form & Framing Lumber            30,000
10 Millwork                         10,000
11 Common Labor                      8,000
12 Carpentry Labor                  52,000
13 Finished Floors                  16,000
14 Cabinets & Vanities              20,000
15 Dry Walls                        20,000
16 Stucco                           14,000
17 Tile & Marble                     8,000
18 Painting                         16,000
19 Plumbing                         40,000
20 Electric                         30,000
21 Finished Hardware                 3,000
22 Electric Fixtures                 4,000
23 Rough Hardware                    2,000
24 A.C. & Heat                      30,000
25 Cleaning                          2,000
26 Med. Cabinets & Bath Access.      2,000
27 Insulation                        4,000
28 Appliances                       16,000
29 Septic Tanks                      6,000
30 Landscaping                       4,000
31 Walks & Drives                   18,000
32 Permits                           3,000
33 Insurance                         4,000
34 Contractors Fee                  70,000
35 Arch. Fee                         6,000
36 Survey                            1,000
37 Supervision                      20,000
38 Sprinkler                         3,000
39 Precast Conc. & Stairs           48,000
40 Luminous Ceilings                 6,000
                                   --------
                                  $626,800
```

SUMMARY OF COST NEW

1.	Cost-Index Trending	$630,584
2.	Segregated Cost Method	$644,354
3.	Quantity Survey Method	$626,800

Method 1 was given the least consideration as the historical cost may be not accurate nor typical for the time period, and the national cost index may not apply to the local area.

Method 2 provides a reasonably accurate estimate and supports the general contractor's estimate.

Method 3 is considered an accurate means of replacement cost and, therefore, was given equal weight with Method 2 in arriving at the final estimate. However, it did not include some of the applicable soft costs.

After analyzing all available data, I estimate the reproduction cost new of the subject improvements to be $650,000, including site improvements valued at $25,000. Site improvements include landscaping, sidewalks, paving, and underground sprinkler system.

DEPRECIATION ANALYSIS

Accrued depreciation is a loss in value from the reproduction
cost new of the improvements from any cause, as of the date of
the appraisal. This loss in value emanates from one or more of
three sources: physical deterioration, functional obsolescence,
and external obsolescence. Depreciation is a penalty only to
the extent that it is recognized as a loss in value by the
market.

There are several methods to estimate accrued depreciation. I
have applied the breakdown method as it reflects the manner in
which an informed buyer would react to the existing conditions
of the subject improvements.

A buyer of an income-producing property is concerned with the
age and utility of the structure, and the remaining years the
real estate can be expected to produce income before major
expenditures must be made for modernization.

The existing improvements are 11 years old and have received
better than average maintenance. The construction and design
are rated above average. I have estimated the effective age to
be 10 years.

Due to all the new construction in Palm Beach, it is imperative
for owners to maintain their properties in order to compete with
the increasing supply of housing and to maximize their income
stream.

I have estimated the total economic life to be 50 years
(Source: Marshall Valuation Service).

BREAKDOWN METHOD

CURABLE PHYSICAL DETERIORATION

The following items of physical deterioration were observed:

    Exterior needs painting
    Landscaping needs general work
    Driveway has drainage problems during heavy rains

These items are immediately curable at a cost of approximately $8,000 (Source: Martin Levine, a general contractor). The $8,000 figure will **not** be deducted from the final values arrived at in the Direct Sales Comparison Approach and Income Approach as the sale and rental comparables all suffer from minor items of physical deterioration. These items were taken into consideration in arriving at the final value estimates in each approach where adjustments were made for condition.

INCURABLE PHYSICAL DETERIORATION

I have estimated all short-lived and long-lived structural elements that are not practical or currently feasible to correct.

Short-Lived Components:

	Replacement Cost*	Effective Age	Useful Life	Depreciation %	Depreciation $
Floor Cover	$16,000	2	6	33%	$ 5,280
Roof Cover	12,000	10	15	67%	8,000
Plumbing	40,000	10	30	33%	13,200
Electrical	30,000	10	30	33%	9,900
Heat & Air Conditioning	30,000	10	25	40%	12,000

Total Incurable Physical Deterioration Short-Lived Components: $48,380

*source: Steve Martin, General Contractor
        Sharpestimator, Inc.

Long-Lived Components

All remaining components are expected to have a remaining economic life the same as the entire structure.

$$\frac{\text{Effective Age}}{\text{Economic Life}} = \frac{11}{50} = 22\%$$

I applied this percentage to the replacement cost new ($650,000) less curable items ($8,000) and incurable components ($128,000), leaving a replacement cost new of $514,000.

    Then: $514,000 x 22% = $113,080

CURABLE FUNCTIONAL OBSOLESCENCE

I observed no defects in design having an adverse effect on value.

INCURABLE FUNCTIONAL OBSOLESCENCE

The subject property has only 1.5 parking spaces per unit. Multi-family dwellings constructed subsequent to 1990 must have 2 1/2 parking spaces per one-bedroom unit. In the Income Approach, I estimated a rent difference of $10.00 per month attributable to better parking. Therefore, this deficiency can be measured by the gross income loss due to poor parking.

The gross annual income loss is calculated as follows:

    10 units x $10.00/month x 12 months = $1,200

The gross income multiplier estimated in the Direct Sales Comparison Approach was 7.4.

    Thus, $1,200 x 7.4 = $8,880

Utilization of gross income was considered acceptable as the majority of expenses would not be affected by the deficiency.

EXTERNAL OBSOLESCENCE

I observed no negative influence in the neighborhood or community that would have a significant adverse effect on the property's value.

Summary of Depreciation

Physical Deterioration
     Physical Curable, Deferred Maintenance $ 8,000
     Physical Incurable, Short-Lived Items   48,380
     Physical Incurable, Long-Lived Items   113,080
     Sub-Total $159,460

Functional Obsolescence:
     Functional Curable   0
     Functional Incurable $ 8,880

External Obsolescence   0

Total Accrued Depreciation $168,340
              Rounded to $168,340

Summary of Cost Approach

Estimated Replacement Cost New - Improvements $650,000
Less Accrued Depreciation   (168,340)

Depreciated Value of the Improvements $481,660
(including site improvements)

Estimated Land Value   130,000

Value Indicated via the Cost Approach $611,660
             Rounded to $610,000

VALUE INDICATED BY COST APPROACH $610,000

STEPS OF THE SALES COMPARISON APPROACH

In this approach the market value is estimated by comparing the subject property to similar properties in the market which have either recently sold or are being offered for sale.

A great number of sales and listings have been examined in the process of making this appraisal. The most comparable sales have been selected for display in this appraisal report.

An attempt was made to verify information about the comparable sales by contacting the buyers, sellers, real estate brokers and closing attorneys. Special attention was given to verify that the transactions were "arm's length" and that any special conditions and special financing were known by the appraiser.

Since this was an apartment building which in this market customarily is priced based on the number of units, it was considered appropriate to select "Number of Units" as the unit of comparison.

Each comparable property was compared to the subject property and adjustments were made significant difference in the elements of comparisons which resulted in an adjusted price of each comparable giving an indication of the value of the subject.

First, I considered whether a time adjustment was needed. All of the Comparable Sales were this year. The market has been very flat during the past year. No data was available to indicate that a time adjustment was required, therefore no time adjustments were made.

No location adjustments were needed as all of the properties were in the same neighborhood and values are similar throughout the neighborhood.

No age or condition adjustments were needed as all the comparable apartments were built about the same time (10 years to 11 years ago) and they all were in average condition.

An adjustment was needed to reflect the special financing of Comparable Sale #3. It was made considering the points saved, lower monthly payment and the convenience of the special financing.

Adjustments were made for the differences in the number of parking spaces per unit and how the units were air conditioned. These adjustments were derived from the market using the matched pair technique.

Finally, the various indicated subject values produced from the analysis of the comparables were reconciled into an indicated value of the subject property via the sales comparison approach.

COMPARABLES SALE LOCATION MAP

SCALE 3" = 1 MILE

A63

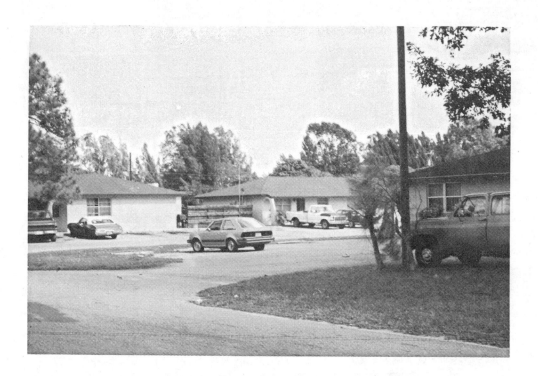

Address:	529 Columbia Drive West Palm Beach, Florida
Grantor:	Henry Starin
Grantee:	Sttaw Evest
Date of Sale:	April 13, 199_ (this year)
Sale Price:	$960,000
Source of Information:	Closing Attorney and Seller
Special Conditions:	None reported
Special Financing:	None reported
Site Area/Density:	1.2 Acres, 13 units per acre
Location:	Six blocks west of subject in same neighborhood

Description of Improvements

Type of Construction:	One story concrete block building. 13,208 G.B.A.
Year Built:	198_ (11 years ago)
Breakdown of Units:	16 one bedroom apartments, each has one bath. Each apartment is 635 sq. ft.
Description of Interior:	Wall to wall carpeting, typical kitchens & baths, central air conditioning
Condition:	Average
Parking:	16 assigned spaces and 8 guest spaces
Recreation Facilities:	None

Current Rentals:	$660 to $665 per month
Potential Gross Income:	$127,000
Net Operating Income:	$86,822 ($5,426 per apartment)
Overall Capitalization Rate:	.0905
Annual Gross Income Multiplier:	7.52
Sale Price per sq. ft.:	$72.68
Sale Price Per Unit:	$60,000

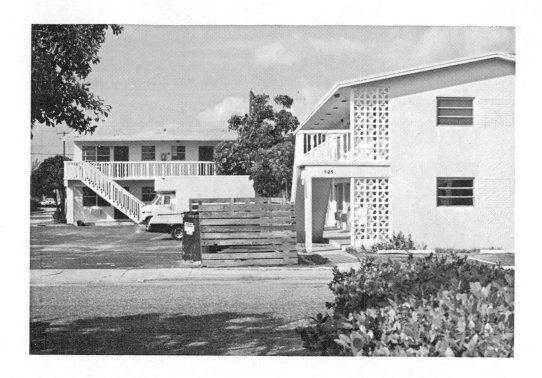

Address:	376 Gulfstream Road West Palm Beach, FL
Grantor:	L. D'Agostino
Grantee:	Eiluj Nosirrah
Date of Sale:	May 20, 199_ (this year)
Sale Price:	$547,000
Source of Information:	Closing attorney and seller
Special Conditions:	Buyers feel that rents were substantially below market rent. The seller had not raised the rents or visited the property for years prior to the sale
Special Financing:	None reported
Site Area/Density:	1.17 acre, 6.8 units per acre
Location:	Eight blocks north of subject in same neighborhood

Description of Improvements:

Type of Construction: Two story concrete block building. 6,760 sq. ft. G.B.A.

Year Built: 198_ (11 years ago)

Breakdown of Units: 8 apartments, 8 one bedroom and one bath units, each 650 sq. ft.

Description of Interior: Wall to wall carpeting, typical kitchens & baths, central air conditioning

Condition: Average

Parking: 16 assigned spaces and 8 guest spaces

Recreation Facilities: None

Current Rentals: $775 to $790 per month

Potential Gross Income: $74,880

Net Operating Income: $48,672 ($6,084 per apartment unit)

Overall Capitalization Rate: .0889

Annual Gross Income Multiplier: 7.30

Sale Price per sq. ft. G.B.A.: $80.91

Sale Price per Unit: $68,375

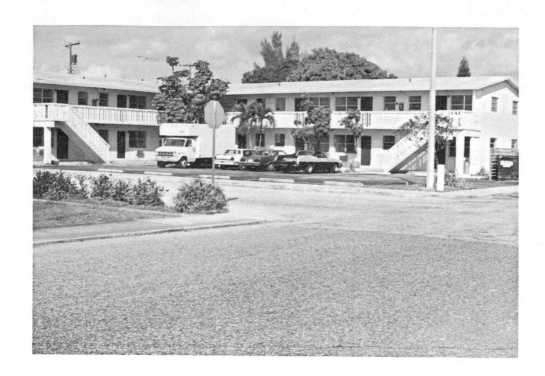

Address:	47 Desoto Drive West Palm Beach, Florida
Grantor:	Ms. Donna Montagnino
Grantee:	Mr. Richard and Mrs. Jessie Kusmit
Date of Sale:	September 20, 199_ (this year)
Sale Price:	$570,000
Source of Information:	Buyer and seller
Special Conditions:	None reported
Special Financing:	Seller took back a $400,000 1st mortgage 8% for 20 years with a balloon payoff at the end of 10 years and no points. The typical mortgage in this market was an 80% mortgage, 20 years at 11% interest with 3 points.
Site Area/Density:	1.17 acre, 6.8 units per acre
Location:	9 blocks north of subject in same neighborhood

Description of Improvements:

Type of Construction:	Two two story buildings both concrete block. Total G.B.A. 6,708 sq. ft.
Year Built:	198_ (11 years ago)
Breakdown of Units:	8 apartments: 4 one bedroom & one bath units, each 650 sq. ft. 4 one bedroom & one bath units, each 640 sq. ft.
Description of Interior:	Wall to wall carpeting, typical kitchens & baths, central air conditioning
Condition:	Average
Parking:	16 assigned spaces and 8 guest spaces
Recreation Facilities:	None
Current Rentals:	$800 to $825 per month
Potential Gross Income:	$77,760
Net Operating Income:	$52,876 ($6,690 per apartment)
Overall Capitalization Rate:	.0927
Annual Gross Income Multiplier:	7.33
Sale Price per sq. ft. G.B.A.:	$84.97
Sale Price per Unit:	$71,250

COMPARABLE SALE NO. 4

Address: 16 Yale Drive
                                 West Palm Beach, Florida

Grantor: Roger & Vera Whait

Grantee: Olive N Court Properties, a
                                 Connecticut Partnership

Sale Price: $738,500

Source of Information: Realtor who sold property and
                                 manages it prior to sale

Special Conditions: None reported

Special Financing: New 80% conventional mortgage

Site Area/Density: 1.17 acre, 6.8 units per acre

Location: Five blocks south of subject in
                                 same neighborhood

Description of Improvements:

Type of Construction: One story concrete block building. Total 10,046 G.B.A.

Year Built: 198_ (10 years ago)

Breakdown of Units: 12 apartments, 12 one bedroom & one bath units, each 644 sq. ft.

Description of Interior: Wall to wall carpeting, typical kitchens & baths, window air conditioning units owned by tenants

Condition: Average

Parking: 24 assigned spaces & 12 guest spaces

Recreation Facilities: None

Current Rentals: $760 to $770 per month

Potential Gross Income: $110,160

Net Operating Income: $71,640 ($5,970 per apartment)

Overall Capitalization Rate: .0970

Annual Gross Income Multiplier: 6.70

Sale Price per sq. ft. G.B.A.: $73.50

Sale Price per Unit: $61,541

EXPLANATION OF ADJUSTMENTS
PARKING ADJUSTMENT

The subject unit is in a high density zone that requires only 2,000 sq. ft. of site per unit. It restricts the available parking to one parking space per unit plus an additional 1/2 parking space for guests. Comparable Sales #2, #3 and #4 are low density zone and there is room for 2 parking spaces per unit plus 1 guest space per unit.

Comparable Sale #1 was similar to Comparable Sale #2 except for the number of parking spaces per unit. (It was not considered proper to also adjust for the density difference as this would be double adjusting for the same difference.)

Comparable Sale #1 (1 1/2 parking spaces per unit)
    Sale price per unit $60,000

Comparable Sale #2 (2 1/2 parking spaces per unut) $68,375

Parking Adjustment (1 1/2 spaces vs. 2 2/1 spaces) $8,000 RD

SPECIAL FINANCING ADJUSTMENT
COMPARABLE SALE #3

Adjustment for 3 points
    $400,000 x .03 = $12,000

Adjustment for below market

Typical Mortgage
    $40,000, 20 yrs, 11% calculates
    to have monthly payments of   4,128.76

Special Financing
    $400,000 20 yrs (10 year balloon)
    8% calculates to have monthly
    payments of   3,345.76

Monthly Savings   783.00

Present Value of $783 per month for
    10 years at 11% market interest rate $56,842.00

Adjustment for saving 3 points   12,000.00

Estimated total dollars saved by
    special financing $68,842

I have also considered the convenience of having
a purchase money mortgage and then estimated the
appropriate financing adjustment to be $70,000
or $8,750 per apartment unit ($70,000 / 8).

AIR CONDITIONING ADJUSTMENT

The subject property has central air conditioning. Some of the
comparable sales do not. Below is how an adjustment was
estimated from the market data available to make an appropriate
per unit air conditioning adjustment.

Comparable Sale #2 and Comparable Sale #4 were similar except
for the number of units and the air conditioning. In Comparable
Sale #2 each unit had a central air conditioning owned by the
landlord. In Comparable Sale #4 window units were owned by the
tenants.

The appropriate air conditioning adjustment was estimated as
follows:

Comparable Sale #2 (central air conditioning)
    Sale price per unit $ 64,125

Comparable Sale #4 (no central air conditioning)
    Sale price per unit   61,541

Air Conditioning Adj. $ 2,584
                                                        ($2,500 RD)

ANALYSIS AND ADJUSTMENT OF SALES DATA

The four sales analyzed in detail on the preceding pages were chosen among many recent apartment building sales. These four sales required the fewest adjustments for difference with respect to the appraised property.

The analysis of these sales produced the following ranges:

G.I.M.	7.30	to	7.52
O.A.R.	.0889	to	.0970
Sale Price/Square Foot	$72.68	to	$84.97
Adjusted Sale Price/Unit	$54,500	to	$60,375

The use of a G.I.M. (Gross Income Multiplier) is valid only for types of properties that are reasonably consistent in net-to-gross income operating ratio and sell with sufficient frequency in the market to produce a descernible pattern.

The G.I.M. is closely related to market action. Its principal advantage is that the reflection of income is direct. Therefore, differences in age, condition, location, and physical characteristics do not require adjustment as these factors have been resolved by the free action of the rental market.

I have given about equal weight to all four sales and selected 7.4 as the gross income multiplier for the subject property.

The potential gross income estimated in the Income Approach was $39,600.

Then: $81,000 x 7.4 = $599,400 rounded to $600,000

The development of an O.A.R. (Overall Capitalization Rate) will be utilized in the Income Approach.

The sale price per square foot ranged fom $72.68 to $84.97. I selected $80.00 for the subject property.

Then: 6,576 sq. ft. x $80.00 = $526,000

This was not considered to be a very good indicator of value as it did not consider the significant adjustments that were made for parking and special financing.

COMPARABLE SALE ADJUSTMENT GRID

COMPARABLE SALES ADJUSTMENT GRID

(All adjustments made on basis of number of apartments unit of comparison)

	Appraised Property	Comparable Sale #1	Comparable Sale #2	Comparable Sale #3	Comparable Sale #4
ADDRESS	700 Duquesne Dr West Palm Beach	529 Columbia Dr W Palm Beach	376 Gulfstream Rd W Palm Beach	47 Desoto Dr W Palm Beach	16 Yale Dr W Palm Beach
SALE PRICE	No sale pending	$960,000	$547,000	$570,000	$738,500
NUMBER OF APARTMENTS	10	16	8	8	12
SALE PRICE PER APARTMENT	--	$60,000	$68,375	$71,250	$61,541
DATE OF SALE	12/16/9_ (this year)	4/13/9_ (this year)	5/20/9_ (this year)	9/20/9_ (this year)	6/8/9_ (this year)
SPECIAL FINANCING	None	None -0-	None -0-	Purchase money mortgage -8,750	None -0-
SPECIAL CONDITIONS	None	None -0-	None -0-	None -0-	None -0-
CONDITION	Average	Same -0-	Same -0-	Same -0-	Same -0-
LOCATION	West Palm Beach Canal	Same -0-	Same -0-	Same -0-	Same -0-
PARKING	1 1/2 spaces per apt. unit	1 1/2 spaces per apt -0-	2 1/2 spaces per apt -$8,000	2 1.2 spaces per apt -$8,000	2 1/2 spaces per apt -$8,000
AIR CONDITIONING	Central	Central -0-	Central -0-	Central -0-	Tenant owned window units +$2,500
TOTAL ADJ.	---	-0-	-$8,000	-$16,750	-$5,500
ADJ SALE PRICE PER APT UNIT	---	$60,000	$60,375	$54,500	$56,041

A 75

SUMMARY OF SALES COMPARISON APPROACH

The best indication of the value of the subject is the sale price per unit. The following adjustment grid displays each sale and how they were adjusted for special financing, parking and air conditioning. No adjustments were needed for time or location.

The four adjusted sales prices ranged from $54,500 to $60,375. Comparable Sale #1 was most similar to the subject and in fact required no adjustments. $60,000 per unit was selected as the indicated value of the subject property.

Then: $60,000 x 10 units = $600,000.

This is well supported by the $600,000 value indicated by the gross income multiplier.

VALUE INDICATED VIA DIRECT SALES COMPARISON APPROACH $600,000

INCOME APPROACH

This type of property is typically purchased as an investment. Therefore, the earning power of the property is an important element affecting its value. An investor who purchases this property is essentially trading his or her present dollars for an income stream of future dollars plus the return of their investment at some date in the future.

STEPS OF THE INCOME APPROACH

The steps of the Income Approach using direct capitalization are summarized as follows:

1. Estimate the Potential Gross Income (P.G.I.) of the property.

2. Add any additional income from sources other than rent.

3. Subtract the typical annual amount of income that will not be collected because of vacancies and collection problems.

4. The result is the Effective Gross Income (E.G.I.).

5. Subtract from the E.G.I., operating expenses, fixed expenses and reserves for the replacement of short lived items.

6. The result is the Net Operating Income (N.O.I.).

7. Develop a direct capitalization rate by dividing the known N.O.I.'s of properties that have sold that are comparable to the subject property by the selling price of the Comparable Sale. Reconcile them into one rate appropriate for the subject property.

8. Divide the N.O.I. of the property being appraised by the appropriate capitalization rate which gives an indicated value of the property via the Income Approach.

COMPARABLE RENTAL LOCATION MAP

SCALE 3" = 1 MILE

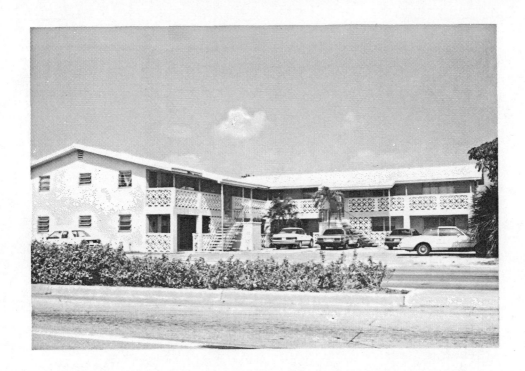

Address:	Auburn Road West Palm Beach, Florida
Location:	Seven blocks south of the subject in the same neighborhood
Source of information:	Exchange Court Properties
Number of units:	12 units each with one bedroom and one bath
Year built/Condition:	198_ (10 years ago)/Average
Type of construction:	Two story concrete block building, central air conditioning
Parking:	1.5 cars per apartment unit
Apartment sizes:	625 to 650 sq. ft.
Vacancy history:	Usually full. One unit available for January rental
Current rents:	$550 to $575 no utilities or furniture
Monthly Rent per sq. ft.:	$.88 to $.92
Remarks:	View of Lake Worth from side

Address:	165 Glen Road West Palm Beach, Florida
Location:	Six blocks south of the subject in the same neighborhood
Source of information:	Jancie Franklin
Number of units:	12 units each with one bedroom and one bath
Year built/Condition:	198_ (12 years ago)/Average
Type of construction:	Two story concrete block building, central air condition
Parking:	1.5 cars per apartment unit
Apartment sizes:	625 to 660 sq. ft.
Vacancy history:	Usually full
Current rents:	$575 no utilities or furniture
Monthly rent per sq. ft.:	$.88
Remarks:	None

Address:	156 18th St. corner of K St. West Palm Beach, Florida
Location:	Nine blocks southwest of the subject in the same neighborhood
Source of information:	James Dew
Number of units:	20 units each with one bedroom and one bath
Year built/Condition:	198_ (11 years ago)/Average
Type of construction:	Two story concrete block building
Parking:	1.5 cars per apartment unit
Apartment sizes:	640 to 660 sq. ft.
Vacancy history:	Approximately 3%
Current rents:	$625 to $650 no utilities or furniture
Monthly rent per sq. ft.:	$.98 to $1.02
Remarks:	There are two tennis courts and a swimming pool on the site

Address:	Sherwood Villas 1755 Fordham Drive West Palm Beach, Florida
Location:	Five blocks southwest of the subject in the same neighborhood
Source of information:	Captain Edward Fink
Number of units:	36 units each with one bedroom and one bath
Year built/Condition:	198_ (12 years ago)/Average
Type of construction:	Concrete block buildings
Parking:	1.5 cars per apartment unit
Apartment sizes:	625 to 675 sq. ft.
Vacancy history:	Approximately 4%
Current rents:	$550 to $575 no utilities or furniture
Monthly rent per sq. ft.:	$.81 to $.96
Remarks:	Coin operated laundry facilities on the premises

EXPLANATION OF ADJUSTMENTS

RENTAL ADJUSTMENT FOR POOL AND COURTS

The subject unit does not have a swimming pool or tennis courts. Comparable Rental No. 3 has a swimming pool and two tennis courts. An appropriate adjustment for a swimming pool and tennis courts was estimated by comparing Comparable Rental No. 3 with Comparable Rental No. 2. The only significant difference between these apartment units were the availability of a swimming pool and two tennis courts.

Monthly Rental Comparable Rental No. 2
    (no swimming pool or tennis court) $575 to $600

Monthly Rental Comparable Rental No. 3
    (swimming pool and two tennis courts) $625 to $650

Estimated rental difference attributable
to availability of swimming pool and
tennis courts $50

AIR CONDITIONING ADJUSTMENT

The subject property has central air conditioning. Some of the comparable sales do not. Below is how an adjustment was estimated from the market data available to make an appropriate per unit air conditioning adjustment.

Comparable Sale #2 and Comparable Sale #4 were similar except for the number of units and the air conditioning. In Comparable Sale #2 each unit had a central air conditioning owned by the landlord. In Comparable Sale #4 window units were owned by the tenants.

The appropriate air conditioning adjustment was estimated as follows:

Comparable Sale #2 (central air conditioning)
    Sale price per unit $ 64,125

Comparable Sale #4 (no central air conditioning)
    (Sale price per unit   61,541

Air Conditioning Adj. $ 2,584
                                    ($2,500 RD)

PARKING ADJUSTMENT

The subject unit is in a high density zone that requires only 2,000 sq. ft. of site per unit. It restricts the available parking to one parking space per unit plus an additional 1/2 parking space for guests. Comparable Sales #2, #3 and #4 are low density zone and there is room for 2 parking spaces per unit plus 1 guest space per unit.

Comparable Sale #1 was similar to Comparable Sale #2 except for the number of parking spaces per unit. (It was not considered proper to also adjust for the density difference as this would be double adjusting for the same difference.)

Comparable Sale #1 (1 1/2 parking spaces per unit) Sale price per unit	$60,000
Comparable Sale #2 (2 1/2 parking spaces per unut)	$68,375
Parking Adjustment (1 1/2 spaces vs. 2 2/1 spaces)	$8,000 RD

COMPARABLE SALE #3

SPECIAL FINANCING ADJUSTMENT

Adjustment for 3 points $400,000 x .03 =	$12,000
Adjustment for below market	

Typical Mortgage
    $40,000, 20 yrs, 11% calculates
    to have monthly payments of
	4,128.76

Special Financing
    $400,000 20 yrs (10 year balloon)
    8% calculates to have monthly
    payments of
	3,345.76

Monthly Savings	783.00
Present Value of $783 per month for 10 years at 11% market interest rate	$56,842.00
Adjustment for saving 3 points	12,000.00
Estimated total dollars saved by special financing	$68,842

I have also considered the convenience of having a purchase money mortgage and then estimated the appropriate financing adjustment to be $70,000 or $8,750 per apartment unit ($70,000 / 8).

ANALYSIS OF COMPARABLE RENTALS

Because there are many one bedroom rental apartments in this market I was able to obtain comparable rentals that required few adjustments. They all were current rentals so no time adjustment was required. They are all in the same neighborhood so no location adjustment was needed. The only significant difference in physical characteristics was that Comparable Rental No. 3 had a swimming pool and two tennis courts. Using the matched pair technique an adjustment of $50 per unit was estimated for a tennis courts and a swimming pool.

The rentals ranged from $560 to $725 per month without utilities or furniture. Those units that rented for $600 or more either had parking for 2.5 cars per apartment unit or a swimming pool and tennis courts.

The rental range for apartments similar to the subject with 1.5 parking spaces per unit and without a swimming pool or tennis courts was $560 to $575.

The owner reported that she was getting $575 per month from each tenant on the anniversary of their renewal. This was confirmed by the rental data to be market rent.

ESTIMATE OF POTENTIAL GROSS INCOME

The first step is to estimate the potential gross income from all sources assuming the property is under competent management.

The following rental information has been obtained from four apartment properties judged to be comparable and competitive with the appraised property. Common to all the rentals is that tenants pay for all utilities except cold water.

First, the rentals of the four comparable sales were considered. Added to these were the rentals of four other apartment buildings in the neighborhood which had not been recently sold. All these rentals were adjusted and reconciled into estimated market rentals of the subject units which when totaled produce the estimated potential gross income.

EXPLANATION OF EXPENSES

In estimating the anticipated expenses for the appraised property, I have analyzed the actual expenses furnished to me and operating statements for similar properties in the area.

Vacancy & Collection Loss
The appraised property has experienced a vacancy level similar to comparable buildings in the area of 1% to 3%. It is my opinion that with competent management, the current rental rates can be maintained in line with the strong occupancy levels and development trends in the market area without experiencing undue vacancy and collection losses. A vacancy and collection loss factor of 3% has been utilized.

Real Estate Taxes
Current taxes are $7,572.56 and have been gradually increasing over the past four years. Based upon comparable properties and my tax analysis, I have stabilized this expense at $7,700 per year.

Insurance
The cost for insurance at the subject property was $1,000. In comparison to similar buildings, this figure falls within an acceptable range.

Management
A survey of local real estate managers revealed management fees range from 4% to 5% of gross income collected. Based upon the comparable properties, the current management fee of 4% is reasonable and acceptable.

Water/Septic
Actual costs have been utilized and include salt for the water softener and annual pumping of the septic tank.

Electricity
The actual charge for electricity was $288. This figure has been increased somewhat to $300 in the stabilized operating statement.

Trash Removal
The actual cost (contract) was $1,200. This fee is not expected to increase during the next year.

Grounds   The actual cost of maintaining the grounds was
                   $160 per month. This cost appears reasonable and
                   in line with other such known costs at similar
                   developments.

Maintenance &
Repairs   Items included in this category include interior
                   and exterior maintenance of the property,
                   supplies, subcontractor's fees, and painting and
                   redecorating. It has been estimated that the
                   subject property will require an average annual
                   maintenance expense of $3,000 or approximately
                   $300 per unit.

Miscellaneous   This category includes any minor interior
                   operating costs such as exterminating or petty
                   cash items. Amounts in this category may vary
                   considerably relative to management practices.
                   However, an amount of $600 per year has been
                   estimated for a property of this size.

Replacement
Allowance   It is customary in this locale to account for
                   replacing short-lived items. Based on the
                   replacement costs arrived at in the Cost Approach
                   and the following life expectancies, this expense
                   has been estimated as follows:

Item	$\dfrac{\text{Cost}}{\text{Life Expectancy}}$	=	Allowance
Appliances	$\dfrac{\$16,000}{10 \text{ yrs.}}$		$1,600
Carpeting	$\dfrac{\$16,000}{6 \text{ yrs.}}$		$2,660
Roof	$\dfrac{\$12,000}{15 \text{ yrs.}}$		$ 800
Heat and A/C	$\dfrac{\$30,000}{25 \text{ yrs.}}$		$1,200
Total Replacement Allowance			$6,266

RECONSTRUCTED OPERATING STATEMENT

Potential Gross Income (10 units x $675/mo. x 12) = $81,000

Less Vacancy & Collection Loss (3%)   (2,430)

Effective Gross Income $78,570

Less Operating Expenses:

    <u>Fixed</u>:
    Real Estate Taxes $ 7,700
    Insurance   1,000
        Sub-Total $ 8,700

    <u>Variable</u>:
    Management (4% of E.G.I.) $ 3,143
    Water/Septic   400
    Electricity   300
    Trash Removal   1,200
    Grounds Maintenance   1,200
    Maintenance & Repairs   3,000
    Miscellaneous   600
        Sub-Total $ 9,843

    Replacement Allowance $ 6,266
        Sub-Total $ 6,266

Total Operating Expenses   32%
(operating expense ratio = 32% of E.G.I.) $24,809

Net Operating Income $53,716

Capitalization Process

The final step in the Income Approach is to capitalize the net operating income into an indication of value. Two methods are available: direct capitalization and yield capitalization.

The major difference between direct capitalization and yield capitalization is that the former does not make an allocation between return on and return of capital. However, a satisfactory rate of return is implicit in the rates derived from the market data.

Direct capitalization converts one year's income into a value indication either by dividing the income by a capitalization rate of multiplying it by a factor derived from the market.

I have derived an overall capitalization rate from the comparable market sales used in the Sales Comparison Approach. A replacement allowance has been deducted as an operating expense for each sale.

Comparable Sale	1	2	3	4
Sale Price	$960,000	$513,000	$510,000	$738,500
Net Oper. Income	$ 86,822	$48,672	$ 52,876	$ 71,640
Indicated O.A.R.	.0905	.0889	.0927	.0970

Most weight was given to Comparable Sale #1 as it had the same parking ratio and central air conditioning. The other Comparable Sales required adjustments for those items. Comparable Sale #3 also required adjustment for special financing. I selected an overall capitalization rate of .09 for the subject property.

Value = Net Operating Income
         Overall Capitaization Rate

Value = $53,716   = $596,844
        .09

A Gross Income Multiplier has also been utilized in this appraisal report. This multiplier was developed in the Direct Sales Comparison Approach to be 7.4. The potential gross income is $81,000, thus:

7.4 x $81,000 = $599,400

As previously explained good income and expense data was available. The final estimate by the Income Approach was $600,000.

RECONCILIATION AND FINAL VALUE ESTIMATE

Value Indicated via Cost Approach $610,000

Value Indicated via Direct Sales
    Comparison Approach $600,000

Value Indicated via Income Approach $600,000

Reconcilation is the step in the valuation process in which the relative significance, applicability, and defensibility of each value indication is weighed. The final conclusion of value is based upon the appropriateness, accuracy, and quality of evidence contained in the appraisal.

The appraised property is improved with an 11 year old, ten unit, rental apartment building in good condition. The property is located in a well established, residential neighborhood, within convenient distance from employment, education, recreation, and shopping facilities. The economic and demographic data of the community has been carefully analyzed. Considering the projected population growth and per-capita income, it is reasonable to expect continued high occupancy levels and the ability of the subject proeprty to command competitive rental rates.

The existing improvements are a legal use. It has been concluded that the highest and best use of the property is the continued use as a ten-unit rental apartment building.

The comparable data found in this appraisal was chosen from a large quantity of data. Data was considered in addition to the data displayed in the report.

All three approaches to value have been developed in this appraisal report. The Cost Approach indicated a value of $610,000, and the Direct Sales Comparison and Income Approaches indicated a value of $600,000. Although there are no great differences to resolve among the value indications, greater confidence has been placed in the Income and Direct Sales Comparison Approaches.

The major weaknesses of the Cost Approach were (1) the lack of multi-family land sales having a similar density of development when compared to the appraised site, and (2) the difficulty in estimating accrued depreciation of an 11-year old building. Thereefore, this approach was used as a guide and check on the values estimated by the other two approaches.

The Direct Sales Comparison Approach was considered appropriate and accurate. The comparable sales were judged to be valid and reliable indicators of market value. The quantity of evidence provided by each comparable was sufficient. The few adjustments that were made were derived from the market. These sales reflect the actions of typical buyers for this type of property and, therefore, led to a logical and well documented conclusion of value.

The Income Approach is considered to be the most applicable method for estimating market value as the subject property is income-producing. The quality of the comparable rental data was particularly good and resulted in a reliable gross income estimate. A reconstructed operating statement was developed based upon expense data obtained from the subject property and from similar properties. The final step was to convert the net operating income into an estimate of value. This process is known as capitalization. Most investment properties in this market are financed with conventional 20 year mortgages at market rates of interest. Typical mortgages are 75% to 80% of the value of the property. With this type of homogeneous financing, direct capitalization gives the best indication of the value of a property being appraised.

As a result of my appraisal and analysis, giving most weight to the Income and Direct Sales Comparison Approaches, and considering all other available facts and circumstances pertinent to an estimate of value, it is my opinion that the estimated market value of the appraised property, as of December 15, 199_, is:

SIX HUNDRED THOUSAND ($600,000) DOLLARS

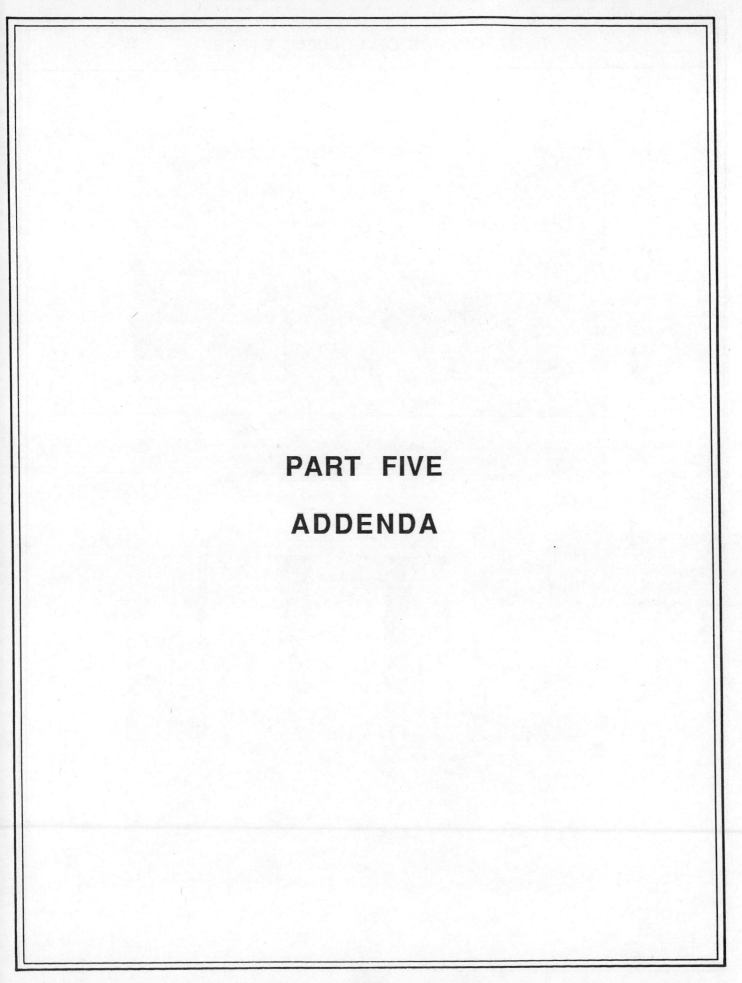

PART FIVE

ADDENDA

SUGGESTED READING

BOOKS AND PAMPHLETS

American Institute of Real Estate Appraisers, Chicago, IL:

–*Appraising the Single Family Residence* by George Bloom and Henry S. Harrison, 1980.

–*The Appraisal of Real Estate*, 9th Edition, 1988.

–*The Condominium Appraisal Report in Communicating the Appraisal* by Arlen Mills, 1988.

–*Historic Properties: Preservation and The Valuation Process*, 1982.

–*The Narrative Report in Communicating the Appraisal Series*, 1988.

–*Residential Condominiums: A Guide to Analysis and Appraisal* by Robert Dombal, 1976.

–*The Uniform Residential Appraisal Report in Communicating the Appraisal* by Arlen Mills, 1988.

–*Valuing the Time Share Property* by Kathleen Conroy, 1981.

Harrison, Henry S.:

–*Houses, The Illustrated Guide to Construction Design and Systems*, rev. ed., Realtors National Marketing Institute, Chicago, IL, 1976.

–*Houses Student Workbook* with Ruth D. Lambert and Bobby Brutton, Realtors National Marketing Institute, Chicago, IL, 1977.

–*Houses Cook Book* with Ruth D. Lambert, Forms and Worms, Inc., New Haven, CT, 1988.

–*Homebuying* with Margery B. Leonard, Realtors National Marketing Institute, Chicago, IL, 1980.

–Illustrated Guide Freddie Mac-Fannie Mae Series, The H^2 Company, New Haven, CT, 1988.
   Single Family Residential Appraisal Report,
   Small Income Properties,
   Individual Condominium Unit

–*Review Appraiser's Handbook*, The H^2 Company, New Haven, CT, 1988.

Laurenti, Luigi. *Property Values and Race: Studies in Seven Cities.* Berkeley, CA, University of California Press, 1960.

O'Flaherty, John D. "An Appraiser's Dilemma: The Cost Approach Value", The Real Estate Appraiser, January-February 1969.

Smith, Halbert C. *Real Estate Appraisal.* Columbus, Ohio: Grid Publishing, 1976.

Building Cost Manuals

Boeckh Building Valuation Manual, Milwaukee: American Appraisal Co., 3 vols.
Vol. 1 - *Residential and Agricultural*; Vol. 2 - *Commercial*;
Vol. 3 - *Industrial and Institutional*. Includes wide variety of building models.
Built up from unit-in-place costs converted to cost per square foot of floor or
ground area. Boeckh Building Cost Modifier is published bimonthly for
updating with current modifiers.

Building Construction Cost Data. Duxbury, Mass.: Robert Snow Means Co., annual.
Lists average unit prices on many building construction items for use in
engineering estimates. Components arranged according to uniform system
adopted by the American Institute of Architects, Associated General
Constractors, and Construction Specification Institute.

Dodge Building Cost Calculator & Valuation Guide. New York: McGraw-Hill
Information Systems Co.
(looseleaf service, quarterly supplements).
Lists building costs for common types and sizes of buildings.
Local cost modifiers and historical local cost index tables included. Formerly
Dow Building Cost Calculator.

Marshall Valuation Service. Los Angeles: Marshall and Swift Publication Co.
(looseleaf service, monthly supplements).
Cost Data for determining replacement costs of buildings and other
improvements in the United States and Canada. Includes current cost
multipliers and local modifiers.

Residential Cost Handbook. Los Angeles: Marshall and Swift Publication Co.
(looseleaf service, quarterly supplements).
Presents square-foot method and segregated-cost method. Local modifiers and
cost-trend modifiers included.

Residential Valuation

The Independent Voice of Residential Appraisers

Volume 4, Number 1   Winter 1989

$3.00

Special
Appraisal Organization Directory
Issue

Nineteenth Century American

BROWNSTONE OR BRICK ROW HOUSE OR EASTERN TOWNHOUSE

APPRAISAL ORGANIZATIONS AND DESIGNATIONS

The following material is reprinted from the November-December 1988 issue of Residential Appraisal Magazine, 315 Whitney Avenue, New Haven, Ct 06511. Information about how to subscribe to R.V. Magazine is at the back of this book.

This introduction also has material from Review Appraiser's Handbook by Henry S. Harrison, H^2 Company, 315 Whitney Avenue, New Haven, CT 06511

DESIGNATIONS

Some Lenders will only use Appraisers who have designations from certain appraisal organizations. They believe that a designated Appraiser will be qualified.

Unfortunately, not all designations are the same. There are at least 30 appraisal organizations which award designations to their members. Requirements vary widely.

Two of these organizations have awarded real estate appraisal designations since before World War II. They both have a long history of rigid standards for awarding their designations. They are the American Institute of Real Estate Appraisers (which awards the RM and MAI designations (and the Society of Real Estate Appraisers) (which awards the SRA, SRPA and the SREA designations). To earn any of these designations an Appraiser must have taken several courses, have years of proven experience, produced demonstration appraisals and passed several examinations.

The designation requirements of the other national appraisal organizations range from those similar to the AIREA and SREA, to none other than making an application and sending in the required fee. To complicate matters further, some of the organizations which have strict designation requirements now have a past history of lax requirements.

There are also some good Appraisers who for various reasons have decided not to belong to any appraisal organization or apply for any designation. Lenders who refuse to consider Appraisers who do not have designations may be eliminating some well-qualified Appraisers who are capable of doing their work.

On the following pages is a reprint of the Directory of Appraisal Organizations from Residential Valuation Magazine.

Directory of Appraisal Organizations

Last year we printed the first Directory of Appraisal Organizations in Residential Valuation Magazine. It was compiled from existing sources, therefore, we requested that our readers tell us of any other organizations which were not on our list. We printed these additions and corrections, as we received them, in our ongoing update column.

For this Special Directory issue of R.V. Magazine we have compiled all of the previously received information. In addition, we have sent a questionnaire to each known organization, requesting verification of, and additions to, this information.

As a result, we believe that we have produced the most accurate and complete directory of appraisal organizations that has ever been compiled.

Once again, we are requesting that you send in any additions or corrections to: R.V. Magazine, 315 Whitney Avenue, New Haven, CT 06511. We will publish the information in future issues of R.V.

RV Editors

Academy of Appraisers and Consultants (AAC)

Information about this organization was obtained from outside sources as the organization did not respond to our questionnaire. The accuracy of the information has not been verified.

Address of National Headquarters: P.O. Box 1, Lenox Hill Station, New York, NY 10021

Designations Awarded: SCAC: Senior Certified Appraiser and Consultant; RFA: Residential Form Appraiser; CIPA: Certified Income Property Appraiser.

Academy of Residential Estate Appraisers

Information about this organization was obtained from outside sources as the organization did not respond to our questionnaire. The accuracy of the information has not been verified.

Address of National Headquarters: 410 Main Street, Longmont, CO 80501

Accredited Review Appraisers Council

Address of National Headquarters: 303 W. Cypress, San Antonio, TX 78212

President: Deborah J. Deane

Executive Director: Mary A. Davila

Telephone: (512) 225-2897

Designations Awarded and Brief Summary of Requirements: AAR: Accredited in Appraisal Review. The AAR designation is awarded after successful completion of educational courses, approval of demonstration report, paying all necessary fees & adherence to standards of practice & code of ethics.

Year Founded and Brief History of Organization: Founded in 1987 to advance the profession of real estate appraisal review; to enhance the competence & performance of all parties concerned through education, professional standards & ethics.

Number of Members: 200 members in thirty four states.

Membership Due: Annual dues $50.00.

American Association of Certified Appraisers (AACA)

Address of National Headquarters: 800 Compton Road, Suite 10, Cincinnati, OH 45231

Executive Director: Anthony J. Brueneman III

Telephone: (800) 543-2222; (513) 729-1400

Designations Awarded and Brief Summary of Requirements: CA-R: Certified Appraiser - Residential; CA-S: Certified Appraiser - Senior; CA-C: Certified Appraiser Consultant.

Year Founded and Brief History of Organization: Founded in 1977 as practical quality designation granting association. Requires combination of education & experience. Narrative report required. References checked.

Number of Members: 2700.

Membership Dues: $135.00 per year, one time $30.00 processing fee.

American Fraternity of Real Estate Appraisers

Address of National Headquarters:
3335 Market Street, P.O. Box 52, Camp Hill PA 17011

President: Dan Barninger

Telephone: (717) 763-1502

Designations Awarded and Brief Summary of Requirements: CSM: Certified Senior Member; CMRA: Certified. Member Residential Appraiser.

Year Founded and Brief History of Organization: Founded in March, 1981 as an independent organization of real estate appraisers. Membership is structured to recognize the individual with emphasis on experience. The "Fraternity" is represented with members throughout the United States and Canada.

Number of Members: 800.

Membership Dues: $70.00.

American Institute of Real Estate Appraisers (The Appraisal Institute)

Address of National Headquarters:
430 North Michigan Avenue, Chicago, IL 60611-4088

President: J. Carl Schultz, Jr., MAI 1989 President

Executive Vice President:
Richard B. Gaskins.

Telephone: (312) 329-8559

Designations Awarded and Brief Summary of Requirements: MAI: Member, Appraisal Institute and RM: Residential Member. College degree, passing a series of examinations, experience and demonstration appraisal reports required. Adherence to strictly enforced Code of Ethics & Standards of Professional Practice. Continuing education as a conditon of membership.

Year Founded and Brief History of Organization: Founded in 1932 in response to a need for appraisal standards as an outgrowth of tremendous real estate losses during the Depression. Began as a department of Ntl. Assn of Real Estate Boards. In 1932 became an independent, affiliated organization of NAR.

Number of Members: Members: 6,947; Candidates: 15,805.

Membership Dues: MAI: $500; RM: $400.
Number of Chapters: 58

Locations of Chapters: Nationwide.

American Real Estate Appraisers Guild

Information about this organization was obtained from outside sources as the organization did not respond to our questionnaire. The accuracy of the information has not been verified.

Address of National Headquarters:
2129 West 8 Mile Road, Detroit, MI 48203

President: S. Thomas Russo

Telephone: (313)891-2755

American Real Estate Society

*Logo
Not Available*

Address of National Headquarters:
University of Kentucky, College of Business and Economics, Department of Finance, Lexington, KY 40506-0034.

Name of Executive Director:
James R. Webb; Finance Dept., University of Akron, College of Business Administration,

Telephone: (606) 257-2968

American Society of Appraisers

Address of National Headquarters:
P.O. Box 17265, Washington, D.C. 20041

International President:
Elizabeth M. Blagbrough, ASA

Executive Director: A.W. Carson

Telephone: (703) 478-2228 or 1-800-ASA-VALU

Designations Awarded and Brief Summary of Requirements: Based on intensive written and oral examinations and submission of acceptable appraisal reports, plus engagment in the appraisal profession, a college degree or its equivalent as deemed by the ASA Int'l. Board of Examiners: two years full time appraisal experience for Accredited Member (AM); five years full time appraisal experience for Accredited Senior Appraiser (ASA).

Year Founded and Brief History of Organization: Originated in 1936, incorporated in 1952, the nation's oldest, multi-disciplinary teaching/testing/certifying appraisal society. Represented by over 5,500 members at home and abroad; 83 chapters. Founding member of The Appraisal Foundation, the parent entity for an Appraisal Standards Board and recent publisher of Uniform Standards of Professional Appraisal Practice.

Number of Members: 5,500

Membership Dues: Senior (ASA) $275; Accredited Member (AM) $225; Candidate $175; Affiliate $100; Student Affiliate $30.

Number of Chapters: 83

Locations of Chapters: The United States, U.S. Virgin Islands, Puerto Rico, Australia, Canada, Central America, Great Britain, Hong Kong, India, Indonesia, Ireland, Israel, Japan, Mexico, Netherlands, Philippines, Portugal, South Africa, South America, Spain, Switzerland, Thailand, and the West Indies.

American Society of Farm Managers and Rural Appraisers (ASFMRA)

Information about this organization was obtained from outside sources as the organization did not respond to our questionnaire. The accuracy of the information has not been verified.

Address of National Headquarters: 950 South Cherry Street, Suite G-16, Denver, CO 80222

Telephone: (303) 758-3513

Designations Awarded: ARA: Accredited Rural Appraiser.

American Society of Professional Appraisers, Inc.

Address of National Headquarters: 100 Galleria Pkwy, Tower 1, Ste 400, Atlanta, Ga 30339

President: Dick Kruger

Executive Director: Lee McCutchan

Telephone: (404) 951-1994

Designations Awarded and Brief Summary of Requirements: CRRA: Certified Residential Real Estate Appraiser; CCRA: Certified Commercial Real Estate Appraiser.

Year Founded and Brief History of Organization: January 1984, formed to help sustain the high standards of the appraisal profession and to give recognition to many deserving, trained, professional appraisers.

Number of Members: 2057

Membership Dues: First year members $110; annual memberhsip $85.

Appraisal Institute of Canada (AIC)

Logo Not Available

Information about this organization was obtained from outside sources as the organization did not respond to our questionnaire. The accuracy of the information has not been verified.

Address of National Headquarters: 309-93 Lombard Avenue, Winnipeg, Manitoba Canada R3B 3B1

Telephone: (204) 942-0751

Designations Awarded: AACI: Accredited Appraiser, Canadian Institute; CRA: Canadian Residential Appraiser; P.App: Professional Appraiser.

Appraisers Common Cause

Information about this organization was obtained from outside sources as the organization did not respond to our questionnaire. The accuracy of the information has not been verified.

Address of National Headquarters: P.O. Box 5798, Scottsdale, AZ 85261

Telephone: (602) 998-2000

California State Association of Real Estate Appraisers, (CSAOREAsm)

CSAOREA^{sm}

Address of National Headquarters: P.O. Box 221488 Sacramento, CA 95822-8488

President: William M. Snyder
Telephone: (916) 427-5196

Designations Awarded and Brief Summary of Requirements: Associate (Professional Interest) Candidate for Designation (Enrolled in or have completed Accredited Basic Appraisal Verified Completion Certificate) Designated Member™; Designated Advanced Member™ (Advanced Course Certificate from accredited higher education institute). Designated Senior Member™ (5 yrs. Appraisal Practice)

Year Founded and Brief History of Organization: Founded in 1981 to provide a vehicle for individuals with an interest in the field of real estate appraisal using/recognizing California Statutes and California accredited appraisal courses.

Membership Dues: Call for membership information.

Locations of Chapters: Call for information about Southern California and Northern California meetings.

Columbia Society of Real Estate Appraisers, Inc. (CSREAI)

Information about this organization was obtained from outside sources as the organization did not respond to our questionnaire. The accuracy of the information has not been verified.

Address of National Headquarters: 82 Edmore Lane, West Islip, NY 11795

President: Charles C. Booth

Director of Ed: Robert A Gregory

Telephone:(516) 422-3603

Federation of Underwriters/ Appraisers, Inc.

Information about this organization was obtained from outside sources as the organization did not respond to our questionnaire. The accuracy of the information has not been verified.

Address of National Headquarters: P.O. Box 1229, Covington, KY 41012

Designations Awarded: URA: Uniform Review Appraiser.

International Association of Assessing Officers

Address of National Headquarters: 1313 East 60th Street, Chicago, IL 60637

President: William S. Carman, Sr.,CAE

Executive Director: Richard R. Almy

Telephone: (312) 947-2064

Designations Awarded and Brief Summary of Requirements: CAE: Certified Assessment Evaluator; RES: Residential Evaluation Specialist. Courses, Exam, Demonstration Appraisal Report.

Year Founded and Brief History of Organization: 1934. A nonprofit educational membership organization dedicated to improving the administration of the property tax and to improving understanding of important property tax issues.

Number of Members: 8000

Membership Dues: $65-$120.

Number of Chapters: 21

Locations of Chapters: Arkansas, Central Arizona, Columbia River, Florida, Illinois, Kansas City Regional, King County (WA), Los Angeles County, Maine, Metro New York, Minnesota, New York Suburban Counties, North California, Oklahoma, Philadelphia, Pima County (AZ), Portland (OR), Tennessee, Utah, Wichita Regional.

International Organization of Real Estate Appraisers (IREA)

Information about this organization was obtained from outside sources as the organization did not respond to our questionnaire. The accuracy of the information has not been verified.

Address of National Headquarters: Wells Fargo Bldg., 44 Montgomery St., San Francisco, CA 94106-USA

International Real Estate Institute

Address of National Headquarters: 8383 East Evans Road, Scottsdale, AZ 85260-3614

Managing Director: Roger Wood
Telephone: (602) 998-8267
Designations Awarded and Brief Summary of Requirements: SCV: Senior Certified Valuer
Year Founded: 1978
Number of Members: 5000

Membership Dues: $150.00 Annually

International Right of Way Association (IRWA)

(Not Available)

Information about this organization was obtained from outside sources as the organization did not respond to our questionnaire. The accuracy of the information has not been verified.

Address of National Headquarters: 9920 La Cienega Blvd., Suite 515, Inglewood, CA 90301

President: George D. Wilkerson

Director of Education: Ralph Brown

Telephone: (213)649-5323

Designations Awarded: SR/WA: Senior Member of the International Right of Way Association.

Massachusetts Board of Real Estate

Address of National Headquarters: 100 Boylston Street, Boston, MA 02116

Name of Executive Director: Mary Ann Jasienowski

Telephone: (617) 542-9823

Designations Awarded and Brief Summary of Requirements: RA: Residential Appraiser and MRA: Certified to appraise all types of real estate. Must pass rigid written examinations, validate appraisal experience; demonstrate proficiency and meet high standards of personal integrity.

Year Founded and Brief History of Organization: Founded in 1934, MBREA educates, trains and certifies men & women as appraisers. Certified MRA qualified to appraise all types of real estate; RA specializes in residential appraisals.

Number of Members: Certified: 131; Provisional: 574.

Membership Dues: Certified: $150; Provisional: $90

Number of Chapters: Statewide organization (Massachusetts)

National Appraisal System

Information about this organization was obtained from outside sources as the organization did not respond to our questionnaire. The accuracy of the information has not been verified.

Address of National Headquarters: P.O. Box 7800, Costa Mesa, CA 92628

President: Vince Pulsipher

Telephone: (800)622-6232

National Association of Certified Real Property Appraisers

Information about this organization was obtained from outside sources as the organization did not respond to our questionnaire. The accuracy of the information has not been verified.

Address of National Headquarters: 4701 Country club Road, Winston-Salem, NC 27104

President: Thomas T. Roberts

Telephone: (919) 760-4177

National Association of Independent Fee Appraisers

Address of National Headquarters: 7501 Murdoch Avenue, St. Louis, MO 63119

Executive Vice President: Robert G. Kaestner;

Director of Education: William H. Steele.

Telephone: (314) 781-6688

Designations Awarded and Brief Summary of Requirements: IFA: Member; IFAS: Senior Member; IFAC: Appraiser - Counselor.

Year Founded and Brief History of Organization: Founded in 1961 in Phoenix, AZ as a non profit professional society of real estate appraisers and is incorporated under the laws of the State of Arizona. Today the Association has chapters throughout the United States and Canada, and continues to grow not only in number but in stature.

Number of Members: 5400

Membership Dues: Associates $100; Candidates $200; Members, Seniors and Counselors $250.

Number of Chapters: 200

Locations of Chapters: All States and Canada.

National Association of Master Appraisers

Address of National Headquarters:
303 West Cypress Street, Box 12617, San Antonio, TX 78212-0617.

President: Marvin T. Deane, MSA

ExecDirector: George R. Harrison

Telephone: (512) 271-0781

Designations Awarded and Brief Summary of Requirements: MRA: Master Residential Appraiser; MFLA: Master Farm and Land Appraiser; MSA: Master Senior Apraiser; CAO: Certified Appraisal Organization.

Year Founded and Brief History of Organization: 1982.

Number of Members: 5000

Membership Dues: $75.00 per year

Number of Chapters: 13 States

Locations of Chapters: Arizona, California, Illinois, Ohio, Iowa, Mississippi, North Carolina, Florida, Texas, Louisiana, Neveda, Minnesota, Oklahoma.

National Associaton of Real Estate Appraisers (NAREA)

Information about this organization was obtained from outside sources as the organization did not respond to our questionnaire. The accuracy of the information has not been verified.

Address of National Headquarters:
8383 East Evans Road, Scottsdale, AZ 85260-3614

Telephone: (602)948-8000

Designations Awarded: CREA: CertifiedReal Estate Appraiser.

National Association of Review Appraisers and Mortgage Underwriters

Address of National Headquarters:
8383 East Evans Road, Scottsdale, AZ 85260

Executive Director: Robert G. Johnson

Director of Ed: Patricia C. Davidson

Telephone: (602) 998-3000

Designations Awarded and Brief Summary of Requirements: CRA: Certified ReviewAppraiser; RMU: Registered Mortgage Underwriter.

Year Founded: 1975

Number of Members: 7500

Membership Dues: $195.00 per year

National Residential Appraisers Institute

Address of National Headquarters:
2001 Cooper Foster Park Road, Amherst, OH 44001

President: Ade Schreiber

Secretary: Wanda Aschenback

National Education Director and Vice President: Jack Braman

Telephone: (216) 282-7925; Ohio Wats 1-800-331-2732; Nat'l Wats 1-800-321-2732

Designations Awarded and Brief Summary of Requirements: CMDA: Certified Market Data Analyst; GSA: Graduate Senior Appraiser; SCA: Senior Certified Appraiser.

Year Founded and Brief History of Organization: Founded in 1977 to improve the efficiency of real estate people in the valuation of residential real estate. The Institute has expanded nationwide and places its emphasis upon education for Realtors™, brokers and appraisers.

Number of Members: 2000 approx.

Membership Dues: $75.00 per year

Number of Chapters: 3

Locations of Chapters: North New Jersey; Toledo, Ohio; Columbus, Ohio.

National Society of Fee Appraisers (NSFA)

Information about this organization was obtained from outside sources as the organization did not respond to our questionnaire. The accuracy of the information has not been verified.

Address of National Headquarters:
4483 N.W. 36 Street, Suite 111,
Miami Springs, FL 33166

President: John C. Fields

Designations Awarded: RA: Residential Appraiser; NFA: National Fee Appraiser; SFA: Senior Fee Appraiaser.

National Society of Real Estate Appraisers, Inc. (NSFA)

Information about this organization was obtained from outside sources as the organization did not respond to our questionnaire. The accuracy of the information has not been verified.

Address of National Headquarters:
1265 East 105th St.,
Cleveland, OH 44108

Executive Vice President:
William J. Hamilton

Director: Otis L. Thorpe

Telephone: (216)795-3445

Designations Awarded: RA: Junior Member; CRA: Senior Member; MREA:Master Member.

Organization of Professional Real Estate Appraisers, Inc.

Logo Not Available

Address of National Headquarters:
P.O. Box 1535, 107 West 7th Street, Columbia, TN 38402

President: Al Thompson,

Executive Director: Ann Evans
Telephone: (615) 381-9446,
Toll Free 1-800-543-7061

Designations Awarded and Brief Summary of Requirements: PRA: Professional Residential Appraiser; PREA: Professional Real Estate Appraiser; PFA: Professional Farm Appraiser; CFFEM: Personal Property

Year Founded and Brief History of Organization: Founded in 1979 by Dr. Terry Evans with first members from Tennessee; evolved with members in 33 states.

Membership Dues: $100.00 per year

Number of Chapters: State chapters presently forming

Professional Women's Appraisal Organization

Address of National Headquarters:
8383 East Evans Road,
Scottsdale, AZ 85260-3614

Executive Director:
Patricia C. Davidson

Telephone: (602) 998-4422

Designations Awarded and Brief Summary of Requirements: PWAA: Certified Member

Year Founded : 1986

Number of Members: 500

Membership Dues: $75.00 per year

Society of Real Estate Appraisers

Address of National Headquarters:
225 North Michigan Avenue, Suite 724, Chicago, IL 60601-7601

Executive Director:
Louie Reese III, SRPA

Telephone: 1-800-331-7732.
Illinois, (312) 819-2400

Designations Awarded and Brief Summary of Requirements: SRA: Senior Residential Appraiser; SRPA: Senior Real Property Appraiser; SREA: Senior Real Estate Analyst

Year Founded and Brief History of Organization: 1935. The largest independent association of real estate appraisers in North America, the Society offers courses, publications and its designation programs for practicing appraisers.

Number of Members: 20,000

Membership Dues: $400: Designated; $250: Candidate; $100 : Associate.

Number of Chapters: With 185 chapters, the Society offers a free nationwide directory of its designated appraisers.

Locations of Chapters: Throughout the U. S., Canada, and Caribbean.

World wide Professional Real Estate Appraisers

Information about this organization was obtained from outside sources as the organization did not respond to our questionnaire. The accuracy of the information has not been verified.

Address of National Headquarters: Suite 2002, Carew Tower, Cincinnati, OH 45202

EMPLOYEE RELOCATION COUNCIL
1720 N Street, N.W.
Washington, D.C. 20036

"THE EMPLOYEE RELOCATION COUNCIL, formed in 1964, is a membership organization of corporations and relocation service companies involved in employee transfer. Of particular concern is adequate relocation assistance to the transferee in the sale of the existing home and the acquisition of the new residence, as well as in various other aspects of the move.

The purpose of the Council, as stated in its bylaws, is "to study, evaluate, and communicate information on practices and procedures in the relocation of employees who are transferred to different geographical locations so that the transfer may be accomplished with maximum efficiency and minimum disruption to the employee, his family and his employer."

The Employee Relocation Council has developed its own Residential Appraisal Report. Many of its members require that appraisers use this form when doing their relocation appraisals.

This form contains its own set of instructions. There are significant differences between these instructions and the Freddie Mac, Fannie Mae, VA and FHA guidelines.

EMPLOYEE RELOCATION COUNCIL
RESIDENTIAL APPRAISAL REPORT

Client File No.: _____

Homeowner: _____

_____

Address: _____

_____

Date: _____

Appraiser File No.: _____

Appraiser: _____

DEFINITIONS RELATING TO THE RELOCATION APPRAISAL

Purpose of the Relocation Appraisal:

To establish the most probable sales price for a relocated employee's primary residence, assuming an arm's length transaction.

Definition of the Relocation Appraisal:

The most probable sales price of a residential housing unit, using the market approach to value.

Definition of Market Data Approach to Value:

The price at which a property would most probably sell, if exposed to the market for a reasonable period of time in an "as is" condition, where payment is made in cash or its equivalent.

Implicit in this definition is the consummation of the sale with passing of title from seller to buyer under conditions whereby:

1. Both parties are well informed and acting in what they consider their best interests.

2. A reasonable amount of time is allowed for exposure in the local market. (A reasonable period is typically up to 120 days unless market conditions indicate otherwise.)

3. Financing, if any, is on terms generally available in the community and typical for the property type in its locale. (If an assumption or special financing is available, justify its specific effect on the appraised value on page four in the "Sales or Financing Concessions" grid section, and discuss the impact if any, on page six in the "Special Financing" section.)

4. Forecasting is applied in making an estimate of a future happening or condition, based on an analysis of trends in the recent past, tempered with analytical judgment concerning the probable extent to which these trends will continue into the future and reflecting an estimated impact, if any, upon value.

INSTRUCTIONS TO APPRAISERS

General Guidelines

The appraiser must observe the following general guidelines in determining the appraised value opinion. The appraiser is to:

1) Estimate the appraised value considering the property in an "as is" condition as of the date of inspection. "As is" condition should reflect the cost of those items (e.g., repairs, decorations, etc.) required to make the subject comparable with similar properties in that market area from a buyer's point of view. If there is a circumstance where the appraiser is unable to determine the "as is" condition (e.g., in-process construction or improvements, suspected structural problems, water related problems, roof, etc.) notify the client immediately.

2) Stress what the property should sell for in the current marketplace. In this regard, give particular attention to the analysis of comparable sales (or homes under contract), competitive listings, supply and demand, and overall market conditions. The appraiser should also consider other factors and make necessary adjustments such as the residence's exposure to the market, availability and terms of financing, over-improvements and location.

3) Reflect in your appraised value opinion as of the date of the appraisal:

    a) An adjustment for any value that may have been created by comparable sale prices (or homes under contract) that were influenced by discount points paid by the seller of FHA, VA, or conventional mortgages; or those comparables which were sold by loan assumption, installment contract, seller carry back, or any form of preferential financing. This also applies to situations where the seller pays certain buyer costs such as buy downs, fees, or credits. In these situations, adjustments should be noted and described for the specific comparable sale.

    b) The difference in discount points between those charged on the comparable sales (or homes under contract) and those charged currently if it is the custom of lenders to charge discount points to sellers on conventional mortgages.

4) Develop the appraised value opinion, assuming the property is free and clear of all non-mortgage encumbrances with the owner responsible for discharging all liens and unpaid installments of special assessments for improvements completed. If the special assessments are still pending and the improvements are not yet completed, the appraiser should include any additional value which may attribute to the pending improvements. If paying off an assessment provides the subject property with an advantage over the comparable sales and competitive listings, this should be reflected in the appraised value.

Procedural Guidelines

In addition to the aforementioned general guidelines, the appraiser must be aware of and follow these specific guidelines:

1. Appraisers are frequently the sole visible representative of the client to the relocated homeowner. Therefore, a professional and courteous manner should be presented.

2. When an appraiser assignment is directed to a specific individual, that appraiser must personally inspect the property and complete the assignment unless approval for a substitution is obtained from the client.

3. On the day the appraiser is contacted with the appraisal request, contact should be made with the employee (or spouse) for an appointment. If the employee (or spouse) cannot be reached on the same day, let the client know so they can assist in locating the homeowner.

4. Inspect the property within two working days and contact the client with the verbal figure within four working days of the original request (unless the transferring employee delays the process). If the appraisal cannot be completed in the required time frame, or if the appraiser will be unavailable to discuss the assignment after completion, the assignment should not be accepted.

5. If access to the property cannot be gained, if valuation problems arise, or if an inspection is required for clarification (such as a structural engineer's report, etc.), the client should be called immediately.

6. Completed copies of the typewritten appraisal report should be mailed within seven working days of the original request (providing there are not delays created by the homeowner).

7. Sufficient time should be taken when inspecting the subject property to impart confidence to the homeowner even if the appraiser is familiar with the property.

8. Consider any information that the homeowner feels is important to the value of his/her home.

9. The appraiser should not discuss his/her appraisal opinions or reveal sensitive information to anyone other than the client. If the homeowner (or spouse) asks general questions as it relates to the appraisal process, feel free to discuss generalities.

10. The appraiser who arrives at the homeowner's property while another appraiser or broker is present, should leave the property immediately and reschedule the appointment.

11. An appraiser will not accept an appraisal assignment if there is a conflict of interest such as: recently appraising the house for another party, an association with the listing agent/company, etc.

12. Appraisers will not solicit a listing or generate a referral as a result of an appraisal assignment.

13. Call the client to clarify the instructions if they are not completely understood.

14. Include the following exhibits:

    a. Photos of the front and rear view of the residence, street scene of the property, factors in near-by vicintiy which affect subject property, either favorably or adversely.
    b. Photos of all comparables. (Please attach all photos separately.)
    c. Sketch of the floor plan of subject property (not necessarily to scale).
    d. Sketch of plot plan showing all improvements (not necessarily to scale).
    e. Map of the subdivision or area depicting locations of the subject, comparable sold properties and competitive listings.

BUILDING SKETCH (if grid is inadequate, please attach separate grid)

ERC-2 Rev. 4/86

D3

VALUATION SECTION

The appraiser has recited three recent sales of properties most similar and proximate to subject and has considered these in the market analysis. The description includes a dollar adjustment, reflecting market reaction to those items of significant variation between the subject and comparable properties. If a significant item in the comparable property is superior to, or more favorable than, the subject property, a minus (-) adjustment is made, thus reducing the indicated value of subject; if a significant item in the comparable is inferior to, or less favorable than, the subject property, a plus (+) adjustment is made, thus increasing the indicated value of the subject.

ITEM	Subject Property	COMPARABLE NO. 1	+(-) $ Adjustment	COMPARABLE NO. 2	+(-) $ Adjustment	COMPARABLE NO. 3	+(-) $ Adjustment
Address							
Proximity to Subj.							
Sales Price		$		$		$	
Closing Date							
Data Source							
Market/Time	DESCRIPTION	DESCRIPTION		DESCRIPTION		DESCRIPTION	
Adjustments							
Location							
Site/View							
Design and Appeal							
Quality of Const.							
Age							
Condition							
Living Area Room Count and Total	Total / B-rms. / Baths	Total / B-rms. / Baths		Total / B-rms. / Baths		Total / B-rms. / Baths	
*Gross Living Area	Sq. Ft.	Sq. Ft.		Sq. Ft.		Sq. Ft.	
Basement & Bsmt. Finished Rooms							
Functional Utility							
Air Conditioning							
Garage/Car Port							
Porches, Patio, Pools, etc.							
Energy Related Items (e.g. solar, heat pumps, etc.)							
Special Features (e.g. fireplaces, kit. equipment, remodeling, etc.)							
Other							
Sales or Financing Concessions							
Net Adj. (Total)		Plus ☐ Minus ☐ $		Plus ☐ Minus ☐ $		Plus ☐ Minus ☐ $	
Indicated Value of Subject		$		$		$	

Describe "other" for Subject: _____

The Market Data Analysis for each comparable sale should include adjustments as appropriate for market condition and **days-on-market** under the heading "Market/Time Adjustment." "Sales or Financing Concessions" should include adjustments for terms of sale.
Reconcile each of the value-related differences between the subject property and the individual comparables, including but not limited to *financing, terms, condition, location, appeal, deferred maintenance, utility, style, view, days-on-market,* and other amenities.

Comparable Sale #1 _____

Comparable Sale #2 _____

Comparable Sale #3 _____

Comments on Market Data and Final Reconciliation: _____

INDICATED VALUE BY MARKET DATA APPROACH . . . . $_____

The above indicated value by the market data approach is also to appear on page 6.

Construction Warranty ☐ Yes ☐ No   Name of Warranty Program _____   Warranty Coverage Expires _____

If yes, is it transferable? ☐ Yes ☐ No

ERC-2 Rev. 4-86

D4

☐ ☐ ☐

EMPLOYEE RELOCATION COUNCIL
RESIDENTIAL APPRAISAL REPORT

SUBJECT INFORMATION

Homeowner

Property Address

City _____ County _____ State _____ Zip Code

Legal Description

Property Rights Appraised ☐ Fee ☐ Leasehold ☐ DeMinimis PUD

Client _____ Address

Occupant _____ Appraiser

NEIGHBORHOOD

Location	☐ Urban	☐ Suburban	☐ Rural
Built Up	☐ Over 75%	☐ 25% to 75%	☐ Under 25%
Growth Rate ☐ Fully Dev.	☐ Rapid	☐ Steady	☐ Slow
Property Values	☐ Increasing	☐ Stable	☐ Declining
Demand/Supply	☐ Shortage	☐ In Balance	☐ Over Supply
Marketing Time	☐ Under 4 Mos.	☐ 4-6 Mos.	☐ Over 6 Mos.

Present Land Use ___ % 1 Family ___ % 2-4 Family ___ % Apts. ___ % Condo ___ % Commercial ___ % Industrial ___ % Vacant ___ %

Change in Present Land Use ☐ Not Likely ☐ Likely (*) ☐ Taking Place (*)

(*) From _____ To _____

Predominant Occupancy ☐ Owner ☐ Tenant ___ % Vacant

Single Family Price Range $ ___ to $ ___ Predominant Value $ ___

Single Family Age ___ Yrs. to ___ Yrs. Predominant Age ___ Yrs.

	Good	Avg.	Fair	Poor
Employment Stability	☐	☐	☐	☐
Convenience to Employment	☐	☐	☐	☐
Convenience to Shopping	☐	☐	☐	☐
Convenience to Schools	☐	☐	☐	☐
Adequacy of Public Transportation	☐	☐	☐	☐
Recreational Facilities	☐	☐	☐	☐
Adequacy of Utilities	☐	☐	☐	☐
Property Compatibility	☐	☐	☐	☐
Protection from Detrimental Conditions	☐	☐	☐	☐
Police and Fire Protection	☐	☐	☐	☐
General Appearance of Properties	☐	☐	☐	☐
Appeal to Market	☐	☐	☐	☐

Comments including those factors, favorable or unfavorable, affecting marketability (e.g. public parks, schools, view, noise)_____

SITE

Dimensions _____ — _____ Sq. Ft. or Acres ☐ Corner Lot

Zoning Classification _____ Present Improvements ☐ do ☐ do not conform to zoning regulations

Highest and Best Use ☐ Present Use ☐ Other (specify) _____

	Public	Other (Describe)	OFF SITE IMPROVEMENTS			Topo
Elec.	☐		Street Access:	☐ Public	☐ Private	Size
Gas	☐		Surface			Shape
Water	☐		Maintenance:	☐ Public	☐ Private	View
San. Sewer	☐		☐ Storm Sewer	☐ Curb/Gutter		Drainage
	☐ Undergrnd. Elect. & Tel.		☐ Sidewalk	☐ Street Lights		Is the property located in a HUD Identified Special Flood Hazard Area? ☐ No ☐ Yes

Comments (favorable or unfavorable including any apparent adverse easements, encroachments or other adverse conditions) _____

IMPROVEMENTS

☐ Existing ☐ Under Constr. VALID PERMIT? ☐ No. Units ___ Type (det., duplex, semi/det., etc.) ___ Design (rambler, split level, etc.) ___ Exterior Walls

Yrs. Actual ___ Effective ___ to ___ No. Stories

Roof Material ___ Gutters and Downspouts ☐ NONE Window (Type): ___ ☐ Storm Sash ☐ Screens ☐ Combination

Insulation ☐ None ☐ Floor ☐ Ceiling ☐ Roof ☐ Wall

☐ Manufactured Housing

Foundation Walls

BSMT. ___ % Basement ☐ Floor Drain Finished Ceiling ___
☐ Outside Entrance ☐ Sump Pump Finished Walls ___
☐ Concrete Floor ___ % Finished Finished Floor ___
Evidence of: ☐ Dampness ☐ Termites ☐ Settlement

☐ Slab on Grade ☐ Crawl Space

Refer comments on improvements and property condition to page 5 in the Supplement under "PROPERTY CONDITION."

ROOM LIST

Room List	Foyer	Living	Dining	Kitchen	Den	Family Rm.	Rec. Room	Bedrooms	No. Baths	Laundry	Other
Basement											
1st Level											
2nd Level											

Finished area above grade contains a total of ___ rooms ___ bedrooms ___ baths. *Gross Living Area ___ Sq. Ft. Bsmt. Area ___ Sq. Ft.

INTERIOR FINISH AND EQUIPMENT

Kitchen Equip.: ☐ Refrigerator ☐ Range/Oven ☐ Disposal ☐ Dishwasher ☐ Fan/Hood ☐ Compact. ☐ Washer ☐ Dryer

HEAT: Type ___ Fuel ___ Cond. ___ AIR COND.: ☐ Central ☐ Other ☐ Adequate ☐ Inadequate

Floors	☐ Hardwood	☐ Carpet Over ___ ☐		
Walls	☐ Drywall	☐ Plaster		
Trim/Finish	☐ Good	☐ Average ☐ Fair ☐ Poor		
Bath Floor	☐ Ceramic			
Bath Wainscot	☐ Ceramic			

Energy related (including energy efficient items) _____

PROPERTY RATING

	Good	Avg.	Fair	Poor
Quality of Construction (Materials and Finish)	☐	☐	☐	☐
Condition of Improvements	☐	☐	☐	☐
Room sizes and layout	☐	☐	☐	☐
Closets and Storage	☐	☐	☐	☐
Insulation - adequacy	☐	☐	☐	☐
Plumbing - adequacy and condition	☐	☐	☐	☐
Electrical - adequacy and condition	☐	☐	☐	☐
Compatibility to Neighborhood	☐	☐	☐	☐
Overall Livability	☐	☐	☐	☐
Appeal and Marketability	☐	☐	☐	☐

ATTIC: ☐ Yes ☐ No ☐ Stairway ☐ Drop-Stair ☐ Scuttle ☐ Floord.

Finished (Describe) ___ ☐ Heated

CAR STORAGE ☐ Garage ☐ Blt. In ☐ Attached ☐ Detach ☐ Car Port

No. Cars ___ ☐ Adequate ☐ Inadequate Condition ___

Describe specialty items (e.g. FIREPLACES, PATIOS, POOL, FENCES, etc.) and detail your comments of functional or physical inadequacies, repairs needed, modernization, etc. on page 5 of the Supplement under "SPECIAL FEATURES" and/or "PROPERTY CONDITION."

*See definition on page 4 and reflect same in the "Gross Living Area" section of the "MARKET DATA ANALYSIS."

ERC-2 Rev. 4/86

D 5

EMPLOYEE RELOCATION COUNCIL SUPPLEMENT TO THE
RESIDENTIAL APPRAISAL REPORT

Describe the value related differences between the subject property and the competing listings (including *financing, terms, condition, location, appeal, deferred maintenance, utility, style, view, days-on-market, and other amenities*). Are seller financing, discount points and/or other seller concessions being offered? *If yes, explain below.*

COMPETING LISTINGS

Listing #1 Address: _____
Original List Price $_____ Current List Price $_____ Date of Most Recent Price Revision _____

Proximity to Subject	Style	Approx. Gross Living Area	Total Rms.	Bed-Rms.	Baths	Garage and Type	Lot Size	Approx. Yr. Blt.	Days-On-Market

Comments: _____

Listing #2 Address: _____
Original List Price $_____ Current List Price $_____ Date of Most Recent Price Revision _____

Proximity to Subject	Style	Approx. Gross Living Area	Total Rms.	Bed-Rms.	Baths	Garage and Type	Lot Size	Approx. Yr. Blt.	Days-On-Market

Comments: _____

Listing #3 Address: _____
Original List Price $_____ Current List Price $_____ Date of Most Recent Price Revision _____

Proximity to Subject	Style	Approx. Gross Living Area	Total Rms.	Bed-Rms.	Baths	Garage and Type	Lot Size	Approx. Yr. Blt.	Days-On-Market

Comments: _____

SPECIAL FEATURES

Specifically describe any special features which affect the appraised value of the subject property such as upgrades, additions, improvements, etc.

_____

PROPERTY CONDITION

Is Urea-Formaldehyde Foam Insulation (UFFI) present or suspected? ☐ Yes ☐ No
Explain _____
Has the owner secured the necessary permits for all additions and improvements? ☐ Yes ☐ No
How was this verified? _____
List any required inspections (e.g., municipal, state, certificate of occupancy, federal, etc.).

List any recommended inspections and why (e.g., structural, mechanical, roof, etc.).

As required in paragraph 1 of the General Guidelines relative to "as is" condition, list in descending order of importance any repairs and improvements you recommend to put the home in marketable condition. Estimate the cost of each recommended repair/improvement. Furnish photographs if warranted.

PROPERTY ACREAGE, TAXES & FEES

Is the property size excessive for the area? ☐ Yes ☐ No   Is the subject comprised of more than one parcel? ☐ Yes ☐ No
Explain: _____

What are the actual real estate taxes? _____
Period covered from _____ to _____
Are taxes typical for the area and price range? ☐ Yes ☐ No
If no, explain: _____

List any special assessments (including municipal, Homeowner Association dues, etc.) or additional encumbrances/liens (existing or pending).

_____

D 6

☐ ☐ ☐

PERSONAL PROPERTY

Note all personal property in your estimated appraised value.
_____
_____
_____
_____
_____

SPECIAL FINANCING

Does the subject property have an assumable loan? ☐ Yes ☐ No

If yes, how was this verified? _____

Is any value for it included in the final appraised value estimate on pages 4 and 6? ☐ Yes ☐ No

If yes, describe the terms of the assumption and discuss its impact on potential purchasers. _____
_____
_____

How does this "Special Financing," if any, compare with the noted COMPETING LISTINGS? (Indicate by listing order)
_____
_____
_____
_____
_____
_____
_____
_____

LISTING INFORMATION

Is the subject property currently listed? ☐ Yes ☐ No

List price(s): Original $_____ Current $_____

Listing company/address _____

Listing agent _____ Phone (_____)_____

How long has property been exposed to market?_____

MARKET CONDITIONS

Describe current local financing availability, interest rates, and terms. _____
_____
_____
_____

Describe current local supply/demand and other pertinent economic issues. _____
_____
_____

Describe future economic trends in these and other pertinent factors and how they may impact on the subject property.
_____
_____
_____
_____
_____
_____

ADDITIONAL COMMENTS

_____
_____
_____
_____
_____
_____
_____
_____
_____
_____
_____
_____
_____
_____

I certify that I have personally inspected both the exterior and interior of the foregoing described property, and I have no interest in such, either present or contemplated. I further certify that I have adhered to the terms of the assignment set forth in the definitions and appraiser instructions. (If more than one appraiser is involved in this assignment, including inspection and review, two signatures are required.) My appraised value estimate (as shown on page 4) for the subject property based on the aforementioned statement is $_____ .

Appraiser(s) Signature _____

Appraiser(s) (please type) _____ Date

Review Appraiser(s) Signature (if applicable) _____

Review Appraiser(s) (if applicable please type) _____ Date

Tax I.D. Number: _____

D 7

EMPLOYEE RELOCATION COUNCIL RESIDENTIAL APPRAISAL REPORT
CONDOMINIUM ADDENDUM

SUBJECT AND COMPLEX INFORMATION

Client _____ Client File No. _____

Homeowner _____

Property Address _____ Unit No. _____

City _____ State _____ Zip Code _____

Project Name/Phase No. _____

Property Rights Appraised: [ ] Condominium [ ] Cooperative [ ] Fee [ ] PUD [ ] DeMinimus PUD

Approximate Year Built **19**___ Original Use _____ Converted **19**___

Type: [ ] High-rise(elevator) [ ] Walk-up: No. of Stories ___ [ ] Row or Town House [ ] Other

If Completed: No. of Phases ___ No. of Units ___ No. Sold ___

If Incomplete: Planned No. Phases ___ No. of Units ___ No. Sold ___

Units in Subject Phase: Total ___ Completed ___ No. Sold ___ No. Rented ___

Approx. No Units for Sale: Subject Project ___ Subject Phase ___

Rate the Unit Mix (i.e. % of eff.; 1,2, & 3 BR): [ ] Good [ ] Avg. [ ] Fair [ ] Poor

COMPLEX PARKING
Total No. Spaces ___ Ratio ___ per Unit
If parking is assigned, rate availability: [ ] Good [ ] Avg. [ ] Fair [ ] Poor
Type(s): [ ] Garage [ ] Built-in [ ] Carport [ ] Attached [ ] Detached [ ] Open Lot

SUBJECT PARKING
No. of Spaces ___ Unit/Space No(s). ___ Type: _____
Is the parking space(s)? [ ] Assigned [ ] Owned
If owned, is the parking space deeded separately?...................... [ ] Yes [ ] No
Is the parking space(s) included in the most probable sales price?.......... [ ] Yes [ ] No
Has the owner(s) leased, rented or otherwise assigned possession of the subject's parking space(s)? .... [ ] Yes [ ] No

MANAGEMENT INFORMATION

Note Type: [ ] Developer [ ] Homeowner's Association [ ] Management Agent [ ] Other

Name and Phone No. of Management Contact: _____

Quality of management group and its enforcement of the bylaws, rules and regulations: [ ] Superior [ ] Good [ ] Adequate [ ] Inadequate

Are all common elements completed and dedicated to the Homeowners Association (e.g. pool, tennis courts, club house, etc.)? ...... [ ] Yes [ ] No

Has the developer formally turned over the control of management to an elected board of directors?................... [ ] Yes [ ] No

Are the officers and directors of the Homeowners Association covered by a fidelity bond? .... [ ] Yes [ ] No

If no, would this affect financing?... [ ] Yes [ ] No

FINANCING

Is the complex at least 50% developed?........................ { These two items are the minimum } .... [ ] Yes [ ] No

Is the complex at least 70% owner-occupied?.................. { requirements for FNMA approval. } .... [ ] Yes [ ] No

Is mortgage financing approved for the subject and complex by:
FHA .... [ ] Yes [ ] No [ ] Pending
VA .... [ ] Yes [ ] No [ ] Pending
FNMA .... [ ] Yes [ ] No [ ] Pending
PMI available? .... [ ] Yes [ ] No [ ] Pending

What is the present monthly condominium/PUD fee for subject? .... $ ___

Note all charges included in the monthly condominium/PUD fee: [ ] None [ ] Heat [ ] Air Conditioning [ ] Electricity [ ] Gas
[ ] Oil [ ] Water [ ] Sewer [ ] Taxes [ ] Parking [ ] Other _____

Are there any other fees charged to the unit that are not included in the monthly condominium/PUD fee? Explain: _____

Compared to the competitive listings and other complexes, are the subject's monthly charges: [ ] Higher [ ] Reasonable [ ] Lower

Explain response: _____

To properly maintain the complex and provide the services anticipated, the budget appears: [ ] High [ ] Adequate [ ] Inadequate

MARKETABILITY

Are there any restrictions on the following:
For-Sale Signs .... [ ] Yes [ ] No
Purchaser's or Occupant's Age .... [ ] Yes [ ] No
Pets .... [ ] Yes [ ] No
Leasing or Renting .... [ ] Yes [ ] No
Sale Subject to Approval .... [ ] Yes [ ] No

Explain any "Yes" response(s): _____

If the recent sales from the complex are *not* being used as comparables on page 4 of 6, explain: _____

If no sales from the complex are used as comparables, note the last sale in the complex, its price and terms. Explain: _____

Appraiser's Name: _____ Date: _____

ERC

Prior to the creation of the Uniform Standards of Professional Appraisal Practice (USPAP), each appraisal organization had its own Code of Ethics. In 1985, an Ad Hoc Committee was formed with representatives of nine national appraisal organizations. to develop the USPAP. The representatives then recommended that their respective organizations officially adopt the USPAP so all appraisers, regardless of what organization they belong to, would be guided by the same standards.

Most of the national appraisal organizations are now in the process of adopting the USPAP. It is suggested that readers keep themselves posted as to the status of the adoption process in their respective appraisal organizations.

The USPAP contains a preamble, preface, competency provision, departure provision and standards together with rules and explanatory comments relating to each standard.

On the following pages are those sections of the USPAP that apply to residential appraising:

Preamble
Competency Provision
Departure Provision
Standard #1
Standard #2
Standard #3

Not included are: Standards #4 & #5 which apply to real estate analysis; Standard #6 which covers mass appraisal; Standard #7 which applies to personal property appraisal; and Standards #8, #9, & #10 which cover business appraisals.

A complete copy of the USPAP may be obtained by sending a stamped, (.85¢) self-addressed #10 envelope to Residential Valuation Magazine, 315 Whitney Ave., New Haven CT 06511.

AD HOC COMMITTEE

on

UNIFORM STANDARDS OF PROFESSIONAL APPRAISAL PRACTICE
Chicago, Illinois
August 24, 1986

To Our Respective Organizations:

The undersigned constitute the Ad Hoc Committee on Uniform Standards of Professional Appraisal Practice. The attached document is a continuing response to the recent concerns of users of appraisal services and the public.

Standards 1 and 2 address real property valuation practice, and have been approved or adopted by each organization. We have now developed Standards 3 through 8 addressing review, analysis, mass appraisal, and personal property appraisal. We recommend immediate adoption by each organization either as a re-stated Standards of Professional Practice document or as an adjunct to the existing Standards of Professional Practice document.

We stand in concert and are ready to discuss and defend the development of the document with the appropriate committees, boards, and/or councils of our respective organizations.

Absent		
Harold N. Butler	Joe S. Durant	John L. Gadd
Appraisal Institute of Canada	American Society of Farm Managers & Rural Appraisers	American Society of Appraisers
William J. Hamilton	Carroll W. Keck	John J. Leary
National Society of Real Estate Appraisers	International Right of Way Association	American Institute of Real Estate Appraisers
Ritch LeGrand	Ian D. McClung	Karl J. Urda
Society of Real Estate Appraisers	International Association of Assessing Officers	National Association of Independent Fee Appraisers

STANDARDS OF PROFESSIONAL PRACTICE AND CONDUCT

Code of Ethics

As Amended February 27, 1987
By the Board of Governors

Uniform Standards of Professional Appraisal Practice © 1987

Adopted February 27, 1987
By the Board of Governors
Effective July 1, 1987

Standards of Professional Conduct

As Amended February 27, 1987
By the Board of Governors

Interpretations of Terminology (Standards of Professional Practice and Conduct)

As Amended February 27, 1987
Effective July 1, 1987

UNIFORM STANDARDS OF PROFESSIONAL APPRAISAL PRACTICE

PREAMBLE

It is essential that a professional appraiser arrive at and communicate his or her analyses, opinions, and advice in a manner that will be meaningful to the client and will not be misleading in the marketplace. These Uniform Standards of Professional Appraisal Practice reflect the current standards of the appraisal profession.

These standards include a Competency Provision which places an immediate responsibility on the appraiser prior to acceptance of an assignment. The standards contain binding requirements, as well as specific guidelines to which a Departure Provision applies under certain conditions. Definitions applicable to these standards are also included.

These standards deal with the procedures to be followed in developing an appraisal, analysis, or opinion and the manner in which an appraisal, analysis, or opinion is communicated. Standards 1 and 2 relate to the development and communication of a real estate appraisal. Standard 3 establishes guidelines for reviewing an appraisal and reporting on that review. Standards 4 and 5 address the development and communication of various real estate analysis functions. Standard 6 sets forth criteria for the development and reporting of mass appraisals for ad valorem tax purposes. Standards 7 and 8 establish guidelines for developing and communicating personal property appraisals. Standards 9 and 10 establish guidelines for developing and communicating business appraisals.

These standards are developed for appraisers and the users of appraisal services. To maintain the highest level of professional practice, appraisers will observe these standards. The users of appraisal services should demand work performed in conformance with these standards.

EXPLANATORY COMMENTS RELATING TO THE UNIFORM STANDARDS OF PROFESSIONAL APPRAISAL PRACTICE

PREFACE

To provide additional information concerning the background, interpretation, or application of a Standards Rule, these Explanatory Comments Relating to the Uniform Standards of Professional Appraisal Practice are adopted.

Explanatory Comments have been developed for Standards Rules for which additional explanation and interpretation might prove to be helpful. There are no Explanatory Comments for Standards Rules that are axiomatic or have not yet required further explanation; however, additional Explanatory Comments will be developed and others supplemented or revised as the need arises.

COMPETENCY PROVISION

Prior to entering into an agreement to perform any assignment, an appraiser must carefully consider the knowledge and experience that will be required to complete the assignment competently and either:

1. have the knowledge and experience necessary to complete the assignment competently; or

2. with regard to appraisal, review, and analysis as defined herein, immediately disclose the lack of knowledge or experience to the client, and take all steps necessary or appropriate to complete the assignment competently; or

3. with regard to mass appraisal as defined herein, immediately take all necessary or appropriate steps to ensure the mass appraisal is developed under the supervision of an appraiser who has the qualifications referred to in Standard 6.

COMPETENCY PROVISION

Comment on Competency Provision

Since the background and experience of appraisers varies widely and a lack of knowledge or experience can lead to inaccurate or inappropriate appraisals, the competency provision requires an appraiser to have both the knowledge and the experience required to perform a specific appraisal service competently. If an appraiser is offered the opportunity to perform an appraisal service but lacks the necessary knowledge or experience to complete it competently, the appraiser must disclose his or her lack of knowledge or experience to the client prior to accepting the assignment and then take the necessary or appropriate steps to complete the appraisal service competently. This may be accomplished in various ways including, but not limited to, personal study by the appraiser; association with an appraiser reasonably believed to have the necessary knowledge or experience; or retention of others who possess the required knowledge or experience. If, in the course of performing an appraisal service, an appraiser discovers that he or she lacks the required knowledge or experience, the appraiser must immediately take all appropriate steps to remedy the deficiency.

The concept of competency also extends to appraisers who are requested or required to travel to geographic areas wherein they have no recent appraisal experience. An appraiser preparing an appraisal in an unfamiliar location must spend sufficient time to understand the nuances of the local market and the supply and demand factors relating to the specific property type and the location involved. Such understanding will not be imparted solely from a consideration of hard data such as demographics, costs, sales and rentals. The necessary understanding of local market conditions provides the bridge between a sale and a comparable sale or a rental and a comparable rental. If an appraiser is not in a position to spend the necessary amount of time in a market area to obtain this understanding, affiliation with a qualified local appraiser may be the appropriate response to ensure the development of a competent appraisal.

DEPARTURE PROVISION

An appraiser may enter into an agreement to perform an assignment that calls for something less than, or different from, the work that would otherwise be required by the specific guidelines, provided that prior to entering into such agreement:

1. the appraiser has determined that the assignment to be performed is not so limited in scope that the resulting appraisal, review, or analysis would tend to mislead or confuse the client, the users of the report, or the public; and

2. the appraiser has advised the client that the assignment calls for something less than, or different from, the work required by the specific guidelines, and therefore the report will include a qualification that reflects the limited or differing scope of the appraisal, review, or analysis.

In the context of this departure provision, exceptions to the following binding requirements are not permitted: S.R. 1-1, S.R. 1-5, S.R. 2-1, S.R. 2-3, S.R. 2-5, S.R. 3-3, S.R. 4-1, S.R. 5-1, S.R. 5-3, S.R. 6-1, S.R. 6-5, S.R. 6-6, S.R. 7-1, S.R. 8-1, S.R. 8-3, S.R. 9-1, S.R. 9-3, S.R. 9-5, S.R. 10-1, S.R. 10-3 and S.R. 10-5.

JURISDICTIONAL EXCEPTION

If any part of these standards is contrary to the law or public policy of any jurisdiction, only that part shall be void and of no force or effect in that jurisdiction.

DEPARTURE PROVISION

Comment on Departure Provision

Before making a decision to enter into an agreement for appraisal services calling for a departure from a specific appraisal guideline, an appraiser must use extreme care to determine whether the scope of the appraisal service to be performed is so limited that the resulting analysis, opinion, or conclusion would tend to mislead or confuse the client, the users of the report, or the public. For the purpose of this provision, users of the report might include parties such as lenders, employees of government agencies, limited partners of a client, and a client's attorney and accountant. In this context the purpose of the appraisal and the anticipated or possible use of the report are critical.

If an appraiser enters into an agreement to perform an appraisal service that calls for something less than, or different from, the work that would otherwise be required by the specific appraisal guidelines, S.R. 2-2(k), 5-2(i), 8-2(h), and 10-2(h) require that this fact be clearly and accurately set forth in the report.

An appraiser must use extreme care in determining whether to enter into an agreement calling for a report that is something less than, or different from, the complete report that would otherwise be required by the specific reporting guidelines. If the limited scope of the report would tend to mislead or confuse the client, the users of the report, or the public, the appraiser must not enter into such agreement.

The requirements of the departure provision may be satisfied by the technique of incorporating by reference. For example, if an appraiser's complete file was introduced into evidence at a public hearing or public trial and the appraiser subsequently prepared a one-page report that (1) identified the property, (2) stated the value, and (3) stated that the value conclusion could not be properly understood without reference to his or her complete file and directed the reader to the complete file, the requirements of the departure provision would be satisfied if the appraiser's complete file contained, in coherent form, all the data and statements that are required by the Uniform Standards of Professional Appraisal Practice. Another example would be an updated report that expressly incorporated by reference all the background data, market conditions, assumptions, and limiting conditions that were contained in the original report prepared for the same client.

EXPLANATORY COMMENTS

STANDARD 1

In developing a real estate appraisal, an appraiser must be aware of, understand, and correctly employ those recognized methods and techniques that are necessary to produce a credible appraisal

General Comment

Standard 1 is directed toward the substantive aspects of developing a competent appraisal. The requirements set forth in S.R. 1-1, the appraisal guidelines set forth in S.R. 1-2, 1-3, 1-4, and the requirements set forth in S.R. 1-5 generally mirror the appraisal process in the order of topics addressed and can be used by appraisers and the users of appraisal services as a convenient checklist.

STANDARDS RULES RELATING TO STANDARD 1

S.R. 1-1

In developing a real estate appraisal, an appraiser must:

(a) be aware of, understand, and correctly employ those recognized methods and techniques that are necessary to produce a credible appraisal;

Comment S.R. 1-1(a)

This rule recognizes that the principle of change continues to affect the manner in which appraisers perform appraisal services. Changes and developments in the real estate field have a substantial impact on the appraisal profession. Important changes in the cost and manner of constructing and marketing commercial, industrial, and residential real estate and changes in the legal framework in which real property rights and interests are created, conveyed, and mortgaged have resulted in corresponding changes in appraisal theory and practice. Social change has also had an effect on app aisal theory and practice. To keep abreast of these changes and developments, the real estate appraisal profession is constantly reviewing and revising appraisal methods and techniques and devising new methods and techniques to meet new circumstances. For this reason it is not sufficient for appraisers to simply maintain the skills and the knowledge they possess when they become appraisers. Each appraiser must continually improve his or her skills to remain proficient in the real estate appraisal profession.

(b) not commit a substantial error of omission or commission that significantly affects an appraisal;

Comment S.R. 1-1(b)

In performing appraisal services an appraiser must be certain that the gathering of factual information is conducted in a manner that is sufficiently diligent to ensure that the data that would have a material or significant effect on the resulting analyses, opinions, or conclusions are considered Further, an appraiser must use sufficient care in analyzing such data to avoid errors that would significantly affect his or her analyses, opinions, and conclusions.

(c) not render appraisal services in a careless or negligent manner, such as a series of errors that, considered individually, may not significantly affect the results of an appraisal, but which, when considered in the aggregate, would be misleading

Comment S.R. 1-1(c)

Perfection is impossible to attain and competence does not require perfection. However, an appraiser must not render appraisal services in a careless or negligent manner. This rule requires an appraiser to use due diligence and due care, and the fact that the carelessness or negligence of an appraiser has not caused an error that significantly affects his or her analyses, opinions, or conclusions and thereby seriously harms a client or a third party does not excuse such carelessness or negligence.

S.R. 1-2

In developing a real estate appraisal, an appraiser must observe the following specific appraisal guidelines:

(a) adequately identify the real estate, identify the real property interest under consideration, define the purpose and intended use of the appraisal, consider the scope of the appraisal, describe any special limiting conditions, and identify the effective date of the appraisal;

(b) define the value being considered;

if the value to be estimated is market value, the appraiser must clearly indicate whether the estimate is the most probable price:

 (i) in terms of cash; or

 (ii) in terms of financial arrangements equivalent to cash; or

 (iii) in such other terms as may be precisely defined;

 if an estimate of value is based on submarket financing or financing with unusual conditions or incentives, the terms of such financing must be clearly set forth, their contributions to or negative influence on value must be described and estimated, and the market data supporting the valuation estimate must be described and explained;

Comment S.R. 1-2(b)

For certain types of appraisal assignments in which a legal definition of market value has been established and takes precedence, the Jurisdictional Exception may apply to this guideline.

(c) consider easements, restrictions, encumbrances, leases, reservations, covenants, contracts, declarations, special assessments, ordinances, or other items of a similar nature;

(d) consider whether an appraised fractional interest, physical segment, or partial holding contributes pro rata to the value of the whole;

Comment S.R. 1-2(d)

This guideline does not require an appraiser to value the whole when the subject of the appraisal is a fractional interest, a physical segment, or a partial holding. However, if the value of the whole is not considered in the analysis, the appraisal must clearly reflect that the value of the property being appraised cannot be used to estimate the value of the whole by mathematical extension.

(e) identify and consider any personal property, fixtures or intangible items that are not real property but are included in the appraisal.

S.R. 1-3

In developing a real estate appraisal, an appraiser must observe the following specific appraisal guidelines:

(a) consider the effect on use and value of the following factors: existing land use regulations, reasonably probable modifications of such land use regulations, economic demand, the physical adaptability of the property, neighborhood trends, and the highest and best use of the property;

Comment S.R. 1-3(a)

This guideline sets forth a list of factors that affect use and value. In considering neighborhood trends, an appraiser must avoid stereotyped or biased assumptions relating to race, age, color, religion, gender, or national origin or an assumption that racial, ethnic, or religious homogeneity is necessary to maximize value in a neighborhood. Further, an appraiser must avoid making an assumption or unsupported premise about neighborhood decline, effective age, and remaining life. In considering highest and best use, an appraiser should develop the concept to the extent that is required for a proper solution of the appraisal problem being considered.

(b) recognize that land is appraised as though vacant and available for development to its highest and best use and that the appraisal of improvements is based on their actual contribution to the site.

Comment S.R. 1-3(b)

This guideline may be modified to reflect the fact that, in various legal and practical situations, a site may have a contributory value that differs from the value as if vacant.

S.R. 1-4

In developing a real estate appraisal, an appraiser must observe the following specific appraisal guidelines when applicable:

(a) value the site by an appropriate appraisal method or technique;

(b) collect, verify, analyze, and reconcile:
   (i) such comparable cost data as are available to estimate the cost new of the improvements (if any);
   (ii) such comparable data as are available to estimate the difference between cost new and the present worth of the improvements (accrued depreciation);
   (iii) such comparable sales data, adequately identified and described, as are available to indicate a value conclusion;
   (iv) such comparable rental data as are available to estimate the market rental of the property being appraised;
   (v) such comparable operating expense data as are available to estimate the operating expenses of the property being appraised;
   (vi) such comparable data as are available to estimate rates of capitalization and/or rates of discount.

   No pertinent information shall be withheld.

(c) base projections of future rent and expenses on reasonably clear and appropriate evidence;

Comment S.R. 1-4(c)

This guideline requires an appraiser, in developing income and expense statements and cash flow projections, to weigh historical information and trends, current market factors affecting such trends, and anticipated events such as competition from developments under construction.

(d) when estimating the value of a leased fee estate or a leasehold estate, consider and analyze the effect on value, if any, of the terms and conditions of the lease(s);

(e) consider and analyze the effect on value, if any, of the assemblage of the various estates or component parts of a property and refrain from estimating the value of the whole solely by adding together the individual values of the various estates or component parts;

Comment S.R. 1-4(e)

Although the value of the whole may be equal to the sum of the separate estates or parts, it also may be greater than or less than the sum of such estates or parts. Therefore, the value of the whole must be tested by reference to appropriate market data and supported by an appropriate analysis of such data.

A similar procedure must be followed when the value of the whole has been established and the appraiser seeks to estimate the value of a part. The value of any such part must be tested by reference to appropriate market data and supported by an appropriate analysis of such data.

(f) consider and analyze the effect on value, if any, of anticipated public or private improvements, located on or off the site, to the extent that market actions reflect such anticipated improvements as of the effective appraisal date;

Comment S.R. 1-4(f)

In condemnation valuation assignments in certain jurisdictions, the Jurisdictional Exception may apply to this guideline.

(g) identify and consider the appropriate procedures and market information required to perform the appraisal, including all physical, functional, and external market factors as they may affect the appraisal;

(h) appraise proposed improvements only after examining and having available for future examination:

(i) plans, specifications, or other documentation sufficient to identify the scope and character of the proposed improvements;

(ii) evidence indicating the probable time of completion of the proposed improvements; and

(iii) reasonably clear and appropriate evidence supporting development costs, anticipated earnings, occupancy projections, and the anticipated competition at the time of completion.

Comment S.R. 1-4(h)

The evidence required to be examined and maintained under this guideline may include such items as contractor's estimates relating to cost and the time required to complete construction, market, and feasibility studies; operating cost data; and the history of recently completed similar developments.

S.R.1-5

In developing a real estate appraisal, an appraiser must:

(a) consider and analyze any current agreement of sale, option, or listing of the property being appraised, if such information is available to the appraiser in the normal course of business;

(b) consider and analyze any prior sales of the property being appraised that occurred within the following time periods:

(i) one year for one- to four-family residential property; and

(ii) three years for all other property types;

(c) consider and reconcile the quality and quantity of data available and analyzed within the approaches used and the applicability or suitability of the approaches used.

STANDARD 2

In reporting the results of a real estate appraisal, an appraiser must communicate each analysis, opinion, and conclusion in a manner that is not misleading.

General Comment

Standard 2 governs the form and content of the report that communicates the results of an appraisal to a client and third parties.

STANDARDS RULES RELATING TO STANDARD 2

S.R. 2-1

Each written or oral real estate appraisal report must:

(a) clearly and accurately set forth the appraisal in a manner that will not be misleading;

Comment S.R. 2-1(a)

Since most reports are used and relied upon by third parties, communications considered adequate by the appraiser's client may not be sufficient. An appraiser must take extreme care to make certain that his or her reports will not be misleading in the marketplace or to the public.

(b) contain sufficient information to enable the person(s) who receives or relies on the report to understand it properly;

Comment S.R. 2-1(b)

A failure to observe this rule could cause a client or other users of the report to make a serious error even though each analysis, opinion, and conclusion in the report is clearly and accurately stated. To avoid this problem and the dangers it presents to clients and other users of reports, S.R. 2-1(b) requires an appraiser to include in each report sufficient information to enable the reader to understand it properly. All reports, both written and oral, must clearly and accurately present the analyses, opinions, and conclusions of the appraiser in sufficient depth and detail to address adequately the significance of the specific appraisal problem.

(c) clearly and accurately disclose any extraordinary assumption or limiting condition that directly affects the appraisal and indicate its impact on value.

Comment S.R. 2-1(c)

Examples of extraordinary assumptions or conditions might include items such as the execution of a pending lease agreement, atypical financing, or completion of onsite or offsite improvements. In a written report the disclosure would be required in conjunction with statements of each analysis, opinion, or conclusion that is affected.

S.R. 2-2

Each written real estate appraisal report must comply with the following specific reporting guidelines:
(a) identify and describe the real estate being appraised;
(b) identify the real property interest being appraised;

Comment S.R. 2-2(a) and S.R. 2-2(b)

These two guidelines are essential elements in any report. Identifying the real estate can be accomplished by any combination of a legal description, address, map reference, copy of a survey or map, property sketch and/or photographs. A property sketch and photographs also provide some description of the real estate in addition to written comments about the physical attributes of the real estate. Identifying the real property rights being appraised requires a direct statement substantiated as needed by copies or summaries of documents setting forth any encumbrances.

(c) state the purpose of the appraisal;
(d) define the value to be estimated;
(e) set forth the effective date of the appraisal and the date of the report;

Comment S.R. 2-2(c), S.R. 2-2(d) and S.R. 2-2(e)

These three guidelines require clear disclosure to the reader of a report the "why, what and when" surrounding the appraisal. The purpose of the appraisal is used generically to include both the task involved and rationale for the appraisal. Defining the value to be estimated requires both an appropriately referenced definition and any comments needed to clearly indicate to the reader how the definition is being applied [cf., S.R. 1-2(b)]. The effective date of the appraisal establishes the context for the value estimate, while the date of the report indicates whether the perspective of the appraiser on the market conditions as of the effective date of the appraisal was prospective, current, or retrospective. Reiteration of the date of the report and the effective date of the appraisal at various stages of the report in tandem is important for the clear understanding of the reader whenever the date of the report precedes the effective date of the appraisal.

(f) describe the scope of the appraisal;

Comment S.R. 2-2(f)

This guideline requires that a written report that sets forth the results of an appraisal contain a clear and accurate description of the scope of the appraisal. This guideline is designed to protect third parties whose reliance on an appraisal report may be affected by this information.

The term "scope of the appraisal" means the extent of the process of collecting, confirming and reporting data. The standards clearly impose a responsibility on the appraiser to determine the extent of the work and of the report in relation to the significance of the appraisal problem. Describing the "scope of the appraisal" is the way in which the appraiser signifies acceptance of this responsibility.

(g) set forth all assumptions and limiting conditions that affect the analyses, opinions, and conclusions;

Comment S.R. 2-2(g)

It is suggested that assumptions and limiting conditions be grouped together in an identified section of the report.

(h) set forth the information considered, the appraisal procedures followed, and the reasoning that supports the analyses, opinions, and conclusions;

Comment S.R. 2-2(h)

This guideline requires the appraiser to summarize the data considered and the procedures that were followed. Each item must be addressed in the depth and detail required by its significance to the appraisal. The appraiser must be certain that sufficient information is provided so that the client, the users of the report, and the public will understand it and will not be misled or confused. The substantive content of the report, not its size, determines its compliance with this specific reporting guideline.

(i) set forth the appraiser's opinion of the highest and best use of the real estate being appraised when such an opinion is necessary and appropriate;

Comment S.R. 2-2(i)

This guideline requires that a written report contain a statement of the appraiser's opinion as to the highest and best use of the real estate being appraised, unless an opinion as to highest and best use is irrelevant or unnecessary. If an opinion as to highest and best use is required, the reasoning in support of the opinion must also be included.

(j) explain and support the exclusion of any of the usual valuation approaches;

(k) set forth any additional information that may be appropriate to show compliance with, or clearly identify and explain permitted departures from, the requirements of Standard 1;

Comment S.R. 2-2(k)

This guideline requires that a written appraisal report or other written communication concerning the results of an appraisal contain sufficient information to indicate that the appraiser complied with the requirements of Standard 1, including the requirements governing any permitted departures from the appraisal guidelines. The amount of detail required will vary with the significance of the information to the appraisal. Information considered and analyzed in compliance with S.R. 1-5 is significant information that deserves comment in any report.

(l) include a signed certification in accordance with Standards Rule 2-3.

S.R. 2-3

Each written real estate appraisal report must contain a certification that is similar in content to the following form:

I certify that, to the best of my knowledge and belief:

— the statements of fact contained in this report are true and correct.

— the reported analyses, opinions, and conclusions are limited only by the reported assumptions and limiting conditions, and are my personal, · unbiased professional analyses, opinions, and conclusions.

— I have no (or the specified) present or prospective interest in the property that is the subject of this report, and I have no (or the specified) personal interest or bias with respect to the parties involved.

— my compensation is not contingent on an action or event resulting from the analyses, opinions, or conclusions in, or the use of, this report.

— my analyses, opinions, and conclusions were developed, and this report has been prepared, in conformity with the Uniform Standards of Professional Appraisal Practice.

— I have (or have not) made a personal inspection of the property that is the subject of this report. (If more than one person signs the report, this certification must clearly specify which individuals did and which individuals did not make a personal inspection of the appraised property.)

— no one provided significant professional assistance to the person signing this report. (If there are exceptions, the name of each individual providing significant professional assistance must be stated.)

S.R. 2-4

To the extent that it is both possible and appropriate, each oral real estate appraisal report (including expert testimony) must address the substantive matters set forth in Standards Rule 2-2.

Comment S.R. 2-4

In addition to complying with the requirements of S.R. 2-1, an appraiser making an oral report must use his or her best efforts to address each of the substantive matters in S.R. 2-2.

Testimony of an appraiser concerning his or her analyses, opinions, and conclusions is an oral report in which the appraiser must comply with the requirements of this Standards Rule.

S.R. 2-5

An appraiser who signs a real estate appraisal report prepared by another, even under the label of "review appraiser," must accept full responsibility for the contents of the report.

Comment S.R. 2-5

This guideline is directed to the employer or supervisor reviewing and signing the appraisal of an employee or subcontractor. The employer or supervisor is as responsible as the individual preparing the appraisal for the content and conclusions of the appraisal and the report. Using a conditional label next to the signature of the employer or supervisor does not exempt that individual from adherence to these standards.

STANDARD 3

In reviewing an appraisal and reporting the results of that review, an appraiser must form an opinion as to the adequacy and appropriateness of the report being reviewed and must clearly disclose the nature of the review process undertaken.

EXPLANATORY COMMENTS RELATING TO STANDARD 3

General Comment

The function of reviewing an appraisal requires the preparation of a separate report or a file memorandum setting forth the results of the review process. These appraisers are normally checking for a level of completeness and consistency in the report and cannot be expected to have first-hand knowledge of the subject property and other data in the report. This is a distinctly different function from that addressed in S.R. 2-5. To avoid confusion in the marketplace between these two functions, appraisers reviewing appraisal reports should not sign the report being reviewed.

Appraisers who engage in the function of reviewing an appraisal report must take appropriate steps to indicate to third parties the precise extent of the review process. A separate report or letter is one method. Another appropriate method is a form or check-list prepared and signed by the appraiser conducting the review and attached to the report being reviewed. It is also possible that a stamped impression on the appraisal report signed by the reviewing appraiser may be an appropriate method for separating the review function from the actual signing of the report. To be effective, however, the rubber stamp must briefly indicate the extent of the review process and refer to a file memorandum that clearly outlines the review process conducted.

STANDARDS RULES RELATING TO STANDARD 3

S.R. 3-1

In reviewing an appraisal, an appraiser must observe the following specific guidelines:

(a) identify the report being reviewed, the real estate and real property interest being appraised, the effective date of the opinion in the report being reviewed, and the date of the review;

(b) identify the scope of the review process to be conducted;

(c) form an opinion as to the adequacy and relevance of the data and the propriety of any adjustments to the data;

(d) form an opinion as to the appropriateness of the appraisal methods and techniques used and develop the reasons for any disagreement;

(e) form an opinion as to the correctness and appropriateness of the analyses, opinions, and/or conclusions in the report being reviewed and develop the reasons for any disagreement.

S.R. 3-2

In reporting the results of an appraisal review, an appraiser must:

(a) disclose the nature, extent, and detail of the review process undertaken;

(b) disclose the information that must be considered in S.R. 3-1 (a) and (b);

(c) set forth the opinions, reasons, and conclusions required in S.R. 3-1 (c), (d) and (e).

No pertinent information shall be withheld.

S.R. 3-3

In reviewing an appraisal and reporting the results of that review, an appraiser must separate the review function from any other functions.

MATHEMATICS IN APPRAISING

INTRODUCTION

In 1970 I taught Appraisal 1A for the American Institute of Real Estate Appraisers. My co-instructor was the late Dr. George Bloom, Professor of Real Estate at Indiana University. When I arrived in the spacious suite that George reserved for me, at the Indiana Student Memorial Union, I found two things on my pillow. There was a book on statistics and a note from George saying that I was teaching all of the math and statistics sections of the course.

In that it had been 20 years since I had taken a college statistics course, that experience required that I spend all of my spare time reviewing. Therefore, I decided to write a primer on the subject of "Mathematics for Appraisers" which would be a little easier to learn from than a college statistics textbook.

Later when George and I co-authored, *Appraising the Single Family Residence*, the material was incorporated into that book. It is also included in the 8th and 9th editions of *Appraising Real Estate*.

In the introduction to *Appraising the Single Family Residence*, Charles B. Akerson, MAI, 1978 President of The American Institute of Real Estate Appraiser, wrote, "Highlights of the book are a math for appraisers feature.".

Printed here, is the first section of this primer, which goes through Simple Linear Regression Analysis. I have not included Step Wise Multiple Regression Analysis, as it is beyond the scope of this book.

Finally, I wish to again thank my father-in-law, Dr. Joseph Lambert who supplied some of the material and illustrations on statistics.

Mathematics of Appraising

Today appraising a single family residence requires the use of a wide variety of mathematical techniques ranging from simple arithmetic through the use of algebraic formulas to the statistical techniques of stepwise multiple regression analyses. Often simple adding, subtracting, multiplying and dividing can be done with only the aid of pencil and paper or a simple calculator. More sophisticated calculators are helpful for solving algebraic formulas and some linear regression analysis. Computers are required for almost all stepwise multiple regression analysis. The trend towards use of the more sophisticated techniques is increasing in the appraisal of single family residences.

This section provides a review of the mathematical techniques and language used by appraisers of single family residences. It begins with a review of basic arithmetic. Familiar processes are shown with the rules that apply to each calculation. They are presented primarily as a basis for the subsequent material on algebra, statistics and regression analysis that follows.

Basic Arithmetic

Data is the information that is collected in the market and analyzed in the appraisal process to produce an estimate of value. Types of data include building dimensions, population figures, reproduction costs, rentals and sales among many others. The numbers that represent this data can be processed to produce other numbers or *results*. There are four basic arithmetic operations known as addition, subtraction, multiplication and division.

Addition is the process of adding two or more numbers together to produce the *sum* of the numbers. The symbol for addition is a plus sign (+).

Example: $120 + $135 + $130 = $385.

Subtraction is the process of deducting one number from another to produce the *difference* between the numbers. The symbol for subtraction is a minus sign (−).

Example: 93 inches − 10 inches = 83 inches

Multiplication is the process of multiplying one number, the *multiplicand,* by another number, the *multiplier,* to produce a result which is called the *product.* The multiplier is also sometimes known as a *coefficient.* The symbols for multiplication are a times sign (×) or a period (·). In algebra it is also a sign to multiply when one number is inside a bracket and the other is outside the bracket.

Example: $4 \times 5 = 20$
$6 \cdot 7 = 42$
$8(9) = 72$

In the above examples 4 could be called the coefficient of 5; 6 the coefficient of 7; and 8 the coefficient of 9.

When a series of different multiplicands are multiplied by the same multiplier, that multiplier is also known as a *constant.*

Example: $6 \times 7 = 42$
$6 \times 8 = 48$
$6 \times 14 = 84$

In this example, 6 can be called a multiplier, coefficient or constant. In algebra the symbol for a constant is "k".

When a series of numbers is multiplied by each other, the results are the same no matter in what sequence the numbers are multiplied.

Example: $6 \cdot 4 \cdot 8 = 192$
$8 \times 6 \times 4 = 192$
$6(8) \times 4 = 192$

Division is the process of dividing one number, the *dividend,* by another number, the *divisor*, to produce a result which is called a *quotient*. The symbol for division is (÷) or a line placed under the dividend and over the divisor.

Example: $18 \div 9 = 2$

$\dfrac{20}{5} = 4$

In the above examples 18 and 20 are the dividends and 9 and 5 are the divisors and 2 and 4 are the quotients. The number 20 is also known as the *numerator* and 5 the *denominator* when the numbers are shown as a fraction. Therefore, the value of a fraction is found by dividing the numerator by the denominator.

Rules for Processing Numbers
- In addition and multiplication the order of the numbers does not affect the results.
- In subtraction the order of the numbers does make a difference in the results.
- In division the sequence of the numbers may affect the results.
- When a series of operations is performed, the ones within brackets (grouping symbols) are done first.

Example: $2 (4 + 6) \times (6 - 2) =$
$2 (10) \times (4) =$
$20 \times 4 = 80$

- When there are brackets within brackets, the innermost operations are done first.

Example: $2 \left[(8 + 2) + (6 - 3) \right] =$
$2 \left[(10) + (3) \right] =$
$2 \left[13 \right] = 26$

- When there are no grouping symbols, all the multiplication and division operations are performed before the addition and subtraction operations.

Example: $4 \times 5 \div 2 \times 10 + 12 =$
$20 \div 2 \times 10 + 12 =$
$10 \times 10 + 12 =$
$100 + 12 = 112$
or
$3 \times 6 + 9 \div 3 - 10 =$
$18 + 3 - 10 = 11$

There are many more rules that apply to the addition, subtraction, multiplication and division operations that cover what to do when the signs are different, how to use absolute numbers, fractions, etc. These are beyond the scope of this introductory material.

Ratios

Ratios are the result of dividing one number by another number. The three different ways to express a ratio are as a whole number (integer), decimal figure or fraction.

Example: In a community school there is a ratio of 58 students to 2 teachers.

The ratio of 58 to 2 is $58 \div 2 = 29$

The ratio of 2 to 58 is $2 \div 58 = .0345$ (rounded)

The ratio of 2 to 58 is $\dfrac{2}{58} = \dfrac{1}{29}$

Percentages

Percentages are ratios multiplied by 100 (or expressed on a base of 100).

Continuing the above example:

$\dfrac{2}{58} = .0345 \times 100 = 3.45\%$ of a teacher for each student.

Rates

Rates are percentages expressed in terms of a time period. $8.00 interest per year on $100 principal = 8% interest per year; $.50 interest per month on $100 = .005 or 1/2% interest per month.

Decimals

Decimals are added, subtracted, multiplied and divided similar to the way whole numbers (integers) are with some additional rules being applied. When decimals are added and subtracted, the number of places to the right of the decimal point is equal to the largest number of places in any of the numbers being added or subtracted.

Example:
$$242.071$$
$$+\ 63.12$$
$$+\ \ 4.2$$
$$+\ \ 2.7983$$
$$\overline{312.1893}$$

$$621.0037$$
$$-\ 11.02$$
$$\overline{609.9837}$$

When decimals are multiplied, the number of places to the right of the decimal point is the total number of places to the right of the decimal point in the numbers being multiplied.

Example: $3.23 \times 7.459 = 24.09257$
$17.31 \times 6.9 \times 41.27 = 4929.24753$

This does not mean the number cannot be rounded in the appraisal process.

When decimals are divided, the decimal points in the dividend (numerator) and divisor (denominator) are moved to the right to make the divisor a whole number (integer); the decimal point is moved the same number of places and in the same direction in both numbers.

Example: $896.487 \div 57.31 =$

$$57.31_{\wedge}\overline{)896.48_{\wedge}7}$$

$$5731\overline{)89648.7}^{\ 15.64\ (rd.)}$$

Algebra

The same rules that apply to basic arithmetic apply to algebra. The main difference is that in algebra letters and symbols are used together with numbers.

Algebra makes use of equations to solve problems. An equation is a statement of fact that a number or group of quantities on one side of an equal sign is equal to another quantity or group of quantities on the opposite side of the equal sign.

Example: $6 + 10 = 16$
$12 - 8 = 3 + 1$
$44 + (5 + 4) = 53$
$15 + (6 \times 5) = 25 + (5 \times 4)$

$$\frac{200}{20} = 10$$

$$\sqrt{36} = 3 \times 2$$

$$(\frac{12}{3} + 1)(11 - 1) = (7 \times 8) - 6$$

The most important rule in solving equations is that with every change in the statement of the equation the integrity or accuracy of the equation must always be maintained. One side of the equation must always equal the other side.

There are three laws or rules that illustrate the application of symbols.

1. The commutative laws state that as with regular addition the sum of two or more symbols is the same no matter in what order they are added together.

Example: $2 + 4 + 10 = 10 + 4 + 2$
$16 = 16$
or
$X + Y + Z = Y + Z + X$

The commutative laws state that as with regular multiplication the product of two or more symbols is the same no matter in what order they are multiplied by each other.

Example: $8 \times 12 \times 5 = 12 \times 5 \times 8$
$480 = 480$
or
$X \cdot Y \cdot Z = Z \cdot X \cdot Y$

2. The associative laws state that as with regular addition and multiplication when brackets are used the operations within the brackets are always performed first. When two or more brackets are used, the operation within the innermost bracket is performed first and then each outer one is performed successively.

Example: $5 \cdot (6 + 3) + 12 - 10 =$
$5 \cdot (9) + 12 - 10 \qquad =$
$45 + 12 - 10 \qquad\qquad = 47$

or

$18 + [(5 \bullet 9) - (18 - 3) + (4 \times 5)] =$
$18 + [(45) - (15) + (20)] \qquad =$
$18 + [50] \qquad\qquad\qquad =$
$18 + 50 \qquad\qquad\qquad\qquad = 68$

or

$$X + (Y + Z) = (X + Y) + Z$$

or

$$X \cdot (Y \cdot Z) = (X \cdot Y) \cdot Z$$

3. The distributive law states that the number or symbol outside the bracket is actually multiplied by each number or symbol within the bracket.

Example: $8(4 + 12) =$
Can be solved:
$= 8(16)$
$= 8 \cdot 16$
$= 128$

but according to the distributive law may also be solved:

$$8(4 + 12) = 32 + 96 = 128$$

or using symbols:

$$X(Y + Z) = XY + XZ$$

(each symbol within the bracket is multiplied by the symbol outside the bracket).

In algebra in order to solve equations it is necessary to simplify them. The commutative, associative and distributive laws are used for this process.

Example of simplification using the commutative law:

$$10 + (2Y + 3Y + 6Y) = 10 + 11Y$$

Example of simplification using the associative law:

$$(7 + 8X) + 3X = 7 + (3X + 8X)$$

This same equation can be simplified using the distributive law:

$$(7 + 8X) + 3X = 7 + (8 + 3)X$$
$$= 7 + 11X$$

Equations are mathematical expressions which relate one group of numbers and symbols to another group of numbers and symbols.

$$3X = 4Y$$

If we know that X equals 4, we can solve the equation to find that Y equals 3:

$$3X = 4Y$$
$$3 \cdot 4 = 4Y$$
$$12 = 4Y$$
$$3 = Y$$

The key to solving algebraic equations is the assertion that two different combinations of numbers and symbols called *groups* or *quantities* are equal to each other. This fact is usually shown in the equation by the use of an equal sign. Groups or quantities are made up of constants, coefficients and variables.

The following are examples of some different types of algebraic equations. In them the variables are unknowns and are represented by letters of the alphabet.

Reflective equation: $X = Y$
Symmetric equation: if $X = Y$ then $Y = X$
Transitive equation: if $X = Y$ and $Y = b$ then $X = b$

Another key to solving algebraic equations is the axiom that both sides of an equation will remain equal after equal amounts are added, subtracted, multiplied by or divided into both sides of the equation.

Example of adding equal amounts to both sides of an equation:

$$X + 15 = 21$$

Add 8 to both sides

$$X + 23 = 29$$

Example of subtracting equal amounts to both sides of an equation:

$$X + 15 = 21$$

Subtract 10 from both sides

$$X + 5 = 11$$

Example of multiplying both sides of an equation by equal amounts:

$$X + 15 = 21$$

Multiply both sides by 7

$$7 (X + 15) = 147$$

Example of dividing both sides of an equation by equal amounts:

$$X + 15 = 21$$

Divide both sides by 7

$$\frac{X + 15}{7} = \frac{21}{7}$$

Another key to solving algebraic equations is that any term may be transposed from one side of an equation to the other side and the sides will remain equal provided that the sign of the transposed term is changed (+ to −, or − to +, or × to ÷, or ÷ to ×).

Example of moving a plus term in an equation to the other side of the equation:

$$9 X + 2 = 29$$

Move the + 2 to the other side: $9 X + \cancel{2} + (−\cancel{2}) = 29 + (−2)$

$$9 X = 29 − 2$$

(the effect is the same as subtracting − 2 from both sides)

Example of moving a minus term in an equation to the other side of the equation:

$$9X - 2 = 25$$

Move the -2 to the other side: $9X - \cancel{2} + (+\cancel{2}) = 25 + (+2)$

$$9X = 25 + 2$$

(the effect is the same as adding $+2$ to both sides)

Example of moving a multiplier in an equation to the other side of the equation:

$$3(9X) = 81$$

Move the multiplier 3 to the other side: $\dfrac{\cancel{3}(9X)}{\cancel{3}} = \dfrac{81}{3}$

$$9X = \frac{81}{3}$$

(the effect is the same as dividing both sides by 3)

Example of moving a divisor in an equation to the other side of the equation:

$$\frac{9X}{3} = 9$$

Move the divisor 3 to the other side: $\cancel{3} \cdot \dfrac{9X}{\cancel{3}} = 9 \cdot 3$

$$9X = 3(9)$$

(the effect is the same as multiplying both sides by 3)

NOTE: In all of the above transposition examples the value of X is 3.

The purpose of this algebra review is to demonstrate the skills needed to solve simple equations of the type encountered by appraisers. Here is an example of how to use the previously explained techniques to solve an equation.

Example: Find the value of X when
$$13X - 6X + 12 = -6X + 3X + 32$$

Step 1: Collect like terms
$$7X + 12 = -3X + 32$$

Step 2: Clear the negative terms by adding equal amounts to both sides.

$$7X + 12 = -3X + 32$$
$$+3X \qquad\quad +3X$$
$$\overline{}$$
$$10X + 12 = \qquad\quad 32$$

Step 3: Clear the equation by adding or substituting equal numbers to both sides.

$$10X + 12 = 32$$
$$- \ 12 \quad -12$$
$$\overline{}$$
$$10X \qquad = 20$$

Step 4: Divide each side of the equation by equal numbers to find the value of the unknown letter (X)

$$10X = 20$$
$$\frac{10X}{10} = \frac{20}{10}$$
$$X = 2$$

This algebra review provides a basis upon which to proceed to statistics, which is a quantitative tool used to analyze data.

Basic Statistics

An appraisal by one popular definition is a supportable estimate of a defined value. Statistics is rapidly becoming an effective tool with which to make and support the value of a single family residence and to better understand available data.

In the language of statistics a *population* is a complete data set or all the data in a certain group. Conclusions must often be reached with incomplete data but if, for example, the group to be studied were houses in Chicago, then the population would be all the houses in Chicago.

Statistics is a field of knowledge that enables an appraiser (or any investigator) to derive and evaluate conclusions about a population from sample data. A sample is only part of the population and conclusions about a population based on a sample may be erroneous.

Observations about a population when they can be measured are called *quantitative*. The numerical value of a quantitative observation is a *variate*.

Observation about a population that cannot be measured is called *qualitative.* They are *attributes.*

For appraisal purposes one of the most useful functions of statistics is to forecast what some variate in a population will be or do. A variate is one item in a population. It is called *discrete* when it can assume only a limited number of values on a measuring scale and *continuous* when it can assume an infinite number of values on a measuring scale.

A continuous variate can become an unlimited number of values.

A typical population of attributes would be house types, i.e., one-story houses, one and one-half story houses, two-story houses, split levels, etc. It is usually easy to display or tell about a population of attributes.

It is much harder to display or tell about a population of variates because there are many different ones.

One of the problems in statistics is to describe a population in universally understandable terms. This is a very difficult thing to do. How does one describe all the houses in a community that have sold in the past year without an individual description of each sale?

One way is to use a single number to describe the whole population. This is called a *parameter.*

One parameter that is used to describe a population is an *aggregate.* It is a sum of all the variates. It is possible to describe all the house sales in a community in any given year by the total dollar amount of all the sales. This is written in statistical language as:

$$A = \Sigma X$$
where
A = aggregate
Σ = sigma = sum of
X = variate

Three other commonly used parameters are the mean, median or mode.

The *mean,* which is denoted by the symbol μ, is commonly called the average. It is obtained by dividing the sum of all the variates in the population by the number of variates.

The mean is by far the most commonly used parameter. In real estate appraising some common uses of the mean are average sale price, average number of days for sale, average apartment rent and average cost per square foot. What is usually meant by each of the statements (unless specifically stated otherwise) is the mean sale price, days for sale, apartment rent, or cost per square foot.

The problem with the use of the mean to describe these and other populations is that it can be distorted by extreme variates. For example, on the following page is a grouping of 36 house sales in a neighborhood. The "average" (or mean) price in this example — $43,494 — does not give a fully accurate picture of the population of houses that have been sold.

The *median* is also used to describe a population or at least the average variate in the population. The median divides the variates of a population into equal halves. To compute the median of a population the variates are arranged in numerical order (as are the 36 sale prices in the example). If the total number of variates is odd, the median is the middle variate. If the total number of variates is even (as it is in this example), the median is the arithmetic mean of the two middle variates.

In the example of 36 house sales the middle two variates are $43,900 and $43,900. The mean of these two variates is $43,900, which is the median of the 36 sales in the example ($43,900 + $43,900 = $87,800 ÷ 2 = $43,900).

$ 36,000
37,300
38,000
38,600
39,000
39,500
39,900
39,900
41,000
41,000
42,000
42,800
42,900
43,000
43,500
43,600
43,700
43,900
43,900 ←—median = Md. = $43,900
43,900
44,000
44,900
45,000 ⎫
45,000 ⎬ mode = Mo = $45,000
45,000 ⎪
45,000 ⎭
45,300
45,500
45,500
46,900
46,900
48,300
48,500
48,600
48,600
49,400
─────────
$1,565,800

A = Sum of the variates
N = Number of variates = 36

$$\text{Mean} = \overline{X} = \frac{A}{N} = \frac{\$1,565,800}{36} = \$43,494$$

Here is another example of an odd number of variates:

Monthly Rent

$180
$180
$190
$200 ◄———— Middle variate (the median)
$210
$215
$220

Like the median and mean, the *mode* is another parameter that describes the typical variate of a population. The mode is the most frequently appearing variate or attribute in a population. The following is an example of a population of monthly rentals showing the mode:

$170
$175
$180
$180
$185
$190 ⎫
$190 ⎬ The most frequent variate is the mode
$190 ⎭
$195
$200

Below is another example showing a population of types of condominium apartments available in a 9-unit complex:

efficiency
efficiency
efficiency
town house ⎫
town house ⎪
town house ⎬ The most frequent attribute is the mode
town house ⎪
town house ⎭
multi-bedroom

In the example of 36 houses, four of them sold for $45,000. This is the most frequent sale price and therefore is the mode. Sometimes two houses of different price may be of the same frequency in the sample or population. Both prices would be modes and the sample would be said to be bi-modal.

One of the problems that must be solved by the appraiser using statistics is to select the appropriate average to describe the population being used. In the previous example the following single numbers can be used to describe the 36 variates in the group of house sales:

$$\Sigma X = \$1,565,800 = \text{sum of all the sales}$$
$$\overline{X} = \$\ \ 43,494 = \text{the mean of all the sales}$$
$$Md = \$\ \ 43,900 = \text{the median of the sales}$$
$$Mo = \$\ \ 45,000 = \text{the mode of the sales}$$

The mean is often selected to describe the sample or population because it is the most commonly used and most people are familiar with it.

Measures of Variation

The parameters mean, median and mode all are used to describe central tendencies of the population. Other sets of parameters are used to provide more information about the population being described. They measure the disparity among values of the various variates comprising the population. These parameters, called *measures of variation* or *dispersion*, are designed to indicate the degree of uniformity among the variates.

One way to measure the disparity between the variates is known as the *range* (denoted by R). It is the difference between the highest and lowest variate.

R = Maximum variate − minimum variate

Using the figures in the example of 36 house sales:

R = $49,400 to $36,000

R = $13,400

The range as a measure of variation is of limited usefulness since it considers only the highest and lowest values and neglects the variation in the remaining values. It also does not lend itself to further statistical treatment.

Average Deviation

Another parameter used to measure deviations between the variates is the *average deviation* which is also known as the average absolute deviation because plus or minus signs are ignored. It is a measure of how much the actual values of the population or sample deviate from the mean or the average. It is the mean of the sum of the absolute (no plus or minus signs) differences of each of the variates from the mean of the variates.

The calculations of the average deviation of the 36 sales, summarized again on page 443, using traditional statistical formula and symbols, follows:

$$\text{A.D. (ungrouped data)} = \frac{\Sigma|X-\overline{X}|}{n}$$

$$\text{A.D. (grouped data)} = \frac{\Sigma f|X-\overline{X}|}{n}$$

where

A.D. = average deviation
Σ = sum of
f = frequency
X = observed value
| | = ignore the + or − signs
n = number of observations in sample (N = population)
$\overline{X}$ = means of sample (σ = population)

$$\text{Mean} = \frac{\$1,565,800}{36} = \$43,494$$

$$\text{Average deviation from the mean} = \frac{\$96,048}{36} = \$2,668$$

Sale price	Absolute deviation between each variate and the mean sale price
$ 36,000	$ 7,494
37,300	6,194
38,000	5,494
38,600	4,894
39,000	4,494
39,500	3,994
39,900	3,594
39,900	3,594
41,000	2,494
41,000	2,494
42,000	1,494
42,800	694
42,900	594
43,000	494
43,500	6
43,600	106
43,700	206
43,900	406
43,900	406
43,900	406
44,000	506
44,900	1,406
45,000	1,506
45,000	1,506
45,000	1,506
45,000	1,506
45,300	1,806
45,500	2,006
45,500	2,006
46,900	3,406
46,900	3,406
48,300	4,806
48,500	5,006
48,600	5,106
48,600	5,106
49,000	5,906
$1,565,800 Total of the sale prices	$96,048 Total deviation from the mean

X	$\lvert X-\overline{X}\rvert$	f	$f\lvert X-\overline{X}\rvert$
$36,000	$7,494	1	$ 7,494
37,300	6,194	1	6,194
38,000	5,494	1	5,494
38,600	4,894	1	4,894
39,000	4,494	1	4,494
39,500	3,994	1	3,994
39,900	3,594	2	7,188
41,000	2,494	2	4,988
42,000	1,494	1	1,494
42,800	694	1	694
42,900	594	1	594
43,000	494	1	494
43,500	6	1	6
43,600	106	1	106
43,700	206	1	206
43,900	406	3	1,218
44,000	506	1	506
44,900	1,406	1	1,406
45,000	1,506	4	6,024
45,300	1,806	1	1,806
45,500	2,006	2	4,012
46,900	3,406	2	6,812
48,300	4,806	1	4,806
48,500	5,006	1	5,006
48,600	5,106	2	10,212
49,400	5,906	1	5,906
		36	$96,048

Mean = $43,494

$$\text{A.D.} = \frac{\Sigma f\lvert X-\overline{X}\rvert}{n} = \frac{\$96,048}{36} = \$2,668$$

This indicates that on the average the individual values in the sample population deviate from the mean $2,668 or about 6%. This is a fairly tight fit and suggests that the mean is an acceptable descriptive representation of this sample.

Like the range, the average deviation does not lend itself to further statistical calculations.

Standard Deviation

The *standard deviation* provides a way of describing a sample or a population that lends itself to further mathematical treatment. In particular it permits application of rules of probability to draw inferences of populations from samples.

In this method the square of the difference between each observation and the mean of the observations is used as a calculation step. This serves to magnify the effects of extreme variance from the mean.

In the illustration, for instance, the mean sale price is $43,494. Therefore, the measure of deviation for a $41,000 sale would be $2,494 squared or $6,220,036.

When standard deviation of a *whole* population is being calculated, it is symbolized by a sigma (σ). Expressed verbally the formula is "standard deviation of a population is the square root of the sum of the squared differences between each observation's value and the mean of all of the observations in the population divided by the number of observations in the population."

When the standard deviation of a *sample* of a population is being calculated, it is symbolized by the letter "s". Expressed verbally the formula is "standard deviation of a sample is the square root of the sum of the squared differences between each observation's value and the mean of all the observations in the sample divided by the number of observations in the sample minus 1."

The reason 1 is subtracted from the number of observations in a sample is to adjust for one degree of freedom that is lost when the mean is calculated. A set of data originally has as many "degrees of freedom" as there are observations. Every time a statistic is calculated directly from the data a degree of freedom is lost.

Formulas for calculating the standard deviation are as follows:

For a population:

$$\sigma = \sqrt{\frac{\Sigma(X-\bar{X})^2}{N}}$$

For a sample:

$$s = \sqrt{\frac{\Sigma (X-\bar{X})^2}{n-1}} \text{ or } \sqrt{\frac{\Sigma f (X-\bar{X})^2}{n-1}}$$

In real estate appraising samples are usually used so the second formula is generally applied as in the example of 36 house sales (see next page).

The standard deviation is an important way to describe the variance of a population or sample. It tells how representative of the whole sample or population the mean is by explaining a standard variance. It is a number that is used and understood by many disciplines. With the availability of electronic calculators it now can be calculated easily. It undoubtedly will become more widely used by appraisers in the future.

When used for this purpose the standard deviation can indicate what percent of the sample of the population may be expected to fall within selected ranges or *confidence intervals* (see page 452).

Approximately 68.2% of the sample or population will generally fall within plus or minus one standard deviation from the mean, if the data meets certain tests of "distribution normalcy" (as discussed later). Many types of real estate data, including residential sales, are commonly found to be approximately normally distributed, or normal distributions can be approximated by appropriate sampling techniques.

In this example, 68.2% of the house sales in the population are expected to be between $40,080 and $46,908 ($43,494 − $3,414 and $43,494 + $3,414), if the data is normally distributed. Also approximately 95% of the sales should fall within two standard deviations from the mean and approximately 99.74% should fall within three standard deviations from the mean.

Because the standard deviation lends itself to further mathematical treatment, it can be used for analytical purposes other than to describe a population.

Statistical Inference

This technique (useful to forecast actions) is based on the assumption that past actions in the market are a valid basis for forecasting present or future actions in the market. In the example past sale prices are used to estimate current sale prices. This technique

Standard Deviation for 36 House Sales

X	f	$(X-\overline{X})$	$(X-\overline{X})^2$	$f(X-\overline{X})^2$
$36,000	1	$7,494	$56,160,036	$ 56,160,036
37,300	1	6,194	38,365,636	38,365,636
38,000	1	5,494	30,184,036	30,184,036
38,600	1	4,894	23,951,236	23,951,236
39,000	1	4,494	20,196,036	20,196,036
39,500	1	3,994	15,952,036	15,952,036
39,900	2	3,594	12,916,836	25,833,672
41,000	2	2,494	6,220,036	12,440,072
42,000	1	1,494	2,232,036	2,232,036
42,800	1	694	481,636	481,636
42,900	1	594	352,836	352,836
43,000	1	494	244,036	244,036
43,500	1	6	36	36
43,600	1	106	11,236	11,236
43,700	1	206	42,436	42,436
43,900	3	406	164,836	494,508
44,000	1	506	256,036	256,036
44,900	1	1,406	1,976,836	1,976,836
45,000	4	1,506	2,268,036	9,072,144
45,300	1	1,806	3,261,636	3,261,636
45,500	2	2,006	4,024,036	8,048,072
46,900	2	3,406	11,600,836	23,201,672
48,300	1	4,806	23,097,636	23,097,636
48,500	1	5,006	25,060,036	25,060,036
48,600	2	5,106	26,071,236	52,142,472
49,400	1	5,906	34,880,836	34,880,836
				$407,938,896

$$s = \sqrt{\frac{\sum f(X-\overline{X})^2}{n-1}}$$

$$s = \sqrt{\frac{\$407,938,896}{36-1}}$$

$$s = \sqrt{\$11,655,397}$$

$$s = \$3,414$$

Mean: $43,494

can also be used to forecast rentals, costs, depreciation, etc., using rules of probability.

The *normal-curve* plots a normal distribution and is a technique to illustrate a distribution of data. Where original data may not be normally distributed, repeated random samples may be drawn with results which approximate a normal distribution. Sales are often treated as though they were normally distributed in competitive, open market situations. The normal curve is often graphed in a form known as a bell curve.

A major characteristic of a bell curve is that it is symmetrical. Both halves have exactly the same shape and contain the same number of observations. The mean, median and mode are the same value and this value is the midpoint (apex) of the curve.

Fig. A illustrates a bell curve and shows that 68.26% of the observations will fall within the range of the mean plus or minus one standard deviation, 95.44% within plus or minus two standard deviations and 99.74% plus or minus three standard deviations. It depicts an analysis of the probable population distribution for the 36 sales, assuming a normal distribution.

In this example the ranges for one, two and three standard deviations are shown. It is also possible to calculate the percentage of the population that will fall within any given distance from the mean.

Continuing the example it is possible to calculate the percentage of sales that will fall within any specified ranges. For example, $2,500 plus or minus the mean of $43,494 (between $40,994 and $45,994) may be estimated by calculating the Z value using the following formula:

Z = the deviation of X from the mean measured in standard deviations

$$Z = \frac{X - mean}{Standard\ deviation}$$

$$Z = \frac{\$45,994 - \$43,494}{\$3,414} = \frac{\$2,500}{\$3,414} = .7323$$

This shows that $45,994 deviates from the mean $43,494 (or $40,994 deviates from the mean $43,494) by .7323 standard deviations.

FIG. A: Area under the Normal Curve

50% of Sales under $43,494
50% of Sales over $43,494
68.26% of the sales between
$40,080 and $46,908
95.44% of the sales between
$36,666 and $50,322
99.74% of the sales between
$32,252 and $53,736

Standard Deviation $3,414

Mean $43,494

FREQUENCY

34.13% — ✕ — 34.13%

68.26%

13.59%   13.59%

2.15%   95.44%   2.15%
99.74%

| $32,252 | $36,666 | $40,080 | $43,494 | $46,908 | $50,322 | $53,736 |
| Minus Three Standard Deviations | Minus Two Standard Deviations | Minus One Standard Deviation | Mean | Plus One Standard Deviation | Plus Two Standard Deviations | Plus Three Standard Deviations |

SALE PRICE

Source: Joseph Lambert, Ph.D.

Areas under the normal curve

z	.00	.01	.02	.03	.04	.05	.06	.07	.08	.09
0.0	.0000	.0040	.0080	.0120	.0160	.0199	.0239	.0279	.0319	.0359
0.1	.0398	.0438	.0478	.0517	.0557	.0596	.0636	.0675	.0714	.0753
0.2	.0793	.0832	.0871	.0910	.0948	.0987	.1026	.1064	.1103	.1141
0.3	.1179	.1217	.1255	.1293	.1331	.1368	.1406	.1443	.1480	.1517
0.4	.1554	.1591	.1628	.1664	.1700	.1736	.1772	.1808	.1844	.1879
0.5	.1915	.1950	.1985	.2019	.2054	.2088	.2123	.2157	.2190	.2224
0.6	.2257	.2291	.2324	.2357	.2389	.2422	.2454	.2486	.2517	.2549
0.7	.2580	.2611	.2642	.2673	.2704	.2734	.2764	.2794	.2823	.2852
0.8	.2881	.2910	.2939	.2967	.2995	.3023	.3051	.3078	.3106	.3133
0.9	.3159	.3186	.3212	.3238	.3264	.3289	.3315	.3340	.3365	.3389
1.0	.3413	.3438	.3461	.3485	.3508	.3531	.3554	.3577	.3599	.3621
1.1	.3643	.3665	.3686	.3708	.3729	.3749	.3770	.3790	.3810	.3830
1.2	.3849	.3869	.3888	.3907	.3925	.3944	.3962	.3980	.3997	.4015
1.3	.4032	.4049	.4066	.4082	.4099	.4115	.4131	.4147	.4162	.4177
1.4	.4192	.4207	.4222	.4236	.4251	.4265	.4279	.4292	.4306	.4319
1.5	.4332	.4345	.4357	.4370	.4382	.4394	.4406	.4418	.4429	.4441
1.6	.4452	.4463	.4474	.4484	.4495	.4505	.4515	.4525	.4535	.4545
1.7	.4554	.4564	.4573	.4582	.4591	.4599	.4608	.4616	.4625	.4633
1.8	.4641	.4649	.4656	.4664	.4671	.4678	.4686	.4693	.4699	.4706
1.9	.4713	.4719	.4726	.4732	.4738	.4744	.4750	.4756	.4761	.4767
2.0	.4772	.4778	.4783	.4788	.4793	.4798	.4803	.4808	.4812	.4817
2.1	.4821	.4826	.4830	.4834	.4838	.4842	.4846	.4850	.4854	.4857
2.2	.4861	.4864	.4868	.4871	.4875	.4878	.4881	.4884	.4887	.4890
2.3	.4893	.4896	.4898	.4901	.4904	.4906	.4909	.4911	.4913	.4916
2.4	.4918	.4920	.4922	.4925	.4927	.4929	.4931	.4932	.4934	.4936
2.5	.4938	.4940	.4941	.4943	.4945	.4946	.4948	.4949	.4951	.4952
2.6	.4953	.4955	.4956	.4957	.4959	.4960	.4961	.4962	.4963	.4964
2.7	.4965	.4966	.4967	.4968	.4969	.4970	.4971	.4972	.4973	.4974
2.8	.4974	.4975	.4976	.4977	.4977	.4978	.4979	.4979	.4980	.4981
2.9	.4981	.4982	.4982	.4983	.4984	.4984	.4985	.4985	.4986	.4986
3.0	.4987	.4987	.4987	.4988	.4988	.4989	.4989	.4989	.4990	.4990

The .7323 can be interpreted from the above table by first finding .7 under the Z column and then looking across the top of the page for the next digits. Accordingly, 26.73% of the sales are shown to fall between $43,494 and $45,994 or between $43,494 and $40,994 and 53.46% of the sales will be between $45,994 and $40,994.

Another question that can be answered using the Z value is the probability of a randomly selected sale falling inside a given range.

Continuing to use the population based on the sample of 36 sales, which has a mean of $43,494 and a standard deviation of $3,414, it is possible to calculate the probability of a randomly selected sale falling in any selected range of values.

For example, the probability of a randomly selected sale falling between $43,494 and $44,494 ($1,000 over the mean) is calculated as follows:

$$Z = \frac{X - \text{mean}}{\text{standard deviation}} = \frac{\$44,494 - \$43,494}{\$3,414} = \frac{\$1,000}{\$3,414} = .29$$

Looking at the table of areas under the normal curve, a Z of .29 = .1141. This indicates an 11.41% chance the sale will fall within $1,000 above the mean. The same process is repeated to find the probability of the sale falling within $1,000 below the mean.

$$Z = \frac{X - \text{mean}}{\text{standard deviation}} = \frac{\$42,494 - \$43,494}{\$3,414} = \frac{\$1,000}{\$3,414} = .29$$

Again, .29 on the table shows .1141, or a 11.41% chance the sale will fall within $1,000 below the mean.

Probability a sale will fall between
$44,494 and $43,494 is: 11.41%
Probability a sale will fall between
$42,494 and $43,494 is: 11.41%
Probability a sale will fall between
$42,494 and $44,494 is: 22.82%

If the range is expanded in the same example to $2,000 plus or minus to the mean of $43,494, to $41,494 and $45,494 respectively, the probability of a randomly selected sale falling within this range woud be increased.

$$Z = \frac{X - \text{mean}}{\text{standard deviation}} = \frac{\$45,494 - \$43,494}{\$3,414} = \frac{\$2,000}{\$3,414} = .59$$

Looking at the areas under the normal curve table .59 = .2224.

Probability a sale will fall between $45,494 and $43,494 is:	22.24%
Probability a sale will fall between $41,494 and $43,494 is:	22.24%
Probability a sale will fall between $41,494 and $45,494 is:	44.48%

In the above two examples, the range being tested is equally above and below the mean sale. However it is also possible to test the probability of a randomly selected sale falling between any selected range in the population. Continuing the example, the probability of a randomly selected sale falling between $40,000 and $50,000 can be calculated as follows:

$$Z\ area_1 = \frac{X_1 - mean}{standard\ deviation} = \frac{\$40,000 - \$43,494}{\$3,414} = \frac{\$3,494}{\$3,414} = 1.02$$

$$Z\ area_2 = \frac{X_2 - mean}{standard\ deviation} = \frac{\$50,000 - \$43,494}{\$3,414} = \frac{\$6,506}{\$3,414} = 1.91$$

Looking at 1.02 on the areas under the normal curve table gives:	.3461
Looking at 1.91 on the areas under the normal curve table gives:	.4719
Probability:	.8180

This indicates the chance a randomly selected sale in this sample will fall between $40,000 and $50,000 is 81.80%.

Confidence Level

Using statistical inference and the laws of probability for a normal distribution, the previous examples have shown how *confidence intervals* may be constructed for a sample where there is a presumption (or approximation) of normally distributed data. These calculations may be valuable in a number of real estate decision-making situations, including loan administration, housing development, and appraising.

As seen in the previous examples, with 36 sales as a sample, an appraiser may say *with a 95% degree of confidence* that any sale randomly selected from the population will fall between $36,664 and $50,332. Similarly, there is a 68% confidence of the sample falling between $40,080 and $46,908. Such measures may be meaningful in connection with other statistical measures.

Since such measures are dependent upon the accuracy of the estimated mean (as a representative of the true population mean), it is also important to establish some degree of confidence about the mean itself. Regardless of population size there is a given sample size which will permit a given level of confidence in the estimated mean.

In the continuing example of 36 sales the standard deviation for price has been calculated as $3,414. The arithmetic mean is $43,494, or about $43,500. If an appraiser wants to be 95% certain that the true mean is within $500 of the estimated mean ($43,494) or between about $43,000 and $44,000, calculations of the necessary sample size are as follows:

n = Sample size required
z = Z statistic at 95% confidence level
s = Standard deviation of the sample
e = Required maximum difference in the mean

And: $n = \dfrac{z^2 s^2}{e^2}$

$$n = \frac{(1.96)^2 (3,414)^2}{(500)^2} = 179 \text{ sales}$$

Thus, with 179 sales in a sample the required standard of confidence could be met. Likewise, for a confidence interval of not more than $750, calculations would be as follows:

$$n = \frac{(1.96)^2 (3,414)^2}{(750)^2} = 80 \text{ sales}$$

In the original sample of 36 sales, an appraiser may ask, "At a 95% confidence, what are the limits between which the true population mean may fall?" By substitution:

$$e^2 = \frac{z^2 s^2}{n}$$

And: $e^2 = \frac{(1.96)^2 (3,414)^2}{36} = \$1,115$

Thus, the appraiser in this case may be statistically 95% certain that the true population mean falls between $42,399 and $44,609.

While such calculations may seem to have obscure reasoning for single family appraising, professional appraisers must have adequate data, knowledge and understanding of the markets in which they appraise. Calculations such as these assist in quantifying change and in performing the neighborhood analyses essential to value estimation. They are also important for appraisal review, loan underwriting and other analyses.

Regression Analysis

Simple Linear Regression Analysis

Trying to estimate the most probable sale price of a residence in the market is the goal of many appraisers. It is seldom sufficient to take a sample of sales and then calculate the standard deviation and base the estimate upon these results. The range of values is usually too great at the confidence level required to be directly useful.

Appraisers long ago discovered that the accuracy of the estimate could be substantially increased by considering in addition to the sale prices of individual properties one or more characteristics of each sale property.

Looking again at the 36 sales in the original example it has been shown there appears to be a relationship between sale price and the number of square feet of living area. The 36 sales with their square feet of gross living area in are exhibited in Table A. In traditional appraisals it is likely that an appraiser would use only those sales

Table A

Comparable Sales Data Set for Simple Regression Analysis

Sale No.	GLA/Sq. Ft.	Sale Price	Price per Sq. Ft. of GLA
1	1,321	$38,000	$28.77
2	1,372	$44,000	$32.07
3	1,394	$39,000	$27.98
4	1,403	$37,300	$26.59
5	1,457	$42,900	$29.44
6	1,472	$43,700	$29.69
7	1,475	$42,000	$28.47
8	1,479	$42,800	$28.94
9	1,503	$36,000	$23.95
10	1,512	$38,600	$25.53
11	1,515	$41,000	$27.06
12	1,535	$39,500	$25.73
13	1,535	$43,900	$28.60
14	1,577	$45,500	$28.85
15	1,613	$45,000	$27.90
16	1,640	$39,900	$24.33
17	1,666	$45,500	$27.31
18	1,681	$39,900	$23.74
19	1,697	$43,600	$25.69
20	1,703	$43,500	$25.54
21	1,706	$44,900	$26.32
22	1,709	$45,300	$26.51
23	1,709	$46,900	$27.44
24	1,720	$46,900	$27.27
25	1,732	$41,000	$23.67
26	1,749	$48,600	$27.79
27	1,771	$48,600	$27.44
28	1,777	$43,000	$24.20
29	1,939	$43,900	$22.64
30	1,939	$45,000	$23.21
31	1,939	$45,000	$23.21
32	1,939	$45,000	$23.21
33	1,939	$48,300	$24.91
34	1,940	$43,900	$22.63
35	2,014	$49,400	$24.53
36	2,065	$48,500	$23.49

which have approximately the same square footage as the appraised property in direct comparison and essentially ignore the others.

Note the appraiser's dilemma in appraising a 1,375 square foot dwelling. Sales 1, 2 and 3 are reported as $28.77, $32.07 and $27.98 per square foot respectively. Other sales may give a clue to the "right answer," but Sales 5 and 6 do little to resolve the conflict. Adjustments will likely be made for other differences, but the complication of multiple hand adjustments has already been noted in Chapter 13.

Sales 1 through 3 indicate a range of $27.98 to $32.07 per square foot, or when applied to the appraised property's 1,375 square feet, an indicated value range of $38,473 to $44,096. (These would be rounded in practice.) However, the remaining market information cannot effectively be applied to the analysis in traditional appraising except to generally reinforce the "appraiser's judgment."

Simple linear regression provides a technique in which more market data may be applied to this analysis — and avoids the zero intercept fallacy illustrated in Chapter 13. For application in the simple linear regression formula, $Y_c = a + bX$, the 36 sales were analyzed by calculator and produced the following:

a = $24,630
b = $11.29
r = .6598 (simple correlation coefficient) ·

Thus, for the 1,375 square foot property appraised:

Y_c = $24,630 + $11.29 (1,375)
Y_c = $40,154
    (or $29.20 per square foot)

The calculated regression line and a plot of the 36 sales is shown in Figure B. Also shown is another statistical measure called the *standard error of the estimate* which allows construction of confidence intervals about the regression line. Calculations in this example produce a standard error estimate of $2,603. When applied to property appraised, the appraiser may now state that the 36 sales in this market support an estimate of about $40,150 for the appraised property (based only upon comparison of square footage). Further, at a

FIG. B: Plot of Sales. Regression Line and Standard Error — 36 Sales

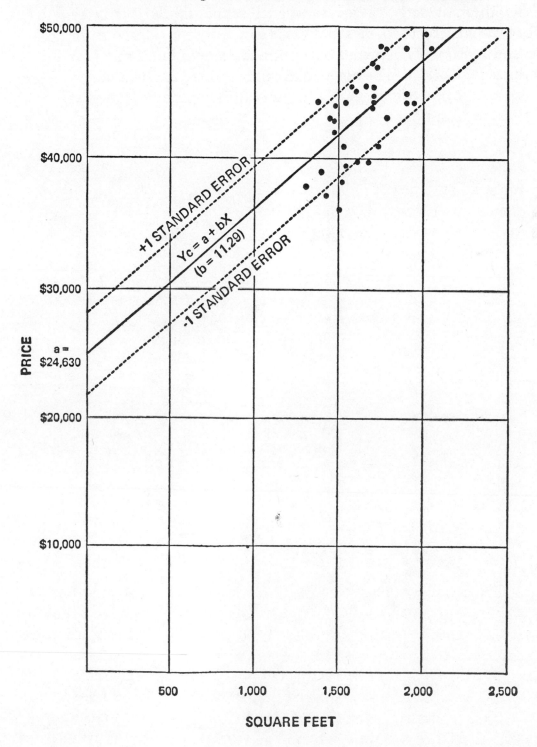

68% confidence level, the market price should lie between $40,150 ± $2,603 (or $37,547 to $42,753). At a 95% confidence level, price should lie between $40,150 ± (2) ($2,603) or $34,944 to $45,356.

Although other statistical measures such as the *standard error of the forecast* may be used, this analysis is generally considered sufficient and reasonably representative of most single family market situations. It should also be noted that a more refined analysis of this data is possible, but this example illustrates the simple application of a regression technique.

☐ My check is enclosed.

☐ MasterCard ☐ VISA ☐ American Express Card

Bill to:

Customer # _____

◁ Please check for your Customer # on mailing label, invoice, or packing slip.

For office use only

Organization _____
Name (please print) _____
Street _____
City/State _____ Zip _____
Telephone(_____)

☐ Please check if this is a new address

Express Delivery available. Call for prices.

FREE SHIPPING AND HANDLING ON PREPAID ORDERS

Ship to: (if different from bill to)

Organization _____
Name (please print) _____
Street _____
(UPS will not deliver to P.O. Box)
City/State _____ Zip _____

Purchase Order # _____

FREE SHIPPING AND HANDLING ON PREPAID ORDERS

Quan.	Item # (see price block)	Description	10 Ch. or 12 Ch.	Unit Price	◆ Imprint Chg. Per 100	Amount

☐ PLEASE BILL ME If you choose to be billed, add the following shipping & handling charges

ORDER TOTAL	FIRST DIGIT OF ZIP CODE			
	0, 1 EXCEPT PR VI GU	2, 3, 4	5, 6, 7	8, 9 EXCEPT HI AK
$ 0.00- 15.00	$ 2.60	$ 2.90	$ 3.25	$ 3.50
15.01- 25.00	4.05	4.40	4.95	5.25
25.01- 50.00	4.90	5.40	6.30	6.75
50.01- 75.00	5.95	6.80	8.05	9.50
75.01-100.00	8.00	9.20	11.30	13.50
100.01-150.00	10.50	11.10	13.80	16.00
150.01-200.00	11.35	13.65	17.40	20.50
200.01-300.00	18.45	21.75	26.95	30.50
300.01-500.00	27.15	29.25	36.00	41.00
500.01 •	34.95	41.05	48.00	55.50

CARD EXPIRES   MO. YR.

MasterCard — also enter 4 digits right above your name

Minimum Charge Order $10.00

Signature _____

☐ I've prepaid my order — please send my **FREE GIFT**	FREE
☐ Prepaid orders of $200.00 or more receive a special gift.	FREE
☐ Please send your FREE Catalogue of Appraisal Forms	FREE
☐ **I've used my customer #, please take off $1.00**	
Shipping and Handling charges (if you did not prepay)	
Alaska, Puerto Rico, Guam, Hawaii: add 15% handling	
$2.25 Additional Charge ON ALL orders under $23.50.	
Connecticut residents add 7½% sales tax	
TOTAL	

forms and worms ® INCORPORATED
P.O. Box 2074 • New Haven, CT 06521

100% Guarantee

All products purchased from Forms and Worms are unconditionally guaranteed. If, for any reason, you are not completely satisfied, simply return merchandise to us for a prompt exchange or full refund. We also offer a full **6-month guarantee** against revisions. If there is an agency form change, we will replace your outdated forms FREE with current revisions.

(Full pads or sets only please)

CALL US!

1 (800) 243-4545

Call us from 8:30 AM 'til 8:00 PM
Eastern Time
For Customer Service
Call 1 (800) 222-6055

Yes! I'll save shipping & handling by pre paying now.

☐ My check is enclosed.

☐ MasterCard ☐ VISA ☐ American Express Card

Bill to:

Customer # _____

◁ Please check for your Customer # on mailing label, invoice, or packing slip.

For office use only

Organization _____
Name (please print) _____
Street _____
City/State _____ Zip _____
Telephone(_____)

☐ Please check if this is a new address

Express Delivery available. Call for prices.

FREE SHIPPING AND HANDLING ON PREPAID ORDERS

Ship to: (if different from bill to)

Organization _____
Name (please print) _____
Street _____
(UPS will not deliver to P.O. Box)
City/State _____ Zip _____

Purchase Order # _____

FREE SHIPPING AND HANDLING ON PREPAID ORDERS

Quan.	Item # (see price block)	Description	10 Ch. or 12 Ch.	Unit Price	◆ Imprint Chg. Per 100	Amount

☐ PLEASE BILL ME If you choose to be billed, add the following shipping & handling charges

ORDER TOTAL	FIRST DIGIT OF ZIP CODE			
	0, 1 EXCEPT PR VI GU	2, 3, 4	5, 6, 7	8, 9 EXCEPT HI AK
$ 0.00- 15.00	$ 2.60	$ 2.90	$ 3.25	$ 3.50
15.01- 25.00	4.05	4.40	4.95	5.25
25.01- 50.00	4.90	5.40	6.30	6.75
50.01- 75.00	5.95	6.80	8.05	9.50
75.01-100.00	8.00	9.20	11.30	13.50
100.01-150.00	10.50	11.10	13.80	16.00
150.01-200.00	11.35	13.65	17.40	20.50
200.01-300.00	18.45	21.75	26.95	30.50
300.01-500.00	27.15	29.25	36.00	41.00
500.01 •	34.95	41.05	48.00	55.50

CARD EXPIRES   MO. YR.

MasterCard — also enter 4 digits right above your name

Minimum Charge Order $10.00

Signature _____

☐ I've prepaid my order — please send my **FREE GIFT**	FREE
☐ Prepaid orders of $200.00 or more receive a special gift.	FREE
☐ Please send your FREE Catalogue of Appraisal Forms	FREE
☐ **I've used my customer #, please take off $1.00**	
Shipping and Handling charges (if you did not prepay)	
Alaska, Puerto Rico, Guam, Hawaii: add 15% handling	
$2.25 Additional Charge ON ALL orders under $23.50.	
Connecticut residents add 7½% sales tax	
TOTAL	

forms and worms ® INCORPORATED
P.O. Box 2074 • New Haven, CT 06521